High Performance TCP/IP
Networking

High Performance TCP/IP Networking

Networking

Concepts, Issues, and Solutions

Mahbub Hassan

The University of New South Wales

Raj Jain

The Ohio State University

An Alan R. Apt Book

PEARSON

Prentice Hall

Upper Saddle River, New Jersey 07458

Library of Congress Cataloging-in-Publication Data on File

Vice President and Editorial Director, ECS: *Marcia Horton*
Publisher: *Alan R. Apt*
Associate Editor: *Toni D. Holm*
Editorial Assistant: *Patrick R. Lindner*
Vice President and Director of Production and Manufacturing, ESM: *David W. Riccardi*
Executive Managing Editor: *Vince O'Brien*
Managing Editor: *Camille Trentacoste*
Production Editor: *Joan Wolk*
Director of Creative Services: *Paul Belfanti*
Cover Manager: *Jayne Conte*
Cover Designer: *Suzanne Behnke*
Cover Image: *Chad Blake/Getty Images, Inc.*
Managing Editor, AV Management and Production: *Patricia Burns*
Art Editor: *Gregory Dulles*
Manufacturing Manager: *Trudy Pisciotti*
Manufacturing Buyer: *Lynda Castillo*
Marketing Manager: *Pamela Hersperger*
Marketing Assistant: *Barrie Reinhold*

© 2004 by Pearson Education, Inc.
Pearson Prentice Hall
Pearson Education, Inc.
Upper Saddle River, NJ 07458

The author and publisher of this book have used their best efforts in preparing this book. These efforts include the development, research, and testing of the theories and programs to determine their effectiveness. The author and publisher make no warranty of any kind, expressed or implied with regard to these programs or the documentation contained in this book. The author and publisher shall not be liable in any event for incidental or consequential damages in connection with or arising out of the furnishing, performance or use of these programs.

Printed in the United States of America
10 9 8 7 6 5 4 3 2 1

ISBN 0-13-064634-2

Pearson Education Ltd., *London*
Pearson Education Australia Pty. Ltd., *Sydney*
Pearson Education Singapore, Pte. Ltd.
Pearson Education North Asia Ltd., *Hong Kong*
Pearson Education Canada, Inc., *Toronto*
Pearson Educación de Mexico, S.A. de C.V.
Pearson Education Japan, *Tokyo*
Pearson Education Malaysia, Pte. Ltd.
Pearson Education, Inc., *Upper Saddle River, New Jersey*

To my parents, my wife, my son, Aaron, and all readers of this book

—Mahbub Hassan

To my wife, Neelu, and my sons, Sameer and Amit

—Raj Jain

Contributing Authors

This book contains contributions from many leading experts actively working on specific performance issues in TCP/IP networks. In addition to the two editors (Hassan and Jain), who themselves wrote parts of the book, there are a total of 24 authors who wrote specific chapters of the book. One of the most challenging tasks was to integrate these individual submissions into a coherent book. As part of the integration effort, the editors have introduced a range of additional materials, including learning objectives, review questions, hands-on projects, and case studies. The editors maintained close liaison with the chapter authors throughout the manuscript preparation process. The manuscript was reviewed and revised twice to address the concerns of the reviewers. Substantial material was added in each revision to further integrate the chapters and improve the quality of the book. While most individual chapter authors were contacted for the revisions, the editors themselves revised some of the chapters. The list of authors who contributed to this book follows (chapters that were substantially revised by the editors are marked with an asterisk).

Chapter 1 Introduction
Mahbub Hassan, University of New South Wales, Australia
Raj Jain, Ohio State University, USA

Chapter 2 TCP/IP Fundamentals*
Sanjay Jha, University of New South Wales, Australia

Chapter 3 Performance Measurement of TCP/IP Networks*
Yukio Murayama, Kurashilki University of Science and Arts, Japan
Suguru Yamaguchi, Nara Institute of Science and Technology, Japan

Chapter 4 TCP/IP Network Simulation
Mahbub Hassan, University of New South Wales, Australia
Sonia Fahmy, Purdue University, USA
Jim Wu, University of Western Sydney, Australia
Abdul Aziz, University of New South Wales, Australia

Chapter 5 TCP Modeling
Sven Östring, University of Cambridge, United Kingdom
Harsha Sirisena, University of Canterbury, New Zealand

Chapter 6 TCP/IP Performance over Wireless Networks
George Xylomenos, Athens University of Economics and Business, Greece
George Polyzos, Athens University of Economics and Business, Greece
Petri Mähönen, Aachen University, Germany
Mika Saaranen, Nokia Mobile Phones, Finland

Chapter 7 TCP/IP Performance over Mobile Networks
Raghupathy Sivakumar, Georgia Institute of Technology, USA

Chapter 8 TCP/IP Performance over Optical Networks
Franco Callegati, Universita' di Bologna, Italy

Maurizio Casoni, Universita' di Modena and Reggio Emilia, Italy
Carla Raffaelli, Universita' di Bologna, Italy

Chapter 9 TCP/IP Performance over Satellite Networks*
Arjan Durresi, Louisiana State University, USA
Sastri Kota, Loral Skynet, USA

Chapter 10 TCP/IP Performance over Asymmetric Networks
Venkata Padmanabhan, Microsoft Research, USA
Hari Balakrishnan, Massachusetts Institute of Technology, USA

Chapter 11 New TCP Standards and Flavors
Sonia Fahmy, Purdue University, USA

Chapter 12 Active Queue Management in TCP/IP Networks
Mohammed Atiquzzaman, University of Oklahoma, USA
Bing Zheng, New Focus, Inc., USA

Chapter 13 Software Implementation of TCP
Jeff Chase, Duke University, USA

Appendix A M/M/1 Queue
Mahbub Hassan, University of New South Wales, Australia
Raj Jain, Ohio State University, USA

Appendix B FreeBSD
Rui Zhao, University of New South Wales, Australia

Appendix C TCP Auto-Tuning
Mahbub Hassan, University of New South Wales, Australia

Preface

The world is undergoing a revolution in information and communication technology. Not only the lives of citizens but also the networking technology are profoundly affected by this revolution. Traditional wired networks are being replaced or complemented by networks based on wireless, optical, satellite, and other media. TCP/IP has emerged as the global Internet-working solution allowing communication over a wide variety of media and networks. These new networking media and the new ways of communication over these networks have given rise to a host of new performance issues and concepts. To adapt and contribute effectively to such changes, engineers and computer scientists must acquire a solid foundation and understanding of the fundamental concepts that affect performance in TCP/IP networks.

Existing texts on TCP/IP focus on the presentation of the protocol details with little coverage of the performance issues and concepts. These texts are good for a first course on TCP/IP networking but do not provide sufficient material for those advanced readers interested in acquiring in-depth knowledge of the performance aspects of TCP/IP, especially in the emerging networking environment. To address this need, we have written *High Performance TCP/IP Networking: Concepts, Issues, and Solutions*, with a clear focus on the performance fundamentals of TCP/IP.

High Performance TCP/IP Networking: Concepts, Issues, and Solutions is a comprehensive guide to the study of its topic. Our book provides an in-depth coverage of (1) tools and techniques for the performance evaluation of TCP/IP networks, (2) performance concepts and issues for running TCP/IP over wireless, mobile, optical, and satellite networks, (3) congestion-control algorithms in hosts and routers, and (4) high performance implementation of TCP/IP protocol stack. This text has been created with an emphasis on fundamental concepts, such as network measurement and simulation techniques, mathematical modeling of TCP dynamics, and management of implementation overhead, which will continue to guide new developments in TCP/IP. Although many specific networks, tools, and protocols are discussed in the text, a continuous effort has been made to emphasize the underlying performance issues and concepts.

ORGANIZATION AND OUTLINE

The book is organized into five parts.

- **Part I: Background.** Part I provides an introduction to the book. It contains two chapters. Chapter 1 provides a rationale for the book. Chapter 2 reviews some of the key features of TCP/IP protocols used in later chapters in the book to explain many performance issues. Chapter 2 reviews only the key features of TCP/IP. A comprehensive treatment of TCP/IP protocol stack is beyond the scope of the book.

- **Part II: Performance Evaluation.** Part II consists of Chapters 3, 4, and 5 and provides detailed coverage of the tools and techniques for performance evaluation of TCP/IP networks. Chapter 3 discusses the performance measurement tools available for monitoring, analyzing, and benchmarking the performance of TCP/IP networks. Chapter 4 introduces simulation techniques and discusses two popular simulation tools. Chapter 5 is devoted to the mathematical modeling of TCP congestion control algorithms.

- **Part III: Performance in Emerging Networks.** Chapters 6 through 10 examine the performance concepts and issues for running TCP/IP in the emerging networking environment. Although many of us think modems and Ethernet when we think Internet and TCP/IP, this is no longer the reality. Yes, it is true that nearly every home has a modem for Internet connection, and nearly every organization has some version of the wired Ethernet connectivity to the desktop. Many homes, however, are subscribing to Digital Subscriber Loop (DSL) technologies for high-speed Internet connection, and many organizations are deploying wireless LANs for flexibility. In the wide area, too, we are witnessing new networking technologies such as mobile cellular data networks (e.g., GPRS), high-speed optical backbones, and increasing use of satellite links for long-distance and global coverage. Each of these new technologies has given rise to some new concepts and issues for TCP/IP performance. We have therefore dedicated a separate chapter to deal with each of these technologies: Chapter 6 for wireless, Chapter 7 for mobility, Chapter 8 for optical, Chapter 9 for satellite, and Chapter 10 for asymmetric networks (e.g., ADSL).

- **Part IV: Congestion Control.** With the increase in networking complexities and traffic dynamics, congestion-control algorithms employed at the end hosts and in the network routers continue to evolve. The new congestion-control algorithms in the TCP protocol resulted in many different TCP flavors (e.g., Tahoe, Reno, Vegas, and so on). Part IV consists of Chapters 11 and 12 and presents an in-depth coverage of the congestion-control algorithms proposed so far. Chapter 11 discusses various TCP flavors, and Chapter 12 examines the new queue management schemes proposed for the network routers to combat congestion in highly dynamic environment.

- **Part V: Implementation.** For emerging high-speed networks (e.g., 10 Gbps Ethernet), the end-system implementation of TCP can become a performance bottleneck. Part V (Chapter 13) summarizes critical performance issues for TCP implementation in end systems and surveys solutions for improving bulk transfer performance.

HOW TO USE THIS BOOK

The book is designed for use in a second course on networking with a prerequisite course on introductory networking or data communications. Some of the possible courses for which this book can be used include Advanced Computer Networks, Advanced TCP/IP Networks, High Performance Networks, and Internet-working. There is enough material in the book for a one-semester or one-quarter course with 12 or 13 weeks of lecture. Depending on the background of the students, two possible course compositions are given here.

Computer science students with limited background in mathematics and hardware design can exclude Chapter 5 (mathematical modeling) and study Chapter

4 (Simulation) in more detail. Engineering students graduating in computer or electrical engineering can spend fewer weeks on Chapter 4 and one extra week on Chapter 5.

Professionals working as network engineers, R & D managers, research scientists, and network administrators will also find this book valuable as a reference to the most recent advances in TCP performance research.

LEARNING AIDS

There are many learning aids in this book:

- **Learning Objectives.** Each chapter starts with a list of learning objectives. The learning objectives highlight the fundamental concepts (skills) students should understand (master) as a result of reading the chapter and help them organize their study goals. They assist instructors in pointing out lecture objectives.

- **Further Reading Lists.** Annotated reading lists at the end of the chapters provide students with valuable resources for independent exploration on specific topics of interest. These lists are particularly useful for professionals.

- **Chapter Summaries.** Summaries offer students a chance to review their understanding of key concepts in the chapter before moving on.

- **Review Questions.** End-of-chapter review questions evaluate the degree to which the student achieved the learning objectives and force the students to think about the key concepts in the chapter. Answers to most of the review questions can be found directly from the chapter; therefore, students are forced to reread parts of the chapter to locate the answers. Such rereading is often required to gain a clear understanding of many difficult concepts. The instructor can use some of these questions for classroom discussions or class tests.

- **Hands-On Projects.** For each chapter, a list of performance evaluation experiments are provided for advanced students seeking to gain a deeper understanding of some of the key concepts and solutions described in the chapter. These experiments can be carried out on open platforms using freely available software. The hands-on projects in this book cover a range of difficulty. Some experiments can be completed in a few weeks using *ns*-2 simulation software, without requiring any kernel-level programming. Other experiments require modification of existing TCP/IP stacks in FreeBSD operating system kernel. These experiments are quite challenging and can be given to students as whole semester projects. Students attempting these experiments are expected to have a good background in programming and operating systems. (Appendix B provides a brief tutorial on FreeBSD for students with no prior background in kernel programming.)

- **Case Studies.** A case study is introduced in Chapter 1 based on a fictitious, but realistic organization with TCP/IP networking infrastructure. The same case study is then used in subsequent chapters with some modifications to introduce new performance problems. The running case study holds together different chapters in the text, provides students a realistic context in which to apply the concepts and techniques learned in the relevant chapters, and yields a classroom discussion topic for the instructor.

- **Figures and Illustrations.** Many concepts throughout the book are explained using illustrations. These illustrations help students understand complex performance issues and concepts.

- **Examples.** Examples have been used where applicable to explain the use of techniques learned from the text.

ACKNOWLEDGMENTS

The book would never exist without the contributions from the individual chapter authors. We take this opportunity to thank all chapter authors for their expertise and time and for putting up with our many requests throughout the preparation of the manuscript. We are indebted to the anonymous reviewers for reading the whole manuscript or part of the earlier versions of the manuscript and making useful comments. Their constructive suggestions significantly influenced the revisions of the manuscript. We thank Professor Krzysztof Pawlikowski of the University of Canterbury, New Zealand, for providing early feedback on Chapter 4. The author of Chapter 11 thanks Tapan Karwa, Venkatesh Prabhakar, Farnaz Erfan, and Minseok Kwon for their help with the simulation experiments in that chapter. Jim Wu, a coauthor of Chapter 4, has been instrumental in fixing some of the problems we faced in preparing the manuscript in LaTex. We gratefully acknowledge the support of the entire production team at Prentice Hall. Finally, the first editor (Hassan) would like to thank Professor Arun Sharma (previous head of school) and Professor Paul Compton (current head of school) at the University of New South Wales for providing a pleasant and stimulating environment in which to work.

Mahbub Hassan
Raj Jain

Contents

High Performance TCP/IP Networking

CHAPTER 1

Introduction

CHAPTER OBJECTIVES

After completing this chapter, the reader should be able to:

- Understand the significance of TCP/IP in the modern era of pervasive computing and communication

- Appreciate the need for designing and building high performance TCP/IP networks

- Gain a clear understanding of the metrics used for performance evaluation of TCP/IP networks

The phenomenal success of the Internet has led to the rapid adoption of the Internet Protocol (IP) technology to build all types of communication networks, including private corporate networks (intranets), military communication networks, home networks, and the emerging Third-generation (3G) cellular networks. Billions of devices worldwide are expected to be IP-capable in the not too distant future to allow for remote access and control through the Internet. Such rapid and unprecedented convergence of communications through IP presents a host of challenging problems in guaranteeing the required performance in such networks. The central theme of this book is to address the performance issues in IP-based communication networks.

Transmission Control Protocol (TCP) is the predominant transport protocol used by IP technology to support popular Internet services. This chapter begins with a history of TCP/IP networks followed by a brief description of the popular TCP-based applications and services. Then we discuss some of the motivating factors that drive the need for mastering the fundamental performance concepts in TCP/IP networks. We also present a comprehensive list of metrics that can be used in performance analysis of TCP/IP networks. The chapter closes with an overview of the remainder of the book.

1.1 HISTORY OF TCP/IP

The first reference to TCP was in a 1973 note entitled "A Partial Specification of an International Transmission Protocol" sent by Dr. Vinton G. Cerf to a few colleagues for a review. The note made a case for avoiding reassembly in network computers (routers). These were early days of networking. The term *router* had not been coined back then, and the concept of layering was not very clear. Most of the networking tasks were handled by Network Control Protocol (NCP).

In 1974, Dr. Vinton G. Cerf and Dr. Robert Kahn, published a paper entitled "A Protocol for Packet Network Interconnection" in which they provided a detailed discussion of several design choices in TCP [68]. The first official specification of TCP was written by Vint Cerf, Yogen Dalal, and Carl Sunshine [91]. The second version of TCP specification was then written by Cerf in March 1977 [89a]. Two months later, Jon Postel observed that Internetwork communication should be viewed as having two components: the hop-by-hop relaying of a message and the end-to-end control of the conversation [271]. In January of 1978, Cerf and Postel split TCP into two protocols: TCP and IP [90]. IP specified routing packets while TCP handled packetization, error control, retransmissions, and reassembly. They argued that simplicity of IP would allow fast and inexpensive gateways to be built. Postel then wrote new specifications for IP and TCP, which were discussed in several IEN meetings and finally published [271a].

In February of 1980, the U.S. Department of Defense (DoD) adopted TCP/IP as the preferred protocol and required that every site connected to Advanced Research Projects Agency (ARPA)net should switch to TCP/IP by 1983. In 1984 the network of networks so connected was later split into MILNET for military-related sites and the regular Internet for other sites. In 1995, National Science Foundation (NSF), which was then in charge of running the Internet, started to turn over its authority to private companies like PSINet, UUNET, ANS/AOL, Sprint, MCI, and AGIS-Net99. By this time, the networking revolution had already begun and it was clear that networking would provide great commercial opportunities.

In the 1980s, there were many other networking protocol stacks that competed with TCP/IP: Digital Equipment Corporation (DEC)net, Systems Network Architecture (SNA), AppleTalk, Xerox Network Systems (XNS), to name a few. Most of these protocols were vendor-specific and proprietary. It was hoped that someday they would all be replaced by a single standard protocol designed by the International Standards Organization (ISO). Knowledge gained from TCP/IP development helped in the development of ISO's transport and networking protocols. ISO developed four different varieties of transport protocols and two varieties of network layer protocols (connectionless and connection-oriented). All this took too long and became too complicated. By this time, TCP/IP had been widely adopted because of its simplicity and the fact that it was an open protocol. Not only are all protocol specifications openly available, but also the source code is available. It is much like UNIX or LINUX. In fact, the implementation of TCP/IP in Berkeley UNIX 4.2 BSD distribution in 1983 may be one reason for the wide adoption of TCP/IP.

1.2 TCP APPLICATIONS AND SERVICES

IP is the baseline protocol of the Internet. To build a service or application on top of IP, additional protocols, namely, transport and application protocols, are required. TCP and UDP are the two *transport layer* protocols in the Internet. TCP provides a reliable transport layer to loss-sensitive applications through retransmission of lost packets, whereas UDP supports a more lightweight transport (without any retransmission) to assist delay-sensitive applications (see Chapter 2 for details on TCP and UDP). Some of the popular Internet applications, together with the associated transport and application protocols, are shown in Figure 1.1. Most popular Internet applications use TCP. Widely used TCP-based applications include:

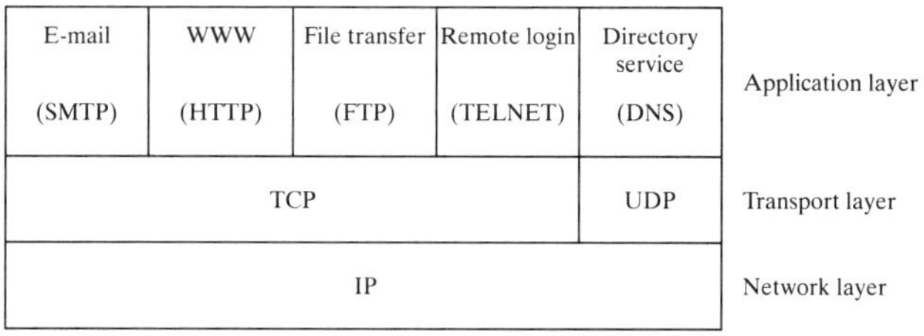

E-mail	WWW	File transfer	Remote login	Directory service	Application layer
(SMTP)	(HTTP)	(FTP)	(TELNET)	(DNS)	
TCP				UDP	Transport layer
IP					Network layer

FIGURE 1.1: TCP- and UDP-based Internet services and applications.

Electronic mail (e-mail). E-mail is a very popular application that allows users to send and receive mails electronically. To send and receive e-mail, one has to open an e-mail account with a network service provider. Many employers run their own TCP/IP networks and provide e-mail accounts to their employees.

World Wide Web (WWW). Users browse the Internet using the WWW. The actual protocol that allows one to download images or other objects from another web site is called Hyper Text Transfer Protocol (HTTP). HTTP uses the reliable service of TCP.

File transfer. TCP/IP networks include a file transfer application that allows users to send and receive arbitrarily large files. These files may contain texts, computer programs, images, or even digitized voice and video clips.

Remote login. Using the remote login application, a user can open an interactive session with a remote machine through the Internet. Every keystroke from the user is sent to the remote machine, and each output character from the remote machine is displayed on the user's screen.

These applications can be used in isolation or in combination to build numerous useful services. For example, Internet banking, stock brokering, or other electronic or mobile (e- or m-) commerce services use the WWW at the front end and may use file transfer in the background.

1.3 MOTIVATION FOR PERFORMANCE STUDY OF TCP/IP

Because of the ongoing convergence of computing, communications, and control through the IP transport technology, we are becoming more and more dependent on TCP/IP services. Many of us access some form of TCP/IP networks several times a day, either from fixed locations (office or home) or from a mobile device while on the move. Today's network services range from traditional information gathering to critical business transactions. Long delays due to network inefficiency can cause user irritation and even loss of profit. To maximize the benefit of being on-line, it is absolutely important to optimize the performance of the TCP/IP networks.

Although the network performance in general can be boosted with high performance hardware, the role of the TCP engine, usually implemented in software, cannot be ignored. The TCP engine has total control over the transport of every single byte of any TCP-based application. TCP is a complex protocol that interacts with many external elements in the end-to-end path. Hardware alone can do little to boost network performance unless the TCP engine is optimized.

The most interesting TCP-related problem is that of congestion and flow control. Hundreds of research articles are published every year analyzing and proposing improvements in TCP's flow control. The algorithms and parameters that are suitable for one environment are not always suitable for other environments, so there is a need for adapting TCP to different environments. High-error-prone wireless networks and high-delay satellite networks are examples of such differing environments. These issues are discussed in detail in this book.

With the emergence of new networking technologies and communication environments, the need for TCP performance studies has never been so intense. In its original form, the traditional TCP simply cannot be expected to perform well with the new communication paradigms. TCP is continuously evolving. Hundreds of Requests for Comments (RFCs) have been written that either add features to TCP or optimize it for a particular environment. This book explains many of these innovations. We should expect TCP to continue to evolve to meet the needs of the future. Understanding the performance issues of the TCP/IPs and their interactions with the external communication elements is crucial for building, analyzing, and maintaining high performance TCP/IP networks.

We are undergoing a major revolution in convergence of communications through TCP/IP technology that will provide ubiquitous and pervasive information access to citizens, wherever they are and whenever they need it. The computing and communication industry requires engineers and scientists who can design new TCP/IP systems, carry out performance analysis of alternative designs, and fully understand the protocol dynamics to guarantee high performance in any situation. Such understanding can only be achieved by mastering the fundamental performance concepts in TCP/IP technology. These concepts are the main subject of this book.

1.4   WHAT DO WE MEAN BY TCP PERFORMANCE?

High performance TCP/IP networking can mean different things to different people depending on the context in which it is used. The following concepts can all be associated with TCP/IP performance:

Round-trip delay. Round trip delay is the total time needed by IP datagrams to travel from source to destination and from destination back to source. Propagation and queuing delays are the two main contributors to its value. Propagation delay depends directly on the distance between the source and the destination. Queuing delay is a function of the traffic load at the intermediate routers and, hence, varies over time. Users of interactive applications (e.g., Remote Login or Telnet) wait for the echo of each character he or she types on the local keyboard. The performance of such applications, therefore, is measured directly as a function of the round-trip delay.

One-way delay. One-way delay is the time needed by IP datagrams to travel from source to destination or from destination to source. Intuitively, one way delay should be half of the round-trip delay. In many cases, however, the forward and backward paths are not symmetric in terms of actual routes, bandwidth, and so on. With such asymmetric paths, the one-way delays for forward and backward paths can be different. One-way delay critically affects the performance of highly interactive applications, such as voice-over IP.

Maximum delay. The maximum possible one-way delay is of great importance to some applications. For example, voice-over IP applications cannot tolerate one-way delays greater than 400 ms.

Delay variation or delay jitter. Because of variable queuing delays, the time it takes for IP datagrams to travel from source to destination varies from one datagram to the next. This variation is called delay variation or delay jitter. Besides queuing delays, other factors, such as dynamic route selections, can also cause variations in one-way delays. A high jitter can have a severe impact on the performance of multimedia applications.

Packet loss rate. Packet loss rate is the ratio of the number of correctly received packets at the destination to the total number of packets transmitted at the source. Major sources of packet loss are (1) buffer overflow at the intermediate routers, and (2) packet corruption caused by transmission errors. A high packet loss rate can severely degrade the performance of data and multimedia applications. Observed packet loss rates can be different for forward and reverse paths.

Bandwidth or effective throughput. Effective throughput is simply defined by the number of application bytes transferred in seconds. For large file transfers, the effective throughput of the application, also called the speed or bandwidth of the connection, is a key performance measure. An inefficient TCP algorithm or implementation can significantly reduce the effective throughput even if the underlying network provides a very high speed communication channel. Observed bandwidth can be different for forward and reverse paths.

Throughput variation. Observed throughput can vary over time. Throughput variation is a metric to measure the variability in the received bandwidth over a given time scale. In general, the larger the time scale, the lower the throughput variability. For a given context, it is important to define a time scale over which throughput variability should be measured.

File transfer time. For short files or object transfers on the WWW, the transfer time of the entire file or object is the key performance factor. File transfer time can be estimated from the effective throughput of the connection.

Fairness. Fairness becomes an important issue when two or more applications compete for resources in a congested router. Fairness can be defined over the long term or short term. Long-term fairness refers to fair allocation of resources in the long run. Short-term fairness is defined in much smaller time scales. A given network algorithm may allocate bandwidth fairly in the long run yet exhibit unfairness in the short term.

Resource consumption. A TCP algorithm or implementation taking less resources is considered a better performer than an implementation that consumes more resources. The resources may include CPU cycles, memory usage, battery power (energy), and so on.

1.5   OVERVIEW OF THE REMAINDER OF THIS BOOK

Chapter 2. Most of the performance issues in TCP/IP networks arise from various interactions between the TCP engine and the surrounding communication environment. To understand these performance issues and the techniques to address them, the reader must be familiar with some of the basic details of TCP/IPs protocols. Chapter 2 reviews TCP/IP protocol fundamentals necessary to follow the subsequent chapters in the book.

Chapter 3. Performance of TCP/IP is affected not only by their protocol specifications but also by their implementations, memory management mechanisms in operating systems, traffic management techniques deployed in network routers, operating characteristics of the underlying communication channels, and the nature of background traffic present in the network. In large networks, therefore, it can be exceedingly difficult to predict accurately the performance of TCP/IP applications. The only way to gauge precisely the performance, and in turn to tune the network for high performance, is to measure performance of live networks. The performance measurement tools can help users to reveal potential bottlenecks, detect inadequate parameter settings, and test component reliability in complex TCP/IP networking environments. Chapter 3 introduces popular TCP/IP performance measurement tools with detailed descriptions of their usage, options, and installations.

Chapter 4. Performance measurement of live networks is not always possible. For example, to evaluate the performance of a proposed router algorithm, temporarily deploying the algorithm in the Internet routers may not be feasible. Additionally, for comparison purposes, we cannot repeat the same traffic and other environment parameters for successive measurements with other algorithms. Because of these difficulties, simulation has emerged as a popular tool for performance evaluation of complex TCP/IP algorithms and protocols. Chapter 4 discusses the fundamental concepts and techniques for network simulation, including validation, verification, and statistical correctness of simulation results. Using several examples, this chapter introduces two popular simulation tools widely used for TCP/IP network simulation.

Chapter 5. Chapter 5 presents the mathematical models that can be applied to gain deeper understanding of TCP dynamics. There are several reasons why we would want to move beyond measurement and simulation and start using mathematical machinery for the performance analysis of TCP/IPs. First, the sheer scale of the Internet is so large that we cannot capture all possible behaviors using simulation or experimental measurements. Second, there still exist many uncertainties in the existing and emerging environments in which TCP operates. These uncertainties can be effectively represented using stochastic processes that drive the responses of TCP. Finally, by modeling the current protocols, we can further determine how close they are to achieving the optimum performance and identify issues that must be addressed in future protocols.

Chapter 6. The current strong drive toward Internet access via mobile terminals makes the inclusion of wireless systems such as Cellular Communications (CC) and Wireless Local Area Networks (WLAN) into the mainstream Internet very desirable. Wireless systems, however, raise a multitude of performance issues, because environmental conditions and terrestrial obstructions and reflections lead to high and unpredictable error rates. CC and WLAN systems mostly share the characteristics of traditional wireless systems (satellite and terrestrial microwave), such as high error rates. They also share some of the characteristics of wired systems, such as low physical layer propagation delays. As a result, to improve their performance, a synthesis of techniques for enhancing the performance of both wired and wireless links is required. Such a synthesis must take into account the requirements of the TCP/IP suite. Chapter 6 explains the TCP/IP performance issues in wireless environments and surveys a wide range of approaches for enhancing TCP/IP performance in such environments.

Chapter 7. While the ability to remain connected to the Internet even when mobile is obviously attractive to an Internet user, it severely exposes the limitations of the different layers of the current Internet's TCP/IP suite, which was designed for a primarily static environment. Chapter 7 illustrates the impact of mobility on the TCP protocol and discusses several approaches that have been proposed to improve TCP's performance.

Chapter 8. Optical networks are being deployed in the Internet backbones paving the way for the next generation of high-speed Internet. The introduction of optical technology in the Internet architecture brings in new challenges and performance issues. Chapter 8 reviews the main proposals for all optical networking with a particular focus on all optical packet switching. This chapter also shows how these requirements affect TCP performance taking into account the end-to-end network performance.

Chapter 9. While optical systems address the ever-increasing bandwidth demand, satellite systems continue to play a significant role in providing ubiquitous access to the Internet. Unfortunately, because of long propagation delays, standard TCP cannot achieve its full potential over satellite connections. Chapter 9 examines the fundamental performance issues in satellite-based TCP/IP communications and discusses solutions to address them.

Chapter 10. The ever-increasing desire of users for high-speed Internet connectivity has led to the deployment of many new network access technologies, such as cable modem and digital subscriber line (DSL). These networking technologies often exhibit *asymmetry* in their network characteristics—the network characteristics in one direction may be quite different from those in the opposite direction. For instance, the *upstream* bandwidth of the cable plant, from the customer premises out to the Internet, is often limited compared to its *downstream* bandwidth toward the customer premises. Bandwidth is not the only source of asymmetry. Asymmetry can also be observed in terms of packet loss rate and media access. Network asymmetry can have an adverse impact on the performance of feedback-based transport protocols such as TCP. The reason for this is that even if the network path in the direction of data flow is uncongested, congestion in the opposite direction can disrupt the flow of feedback. This disruption can lead to poor performance. Chapter 10 provides an in-depth discussion of the performance problems caused by network asymmetry in the context of TCP. Solutions to achieve near-optimal TCP performance under a variety of asymmetric conditions are described.

Chapter 11. Although the original design of TCP was capable of sustaining rapid growth and diversity in the Internet, it had some "flaws" in its congestion control engine. Congestion collapse first occurred in the Internet in 1986 [179]. An investigation resulted in the design of new congestion control algorithms, now an essential part of TCP. Since the development of the basic TCP congestion control algorithm, known as TCP Tahoe in 1988 [44, 179], a number of variations of the TCP congestion control algorithm have been proposed and studied. Chapter 11 discusses the most prominent variants or flavors of TCP and presents performance comparisons using simulations.

Chapter 12. Performance of TCP-based applications depends not only on TCP's congestion control algorithms but also on the choice of queue management in the network routers. Queue management is defined as the algorithms that manage the length of packet queues by dropping packets when necessary or appropriate [69]. From the point of dropping packets, queue management can be classified into two categories. The first category is *passive queue management* (PQM), which does not employ any preventive packet drop before the router buffer gets full or has reached a specified value. The second category is *active queue management* (AQM), which employs preventive packet drop before the router buffer gets full. The expected advantages of AQM include increased throughput, reduced delay, and reduced jitter. Chapter 12 discusses the background, objective, and motivation of AQM. It also surveys a number of AQM schemes.

Chapter 13. On high-speed networks, performance of TCP-based applications is often limited by the capability of the end systems to generate, transmit, receive, and process the data at network speeds. Most traditional implementations, such as BSD implementation, cannot cope with the emerging high-speed networks (e.g., Giga bits per second (Gbps) Ethernet) at line-speed. Chapter 13 gives a structural overview of a typical TCP implementation followed by a discussion of the protocol-related extensions for high performance networks, end-system techniques for low-overhead TCP/IP networking, and approaches to avoid excessive data copying. Many of the implementation issues and techniques discussed in this chapter concern the relationship between the TCP stack and the surrounding system, rather than the protocol implementation itself. Some do not affect interoperability, and, thus, fall outside the scope of the TCP-related RFCs. Even so, they are increasingly important as Ethernet and other IP network technologies advance. As a result of these advances, TCP often serves as a standard transport for storage access and server-server coordination in datacenter environments, which were previously the domain of more specialized networking technologies such as FibreChannel. This places additional pressure on TCP/IP implementations to deliver competitive end-to-end (application-to-application) performance.

1.6   FURTHER READING

In Section 1.4, we have discussed many performance metrics without providing their mathematical definitions. Without common definitions, different analysts may use different formulas to measure the same metrics, which may lead to confusion. At the time of this writing, both the International Telecommunications Union (ITU) and the Internet Engineering Task Force (IETF) were working on achieving standard definitions of IP performance metrics [171, 175]. IETF has already defined five metrics: connectivity [229], one-way delay [45], one-way packet loss [46], round-trip delay [47], and bulk-transfer capability [234].

Although not yet defined by IETF, throughput variation is used in the research community to measure the smoothness of a flow [144, 325]. Coefficient of variation (CoV) is a popular method used to define throughput variation in the following way. Consider a time scale of δ seconds. For a given flow F, compute the average throughput in each successive interval of δ seconds as the number of bytes transmitted during the interval divided by δ, for n intervals. This gives a time series of $\{G_i\}_{i=1}^{n}$, where G_i is the average throughput of interval i. CoV is defined as the standard deviation of the time series divided by the mean of the time series. For TCP connections, δ is usually a multiple of round-trip times (RTTs). For example, $\delta = 1$ means that throughput variation is measured over the time scale of one RTT of the connection.

Fairness is another metric widely used for evaluating TCP congestion control algorithms. There are several definitions of fairness. One popular definition, known as Jain's fairness index [186], computes a single dimensionless fraction between 0 and 1 to obtain the fairness among N flows as:

$$F = \frac{(\sum_{i=1}^{N} x_i)^2}{N \sum_{i=1}^{N} x_i^2} \tag{1.1}$$

where x_i is the resource (e.g., throughput, buffer space, etc.) allocation for flow i. Other definitions that are slightly different from Jain's fairness index are also used by researchers and analysts [144, 205]. As mentioned in Section 1.4, studies have shown that short-term fairness may not be the same as long-term fairness in some systems [144, 205, 325].

Protocol overhead (or protocol-related extra bytes) sometimes can be a concern for TCP/IP networks. For example, protocol overhead can be as high as 20% if Asynchronous Transfer Mode (ATM) networks are used to connect IP routers. There are techniques to reduce such overhead. Hassan and Atiquzzaman [158] dedicated an entire book to explaining a comprehensive list of TCP/IP performance issues over ATM networks.

1.7 SUMMARY

Installations of TCP/IP networks continue to grow exponentially. We are using TCP/IP services more than ever before, and this trend is likely to continue in the future with the advancement in wireless technology. There are millions of businesses worldwide that have some form of on-line presence using TCP/IP technology. The ever-increasing dependence on TCP/IP networks dictates designing, building, and maintaining high performance TCP/IP networks to maximize the benefits of being on-line. Good understanding of the TCP engine, its implementation in end systems, and its complex interactions with external communication environment holds the key to designing and implementing high performance TCP/IP networks in home, corporate, or public domains.

1.8   REVIEW QUESTIONS

1. Name five TCP/IP-based applications.

2. Consider the things you usually do at home or office. Try to identify the ones that use TCP/IP networking in some way, directly or indirectly. Is TCP/IP performance important to you? If so, in what ways?

3. Name five performance measures of TCP/IP networks.

4. Consider a network in which two TCP flows, TCP-1 and TCP-2, are sharing a bottleneck link. The same link is also shared by other UDP flows. The RTT of the link is 50 ms. We are interested in measuring performance of TCP-1 and TCP-2. TCP traffic is captured for the first 3000 ms. Table 1.1 gives packet arrival times at destinations for TCP-1 and TCP-2. Using the CoV method, compute throughput variation of TCP-1 for the following two time scales:

   (a) $\delta = 1 \times RTT$

   (b) $\delta = 2 \times RTT$

   Explain the differences in throughput variances for two time scales.

5. Consider Table 1.1. Using Eq. (1.1), compute long-term fairness (over 3000 ms) between TCP-1 and TCP-2. Do we have fair sharing of bandwidth?

6. What is the difference between long-term fairness and short-term fairness? Give an application scenario in which network operators may be interested in short-term fairness.

7. Give three motivating factors for measuring one-way performance metrics.

8. Provide an example of TCP/IP networking scenario in which delay in the forward direction may be significantly different from the one in the reverse direction.

9. One-way delay measurement of a corporate TCP/IP network spanning two distant sites reveals that the mean one-way delay is 500 ms. Which of the following applications can run satisfactorily over this network?

TABLE 1.1: Packet arrival times for review questions 4 and 5.

TCP Flow	Packet Arrival Time (ms)
TCP-1	25 51 78 120 141 181 202 240 305 360 380 401 420 448 505 520 560 605 655 710 760 780 860 910 930 960 1010 1030 1110 1140 1165 1206 1266 1285 1305 1401 1449 1499 1502 1551 1604 1655 1675 1705 1755 1801 1858 1899 1903 1999 2055 2075 2103 2153 2205 2249 2298 2312 2332 2349 2401 2420 2455 2501 2555 2601 2620 2655 2701 2720 2735 2855 2875 2955 2975 2995
TCP-2	1 63 99 106 128 135 149 280 390 455 475 530 540 575 675 730 751 770 791 820 875 940 980 1040 1101 1130 1152 1190 1230 1251 1295 1360 1412 1421 1435 1475 1575 1620 1631 1690 1720 1735 1775 1791 1815 1825 1841 1931 1975 2090 2125 2140 2165 2181 2230 2275 2375 2435 2475 2530 2634 2675 2746 2776 2830 2930 2986

(a) Voice-over IP

(b) File transfer

(c) Web browsing

(d) E-mail

(e) Video on demand

10. Explain how an efficient TCP/IP implementation can extend the battery life of a mobile device.

1.9 CASE STUDY: INTRODUCTION TO WIRELESS CORPORATION

Wireless Corporation (WCORP) is a high-tech research and development (R&D) organization with its headquarters in Sydney, Australia. The major source of revenue for WCORP is contract research for large telecommunication vendors. To capitalize on the unprecedented growth in the wireless market, the CEO of the company has recently opened another office in Melbourne, Australia. Currently, WCORP employs 70 research scientists in Sydney and 50 in Melbourne. In addition, each office has several support staff for smooth operation of the business. Each office has installed Local Area Network (LAN)s based on 100 Mbps Ethernet technology. A 256 Kbps leased line connects the Sydney office and the Melbourne office.

Over the years, WCORP has installed a large number of different systems to meet its ever-growing computing and communication needs. At present, supported systems include Microsoft Windows–family PCs and compatibles (including NT), IBM AS/400, Novell Netware, DEC VAX VMS, and UNIX-based systems. Major applications include e-mail, file transfer, and remote terminal access. To support interconnectivity between all computers, WCORP had installed multiple protocol stacks on each PC. Table 1.2 shows the stacks (and the corresponding systems) loaded on each PC.

Currently, the volume of intra- and interoffice traffic is low, and network users are happy with the network performance. In subsequent chapters, we will witness significant growth and diversity in the company that will bring changes in traffic volume, networking technology, and communication patterns. These changes will call for performance evaluation of the network to identify appropriate solutions for high performance TCP/IP networking.

TABLE 1.2: Protocol stacks loaded on each PC at WCORP.

Protocol Stack	System
MS-DOS	MS-DOS and Windows
SNA	IBM AS/400
IPX/SPX	Novell Netware
DECnet	DEC VAX VMS
TCP/IP	UNIX

CHAPTER 2

TCP/IP Fundamentals

CHAPTER OBJECTIVES

After completing this chapter, the reader should be able to:

- Gain an understanding of the basic services provided by TCP, UDP, and IP

- Explain the congestion control algorithms employed by TCP

- Describe protocol details of TCP necessary to ensure reliable data transfer over unreliable networks

Most of the performance issues in TCP/IP networks arise from various interactions between the TCP engine and the surrounding communication environment. To understand these performance issues and the techniques to address them, the reader must be familiar with some of the basic details of TCP/IP protocols. This chapter reviews the TCP/IP protocol fundamentals necessary for understanding the subsequent chapters in the book. Many details, not directly referenced in the rest of the book, are deliberately left out. For more comprehensive coverage of TCP/IP, readers should consult books dedicated to TCP/IP protocols, such as that by Comer [113].

2.1 TCP

TCP is a very complex protocol. To understand the performance dynamics of TCP, one has to learn its basic operations. In this section, we explain some of the key features of TCP, including the flow control and congestion control.

2.1.1 TCP Services

TCP provides several useful services to its applications. These services are briefly described in this section.

Connection-Oriented Service. TCP is a connection-oriented protocol. Before two application processes can start sending data to each other, they must establish a TCP connection between them. If multiple application processes are running on a given IP host, each process is identified by a unique port number in that host, so each of them can establish a separate TCP connection. Each TCP connection is identified by a 4-tuple, source IP address, source TCP port number, destination IP address, and destination TCP port number. The connection is terminated upon completion of the communication session. Connection establishments and terminations are explained later in the section.

Streaming Service. TCP provides a *streaming* service to its applications. Once a TCP connection is established between two application processes (one is a sending process, the other is a receiving process), the sender writes a stream of bytes (or characters) into the connection and the receiver reads these bytes out of the connection. The stream-oriented abstraction is visible only to the applications; the TCP layer itself operates on a *packet mode*. The sending TCP accumulates a certain amount of application bytes, forms a packet called a TCP segment, and sends the segment to the receiving TCP. The receiving TCP extracts application bytes from the segment, orders them if necessary, and delivers them as a stream of bytes to the appropriate receiving application process. The format of a TCP segment is explained later in the section.

Full-Duplex Service. TCP is a full-duplex protocol supporting data flow in both directions. This means that once a TCP connection has been established between two application processes, either process can send data to the other over the same connection at the same time.

Reliable Service. TCP guarantees delivery of every single byte, in order, without any duplication. To achieve reordering of any out-of-order arrival and to eliminate any duplicate delivery, the receiving TCP buffers the incoming data before delivering them to the application process. To guarantee the delivery of data, TCP uses the acknowledgment mechanism to check if the transmitted data have been received correctly by the receiver. Details of the acknowledgment procedure are described in a later section. Unacknowledged data are retransmitted later. If the underlying communication channel is noisy and error-prone, several retransmissions of the same segment may be necessary for correct delivery of data to the receiver. For most data applications, such as file transfer and the World Wide Web, the reliability feature is extremely important as the applications do not have to worry about the lost or disordered data.

End-to-End Semantic. TCP's reliability is based on an end-to-end semantic. Acknowledgments (ACKs) are generated only by the receiving TCP and only after the data are received correctly by the receiver. Therefore, when a TCP sender receives an ACK, it is guaranteed that the data have reached the receiver safely. It is this end-to-end semantic that provides the ultimate reliability at the TCP layer. The end-to-end semantic would be violated if any intermediate node (not the TCP destination) generates ACKs on behalf of the destination.

2.1.2 Header Format

Each TCP segment has two parts, a standard 20-byte header followed by a variable payload containing the application data. The header contains much useful information, such as the advertised window size, ACK number, and so on. To understand TCP operations, it is necessary to examine the meanings and purposes of these fields. In this section, we describe the header format (Figure 2.1), the fields in the header, and their meanings.

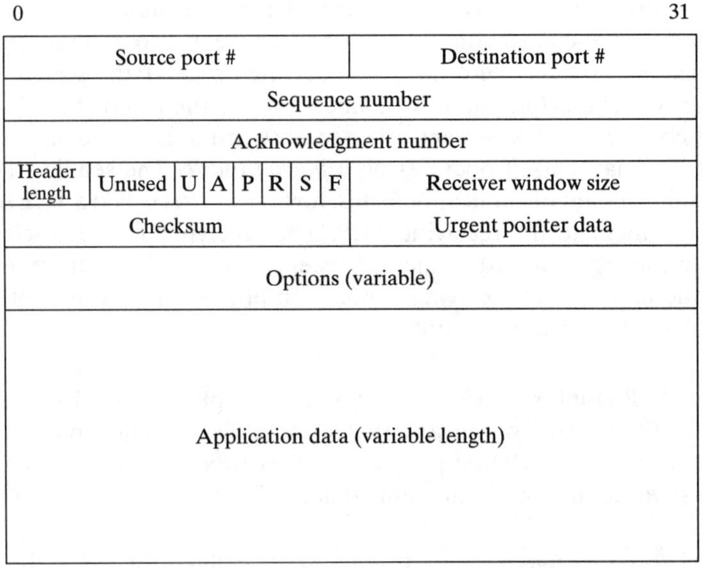

0   31

Source port #	Destination port #
Sequence number	
Acknowledgment number	

Header length	Unused	U	A	P	R	S	F	Receiver window size

Checksum	Urgent pointer data
Options (variable)	

Application data (variable length)

FIGURE 2.1: TCP segment format.

Source port number (16 bits). Each TCP application at the source host is uniquely identified by the source port number. The port identification allows multiplexing and demultiplexing multiple TCP connections over the same TCP protocol process.

Destination port number (16 bits). It identifies a TCP application at the destination host. When a TCP segment is received at the destination host, this port number is used to deliver the segment data to the correct application.

Sequence number (32 bits). The 32-bit sequence number field contains the sequence number of the first byte of data carried in the TCP segment. As an example, if the preceding segment started with a sequence number of 2001 and contained 1460 bytes of data, then the sequence number of the next TCP segment is set to 3461.

Acknowledgment number (32 bits). The destination uses this field to acknowledge the correctly received data.

Header length (4 bits). This field is used to indicate the length of TCP header in multiples of 32-bit words. In most cases the header length of a TCP segment is 20 bytes; however, this may vary if the options field is used. Because the header can be of variable length, the length field also helps to identify the start of the payload.

Reserved (6 bits). These six bits are reserved for future or experimental use.

Flags (6 bits). A TCP segment may carry several different types of protocol messages, such as ACK, start signal of a connection, end signal of a connection,

TABLE 2.1: TCP flags.

Flag	Description
ACK (A)	Acknowledgment field valid
FIN (F)	Final segment from sender
PSH (P)	Push operation invoked. Receiving process needs notification.
RST (R)	Connection to be reset
SYN (S)	Start of a new connection
URG (U)	Urgent pointer field valid

and so on. Each bit in the flag field is used to identify a given type. Table 2.1 shows the purpose of each of the six flag bits. The multiple flag bits may be set at the same time. For example, if an end signal is carried along with an ACK, both ACK and final (FIN) flags must be set in that segment.

Receiver window size (16 bits). The receiver advertises its window (available buffer space) to the sender using this field. The receiver window is used by the sender for the purposes of flow control.

Checksum (16 bits). The checksum field is computed over the TCP header, the TCP payload, and the pseudoheader consisting of the source and destination IP addresses as well as the length field of the IP header. The checksum field protects the header and the payload of the TCP segment.

Urgent pointer (16 bits). A TCP segment may carry data that need priority treatment (the urgent [URG] flag would be set for this segment). For example, an URG pointer may be used to pass escape characters to cancel an operation on a remote computer. The URG data is processed before any other data waiting in the buffer. The 16-bit URG pointer points to the last byte of URG data in the segment, so that the receiving TCP can easily locate the URG data for immediate processing.

Options (variable). Options are to be specified using multiples of bytes. There are two extra bytes preceding each option. The first byte indicates the option type followed by the second byte indicating the length of the option in bytes (including these two preceding bytes). Examples of options are:

- **Maximum Segment Size (MSS) (16 bits).** This option is used by the originating TCP during connection establishment (in the start-of-a-new-connection [SYN] segment) to negotiate the MSS to be used for the connection. The 16 bits used for this field limit the MSS to 64 KB.

- **Timestamp (8 bytes).** The timestamp option is to be used for more accurate round-trip time (RTT) calculations. Two four-byte timestamp fields are used for this option. The sending TCP fills the first field with the current time. The receiver echoes back the timestamp value received in the second field in an ACK segment. This facilitates the sender for more accurate calculation of the RTT.

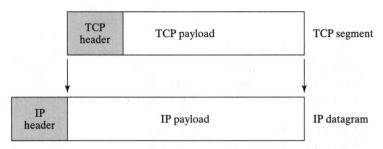

FIGURE 2.2: Encapsulation of TCP segments into IP datagrams.

2.1.3 Encapsulation in IP

Once a TCP segment is ready for transmission, it is passed on to the IP layer. The IP layer encapsulates the entire TCP segment, the TCP header, and the TCP payload into the IP datagram payload. Figure 2.2 illustrates the encapsulation of a TCP segment in an IP datagram. Given this encapsulation method, the first 20 bytes of an IP datagram payload contain all fields of a standard (no options used) TCP header.

2.1.4 Acknowledgment Mechanism

TCP relies on acknowledgments from the receiver to confirm correct delivery of data. Some of the important features of TCP's ACK mechanism are described below.

Cumulative Acknowledgment. Each ACK is a confirmation that all bytes up to the ACK number has been received correctly. For example, if the destination sends an ACK of 2001, it means that all bytes up to and including 2000 have been received. One obvious benefit of such cumulative ACK is that many lost ACKs are easily compensated for by the subsequent ACKs of higher numbers.

ACK-Only Segment and Piggybacking. The ACK is indicated through an ACK field in the TCP header. Therefore, to acknowledge correctly received bytes, a receiver can either create an ACK-only segment (the segment carries only the header containing the ACK number, no data are sent in this segment), or it can send the ACK in a data segment (segment carrying data in the reverse direction). When an ACK travels in a data segment, the process is called *piggybacking*. Piggybacking reduces ACK traffic in the reverse direction.

Delayed ACK. The receiving TCP has the choice of either generating an ACK as soon as it receives a segment or delaying the ACK for a while. By delaying the ACK, the receiver may be able to acknowledge two segments at a time and reduce ACK traffic; however, delaying an ACK for too long may cause a timeout and retransmission at the sender. A TCP receiver should not delay ACKs more than 500 ms.

Duplicate ACK. If a segment gets lost in the network, but the following segment arrives safely at the receiver, it is possible for a receiving TCP to receive data with a sequence number beyond the expected range. In that case, the receiving

TCP buffers the incoming bytes and regenerates the ACK for the bytes received so far in sequence. The regeneration of the same ACK number causes the duplicate ACK phenomenon at the sender, that is, the sender can receive the same ACK more than once. In the original TCP, the sender simply ignores the duplicate ACK. As we will see in a later chapter, some later variants of TCP take special actions based on duplicate ACKs.

2.1.5   Retransmission Mechanism

Retransmission is the basic tenet of TCP's reliable data transfer service. If a segment is lost, it has to be retransmitted. To detect the loss of a segment, TCP maintains a *retransmission timer* for each segment sent. The timer is set for a duration called the retransmission timeout (RTO) period. If an ACK is received during the RTO, the timer is cleared; otherwise the timer expires. On expiration of the retransmission timer, the segment is retransmitted.

Setting an optimum value for the RTO is very significant from the performance point of view. The timeout period should be greater than the round-trip time (RTT) to accommodate various delays, such as the transmission delay, the link propagation delay, the header processing time, the ACK generation time, and so on. In a dynamic environment, however, the actual RTT may vary over time. On the one hand, setting the RTO longer than necessary would result in longer delay for applications if losses are frequent. On the other hand, smaller values may result in premature retransmissions causing waste of communication resources such as bandwidth and processing time.

To address this problem, the TCP sender maintains an estimate of RTT for each of its connections. Let us use the variable `EstimatedRTT` to represent this estimate. `EstimatedRTT` is calculated from a sample RTT (`SampleRTT`) of the connection, where `SampleRTT` is defined as the time from the moment a TCP segment is transmitted until an ACK is received for the segment. Because `SampleRTT` usually varies between measurements (the variation is usually caused by the variable queuing delays in intermediate routers), an exponential weighted moving average is used to calculate the `EstimatedRTT`:

$$\text{EstimatedRTT} = (1 - \alpha) * \text{EstimatedRTT} + \alpha * \text{SampleRTT} \qquad (2.1)$$

A typical value used for α is 0.125, which has the impact of giving a low weight to the `SampleRTT` value measured in the previous period and a high weight to the historical data represented by `EstimatedRTT`. Lower α value avoids an RTT estimate being skewed by any spikes in the measured samples.
Once RTT is known, the RTO is estimated as:

$$RTO = \text{EstimatedRTT} + 4 * \text{deviation} \qquad (2.2)$$

where

$$\text{deviation} = (1 - \alpha) * \text{Deviation} + \alpha * |\text{SampleRTT} - \text{EstimatedRTT}| \qquad (2.3)$$

The deviation factor in Equation (2.2) accommodates any fluctuations in `SampleRTT` from `EstimatedRTT`. For links with consistent `SampleRTT`, this factor will be negligible. Equation (2.3) is used to maintain the exponentially weighted moving average of the deviation.

Most TCP implementations represent the RTO as a multiple of clock "ticks." The retransmission timer is then decremented every clock tick. The timer expires when the value reaches zero. A retransmission timer should be set to at least two ticks. In many popular implementations a tick equals 500 milliseconds yielding a minimum RTO of 1 second. Recent operating systems, such as Solaris, have smaller tick values.

2.1.6　Connection Establishment and Termination

TCP provides the connection-oriented service through two procedures, connection establishment and connection termination. A connection is established before starting the data transfer. When the data transfer completes, the connection is explicitly terminated. In this section we show the steps involved in connection establishment and termination.

Connection Establishment.　　The process of establishing a TCP connection is called *three-way handshaking*. Figure 2.3 illustrates the steps of three-way handshaking using a *client-server* model (e.g., a web client tries to establish a TCP connection with a web server to download a file):

1. The client sends a SYN segment (SYN-bit set in the header) to the server with an initial sequence number (e.g., SeqNo = 88) that it is going to use for this connection.

2. The server sends a segment that has both SYN and ACK bits set in the flag (SYN + ACK, AckNo = 89, SeqNo = 155). The ACK number (AckNo) indicates that the server has received bytes up to 88 correctly and the next byte it expects has sequence number 89. The sequence number (SeqNo) tells the client that the server will use 155 as the starting sequence number for its data. The client and the server may use different initial sequence numbers.

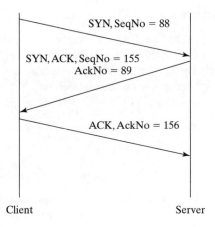

FIGURE 2.3: TCP connection establishment using three-way handshaking.

3. Finally, the client acknowledges the server's sequence number (AckNo = 156) with an ACK segment. Now the client and the server have successfully established a TCP connection between them and are ready to exchange data over this connection.

Connection Termination.   The process of terminating a TCP connection is called *four-way handshaking* (Figure 2.4). The steps of four-way handshaking are:

1. The client sends a FIN segment (FIN-bit set in the header) to the server to indicate that it wishes to terminate the connection.
2. The server sends an ACK to confirm the receipt of the FIN segment. At this stage the TCP client stops communication in the client-server direction. The server, however, may need to continue the communication in the server-client direction (e.g., part of a file is yet to be transmitted).
3. When the server is ready to close the connection, it sends a FIN segment to the client. Because the server is not necessarily ready to terminate the server-client communication when it receives a FIN segment from the client, steps 2 and 3 may not be combined.
4. The client acknowledges the receipt of the FIN segment with an ACK segment. Now the connection is terminated from both ends.

Each handshake introduces some delays (the SYN or FIN segments need to travel to the other ends). The handshaking is the major source of delay in establishing and terminating TCP connections for long-distance communications (e.g., in satellite TCP/IP networks).

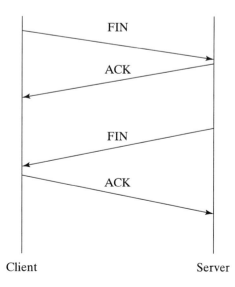

FIGURE 2.4: TCP connection termination using four-way handshaking.

2.1.7 Flow Control and Sliding Window

Flow control is the mechanism that prevents a fast sender from swamping a slow receiver. Each TCP receiver allocates some buffer for a TCP connection. Data received (correctly and in order) are placed in this buffer for the corresponding application to read them and clear the buffer as soon as possible. However, in many situations (e.g., a slow laptop downloading a file from a high-speed server on the LAN), the application in the receiving host may not be able to keep up with the data-arriving rate, leading to buffer overflow at the receiver. In such situations, TCP exercises flow control to adjust the transmission rate of the sending TCP to prevent buffer overflow at the receiver.

Sliding Window.   TCP implements a sliding window scheme to accomplish the flow control. The size of the window controls the number of bytes in transit (transmitted but not yet acknowledged). When a window full of data is in transit, TCP must stop transmitting any further segments and wait for acknowledgment from the receiver. When an acknowledgment arrives, TCP can transmit new bytes not exceeding the number of bytes acknowledged.

The sliding window concept is illustrated in Figure 2.5. In this example, the window size is six bytes (TCP's flow control is byte-based), which will allow a maximum of six bytes to be in transit. We have the following steps:

- **Step 1.** Bytes 0, 1, and 2 have already been transmitted and acknowledged by the receiver. Bytes 3, 4, and 5 have already been sent, and the sender is waiting for ACK. Since the window size is 6, bytes 6, 7, and 8 are allowed to be transmitted. Bytes 9 and above cannot be sent because of the window size limitation.

- **Step 2.** TCP has sent bytes 6, 7, and 8, and it is waiting for ACK for all segments in its current window. A window full of data is in transit; no more data can be sent at this stage.

- **Step 3.** ACK for bytes 3 and 4 has been received. At this stage, the sliding window slides by two to the right, making bytes 9 and 10 eligible to be sent.

- **Step 4.** TCP sends bytes 9 and 10 and again starts waiting for ACK.

In summary, the right-hand side of the window slides when a byte is sent, whereas the left-hand side of the window slides when an ACK is received. The maximum number of bytes waiting for ACK is determined by the window size.

Window Size Adjustment.   In the example of Figure 2.5, we used a *fixed* window size of six bytes. In practice, the window size is adjusted dynamically according to the available buffer space in the receiving TCP. The receiving TCP can increase or decrease the size of the window in an ACK segment (using the Receiver Window Size field in the TCP segment header). The sending TCP maintains a variable called *AdvertisedWindow* to keep track of the current window size for the purposes of flow control.

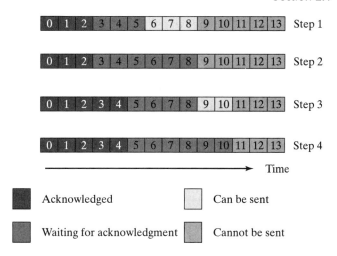

FIGURE 2.5: TCP's sliding window.

2.1.8 Congestion Control

Flow control effectively prevents buffer overflow at the receiver by dynamically adjusting the *AdvertisedWindow* according to the available buffer space at the receiver. The flow control mechanism, however, does not address the buffer overflow problem in the intermediate routers during network congestion. To address network congestion, TCP implements a set of mechanisms collectively called *congestion control*.

The fundamental principle behind congestion control is to adjust the transmission window of the sender in such a way that buffer overflow is prevented not only at the receiver but also at the intermediate routers. To achieve this, TCP uses another window control variable called *CongestionWindow*. The idea is that if somehow we could learn the available buffer space in the most congested (bottleneck) router in the end-to-end path of the TCP connection, we could set the *CongestionWindow* accordingly and select the actual transmission window as the minimum of *AdvertisedWindow* and *CongestionWindow*. This would prevent buffer overflow both at the receiver and in the network.

The challenge is how to learn the available buffer space in the network routers. Routers do not participate at the TCP layer and, hence, cannot use the TCP ACK segments to adjust the window. To overcome this problem, TCP assumes network congestion whenever a retransmission timer expires and reacts to network congestion by adjusting *CongestionWindow* using three algorithms, *slow-start*, *congestion avoidance*, and *multiplicative decrease*. Several modifications of these algorithms are currently available. In this section, we describe the original versions; modifications are discussed in Chapter 11.

Slow Start.   The principle behind the slow-start mechanism is to start with a small window size and increase it "slowly" (we will later see that it is not so slow) when ACKs arrive. This has the effect of *probing* the available buffer space in the network. The actual window increase mechanism is as follows.

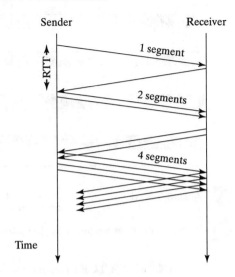

FIGURE 2.6: TCP slow-start.

Initially, the *CongestionWindow* is set to one segment. The window size is increased by one each time a segment is acknowledged. Assuming a large *AdvertisedWindow* (i.e., *AdvertisedWindow* remains greater than the *CongestionWindow*), the transmission of segments during a slow-start is illustrated in Figure 2.6. At first TCP sends one segment. After receiving the ACK for this segment, it sends two more segments (*CongestionWindow* is incremented to two). When these two new segments are acknowledged in the following RTT (*CongestionWindow* is now incremented to four), it sends four new segments and so on.

Congestion Avoidance. We have seen in the example of Figure 2.6 that after each RTT, the window size practically gets doubled, allowing twice as many segments to be transmitted. The exponential growth of the *CongestionWindow* (against RTT) is illustrated in Figure 2.7. Unless the exponential growth is checked at some point, it can quickly lead to congestion. To avoid congestion before it happens, TCP implements the *congestion avoidance* algorithm, which forces a linear increase of the *CongestionWindow* after it reaches a threshold. This threshold is dynamically adjusted through a variable called *ssthresh*.

The linear increase during congestion avoidance is achieved by incrementing the *CongestionWindow* by *1/CongestionWindow* each time an ACK is received. This way the *CongestionWindow* is effectively increased by one every RTT. Figure 2.7 shows an example of how the *CongestionWindow* is controlled by the slow-start and the congestion avoidance algorithms for an *ssthresh* of 8. It shows the increase of the *CongestionWindow* as a function of RTT. The *CongestionWindow* increases exponentially during slow-start phase until it reaches the value of *ssthresh* (8 in this case). After this period, it enters the congestion avoidance phase and starts to grow linearly.

Multiplicative Decrease. Transition from slow-start phase to congestion avoidance phase is controlled by the variable *ssthresh*. *Multiplicative decrease* is

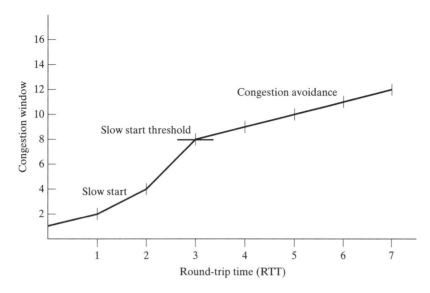

FIGURE 2.7: Congestion avoidance.

the algorithm that controls this variable. With multiplicative decrease, TCP sets *ssthresh* to half of the current *CongestionWindow* each time a timeout occurs (at timeout *CongestionWindow* itself is set to one segment to force a slow-start) down to a minimum of two segments. Therefore, if there are consecutive timeouts (severe network congestion), multiplicative decrease reduces the sending rate exponentially. The *additive increase* of the *CongestionWindow* during the congestion avoidance phase and the *multiplicative decrease* of *ssthresh* is often referred to as the additive increase, multiplicative decrease (AIMD) algorithm.

2.2   UDP

In addition to TCP, the TCP/IP protocol stack provides another transport protocol called User Datagram Protocol (UDP). In this section, we present an overview of UDP.

2.2.1   UDP Services

Unlike TCP, UDP provides a much simpler, bare minimum service to the applications. All UDP provides is a mechanism for the application to send a short message to a given destination. UDP is connectionless, unreliable, and not stream-oriented (it is datagram-oriented). With the datagram-oriented service, UDP cannot accept a stream of data from the application and segment them for transmission. The application is supposed to supply segmented data to UDP for transportation as an independent datagram.

Because UDP is connectionless, it does not implement connection establishment and connection termination. Lack of reliability means that there is no ACK and retransmission mechanisms and no sequence numbers to identify each datagram; therefore, a UDP sender will not know if a datagram was lost on the way.

TABLE 2.2: Key differences between TCP and UDP.

TCP	UDP
Connection-oriented	Connectionless
Stream-oriented	Datagram-oriented
Reliable	Unreliable
Implements flow control	No flow control
Implements congestion control	No congestion control

There is no flow control either, meaning that a UDP receiver may experience buffer overflow. Table 2.2 summarizes the key differences between TCP and UDP.

One might be wondering about the practical uses of UDP given its simplicity. The simplicity of UDP actually turns out to be its strength for many applications that do not require the heavyweight services of TCP. Some of the traditional and emerging uses of UDP are:

- **Multicasting.** Multicasting is an application that sends the same piece of data to many receivers (e.g., video conferencing, web casting, etc.). Because TCP is a point-to-point connection-oriented protocol, it is not practical to use TCP for multicasting with a large number of receivers. UDP is connectionless, so UDP does not have this scalability problem with multicasting.

- **Network management.** Network management protocols, such as Simple Network Management Protocol (SNMP), use short request-response messages suitable for UDP. The overhead of connection establishment and connection termination for each of these short messages would be overkill.

- **Routing table update.** Like network management, the routing applications, such as Routing Information Protocol (RIP), rely on query-response type of communications. These applications sometimes use UDP for its simplicity.

- **Real-time multimedia.** The emerging audio and video applications, such as Netmeeting and RealAudio, use UDP. These real-time applications can tolerate occasional packet losses but cannot tolerate long delays caused by retransmissions of lost packets. By the time the retransmitted packet would arrive at the destination, it would become useless and be discarded anyway. TCP, therefore, is rarely used by real-time multimedia applications.

2.2.2 Header Format

Like TCP, UDP datagram has a header and a payload. The payload carries the application message and the header carries the information necessary for the correct operation of the UDP protocol. However, unlike TCP header, which has a standard size of 20 bytes and contains a large number of fields, the UDP header is very simple, only eight bytes long. Figure 2.8 shows the UDP header, which consists of four fields:

FIGURE 2.8: UDP header format.

- Source and destination port numbers (16 bits each). UDP provides port numbers to let multiple application processes share the same UDP services on the same host. With 16 bits, there are a total of 65,535 possible ports.

- Length (16 bits). The length field represents the total length of the UDP datagram (including header) in bytes.

- Checksum (16 bits). UDP provides a checksum field to check the integrity of its data. A packet with incorrect checksum is simply discarded at the receiver, with no further actions taken.

2.2.3 Encapsulation in IP

Like TCP, UDP datagrams also travel in the payload of IP datagrams. The entire UDP datagram, the header and the payload, is inserted in the IP payload; thus, the first eight bytes of the IP payload contain the UDP header.

2.3 IP

IP is the network layer protocol used by both TCP and UDP. In this section, we provide an overview of the IP protocol.

2.3.1 IP Services

The IP protocol provides a connectionless unreliable datagram model of communication. IP encapsulates the higher layer protocol units, such as TCP segments and UDP datagrams, within the IP datagram payload, creates the IP header, and forwards the complete IP datagram to the next hop router toward the destination. Each intermediate router processes the IP datagram header and forwards it to the next router along the path until it reaches the destination.

The connectionless model used by IP in the Internet has several advantages. First of all, there is no need for explicit connection establishment and termination. This simplifies the router design as the routers do not need to maintain any connection-related information; therefore, the connectionless model scales well for a large number of hosts in the Internet. Routers also have flexibility of choosing an appropriate path for each IP datagram based on the congestion level or link availability in the Internet.

The connection-less model of IP, however, has its price. IP cannot guarantee the delivery of data to the destination. The service it provides is often referred to as the "best-effort" service. This means that routers will try their best to deliver a datagram, but if there is congestion and routers cannot process datagrams fast enough, they may drop them. IP does not implement any retransmission of lost datagrams. There is also the possibility of datagrams arriving out of order at the destination, as routers may send different datagrams via different routes. Higher layer protocols, such as TCP, are used to build a reliable service on top of the unreliable IP.

2.3.2   Fragmentation and Reassembly

For ultimate transmission of IP datagrams over a given physical link, the datagrams must be encapsulated in the payload of the link layer frames as shown in Figure 2.9. The frame payload has to be large enough to hold a given IP datagram. For most physical network technologies, the payload size has an upper bound, which imposes a limit on the datagram size the frame can carry. The upper bound is called the Maximum Transfer Unit (MTU) of the network.

Because routers sometimes connect dissimilar networks, the MTU of one port may be larger than the MTU of the other port. For example, the Ethernet MTU is 1500 bytes, but a serial Point-to-Point Protocol (PPP) link has an MTU of 296. In that case, if a router receives a 1500-byte IP datagram from its Ethernet port and tries to send it over the PPP port, it must segment the original IP datagram into several pieces. The process of segmentation of IP datagrams is called *fragmentation*.

IP datagrams are fragmented in such a way that each fragment becomes a complete IP datagram that can travel to its destination independently of the other fragments. Once all fragments are received at the destination, the process of putting them all together to reconstruct the original datagram is called *reassembly*. Fragmentation can be done at the source or at any intermediate router, but reassembly is done only at the destination.

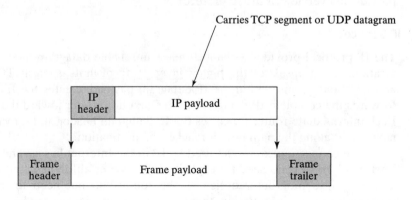

FIGURE 2.9: Encapsulation of IP datagram into link layer frame.

Fragmentation could be avoided if the minimum MTU in the end-to-end path could be discovered before the start of a communication. TCP has a variable called Maximum Segment Size (MSS) that determines the number of data bytes to be sent in a segment. TCP can select a MSS small enough to avoid fragmentation anywhere in the path. For example, if TCP can learn that it is going to communicate over an Ethernet network, it would select a MSS of 1460 bytes (1500 minus the 40 bytes for TCP and IP headers) to avoid fragmentation.

2.3.3 Header Format

Figure 2.10 shows the header format of the current IP version (version 4). Some of the key fields of the IP header are described below.

Version. This field indicates the version number of the IP datagram. Currently only version 4 is used, but version 6 will be available in the future. If a router or a host supports both versions 4 and 6, the datagram can be directed to the correct process using this field.

Header length. This field is used to indicate the length of header in multiples of 32-bit words. In most cases the header length of IP datagrams is 20 bytes (if options field is not used). Because the header can be of variable length, the length field helps to identify the start of the payload.

Type of service (TOS). This field was included in IP version 4 so that a source could request some form of privileged treatment from the routers. For example, control packets could get preferential treatment in the wake of congestion in the network. It could also be used to specify quality of service requirements, such as delay and throughput. However, it is not mandatory for the routers to support this feature. The Internet Engineering Task Force (IETF) is currently

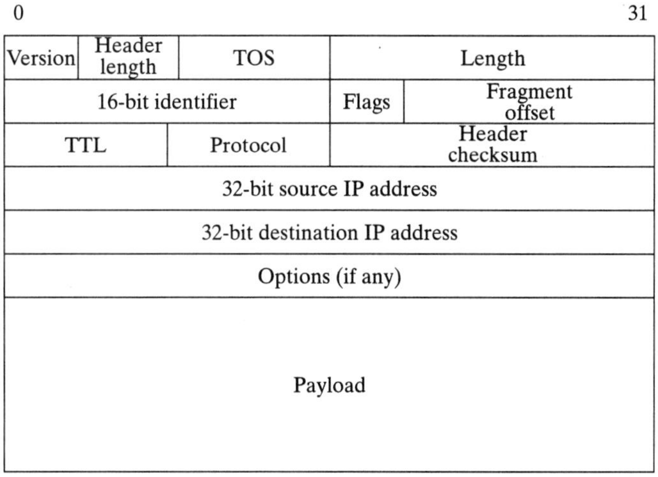

0				31
Version	Header length	TOS	Length	
16-bit identifier		Flags	Fragment offset	
TTL		Protocol	Header checksum	
32-bit source IP address				
32-bit destination IP address				
Options (if any)				
Payload				

FIGURE 2.10: IP version 4 header format.

working on standardizing these bits to support multiple services (as opposed to only best-effort service) in TCP/IP networks [254].

Total length. As the name suggests, total length field indicates the total length of a datagram in bytes including the header.

Identifier. This field is used to uniquely identify a datagram.

Flags and fragment offset. These two fields are used for fragmentation and reassembly. The flags field consists of three bits. The Don't Fragment (DF) bit is set by a source to indicate that this datagram should not be fragmented. The More Fragments (MF) bit indicates the last fragment of the datagram to facilitate reassembly at the destination. The third bit is currently unused. The Fragment Offset field indicates the exact position of the fragment in the original datagram.

Time to live. Because of the possible routing loops in the IP networks, datagrams can keep circulating in the network. This may result in a waste of resources. The time-to-live (TTL) field restricts the life of a datagram in the network. The TTL field indicates the maximum number of hops a datagram can traverse in the network. Each router decrements this counter by one. Once the value of this field reaches zero, the datagram is discarded by the router.

Protocol. The protocol field identifies the transport layer protocol at the receiver that should receive the data portion of the IP datagram. As an example, a value of six indicates that the IP datagram is destined for TCP, whereas a value of 17 indicates that it should be passed to a UDP. In essence, this field helps multiplexing and demultiplexing multiple higher layer protocols over the same IP layer.

Header checksum. The header checksum is used by routers to detect bit errors in a received IP datagram header. An error in the header may potentially result in delivery of the datagram to a wrong destination. Routers simply discard a datagram for which the checksum gives error. The data part of IP protocol is not protected by this checksum. It is up to the higher layers to recover from errors in the data field.

Source and destination addresses. These fields are used to identify the source and destination of the IP datagram. They contain 32-bit IP addresses.

Options: The option field can extend the IP header. As the name suggests, this field is not compulsory. This field can be used to support options such as security, source routing, route reordering, and timestamping. This field is of variable length as the number of options used in a datagram is not fixed.

Payload. This field encapsulates higher layer protocol units, such as TCP segments or UDP datagrams.

Padding. Padding field can be used to align the datagram to 32-bit words.

2.3.4 IP Version 6

To combat the IP address depletion problem, the IETF has recently defined a new version, version 6, for IP. The new version, referred to as IPv6, has a much larger address space; each address is 128 bits long. As a result, IPv6 has a much larger header size. The standard or base header size is 40 bytes, which is twice as much as the current 20 bytes in version 4.

Although IPv6 was originally designed to support large address space, it includes a number of new features. IPv6 supports authentication, data integrity, and confidentiality at the network layer. It has mechanisms to facilitate real-time audio and video transmission. However, the performance issues and concepts discussed in the later chapters are mainly concerned with the TCP layer. Whether IP version 4 or version 6 is used below TCP makes little difference to the material presented in these chapters. Detailed discussion of IPv6, therefore, is outside the scope of this book.

2.4 FURTHER READING

Comer's *Internetworking with TCP/IP* [113] is a classic book on TCP/IP. It covers the entire TCP/IP protocol stack with good details.

Forouzan's *TCP/IP Protocol Suite* [149] explains the entire TCP/IP suite with many easy-to-understand illustrations and examples.

Stevens's *TCP/IP Illustrated, Volume 1* [302], explains many concepts and operations of TCP by analyzing packet traces on live networks.

2.5 SUMMARY

TCP and UDP are two transport layer protocols used in the TCP/IP networks. TCP provides a connection-oriented reliable service to its applications. The reliability is achieved through acknowledgments of correctly received data and retransmission of lost data. TCP is used by most applications on the Internet, such as e-mail, file transfer, and the World Wide Web. TCP uses sophisticated congestion control algorithms to adjust its sending rate according to the observed network state. It uses a sliding window mechanism to prevent buffer overflow at a slow receiver. UDP is a lightweight protocol that does not guarantee delivery of data. Multimedia applications usually use UDP, as they can tolerate occasional packet losses. Both TCP and UDP run over the IP layer, which provides an unreliable datagram service.

2.6 REVIEW QUESTIONS

1. TCP/IP has two transport protocols, TCP and UDP. What are the key differences between them?

2. UDP does not have any built-in reliability. Why would one use UDP instead of TCP?

3. Why does TCP connection termination need four-way handshaking, whereas TCP connection establishment needs only three-way handshaking?

4. Using an example, explain how cumulative acknowledgment can compensate for a lost ACK.

5. What is the purpose of TCP timeouts, and why is the timeout duration important?

6. When a timeout occurs, TCP sets its slow-start threshold to half its current congestion window size (multiplicative decrease). Can you think of the consequences if multiplicative decrease were replaced by additive decrease (say, for example, that current congestion window is decreased by one)?

7. In most cases, TCP retransmission timer expires whenever a router drops a packet due to buffer overflow (the packet never reaches receiver). Can you think of situations when RTO occurs even though packets reach receiver?

8. Fragmentation can be done at the source or any intermediate routers, but reassembly is done only at the destination. Why do intermediate routers not reassemble IP fragments?

9. Can you think of any disadvantages of IP fragmentation?

10. What role can TCP play to avoid IP fragmentation?

2.7 CASE STUDY: WCORP ADOPTS TCP/IP

Although multiprotocol stacks had been meeting the interconnecting needs of WCORP in the past, the following costs were identified for maintaining multiple stacks:

Increased load on memory. As each PC loads four protocol stacks, very little memory is left for running applications.

Reduced performance. Multiple protocols draw more CPU cycles, causing adverse effect on performance.

Multiple address management. Different protocols use different addresses for identifying and communicating between computers. When multiple protocol stacks are loaded on a PC, multiple addresses have to be assigned and managed for each PC, making the address management much harder. Communication errors caused by incorrect address assignment become difficult to isolate and correct.

Multiple routing systems. Different stacks use different routing protocols and systems. With multiple stacks, routers must maintain multiple routing systems. These multiprotocol routers are very costly to purchase and maintain.

Because of the above costs associated with multiple stacks, WCORP has decided to adopt a *single protocol* strategy to meet its interconnecting requirements. As discussed in the previous case study (see Chapter 1), the four major stacks currently in use are SNA, IPX/SPX, DECnet, and TCP/IP. To adopt a *single protocol* strategy, WCORP must select one of these four stacks. As a first step toward making this selection, the network administrator identifies six important communication requirements to be fulfilled by the single protocol stack: native connectivity to the public Internet, nonproprietary ownership, reliable communication, connectionless communication, client-server communication, and routing between different subnets. Table 2.3 shows the comparison of different stacks against these

TABLE 2.3: Comparison of different protocol stacks.

Protocol Stack	Internet Connectivity	Ownership	Reliable	Connectionless	Client-Server	Routing
SNA	Difficult	IBM	Yes	Yes	Yes	Yes
IPX/SPX	Difficult	Novell	Yes	Yes	Yes	Yes
DECnet	Difficult	Digital	Yes	Yes	Yes	Yes
TCP/IP	Easy	Open	Yes	Yes	Yes	Yes

six requirements. After careful consideration, WCORP has finally decided to adopt TCP/IP as the single stack to support interconnectivity. The driving factors for this selection were the open standard of TCP/IP (not owned by any specific vendor) and seamless connectivity to the public Internet.

CHAPTER 3

Performance Measurement of TCP/IP Networks

CHAPTER OBJECTIVES

After completing this chapter, the reader should be able to:

- Appreciate the role of measurement in building and maintaining high performance TCP/IP networks

- Explain the types of tools available for performance measurement of TCP/IP networks

- Know the capabilities of freely available performance measurement and testing tools for TCP/IP networks

- Select an appropriate tool for a given measurement task at hand

The performance of TCP is affected not only by its protocol specification and internal algorithms but also by its implementation, memory management mechanism in its underlying operating system, system architectures, and the communication channels we use. Network measurement can, therefore, help users to reveal potential bottlenecks, detect inadequate parameter settings, and test component reliability in complex TCP/IP networking environments. In this chapter, we discuss the role of network measurement and introduce several popular performance measurement tools with detailed descriptions of their usage, options, and installations. Because many Computer Science (CS) and Electrical Engineering (EE) students have access to only UNIX machines, the chapter is mainly based on UNIX tools. Most of these tools, however, are also available in Windows, and their usage is very similar to their UNIX counterparts.

3.1 REASONS FOR NETWORK MEASUREMENT

Measurement of TCP/IP networks is used not only by performance analysts but also by programmers implementing TCP/IP stacks. Some of the reasons for measurement are:

1. A network manager may measure link utilizations to find the performance bottleneck.
2. A network manager may carry out extensive measurements with an objective to tune the TCP/IP stack.

3. A network analyst may measure details of peak traffic to characterize the workload. The derived workload can be used for testing alternate network systems or for carrying out simulations of alternative network designs (see Jain [186] for details on types of workloads, workload selection, and workload characterization techniques).

4. A network researcher may wish to collect traffic traces to drive simulations (more on trace-driven simulation in Chapter 4).

5. A mathematician may need to collect data from operational TCP/IP networks to validate a TCP model (see Chapter 5 for details on mathematical modeling of TCP).

6. A TCP/IP protocol implementor may need to capture and inspect headers and/or payloads of packets transmitted over the network. The information gathered will enable the implementor to debug and verify correct implementation of the protocol.

3.2 MEASUREMENT TASKS

Network measurement is a complex task. It has several subtasks, each relying on the other:

1. **Data collection.** This component collects raw data from the operational network. The type and amount of data collected depends on the ultimate use of the data. For example, data needed to drive a (trace-driven) simulation may contain the arrival time of each packet and the size of the packet (in bytes).

2. **Analysis.** Sometimes it is necessary to analyze raw data to obtain certain characteristics (e.g., average throughput, average delay, etc.) of collected data.

3. **Presentation.** It produces graphs and charts to present performance metrics for visual use.

4. **Interpretation.** Meaningful interpretation of data is the ultimate goal of a measurement exercise.

To assist the performance analyst with these tasks, there exist many measurement tools. In the next section, we discuss various types of tools that are available to us.

3.3 CLASSIFICATION OF MEASUREMENT TOOLS

Since the birth of the Internet, many tools have been developed to measure and evaluate the performance of TCP. These performance measurement tools are invaluable in assessing, monitoring, managing, and benchmarking various implementations of TCP. Measurement tools can be classified based on a number of characteristics, such as purposes of measurement, the level of tasks accomplished, and the type of implementation.

Depending on the purposes of measurement, there are two types of tools (Figure 3.1), *monitoring tools* and *benchmarking tools*. Monitoring tools are widely used by TCP protocol stack implementors. These tools capture and show the packet headers transmitted over the network. Primarily, these tools were developed for

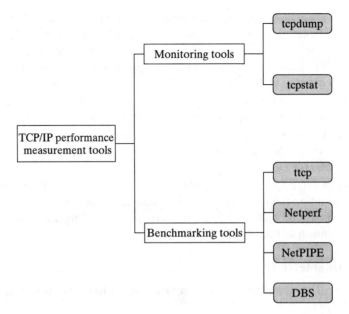

FIGURE 3.1: Types of TCP/IP performance measurement tools.

helping protocol implementations, but currently they are widely used for network management purposes as well. Tcpdump and tcpstat are two widely used traffic monitoring tools. The benchmarking tools generate test traffic over the networks and measure various performance indices such as throughput, delay, jitter, and estimated available bandwidth. These tools are normally used for network management purposes, but they are also valuable to the TCP protocol implementors for tuning the TCP implementations. Examples of benchmarking tools include ttcp, NetPerf, NetPIPE, and DBS.

Depending on the level of tasks accomplished, a tool may be classified into two categories: *collector* and *analyzer*. A collector is used to capture and dump raw data. Tcpdump is a good example of such tools. An analyzer reads the raw data file captured by a collector and summarizes the data. A third category of *associated* tools, such as gnuplot, can be used for presentation of results in graphs or charts if the analyzer does not have such capabilities.

Another way to classify measurement tools is according to their implementations. *Software tools* are implemented inside the network hosts, whereas *hardware tools* are exogenous instruments separately attached to the network. Hardware tools are mainly used for high-speed and high-resolution measurements. Jain presents a good discussion on the pros and cons of software tools versus hardware tools [186].

3.4 POPULAR MEASUREMENT TOOLS AND THEIR APPLICATIONS

In this section, we take an in-depth look at six popular, freely available software tools. Using examples, we show how these tools can be applied to performance measurement of TCP/IP networks.

3.4.1 Tcpdump

The major function of tcpdump [184] is to monitor packets on the attached network and dump headers and payloads of packets to a human-readable format. The use of tcpdump is illustrated in Figure 3.2. To monitor the traffic, tcpdump sets the network interface in the *promiscuous* mode to capture all packets on the attached network. It uses Packet Capture library (libpcap), which was originally developed by Van Jacobson and is used by many other traffic monitoring applications. This library provides an Application Program Interface (API) to a packet capture system implemented in UNIX kernel and supports *filtering* of packets captured by the interface. Tcpdump program obtains filtering specifications from command line arguments and passes a compiled version of these specifications to the in-kernel packet capturing mechanism through the API provided by libpcap.

Tcpdump was originally implemented on BSD UNIX system and is now available on almost all UNIX platforms. The original version of tcpdump was developed by Van Jacobson and his network research group in Lawrence Berkeley National Laboratory in the late 1990s. Because of its simplicity and easy-to-use features, tcpdump remains a popular performance monitoring tool for the network operators and protocol implementors.

Usage and Options. Tcpdump is a simple and easy-to-use tool. It supports many command line options for flexibility and convenience. The command line options of tcpdump are shown in Figure 3.3. Table 3.1 summarizes the meanings of these options. To effectively use tcpdump for actual protocol development and network trouble-shootings, it is necessary to understand the meanings and effects of these command line options. In this section, we describe some of the most useful options and later illustrate these options using several practical examples.

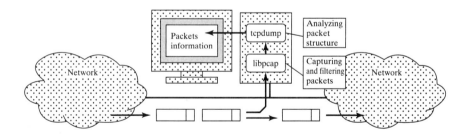

FIGURE 3.2: Program structure of tcpdump.

```
tcpdump [ -adeflnN0pqStvx ] [ -c count ] [ -F file ]
        [ -i interface ] [ -r file ] [ -s snaplen ]
        [ -T type ] [ -w file ] [ expression ]
```

FIGURE 3.3: Command line options for tcpdump.

TABLE 3.1: Brief descriptions of `tcpdump` options.

Option	Description
-i	Listen on interface. If unspecified, tcpdump searches the system interface list for the lowest numbered, configured up interface (excluding loopback). Ties are broken by choosing the earliest match.
-p	Don't put the interface into promiscuous mode.
-s	Snarf snaplen bytes of data from each packet rather than the default of 68.
-r	Read packets from file (which was created with the -w option). Standard input is used if file is "-."
-w	Write the raw packets to file rather than parsing and printing them out. They can later be printed with the -r option. Standard output is used if file is "-."
-c	Exit after receiving count packets.
-F	Use file as input for the filter expression. An additional expression given on the command line is ignored.
-T	Force packets selected by "expression" to be interpreted the specified type.
-a	Attempt to convert network and broadcast addresses to names.
-e	Print the link-level header on each dump line.
-f	Print "foreign" internet addresses numerically rather than symbolically.
-n	Don't convert addresses (i.e., host addresses, port numbers, etc.) to names.
-N	Don't print domain name qualification of host names.
-q	Quiet output. Print less protocol information so output lines are shorter.
-S	Print absolute, rather than relative, TCP sequence numbers.
-t	Don't print a timestamp on each dump line.
-tt	Print an unformatted timestamp on each dump line.
-v	Verbose output. For example, the time to live and type of service information in an IP packet is printed.
-vv	Even more verbose output. For example, additional fields are printed from NFS reply packets.
-x	Print each packet (minus its link level header) in hex. The smaller of the entire packet or snaplen bytes will be printed.
-l	Make stdout line buffered. Useful if you want to see the data while capturing it; e.g., "tcpdump -l\break |tee dat" or "tcpdump -l > dat & tail -f dat."
-d	Dump the compiled packet-matching code in a human-readable form to standard output and stop.
-dd	Dump packet-matching code as a C program fragment.
-ddd	Dump packet-matching code as decimal numbers (preceded by a count).
-O	Don't run the packet-matching code optimizer. This is useful only if you suspect a bug in the optimizer.

Network Interface.   For gateways and hosts having multiple interfaces, option -i specifies a network interface that tcpdump will watch. On an ordinary host with single network interface, this option is not required.

Off-Line Analysis.   Options -w and -r are useful for off-line analysis. Option -w allows us to dump raw packets into a specified file. We can then read raw packet data from this file with option -r for later analysis. This off-line style of analysis is good for either debugging protocols or seeking specific packets in network trouble-shooting, especially for the case in which we have to deal with a huge number of packets and the ones we need are very few. The important option is -tt, which allows us to record the time of each packet. The timestamp later can be used for trace-driven simulation (see Chapter 4).

Output Style.   Tcpdump provides several options for selecting an appropriate output style. For example, in some cases we may prefer to see an IP address in dotted-decimal notation rather than converted into a canonical name through Domain Name Server (DNS). We can control this kind of output style with options provided by tcpdump. See options -a, -f, and -n in Table 3.1.

Parsing Length.   Number of bytes parsed in the header of a captured packet determines the level of information we can gather. The longer the parsing length, the more we can discover. This is a direct consequence of packet encapsulation at each protocol layer; the higher layer header is concealed in the payload of the lower layer payload. With option -s, we can specify the number of bytes (from the beginning of the packet) to be parsed. Default length is 68, which is adequate for IP, Internet Control Message Protocol (ICMP), TCP, and User Datagram Protocol (UDP). However, if someone is interested in analyzing application layer protocols, such as Hyper Text Transfer Protocol (HTTP) and File Transfer Protocol (FTP), he or she will need to specify a longer parsing length. Specifying more bytes in this option, however, will occupy larger buffer space for holding the packets.

Filtering.   Tcpdump has a filtering mechanism to dump *selected* packets. The filter is specified as an *expression* in a command line option. When a filter is specified, only packets that make the expression "true" are dumped. If no filtering expression is specified, all packets on the attached network are captured and dumped. Sometimes the filter specification may be complicated and too long to specify as a command line option. In that case, one can use option -F to read an expression from a file.

In its simplest form, an expression contains one or more *primitives*. Primitives consist of an identifier, such as a name or a number, preceded by one or more *qualifiers*. There are three different kinds of qualifiers:

type. This qualifier specifies to what kind of thing the name or number refers. Possible types we can use are host, net, and ports. For example, net 192.168.1 means a network with 192.168.1 as its prefix; host site.foo.com points to a host that has site.foo.com as its name. If there is no type qualifier, the name or number refers to a host.

dir. This qualifier specifies originating and forwarding directions of packets. For example, dst net 163.221 focuses packets directed to a network 166.221. src site.foo.com specifies packets with source address of site.foo.com. We can use "and" and "or" operators to specify more complex qualifiers. For example, src or dst port 35 specifies any packets to or from port 35 (but because it does not specify any transport layer protocols, it will capture both TCP and UDP packets with port 35.) If there is no dir qualifier, src or dst is assumed.

proto. This qualifier restricts the match to a particular protocol. Possible protocols are ether, fddi, ip, arp, rarp, decnet, lat, sca, moprc, mopdl, tcp, and udp. In the absence of a proto qualifier, all protocols consistent with the type are assumed. For example, port 25 means port 25 in both TCP and UDP protocol.

More complex filter expressions can be created by using concatenation (and or &&), alternation (or or ||), and negation (not or !) to combine primitives. A parenthesized group can also be used, but parentheses are special to shell program so that they must be escaped if expression is in command line option. Other special primitive keywords, such as gateway, broadcast, less, and greater, are also available. Allowable primitives used for TCP/IP networks are listed in Table 3.2.

Tcpdump Output Format. Tcpdump prints information from a TCP header in a single line in the following format:

```
src > dst: flags data-seqno ack window urgent options
```

Src and dst are the source and destination IP addresses and TCP port numbers. Flags are some combinations of S (SYN), F (FIN), P (PUSH), or R (RST) or a single "." (no flags). Data-seqno describes the portion of the sequence space covered by the data in this packet. Ack is the sequence number of the next data byte expected from the other end of this connection. Window is the number of bytes available in the receiver buffer. Urgent indicates that there is "urgent" data in the packet. Options are TCP options enclosed in angle brackets (e.g., <mss 1024> in Figure 3.4). Note that src, dst, and flags are always present in the output, but the other fields may or may not be present (depending on the contents of the TCP header).

Performance Measurement Examples. In this section, we give several examples to help readers understand how tcpdump can be used for network performance

```
host-a.1023 > host-b.login: s 768512:768512(0) win 4096 <mss 1024>
host-b.login > host-a.1023: s 947648:947648(0) ack 768513 win 4096 <mss 1024>
host-a.1023 > host-b.login: . ack 1 win 4096
```

FIGURE 3.4: Tcpdump output of an rlogin session (first three lines).

TABLE 3.2: Primitives for TCP/IP networks.

Option	Description
host *host*	Specify a source or destination IP address.
dst host *host*	Specify a destination IP address or a name.
src host *host*	Specify a source IP address or a name.
ether dst *ehost*	Specify a destination Ethernet address.
ether src *ehost*	Specify a source Ethernet address.
ether host *ehost*	Specify a source or destination Ethernet address.
gateway *host*	Specify a name of gateway that transfers the packet.
net *net*	Specify a source or destination network address.
dst net *net*	Specify a destination network address.
src net *net*	Specify a source network address.
net *net* mask *mask*	Specify the netmask of *net*.
net *net*/*len*	Specify the length of the netmask.
port *port*	Specify a source or destination port number.
dst port *port*	Specify a destination port number of TCP or UDP. The port can be a number or a name used in /etc/services.
src port *port*	Specify a source port number of TCP or UDP.
less *length*	Specify a length of the packet that is captured if less than or equal to.
greater *length*	Specify a length of the packet that is captured if greater than or equal to.
ip proto *protocol*	Specify a protocol number or name that is upper layer of IP such as: tcp, udp, icmp, igrp, nd.
ether proto *protocol*	Specify a protocol number or name that is upper layer of Ethernet such as: ip, arp, or rarp.
ether broadcast	Capturing if the packet is an Ethernet broadcast packet.
ip broadcast	Capturing if the packet is an IP broadcast packet.
ether multicast	Capturing if the packet is an Ethernet multicast packet.
ip multicast	Capturing if the packet is an IP multicast packet.
expr relop expr	*relop* is one of >, <, >=, <=, =, !=, and *expr* is an arithmetic expression composed of integer constants (expressed in standard C syntax), the normal binary operators [+, -, *, /, &, |], a length operator, and special packet data accessors.
proto [*expr* : *size*]	To access data inside the packet. The byte offset, relative to the indicated protocol layer, is given by *expr*. Size is optional and indicates the number of bytes in the field of interest; it can be either one, two, or four and defaults to one. The length operator, indicated by the keyword *len*, gives the length of the packet.

measurement. Some of these examples are quite simple, while others are more advanced to address more practical situations.

EXAMPLE 3.1   Capture all traffic to and from a given host.

If we want to analyze the traffic load on a given server, we must first capture and print all packets arriving at or departing from this server. The following tcpdump command captures all packets to and from a server called alpha and dumps the first 68 bytes of each packet:

```
# tcpdump host alpha
```

In this case, hostname alpha can be mapped to an IP address through either DNS or static database (such as /etc/hosts) lookups. As mentioned earlier, the first 68 bytes of a captured packet contain useful TCP/IP header fields for further analysis of the captured data.

EXAMPLE 3.2   Print communication between selected hosts.

Sometimes it is necessary to monitor traffic dynamics between specific hosts to better understand the communication patterns in a given TCP/IP network. To print traffic details between host alpha and either host beta or host delta, the following tcpdump command can be used:

```
# tcpdump host alpha and \( beta or delta \)
```

or just using single quote as

```
# tcpdump 'host alpha and (beta or delta)'
```

To print all IP packets between host alpha and any host except host beta, the tcpdump command is:

```
# tcpdump ip host alpha and not beta
```

EXAMPLE 3.3   Monitoring traffic between two networks.

The previous example showed how to monitor traffic between *hosts*. Network engineers also often need to monitor traffic dynamics between specific *networks*. To print all traffic between any hosts attached to the local network and hosts at network 163.221/16, one can use tcpdump as shown here:

```
# tcpdump net 163.221
```

Instead of using numeric values for a given network, tcpdump also allows the use of mnemonic names. For example, if network 163.221 is defined as naist-net in /etc/networks, the network name in command line option can be specified as:

```
# tcpdump net naist-net
```

EXAMPLE 3.4   Monitoring of specific TCP/IP applications.

This example shows how tcpdump can be used to monitor traffic from specific TCP/IP applications at strategic locations of a given TCP/IP network. One can use a special keyword "gateway" as a primitive (see Table 3.2) to specify all FTP traffic through a gateway called gw as follows:

```
# tcpdump 'gateway gw and (port ftp or ftp-data)'
```

FTP uses two ports (20 for data transfer and 21 for FTP protocol itself) for interactions between FTP client and server.

EXAMPLE 3.5   Capturing the starts and ends of TCP connections.

For performance monitoring of TCP/IP application servers, information we need to know is the duration of TCP connections accessing the servers. To achieve this, capturing the start and end packets (the SYN and FIN packets) of a TCP connection is required. The following tcpdump command can be used for this purpose:

```
# tcpdump 'tcp[13] & 3 != 0 and not src and dst net localnet'
```

Here we assume that localnet is defined in /etc/networks; otherwise we need to use a numerical network address such as 192.168.1. Note that 'tcp[13] & 3' checks if SYN or FIN bit is set in the *control bit* field in the TCP header. This notation is equivalent to 'tcp[13:1] & 3' or

```
tcp[tcpflags] & (tcp-syn|tcp-fin)
```

For details of this notation see Table 3.2 (last option "proto").

EXAMPLE 3.6   Monitoring long datagrams.

Long IP datagrams need fragmentation at the gateways. Monitoring long datagrams is helpful for performance tuning as well as trouble-shooting of datagram forwarding mechanisms. This example shows how one can use tcpdump to monitor long datagrams transmitted through a given gateway. To print IP datagrams longer than 1500 bytes sent through the gateway called gw, one can use:

```
# tcpdump 'gateway gw and ip[2:2] > 1500'
```

Once again, ip[2:2] can be interpreted from the last option ("proto") in Table 3.2. The first 2 means that we have to examine bytes starting from three. The second 2 refers to two bytes, that is, the length field in the IP header.

EXAMPLE 3.7   Packet filtering.

This example shows how the packet filtering of tcpdump can help us monitor specific network conditions. Tcpdump can set a filter with conditions on the values of specific fields in the Ethernet header. The following example can print IP broadcast or multicast packets that were not sent via Ethernet, broadcast or multicast:

```
# tcpdump 'ether[0] & 1 = 0 and ip[16] >= 224'
```

EXAMPLE 3.8   Monitoring connection establishment of a TCP session.

In Figure 3.4, we show an example of a tcpdump output. This example illustrates the operation of an **rlogin** session from host-a (client) to host-b (server). The first three lines of the tcpdump output represent the three-way handshake process to establish a TCP connection between host-a and host-b. These three lines are further explained below.

Line 1. host-a sends a SYN packet from TCP port 1023 to port rlogin (513 defined in /etc/services) on host-b. S indicates that the SYN flag in TCP header was set. The initial sequence number is 768512, and the TCP segment contains no data. The notation used for data-seqno is first:last (nbytes) where first and last represent the first and last sequence numbers covered by the data carried in this segment. The actual number of data bytes (zero in this case) carried is shown in the parentheses. Available receiver window size (4096 bytes) is notified using this SYN packet, and a Maximum Segment Size (MSS) option is attached to this packet to request a 1024-byte MSS.

Line 2. host-b replies with a similar packet, but it includes a piggybacked acknowledgment (ACK) for host-a's SYN packet (SYN-ACK packet). This packet also contains host-b's initial sequence number (947648).

Line 3. host-a then returns an ACK for host-b's SYN packet (completion of the three-way handshake). The "." means no flags were set. Instead of the large raw sequence number, the ACK here is a small integer (1). The reason is as follows. The first time tcpdump sees a TCP "conversation," it prints the sequence number from the packet as it is. On subsequent packets in the conversation, the difference between the current packet's sequence number and this initial sequence number is printed. In other words, the sequence numbers after the first observation is interpreted as relative "byte positions" in the data stream in each direction where the first data byte in each direction is 1. With the option -S in the command line option, this feature can be overwritten to print raw sequence numbers.

Related Tools.   Because of the popularity of tcpdump, several advanced tools complementing tcpdump have been developed. In many cases, tcpdump is simply used as a packet-capturing tool feeding raw data to these advanced tools. The format of the files generated by tcpdump (using option -w) is called *pcap*. For advanced analysis of captured packets, we can use tools, such as Tcpillust and tcptrace, which can handle *pcap* file format.

Tcpillust [18] is a graphical TCP connection analysis tool developed by Yoshifumi Nishida at SONY Computer Science Laboratory. This tool takes the data file generated by tcpdump, and then draws pictures to show interactions between clients and servers. These pictures can significantly aid the detection of unexpected behaviors in a TCP/IP implementation. Interestingly, Tcpillust was named after the well-known TCP book series called *TCP/IP Illustrated* by Stevens. Source codes and other related information about Tcpillust are freely available from its official web site [18]. Tcptrace [19] was developed by Shawn Ostermann at Ohio University. This tool can analyze data in *pcap* file to obtain performance indices such as round-trip time (RTT), window size changes, throughput, and many more. One of the salient features of tcptrace is the wide range of output styles. It can also generate graphical data that can be viewed by *xplot*. Source codes and other related information on tcptrace are freely available from its official web site [19].

Installation.   All major UNIX platforms, such as FreeBSD, NetBSD, OpenBSD, Linux, and MacOS X, include tcpdump in their recent releases. Users on these platforms, therefore, do not have to install tcpdump. On other platforms, one may have to install tcpdump on his or her own; however, installation of tcpdump is quite easy. Source code archives of tcpdump and libpcap can be downloaded from the following URL:

```
http://www.tcpdump.org/
```

Because tcpdump uses libpcap, libpcap should be installed before the installation of tcpdump. Installation of libpcap (and later tcpdump) can be completed in a few steps:

1. Go ("cd") to the directory containing the source code of tcpdump.
2. Run "./configure" to configure the package for your system.
3. Run "make" to compile the package.
4. Obtain the *super user* privilege through "su," then run "make install" to install the programs and any data files and documents.

3.4.2 Tcpstat

Tcpstat [166] periodically reports TCP-related statistics on a given network interface. These statistics include bandwidth being used, number of packets exchanged, average packet size of a TCP stream, and so on. Like tcpdump, tcpstat also makes use of the *libpcap* library. The functional structure of tcpstat is shown in Figure 3.5.

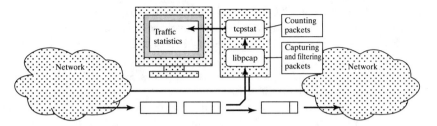

FIGURE 3.5: Functional diagram of `tcpstat`.

Usage and Options.   In this section, we briefly explain how to use `tcpstat`. The default behavior of `tcpstat` can be described as follows. First it finds an appropriate network interface to be monitored, then it captures packets that appear on the network interface, and lastly it presents a summary of statistics every 5 seconds. Like `tcpdump`, `tcpstat` also sets the network interface to the *promiscuous* mode; therefore, `tcpstat` has to be invoked from the *super user* privilege.

To find out an appropriate network interface, `tcpstat` scans a list of network interfaces and selects an active (up and running) interface (except loopback interface), if it finds one. On a gateway with multiple active network interfaces, the interface to be monitored should be specified by option `-i`.

There are many options for `tcpstat`. The command line options are shown in Figure 3.6. Table 3.3 provides a brief description of each of these options. Through several examples later in the section, we will show how to use these options for practical performance monitoring purposes.

Output Format.   With option `-o`, we can customize the format of the output generated by `tcpstat`. The string following option `-o` can be any quoted string, and `tcpstat` will write this string to the standard output. If the string includes any special substrings that begin with a "%," `tcpstat` tries to substitute certain values for them. Table 3.4 shows a list of all substitution strings defined in `tcpstat`. In addition, `tcpstat` can handle almost all standard `printf` escape characters such as "\n." The default format string for `tcpstat` is:

`Time:%S\tn=%n\tavg=%a\tstddev=%d\tbps=%b\n,`

```
tcpstat [-?haeFlp] [-B bps] [-b bps] [-F filter expr]

        [-i interface] [-o output]

        [-r filename] [-s seconds] [interval]
```

FIGURE 3.6: Command line options of `tcpstat`.

TABLE 3.3: Command line options of `tcpstat`.

Options	Description
-i interface	Do a live capture (rather than read from a file) on the `interface` interface given on the command line. In the event you specify `auto` as an interface, then `tcpstat` tries to find an appropriate one by itself.
-p	Set the interface into nonpromiscuous mode (promiscuous is the default) when doing live captures.
-r filename	Read all data from `filename`, which may be a regular file, a named pipe, or "-" to read its data from standard input. Acceptable file formats include pcap (tcpdump files) and "snoop" format files. `filename` is usually a file created by the `tcpdump` command using the "-w" option.
-s sec	When monitoring an interface, `tcpstat` runs for only `sec` seconds and then quits. Has no effect when reading data from a file.
-F	Flush the output streams after printing each interval. Sometimes useful when redirecting output into a file or piping `tcpstat` into another program such as `grep`.
-f filter expr	Filter the packets according to the rules given by `filter expr`. Its syntax is identical to filtering expression in `tcpdump`. See Section 3.4.1.
-b bps	Bandwidth mode. Displays the total number of seconds the data-throughput exceeded `bps` and the percentage of total time this was, as if the interface were limited to bps bits per second.
-B bps	"Dumb" bandwidth mode. Displays the total number of seconds the data-throughput exceeded `bps`, and the percentage of total time this was.
-l	Include the size of the linklayer header when calculating statistics. (Ethernet only, right now. Usually 14 bytes per packet.)
-a	Accounting mode. Displays the estimated number of bytes per second, minute, hour, day, and month.
-e	Suppresses the display of empty intervals.
-o format	Set the output format when displaying statistics.
-h, -?	Display version and a brief help message.

which will produce an output similar to the one shown in Figure 3.7 (the exact meaning of the output will be explained later).

Performance Measurement Examples.   In this section, we show several examples illustrating the ideas and concepts of performance measurement using `tcpstat`.

EXAMPLE 3.9   Printing packet and bandwidth statistics on a network interface.

Using `tcpstat`, one can learn various statistics, such as the average packet size, average bandwidth achieved, and so on, on a given network interface of a

```
Time:940948785    n=107    avg=251.81    stddev=422.45    bps=43110.40

Time:940948790    n=99     avg=400.21    stddev=539.39    bps=63393.60

Time:940948795    n=43     avg=257.16    stddev=352.83    bps=17692.80
```

FIGURE 3.7: Default output of `tcpstat`.

TABLE 3.4: Output formatting.

Substitution Strings	Description
%A	The number of ARP packets
%a	The average packet size
%B	The number of bytes per second
%b	The number of bits per second
%C	The number of ICMP and ICMPv6 packets
%d	The standard deviation of the size of each packet
%I	The number of IPv4 packets
%l	The network "load" over the last minute, like in uptime
%M	The maximum packet size
%m	The minimum packet size
%N	The number of bytes
%n	The number of packets
%p	The number of packets per second
%R	Same as \%S but relative to the first packet seen
%r	Same as \%s but relative to the first packet seen
%S	The timestamp for the interval in seconds after the "UNIX epoch"
%s	The timestamp for the interval in seconds.microseconds after the "UNIX epoch"
%T	The number of TCP packets
%U	The number of UDP packets
%V	The number of IPv6 packets
%number	Switch the output to the file descriptor number at this point in the string. All output for each interval before this parameter is by default the standard output (file descriptor 1). Useful when redirecting the output into more than one file (or fifo) for separate statistics. Be sure you know where they are going. Writing to "dangling" file descriptors (without directing them to a specific destination) may produce unexpected results.
%%	The "%" character

gateway or a host. The following `tcpstat` command displays (the output is shown in Figure 3.7.) the default statistics (timestamp, the number of packets passed through the interface, average packet size, standard deviation of the packet size, and the bandwidth in bits per second) every 5 seconds for all traffic passing through the network interface called `eth0`:

```
# tcpstat -i eth0
```

EXAMPLE 3.10   Printing SMTP and HTTP statistics using packet filtering.

This example demonstrates the usefulness of the packet filtering option in `tcpstat`. Using packet filtering, one can zoom into specific TCP applications, such as SMTP and HTTP. Because `tcpstat` uses `libpcap` library for capturing packets on a network interface, we can specify packet filtering in the same way we do it with `tcpdump`. Table 3.3 shows that we can set a filter with option `-f`. The following `tcpstat` command prints SMTP and HTTP throughput every second.

```
# tcpstat -f 'port (smtp or http)' 1.0
```

EXAMPLE 3.11   Statistics through postprocessing of `tcpdump` data file.

In this example, we show how `tcpstat` can be used as a postprocessing tool for the raw data captured by `tcpdump`. Tcpstat can read data from a file that was generated by `tcpdump` (with option `-w`). To display the default statistics every 5 seconds from the file "file.dump" generated by `tcpdump`, we can use the following commands:

```
# tcpdump -w file.dump
# tcpstat -r file.dump
```

EXAMPLE 3.12   Monitoring bandwidth utilization.

Sometimes it is necessary to know if the network traffic is exceeding a given bandwidth threshold and, if so, what percentage of the traffic stays over the threshold and what percentage stays under, and so on. This can be achieved with option `-b`. With this option, `tcpstat` does not generate periodic reports but continues to monitor packets on the network interface and waits for a terminating signal from the user or another process. Upon receiving the signal, it reports how long the data-throughput exceeded the specified bandwidth and the percentages. For example, we can use `tcpstat` to display what percentage of the traffic exceeded the speed of 64 Kbps as follows:

```
# tcpstat -b 64000 0.5
```

```
Listening on fxp0
^C
Time exceeding 64000.00 bps:   186.50 sec.       (67.45% of the time)
Peak Bandwidth: 563648.00 bps
#
```

From these results, we learn that most of the time (67.45%) the bandwidth was above the 64 Kbps threshold and the peak bandwidth was 563 Kbps.

EXAMPLE 3.13   Working with Tcpdump **and** Gnuplot.

As mentioned earlier, tcpstat can be used for postprocessing the data captured by tcpdump. A typical postprocessing task is to classify all packets according to their types (TCP, UDP, etc.) and compile various statistics of the individual packet types (e.g., what percentage of the traffic is TCP, etc.). Such statistics generated by tcpstat are often plotted as graphs for more visual effect. Gnuplot is a tool freely distributed with most UNIX operating systems, and it can be used to create the graphs from the data generated by tcpstat. Figure 3.8 illustrates how tcpdump, tcpstat, and gnuplot all work together to create the graphs of traffic statistics.

Now we consider a specific performance monitoring example where all three tools are used. The task is to determine how many packets of ARP, TCP, and UDP are observed on a given network and to plot these statistics on a graph. In addition to this, we wish to create another graph showing the throughput and load of the observed traffic. The task can be carried out in several steps:

Step 1. Dump network traffic using tcpdump as follows:

```
# tcpdump -w rawdata.dmp
```

Tcpdump creates a file rawdata.dmp and continues to store dumped packet information until stopped.

Step 2. Classify packets according to their types, and compute packets per second statistics for each type using tcpstat. In this step, we make use of several tcpstat options, option -r to read data file (generated by tcpdump in Step 1) and option -o for specifying the output format suitable for later processing by gnuplot:

```
% tcpstat -r rawdata.dmp -o "%r %A %T %U %l %b\n" > tcpstat.log
```

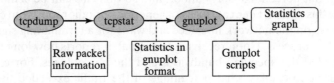

FIGURE 3.8: The creation process for traffic statistics graphs using tcpdump, tcpstat, and gnuplot in tandem.

```
set term pbm small color

set data style lines

set xlabel "Time (seconds)"

set ylabel "packets/s"

plot [00:500] "tcpstat.log" using 1:2 title "ARP," \
              "tcpstat.log" using 1:3 title "TCP," \
              "tcpstat.log" using 1:4 title "UDP"
```

FIGURE 3.9: Gnuplot script file for generating the graph in Figure 3.11 (script1).

Step 3. Now all we need to do is to tell gnuplot where to get its data and how to display it. This is usually done by preparing a gnuplot *script file*. Figure 3.9 shows the script file (script1) that generates a graph showing the number of ARP, TCP, and UDP packets in every 5 seconds. Once the script is written, call gnuplot to save the graph in a Portable Bit Map (PBM) file:

% gnuplot script1 > graph1.pbm

Figure 3.11 shows graph1.pbm.

To create the graph for throughput and traffic load, we need to repeat Step 3 with a different gnuplot script (shown in Figure 3.10):

% gnuplot script2 > graph2.pbm

The second graph, graph2.pbm, is shown in Figure 3.12.

Installation.   Like tcpdump, tcpstat can be installed using a few simple steps (see the installation steps under tcpdump in the previous section). Source-code archive of tcpstat is available freely from the following web site:

http://www.frenchfries.net/paul/tcpstat/

3.4.3 Ttcp

Ttcp [22], developed in the mid 1990s, is a classic throughput benchmarking tool for TCP/IP networks. Using ttcp, we can measure TCP throughput on any given

```
set term pbm small color

set data style lines

set ytics nomirror

set ylabel "Throughput (Kbps)"

set y2label "Load"

set xlabel "Time (seconds)"

plot [0:500] "tcpstat.log" using 1:5 axes x1y2 title "Load," \
             "tcpstat.log" using 1:(\$6/1000) title "Throughput"
```

FIGURE 3.10: Gnuplot script file for generating the graph in Figure 3.12 (script2).

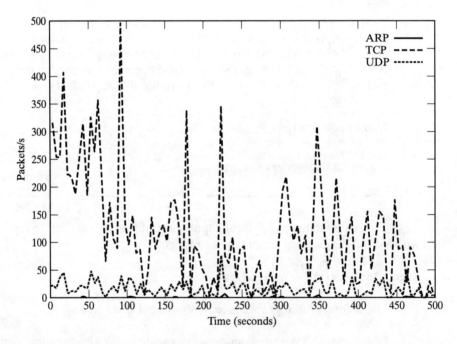

FIGURE 3.11: Number of ARP, TCP, and UDP packets per seconds (graph1.pbm).

network segment. For this measurement, we have to install `ttcp` on two hosts; one serves as a transmitter that generates TCP traffic, and the other is a receiver that receives the traffic and calculates the effective throughput between these two hosts (Figure 3.13). Ttcp is simple, is light-weight, and does not require the *super user* privilege.

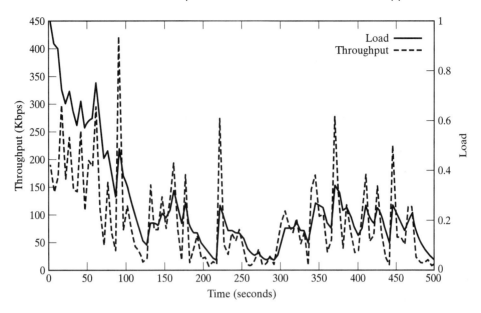

FIGURE 3.12: Throughput and load of the observed traffic (graph2.pbm).

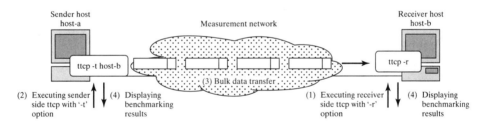

FIGURE 3.13: Performance measurement with ttcp.

Usage and Options.   For throughput measurement, ttcp is first started on the receiver and then on the transmitter. In the receiver, option -r is used to open the connection in passive mode. Option -t is used in the transmitter to force an active mode (traffic generating mode). To generate traffic automatically, option -s is used; without this option, ttcp tries to read data from stdin. The same option for the receiver turns off the printing of the received data on to the display. Option -s, therefore, must be used both at the transmitter and at the receiver for such throughput measurement experiments. Once invoked with option -s, ttcp generates and transmits certain amount of traffic to the receiver and then calculates the following performance indices:

- Total CPU time for sending data

- Total amount of data sent

- Throughput based on CPU time

- Throughput based on actual time (time from when first packet was sent to when last packet was processed).

Performance Measurement Examples.   The following examples show how to use ttcp for throughput measurement between two hosts.

EXAMPLE 3.14   Throughput measurement using TCP.

This example shows how to measure throughput between the current host and the host called target.wide.ad.jp using TCP. Figures 3.14(a) and 3.14(b) show ttcp commands and outputs in the transmitter and in the receiver, respectively. The results show that a throughput of 420 Kbps can be achieved between these two hosts.

(a) Transmitter process

```
% ttcp -t -s target.wide.ad.jp
ttcp-t: nbuf=1024, buflen=1024, port=2000
ttcp-t: socket
ttcp-t: connect
ttcp-t: 0.0user 0.2sys 0:19real 1% 0i+0d 0maxrss 0+0pf 550+0csw
ttcp-t: 1048576 bytes processed
ttcp-t:  0.246749 CPU sec  = 4149.97 KB/cpu sec,  33199.7 Kbits/cpu sec
ttcp-t:   19.4936 real sec = 52.5302 KB/real sec, 420.241 Kbits/sec
%
```

(b) Receiver process

```
% ttcp -r -s
ttcp-r: nbuf=1024, buflen=1024, port=2000
ttcp-r: socket
ttcp-r: accept
ttcp-r: 0.0user 0.7sys 0:19real 4% 0i+0d 0maxrss 0+0pf 759+2csw
ttcp-r: 1048576 bytes processed
ttcp-r:  0.781702 CPU sec  = 1309.96 KB/cpu sec,  10479.7 Kbits/cpu sec
ttcp-r:   19.5011 real sec = 52.5098 KB/real sec, 420.078 Kbits/sec
%
```

(c) Performance measurement using UDP
- Transmitter

```
ttcp-t: 0.0user 0.3sys 0:00real 38% 0i+0d 0maxrss 0+0pf 86+1csw
ttcp-t: 1048576 bytes processed
ttcp-t:  0.358669 CPU sec  =    2855 KB/cpu sec,    22840 Kbits/cpu sec
ttcp-t:  0.911927 real sec = 1122.9 KB/real sec,  8983.18 Kbits/sec
```

- Receiver

```
ttcp-r: 0.0user 0.9sys 0:00real 93% 0i+0d 0maxrss 0+0pf 2+14csw
ttcp-r: 337920 bytes processed
ttcp-r:  0.922761 CPU sec  = 357.622 KB/cpu sec,  2860.98 Kbits/cpu sec
ttcp-r:   0.96634 real sec = 341.495 KB/real sec, 2731.96 Kbits/sec
```

FIGURE 3.14: Output of ttcp.

EXAMPLE 3.15   Throughput measurement using UDP.

Because TCP exercises its own flow and congestion control, the throughput measured by `ttcp` using TCP does not always represent the true link performance. TCP throughput is usually much lower than the actual link capacity. Instead of TCP, UDP can be used with `ttcp`. To use UDP, option -u, instead of -t or -r, should be specified in the command line option. Since UDP does not have any congestion control, more precise link performance measurement is sometimes possible using UDP. Figure 3.14(c) shows link throughput performance with UDP between the same hosts used in (a) and (b) with TCP. With UDP, the receiver shows a throughput of 2.7 Mbps, much higher than the 420 Kbps throughput achieved with TCP.

Installation.   Source code of `ttcp` is freely available from several anonymous FTP sites, such as `ftp://ftp.arl.mil/pub/ttcp`. In the above directory, there are two files, `ttcp.c` for the source code and `ttcp.1` for the manual page. This source code was developed for BSD platforms on which the program could be used for BSD socket interface. Therefore, one can compile and use it on any platform where BSD socket system calls are available. On FreeBSD / NetBSD, it can be compiled as:

```
% cc -O ttcp.c -o ttcp
```

3.4.4   Netperf

`Netperf` [188] is another benchmarking tool for TCP/IP networks that can be used to measure various aspects of network performance. This tool was developed by Rick Jones of Hewlett-Packard (HP), and its initial version was released in the mid 1990s. Similar to `ttcp`, this tool measures a performance index such as available throughput between two specified hosts by means of active testing. Major features of `Netperf` are:

- It can generate different traffic patterns, such as bulk data transfer and interactive (request/response) data exchange, for measuring different aspects of network performance.

- It supports more detailed and precise performance measurement than `ttcp`.

- It can be used as a performance measurement tool not only for transport layer protocols such as TCP or UDP but also for datalink and other network protocols. Its current version can test and perform performance measurement on DLPI, the Fore ATM API, UNIX Domain Sockets, and HP's HiPPI LLA.

The `Netperf` tool actually includes two different programs: `netserver` and `netperf`. Netserver runs as a server on the receiving host and is normally invoked by `inetd` super daemon. `Netperf` is invoked on the transmitting host and works as a client program for `netserver`. When invoked, `netperf` generates traffic to be sent to `netserver` and conducts performance measurement. These client-server interactions of the `Netperf` system are depicted in Figure 3.15.

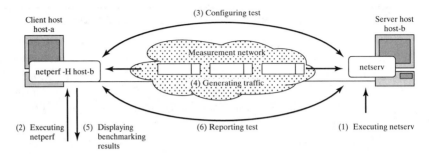

FIGURE 3.15: Use of Netperf in network performance measurement.

Usage and Options. At first, one must make sure that netserver is running at the receiving host. If netserver is configured to be invoked from inetd super daemon, no special action is required; otherwise one has to start the server process as follows:

```
% netserver
Starting netserver at port 12865
%
```

After turning the netserver on, netperf has to be started at the transmitting host. Once the client and the server have been turned on, we have the option to use either the *bulk data transfer* or the *interactive data exchange* model for performance measurement.

Performance Measurement Examples. In this section, we give examples illustrating two different concepts of performance measurement, *bulk data transfer* and *interactive data exchange*, using the netperf tool.

EXAMPLE 3.16 Bulk data transfer.

Bulk data transfer model is used to measure the available bandwidth or the effective throughput in the network segment between the transmitting and the receiving hosts. Either TCP or UDP can be used for this purpose. A typical TCP-based experiment is shown in Figure 3.16(a). In this case, the server process is running on the host testsite.wide.ad.jp. The client program netperf is invoked with -H option to specify the target (receiver) host. After several seconds, the netperf shows the following performance indices:

- Socket buffer size in bytes at the receiving host

- Socket buffer size in bytes at the transmitting host

- Message size in bytes

- Elapsed time in seconds (length of this performance measurement)

- Effective (available) throughput between the two hosts

(a) TCP

```
% netperf -H testsite.wide.ad.jp
TCP STREAM TEST to testsite.wide.ad.jp
Recv    Send    Send
Socket  Socket  Message  Elapsed
size    size    size     time       Throughput
bytes   bytes   bytes    secs       10^6bits/sec

 8192   8192    8192    10.64         0.43
%
```

(b) UDP

```
% netperf -H testsite.wide.ad.jp -t UDP_STREAM -- -m 1024
UDP UNIDIRECTIONAL SEND TEST to shower.nara.wide.ad.jp
Socket  Message  Elapsed  Messages
size    size     time     Okay Errors  Throughput
bytes   bytes    secs       #      #   10^6bits/sec

 9216   1024     10.00    10747 36610     8.81
41600            10.00     3013           2.47
%
```

(c) Transactions

```
% netperf -H testsite.wide.ad.jp -t TCP_RR
TCP REQUEST/RESPONSE TEST to testsite.wide.ad.jp
Local /Remote
Socket  Size    Request  Resp.  Elapsed  Trans.
send    recv    size     size   time     rate
bytes   bytes   bytes    bytes  secs     per sec

8192    8192    1        1      10.00    187.26
8192    8192
%
```

FIGURE 3.16: Output of `netperf`.

Instead of TCP, we can use UDP. The command line option -t can be used for setting the traffic type. The following command selects the UDP stream:

`% netperf -t UDP_STREAM -H target`

The default settings for UDP stream uses 9216-byte messages for performance measurement. However, since this message size is larger than the MTU of the major datalinks, almost all UDP packets generated in default settings are later fragmented at the IP layer. Furthermore, this message size is considered large in terms of buffer management in UNIX kernel, which in turn may cause buffer overflow and loss of packets at the receiver. In the presence of too many packet losses, the estimated bandwidth by Netperf would be unrealistically small. To avoid this situation, use of smaller messages for performance evaluation is highly recommended. Option -m can set the message size as shown in Figure 3.16(b). Note that -- is a delimiter to tell `netperf` that this option should be passed to protocol modules such as `UDP_STREAM`. As shown in Figure 3.16(b), `netperf` prints several performance indices for UDP as well, but they are slightly different from the ones we get for TCP:

- Socket buffer size in bytes.

- Message size in bytes.

- Elapsed time for performance measurement.

- Number of messages sent and messages dropped.

- Throughput.

EXAMPLE 3.17   Interactive data exchange.

Bulk data transfer is an effective model for measuring average throughput, but it cannot measure network performance for bursty traffic, such as short web transactions. Netperf's transaction model allows us to measure the performance of such request/response traffic.

Using the transaction model, Netperf measures network performance in *transactions per second*. A transaction is defined as a single sequence of data exchange between Netperf's client (netperf) and its server (netserver). The transaction time starts at the issuing of a request at the client and ends when the client receives a response from the server. A single interaction, therefore, includes the round-trip time between the client and the server and the data processing time at the server.

Figure 3.16(c) shows an example of Netperf's transaction-based performance measurement. To use TCP transaction, we have to set its traffic type to TCP_RR. The output is similar to the one for other traffic types, but with the TCP_RR type two new parameters are shown, the request/response size and the transaction rate per second (TPS). In this example, message size for both request and response was set to one byte. We can specify the size of request and response in command line options. For example, for a 64-byte request and a 1024-byte response, one should run the test as:

```
netperf -H target -- -r 64, 1024
```

There are many command line options for running netperf tests. A brief description of these options is provided in Table 3.5 (for netperf) and Table 3.6 (for netserver).

Installation.   The source code and manual for netperf is freely available from its official web site at:

```
http://www.netperf.org/netperf/NetperfPage.html
```

Installation of netperf is similar to the other open source packages; the steps are:

1. Extract source code archive.

TABLE 3.5: Options for `netperf`.

Option	Description
-a sizespec	Alter the send and receive buffer alignments on the local system. This defaults to 8 bytes.
-A sizespec	As -a but for the remote system.
-c [rate]	Request CPU utilization and service demand calculations for the local system. If the optional rate parameter is specified, netperf will use that instead of calculating the rate itself.
-C [rate]	As -c but for the remote system.
-d	Increase the quantity of debugging output displayed during a test (possibly at the expense of performance).
-f GMKgmk	Change the units of measure for stream tests. Capital letters are powers of two, lowercase are powers of 10.
-F fill_file	Prefill the send buffers with data from the named file. This is intended to provide a means for avoiding buffers that are filled with data, which is trivially easy to compress.
-h	Display a usage string, and exit.
-H remote_host	Set the hostname (or IP address) of the remote system.
-i max,min	Set the maximum and minimum number of iterations when trying to reach certain confidence levels.
-I lvl,[,intvl]	Specify the confidence level (either 95 or 99—99 is the default) and the width of the confidence interval as a percentage (default 10)
-l testlen	Specify the length of the test (default 10 seconds). A negative value sets the number of request/response transactions or the number of bytes for a stream test.
-n numcpus	Specify the number of CPUs in the system on those systems for which netperf has no way to find the number of CPUs automatically (all but HP-UX).
-o sizespec	Set an offset from the alignment specified with -a.
-O sizespec	As -o but for the remote system.
-p portnum	Connect to a listening server on the specified port rather than using /etc/services.
-P 0|1	Show (1) or suppress (0) the test banner.
-t testname	Specify the test to perform. Valid test names are (but not always compiled-in): TCP_STREAM, TCP_RR, TCP_CRR, UDP_STREAM, UDP_RR, DLCO_STREAM, DLCO_RR, DLCL_STREAM, DLCL_RR, STREAM_STREAM, STREAM_RR, DG_STREAM, DG_RR, FORE_STREAM, FORE_RR, HIPPI_STREAM, HIPPI_RR, LOC_CPU, REM_CPU.
-v verbosity	Set the verbosity level for the test (only with -P).
-V	Enable the copy-avoidance features (HP-UX 9.0 and later only).
-h	Display a usage string based on the test name set with -t, and exit.

TABLE 3.6: Options for `netserver`.

Option	Description
-h	Display a usage string, and exit.
-n numcpus	Specify the number of CPUs in the system on those systems for which netperf has no way to find the number of CPUs automatically (all but HP-UX).
-p portnum	Listen on the specified port. This is used when running as a stand-alone daemon.

2. Edit `Makefile`. In this file, there are two variables, `NETPERF_HOME` and `CFLAGS`, which may need to be modified.

   - `NETPERF_HOME`
     For this variable, we have to define a directory in which Netperf's tools and scripts are installed. Because Netperf uses its own scripts and tools, it is better to create a separate directory, such as `/usr/local/netperf`, then install the codes in this directory.

   - `CFLAGS`
     This variable needs to be modified if ATM API or other modules are used.

3. Run `make`.
4. Run `make install` (super user privilege may be required).
5. Add entries for configuration and database files in `/etc` directory. For netperf to be invoked automatically from `inetd` super daemon with TCP as its default transport protocol, one has to add

   ```
   netperf 12865/tcp
   ```

   to `/etc/services` database file and

   ```
   netperf stream tcp nowait root /home/netperf/netserver netserver
   ```

   to `/etc/inetd.conf` configuration file, if Netperf's `netserver` is installed in the directory `/home/netperf/netserver`. Note that if Netperf is installed on the host that can be directly accessed from either the global Internet or other external networks, setting up the `netserver` to be invoked via `inetd` is not a good idea from a security point of view (unless some sort of access control is implemented). In that case, it may be better (safer) to execute `netserver` manually.

3.4.5 NetPIPE

NetPIPE [298] is yet another network performance measurement tool. It was developed by Quinn O. Snell and other members in the U.S. Department of Energy's (USDOE) Ames Laboratory in Iowa. The acronym NetPIPE stands for Network Protocol Independent Performance Evaluation tool. Like `ttcp` and netperf, NetPIPE is also based on the popular benchmarking model in which a transmitting host sends test traffic to a receiving host over a given communication network. However, what makes NetPIPE different from ttcp and netperf is its focus on *application-oriented* performance measurement.

With the application performance in mind, what one wants to know in regard to network communication is not the available throughput but, for example, the optimal message size that gives the best application performance. Another performance evaluation objective could be to observe the network saturation (congestion) level with a particular message size. Developers of clustered computer systems, networked virtual reality systems, and other systems that require high performance TCP/IP networking infrastructure need to know the answers to these performance questions for optimum system design and operation. These answers are not easy to obtain with other benchmarking tools such as ttcp and Netperf.

NetPIPE has two modules, a protocol-specific communication module and a protocol-independent module. The protocol-specific module contains the necessary functions to establish a connection, send and receive data, and close a connection for a given protocol. This module may differ for each protocol. Current support includes TCP, MPI, RPC, and AAL5. The protocol-independent module implements block and streaming data transfer over a connection established by the protocol-dependent communication module.

Usage and Options.   As mentioned earlier, NetPIPE must run a transmitter process in a transmitting host and a receiver process in a receiving host. The command NPtcp is used for both hosts, with option -t at the transmitter and -r at the receiver. The receiver process is executed before the transmitter process. Since the default action of NetPIPE is to carry out a sequence of tests without any output displayed on the screen, option -P (in the transmitter) would be a help to know if the NetPIPE process is running.

There are many options to set a variety of test parameters, such as the increment steps of the message size, buffer size, destination port number, and so on. Table 3.7 gives brief descriptions of these options. If an option is used to modify a test parameter, including options -i, -l, -p, -s, and -u, one has to set the options on both the transmitter and the receiver, otherwise the test will not run properly.

At the completion of the tests, the results are stored in the file NetPIPE.out. The name of this output file can be changed with option -o. The typical procedure of performance evaluation with NetPIPE is depicted in Figure 3.17.

Performance Measurement Examples.   In this example, we show how NetPIPE can assist the network analyst to maximize application throughput by selecting the optimum message size. Figure 3.18 shows a sample output file NetPIPE.out. One line of output is generated for each message transfer. Each line contains five items: (1) transfer time (in seconds) for this message, (2) estimated throughput (in Mbps) for this message, (3) message size in bits, (4) message size in bytes, and (5) variance. In this example, we will use items (2) and (4) to determine the optimum message size.

TABLE 3.7: Options for NetPIPE.

Option	Description
-A alignment	Align buffers to the given boundary. For example, a value of 4 would align buffers to 4-byte (word) boundaries.
-a	Specify asynchronous receive, if the underlying protocol supports it.
-b buffer_size	[TCP only] Set send and receive TCP buffer sizes.
-h hostname	[TCP transmitter only] Specify name of host to which to connect.
-i increment	Specify increment step size (default is an exponentially increasing increment).
-l start_msg_size	Specify the starting message size. The test will start with messages of this size and increment, either exponentially or with an increment specified by the -i flag, until a block requires more than 1 second to transmit or the ending message size specified by the -u flag is reached, whichever occurs first.
-O buffer_offset	Specify offset of buffers from alignment. For example, specifying an alignment of 4 (with -A) and an offset of 1 would align buffers to the first byte after a word boundary.
-o output_filename	Specify output filename. By default, the output filename is NetPIPE.out.
-P	Print results on screen during execution of the test. By default, NetPIPE is silent during execution of the test.
-p port_number	Specify TCP port number to which to connect (for the transmitter) or the port on which to listen for connections (for the receiver).
-r	This process is a TCP receiver.
-s	Set streaming mode: data are only transmitted in one direction. By default, the transmitter measures the time taken as each data block is sent from the transmitter to the receiver and back, then divides the round-trip time by two to obtain the time taken by the message to travel in each direction. In streaming mode, the receiver measures the time required to receive the message and sends the measured time back to the transmitter for posting to the output file.
-t	This process is a TCP transmitter.
-u ending_msg_size	Specify the ending message size. By default, the test will end when the time to transmit a block exceeds 1 second. If -u is specified, the test will end when either the test time exceeds 1 second or the ending message size is reached, whichever occurs first.

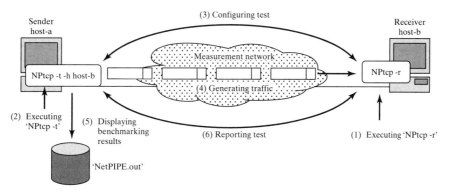

FIGURE 3.17: Performance measurement with NetPIPE.

```
0.000162 0.047086 8 1 0.000000
0.000162 0.094118 16 2 0.000000
0.000162 0.140886 24 3 0.000000
0.000162 0.187954 32 4 0.000000
0.000162 0.283345 48 6 0.000000
0.000160 0.382024 64 8 0.000000
0.000162 0.563728 96 12 0.000000
0.000161 0.616017 104 13 0.000000
........
........
0.503792 63.518332 33554432 4194304 0.000002
0.503379 63.570374 33554456 4194307 0.000001
0.753840 63.673941 50331624 6291453 0.000004
0.754975 63.578258 50331648 6291456 0.000002
0.755454 63.538006 50331672 6291459 0.000003
1.007394 63.530252 67108840 8388605 0.000008
1.009570 63.393353 67108864 8388608 0.000021
1.007363 63.532235 67108888 8388611 0.000005
```

FIGURE 3.18: A sample of NetPIPE output file.

The output file of Figure 3.18 is plotted in a graph (Figure 3.19) using `gnuplot` to help interpret the performance results. The throughput versus message-size graph shows that the throughput increases almost linearly with the increase in message size up to a message size of 10 Kb; after that the impact of message size increase on network throughput is negligible. This graph, therefore, suggests that under the conditions used for the experiment, the optimum message size would be around 10 Kb.

Installation.   Source code archive and other related documentations of Net-PIPE are freely available from the following web site:

```
http://www.scl.ameslab.gov/netpipe/.
```

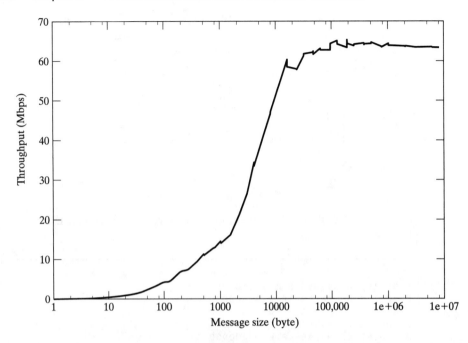

FIGURE 3.19: Gnuplot graph using NetPIPE output data.

Upon extracting the source code in a separate directory, one should complete the following steps to install NetPIPE.

1. Change directory (cd) to the directory containing the source code.
2. Edit Makefile, if needed. For example, the Makefile should be edited to compile NetPIPE with NPmpi and NPpvm, if testing of MPI and Parallel Virtual Machine (PVM) interfaces is desired.
3. Run "make" to compile the package.

3.4.6   Distributed Benchmark System

The TCP/IP measurement tools discussed so far in this chapter are used primarily to measure the average throughput of a *single* TCP connection between two points of a given network. The throughput measurement mainly evaluates the *flow control* mechanism of TCP. Distributed Benchmark System (DBS) [249] is a more advanced measurement tool that allows us to carry out comprehensive TCP performance tests to evaluate *multiple* TCP connections in parallel among many different points in the network. DBS also supports more sophisticated test traffic patterns to exercise realistic network conditions. Through more control over the network load patterns and traffic dynamics, DBS allows the performance engineers to evaluate other important aspects of TCP, namely, *retransmission control* and *congestion avoidance control*, which have significant influence on the overall performance of a TCP/IP network.

Usage and Options. The DBS software package is slightly more complex than the other packages discussed so far. An experiment in DBS is first specified in a script language and saved in a *command file*. The command file contains details, such as the number of TCP connections, the participating hosts in the network, network load patterns, and so on. DBS has three main components, dbsc (the DBS controller), dbsd (the DBS daemon), and dbs_view (the DBS viewer). Dbsc orchestrates the entire experiment by reading the experiment specifications from the command file, dispatching jobs to the dbsds running in different hosts in the network under test and collecting (collating) experimental results from the dbsds. Dbs_view uses Perl and gnuplot to visually depict the results collected by the dbsc. Figure 3.20 provides a step-by-step illustration of a typical DBS experiment. The steps involved are:

(0) Starting up the experiment. Start dbsd on all experimental hosts (not necessary if dbsd is registered in inetd.conf, as described later). Start dbsc on the controlling host and wait for the experiment to be completed.

(1) Reading command file. Dbsc interprets the configurations of the experiment from the command file.

(2) Sending commands. Dbsc sends commands to dbsds running in the specified experimental hosts.

(3) Data transmission. Each dbsd generates traffic according to the instructions given by the dbsc.

(4) Receiving results. Dbsds return the experimental results to the dbsc.

(5) Writing results files. Dbsc saves the results received from the dbsds in output files.

(6) Analyzing traffic data. Dbs_view draws graphs and charts of various performance measures (delay, jitter etc.) using the data in the output files.

Because all details of a DBS experiment are specified in a command file, only a few command line options are available for dbsc and dbsd:

```
dbsc [-p port_number] [-d] command_file
dbsd [-p port_number] [-d] [-D] [-h allow_host]
```

Command_file is the name of the command file created before the start of the experiment. Option -p is used to change the default port number (10710) for the DBS. For trouble-shooting purposes, one may use option -d to display the running status of the DBS experiment. Options '-D' and '-h allow_host' may be useful to execute dbsd from inetd automatically as described later in this section.

Unlike dbsc and dbsd, dbs_view has many options. Note that dbs_view is not a tool that merely draws graphs (in fact, it uses gnuplot to actually draw the graphs), but it performs a variety of processing on the "raw" data in the output file before generating graphs of interests. The major options are described in Table 3.8.

Performance Measurement Examples. In this section, we give examples to show how dbsc, dbsd, and dbs_view can be used to measure TCP/IP network performance under more realistic traffic conditions.

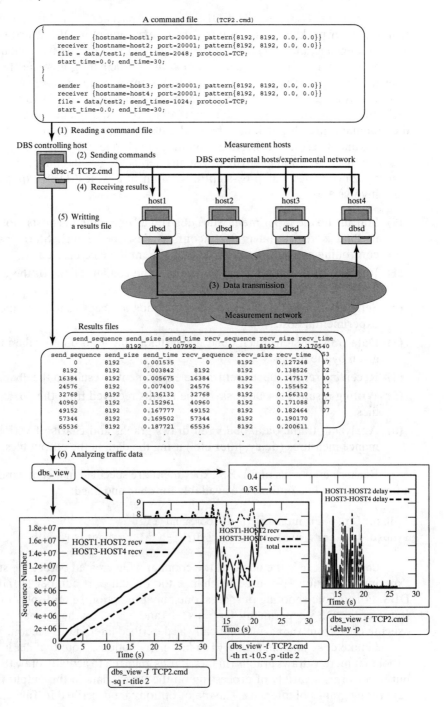

FIGURE 3.20: Data flow of DBS.

TABLE 3.8: Options of `dbs_view`.

Option	Description
`-f file file . .`	Specify the name of command file (multiple designation is possible). This is NOT an output file. This is the file that is specified when you execute dbsc.
`-a area`	Describes the area of drawing the graph. Specify like "`[0:20][0:1000]`" (double quotation is needed).
`-sq s|r|u|S|R|U`	Displays sequence numbers on the application level s: display sending sequence number with Step Line r: display receiving sequence number with Step Line u: display UDP lost packet with Step Line S: display sending sequence number with Dot R: display receiving sequence number with Dot U: display UDP lost packet with Dot
`-th s|r|t|S|R|T`	Displays throughput on the application level s: display sending throughput with Line r: display receiving throughput with Line t: display the total receiving throughput with Line S: display sending throughput with Step Line R: display receiving throughput with Step Line T: display the total receiving throughput with Step Line
`-delay`	Displays transmission delay time on the application level
`-jitter s|r`	Displays jitters on the application level s: display sending jitter with Step Line r: display receiving jitter with Step Line
`-ulost`	Calculates lost packets of UDP.
`-t time (sec)`	Specify the grain degree of the time interval (default is 0.1 seconds).
`-p`	calculating option '-tth', '-tlost', '-trtt', '-tdelay', '-tjitter' and '-ulost'
`-ps`	Outputs as a PostScript file.
`-eps`	Outputs as an EPS file.
`-color`	Outputs as color PS or EPS file (specify -ps or -eps same time)
`-title #`	Specify the number of words in the command file to be used as title of data. Examples are as follows: `-title` isn't specified → 'test1/host1_host2/data1' `-title -1` → no title `-title 1` → 'test1' `-title 2` → 'host1_host2' `-title 3` → 'data1'

The first step with DBS is to write a command file specifying a given experiment in detail. Writing such a command file for the first time may not be easy for a beginner. The DBS distribution package includes several sample command and result (output) files to help a beginner understand the format of a command file. In this example, we use one of the sample command files, named 'TCPvsMPEG.cmd' (shown in Figure 3.21) to illustrate the operation of DBS experiments. Details of how to write a command file can be found in the manual pages distributed with the DBS package.

```
# TCP
{
    sender {
        hostname    = host1;
        port        = 0;
        so_debug    = OFF;
        tcp_trace   = OFF;
        no_delay    = OFF;
        send_buff   = 32768;
        recv_buff   = 32768;
        mem_align   = 2048;
        pattern {8192, 8192, 0.0, 0.0}
    }
    receiver {
        hostname    = host2;
        port        = 20000;
        so_debug    = OFF;
        tcp_trace   = OFF;
        no_delay    = OFF;
        recv_buff   = 32768;
        send_buff   = 32768;
        mem_align   = 8192;
        pattern {8192, -1, 0.0, 0.0}
    }
    file            = data/TCP;
    protocol        = TCP;
    start_time      = 0.0;
    connection_mode = BEFORE;
    end_time        = 30;
    send_times      = 2048;
}
# UDP
{
    sender {
        hostname    = host3;
        port        = 20000;
        so_debug    = OFF;
        tcp_trace   = OFF;
        no_delay    = OFF;
        send_buff   = 32768;
        recv_buff   = 32768;
        mem_align   = 8192;
        pattern {40960, 1024, 0.033333333, 0; # I frame
                  2048, 1024, 0.033333333, 0; # B frame
                  2048, 1024, 0.033333333, 0; # B frame
                 10240, 1024, 0.033333333, 0; # P frame
                  2048, 1024, 0.033333333, 0; # B frame
                  2048, 1024, 0.033333333, 0; # B frame
                 10240, 1024, 0.033333333, 0; # P frame
                  2048, 1024, 0.033333333, 0; # B frame
                  2048, 1024, 0.033333333, 0; # B frame
                 10240, 1024, 0.033333333, 0; # P frame
                  2048, 1024, 0.033333333, 0; # B frame
                  2048, 1024, 0.033333333, 0; # B frame
        }
    }
    receiver {
        hostname    = host4;
        port        = 20000;
        mem_align   = 2048;
        pattern {8192, 8192, 0.0, 0.0}
    }
    file            = data/UDP;
    protocol        = UDP;
    start_time      = 2.0;
    end_time        = 30;
    send_times      = 20;
}
```

FIGURE 3.21: Sample command file (TCPvsMPEG.cmd).

Command file 'TCPvsMPEG.cmd' specifies two types of data transmissions: one is TCP bulk data transfer, and the other is UDP stream simulating MPEG 1. Host1 and host2 establish a TCP connection, where host1 is a sender and host2 is a receiver. Host3 and host4 send and receive UDP traffic. For actual tests, one needs to replace host1 to host4 by actual names of the hosts in a given network. To run the experiment, the following steps are executed:

(1) Replace host1 ~ host4 in the command file with actual names.

(2) Create a directory called 'data' (it is specified in the lines starting with 'file='`).

(3) Run dbsd in each host as follows:

```
% dbsd
```

(4) Run dbsc as follows:

```
% dbsc TCPvsMPEG.cmd
```

(5) After dbsc completes, check the creation of the result files (one for TCP and one for UDP):

```
% ls data
TCP.t     UDP.t
```

(6) Draw necessary graphs using dbs_view.

Depending on the requirements, many different graphs can be created using dbs_view. Here we show some examples of what can be achieved.

EXAMPLE 3.18   Throughput measurement.

In this example, we are interested in comparing instantaneous (NOT *average*) throughput of TCP and UDP measured as Mbps in intervals of 0.1 seconds (-t 0.1 from Table 3.8). To achieve this, we run dbs_view as follows:

```
% perl ../script/dbs_view -f TCPvsMPEG.cmd -title 2
-th r -t 0.1 -p
```

Figure 3.22 shows the graph created by the above command. The graph shows that the MPEG application has activities in the 2- to 10-second interval, causing throughput drop for TCP. MPEG remains idle the rest of the time, letting TCP consume the entire link bandwidth.

EXAMPLE 3.19   Sequence number graph.

This example compares the rate of sequence number increase between TCP and UDP. The following dbs_view command is executed (see Table 3.8 for option details):

```
% perl ../script/dbs_view -f TCPvsMPEG.cmd -title 2
-sq r -p
```

Figure 3.23 shows sequence number versus time graph. We can see that the UDP sequence increases slower than TCP. In the interval of 2 to 10 seconds, where MPEG is active, TCP sequence increases slower than that in the interval of 10 to 20 seconds.

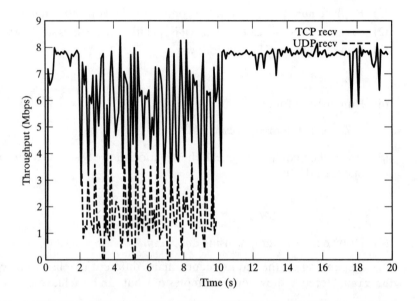

FIGURE 3.22: Throughput.

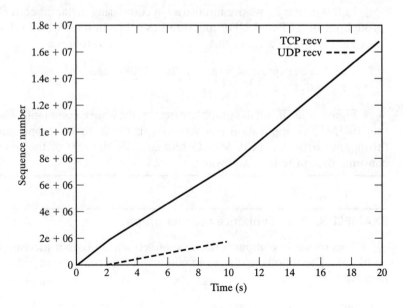

FIGURE 3.23: Sequence number.

EXAMPLE 3.20   Packet delay comparison.

In this example, end-to-end packet delay is compared for TCP and UDP packets. The delay graph of Figure 3.24 is achieved by executing

```
% perl ../script/dbs_view -f TCPvsMPEG.cmd -title 2
-delay -p
```

The graph shows that TCP experiences very low delay when there is no MPEG traffic. With MPEG traffic in the background in the 2- to 10-second interval, TCP experiences a delay of around 50 ms. Delay experienced by UDP sometimes exceeds 150 ms, which may cause severe performance problem for the MPEG video.

To have a closer look at the delay comparisons, it is desirable to magnify a small part of the graph. The following dbs_view command plots the delay curves between 5 and 6 seconds:

```
% perl ../script/dbs_view -f TCPvsMPEG.cmd -title 2
-a "[5:6]" -delay -p
```

Figure 3.25 shows the magnified curves. We can see that MPEG traffic experiences variable delay with large spikes from time to time. These large spikes cause large jitter.

Installation.   One must install xntp for synchronizing the time between all experimental hosts before using DBS. Xntp is freely available from the following URL:

```
http://www.xntp.org/
```

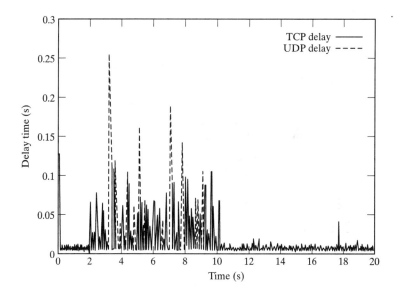

FIGURE 3.24: Delay.

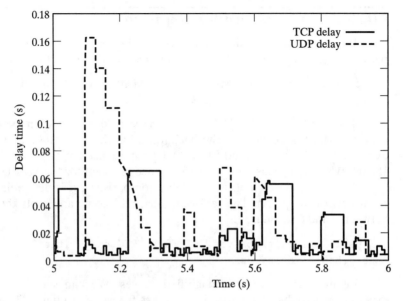

FIGURE 3.25: Delay in detail.

The source code and manual pages of DBS are freely available from the following URL:

```
http://www.ai3.net/products/dbs/
```

The steps to install DBS are:

1. Switch ('cd') to the directory containing the source code.
2. Check 'Makefile' and edit it if necessary.
3. Run 'make' to compile the package.
4. Obtain the *super user* privilege using the command 'su', then run 'make install' to install the programs, data files, and documentations.

Running DBS through inetd. To get dbsd executed automatically through inetd, the following configurations are necessary:

1. Copy dbsd to /usr/local/etc/dbsd.
2. Add the following line to /etc/services.

   ```
   dbs 10710/tcp
   ```

3. Add the following line to /etc/inetd.conf.

   ```
   dbs stream tcp nowait root /usr/local/etc/dbsd dbsd -D
   ```

4. Locate the process number of inetd and execute:

   ```
   kill -HUP 'process number'
   ```

To address the security problem, one can restrict dbsd accepting commands only from specific hosts by appending "-h hostname" as follows:

```
dbs stream tcp nowait root /usr/local/etc/dbsd dbsd -D -h allow_host
```

3.5 SELECTING THE RIGHT TOOL

In the previous section, we discussed six TCP performance measurement tools. There are situations when one tool may be more appropriate than others. Besides measurement capabilities, there are features, such as availability on a given platform, that can also influence the selection of a particular tool. Table 3.9, which compares

TABLE 3.9: Comparison of TCP measurement tools.

Feature/Capability	Tcpdump	Tcpstat	Ttcp	Netperf	NetPIPE	DBS
Price	Free	Free	Free	Free	Free	Free
Platform	Unix, Windows (windump)	Unix	Unix, Windows (wsttcp)	Unix, Windows	Unix, Windows	Unix
Root access needed for installation	Yes	Yes	No	No	No	Yes
Dump packet headers?	Yes	No	No	No	No	No
Measure instantaneous throughput?	No	No	No	No	No	Yes
Measure behavior of TCP slow start?	No	No	No	No	No	Yes
Measure overhead of connection establishment?	No	No	No	Yes	No	Yes
Multiple connections between two hosts?	No	No	No	No	No	Yes
Multiple connections between multiple hosts?	No	No	No	No	No	Yes
Specify traffic pattern?	No	No	No	Yes	No	Yes

TABLE 3.10: URLs for TCP measurement tools.

Tool	URL (Unix)	URL (Windows)
Tcpdump	www.tcpdump.org	windump.polito.it
Tcpstat	www.frenchfries.net/paul/tcpstat	
Ttcp	ftp.arl.mil/pub/ttcp	www.winsite.com
Netperf	www.netperf.org	www.netperf.org
NetPIPE	www.scl.ameslab.gov/netpipe	ftp.scl.ameslab.gov/pub/netpipe/NT
DBS	www.ai3.net/products/dbs	

these six tools, can help in making a selection. For example, someone interested in measuring TCP throughput under specific input traffic patterns, would select either Netperf or DBS (both capable of handling specific traffic patterns). However, if *instantaneous* throughput is of interest, DBS would be more appropriate (`Netperf` cannot show instantaneous throughput).

One good aspect of all these tools is that they are freely available. Table 3.10 lists the URLs that contain information on how to download the free software tool.

3.6   FURTHER READING

There are numerous white papers and published articles (too many to list all of them here) that present TCP/IP performance measurement case studies using the tools discussed in this chapter. The reader will gain a deeper understanding of the application of these tools from these case studies. Here we refer to some of the studies.

Many examples of TCP analysis using `tcpdump` can be found in [302]. Using `ttcp`, Charalambos et al. [101] measured TCP performance on an ATM network over a high-speed satellite link. Netperf was used by Kim et al. [200] to carry out a benchmark performance test of an ATM test bed that was built to simulate advanced C^4I applications such as real-time battle management, SAR image processing and analysis, and air tasking order monitoring. Park et al. [259] use NetPIPE to study Gigabit Ethernet performance for different versions of Linux. Murayama and Yamaguchi [250] describe experiments using DBS to measure and compare TCP end-to-end performance for different types of LANs, including FDDI, ATM, and HIPPI over ATM networks, and WANs, including VSAT satellite channels. An example of high-resolution traffic measurement using a specialized hardware tool can be found in [216].

RFC 2525 [266] shows several problems in existing TCP implementations using data captured by `tcpdump`.

The IP Performance Metrics (IPPM) Working Group in the International Engineering Task Force (IETF) produces standards that define specific metrics and procedures for accurately measuring and documenting these metrics. These documents are freely available on the IETF web site [175].

The Cooperative Association for Internet Data Analysis (CAIDA) [2] has references to many measurement and network visualization tools for the global Internet infrastructure, including hardware tools for high-speed and high-resolution measurement.

Surveyor [15] (`http://www.advanced.org/surveyor/`) is a large-scale measurement infrastructure deployed at many participating sites around the world. Based on standards developed by IETF's IPPM WG, Surveyor measures the performance of the Internet paths among participating sites. The project also develops methodologies and tools to analyze the performance data.

In this chapter, we have discussed TCP performance measurement using six tools. Several other tools are sometimes used for performance monitoring and measurement. Some of them include traceroute [21], ping (comes with standard distributions of UNIX and Windows), nettest (a *secure* network testing tool) [12], netspec [11], pathrate [13], analyzer [1], and speedy [6].

3.7   SUMMARY

Live measurement of operational networks is a vital part of building and maintaining high performance TCP/IP networks. In this chapter, we have discussed six TCP performance measurement tools and explained their usage through practical examples. All these tools are freely available on the web.

The measurement tools are of two types, monitoring and benchmarking. Network monitoring tools, such as `tcpdump` and `tcpstat`, help us capture details of packets transmitted on the network. We can learn key traffic dynamics, for example, the actual percentage of traffic that comes from TCP or UDP, on a given network by analyzing such captured data. To measure the available throughput in the network, we need to use the benchmarking tools. In this chapter, we have discussed four benchmarking tools, `ttcp`, `Netperf`, `NetPIPE`, and `DBS`. These tools generate traffic at a *transmitting* host and measure the throughput at a *receiving* host.

Tools discussed in this chapter were developed in the late 1990s. These tools are implemented in software and they run in general-purpose operating system environment. Software-based tools are adequate for most existing TCP/IP networks operating under the Gbps mark. However, for Gbps networks, there are some commercial performance measurement devices that use real-time operating systems, such as QNX, and specially designed hardware drivers to generate large amounts of traffic at Gbps speed. Given the high-speed trend of future TCP/IP networks, the existing software-based tools must evolve to be effective in the future. The growing popularity of the wireless Internet, however, means that we are going to see large-scale deployments of wireless TCP/IP networks operating way below the Gbps mark. The tools discussed in this chapter, therefore, will continue to be useful to many network operators and engineers in the future.

3.8   REVIEW QUESTIONS

1. How can TCP measurement tools help build and maintain high performance TCP/IP networks?
2. What types of measurement tools are available? Name two tools of each type.
3. What additional measurements can be achieved with DBS compared to other benchmarking tools described in this chapter?
4. Visit `http://www.acm.org/sigcomm/ITA`, an Internet site that holds a large volume of Internet traffic trace. Find out which tool was used to collect traces. Identify the additional tools used to process the traces further.
5. Consider a measurement scenario in which we need to monitor network performance when multiple TCP connections are in progress. We are interested in monitoring the slow-start behavior of all TCP connections. Which of the following tools is most suitable for this task and why?

(a) ttcp

(b) netperf

(c) netpipe

(d) dbs

(e) tcpdump

6. Is there any capability difference between ttcp and netperf? Can you give an example in which one tool has an advantage over the other?

7. Make a list of tools that do not need super user (su) access to install and run. Make a similar list for those tools that *do* need su access.

8. What are the limitations of software-based tools discussed in this chapter? When do we need hardware-based, special-purpose tools for performance measurement?

9. The benchmarking tools must have a daemon running in the receiving hosts. It either can be started manually or can be configured to run automatically through the inetd super daemon. Discuss the advantages and disadvantages of running the daemon through inetd.

10. Can we effectively use the tools discussed in this chapter for future TCP/IP networks? Why or why not? (Hint: what are the characteristics of future TCP/IP networks?)

3.9   HANDS-ON PROJECTS

1. Install Tcpdump and Tcpstat in your system. Now compare the distribution of UDP and TCP traffic on your LAN. Show the distributions using a graph similar to the one shown in Figure 3.11.

2. If you have access to any multimedia applications (e.g., Netmeeting), start a few of them on your LAN. Repeat the measurement of UDP and TCP traffic. Can you notice any difference in the percentages?

3. Install DBS on your system. Experiment with some of the examples illustrated in Section 3.4.6.

3.10   CASE STUDY: WCORP MONITORS NETWORK TRAFFIC

With the emergence of inexpensive cameras and network videoconferencing tools, more and more scientists at WCORP started using videoconferencing as an effective communication tool with their colleagues in the remote office. A direct consequence is in the increase of traffic on the network that at times slowed down the performance of other applications, namely, FTP and WWW. The network administrator of WCORP wanted to restrict the use of videoconferencing but was not sure how much restriction would be appropriate. A total ban on videoconferencing may be an inappropriate action if the traffic generated by videoconferencing is only a very small fraction of the total traffic.

The network administrator has decided to monitor all traffic on the LAN using tcpdump and compute the percentage of UDP and TCP traffic. Because videoconferencing uses UDP and all other applications (e-mail, FTP, and WWW) use TCP, a breakdown of UDP and TCP would give a breakdown of traffic generated by videoconferencing and other data applications. Using `tcpdump` and `tcpstat`, UDP and TCP packet generation on the LAN was displayed in a graph like the one in Figure 3.11. The graph showed that almost 30% of the total traffic was generated by the videoconferencing applications. After consulting with the CEO, the network administrator felt that video traffic is a little too much, and the users must be warned to reduce the use of videoconferencing. One week after the warning was circulated, the traffic was monitored once again. The network administrator was quite happy to see that UDP traffic had decreased from 30% to 10% and as a result the performance of FTP and WWW had also increased.

C H A P T E R 4

TCP/IP Network Simulation

CHAPTER OBJECTIVES

After completing this chapter, the reader should be able to:

- Appreciate the role of simulation in performance evaluation of TCP/IP networks

- Gain good understanding of the steps of a systematic simulation study

- Acquire the knowledge needed to conduct *steady-state* simulations

- Learn the steps of *trace-driven* simulations

- Master the basic skills needed for analyzing confidence level of simulation results

- Describe the types of simulation tools available for simulating TCP/IP networks

- Become familiar with the capabilities of popular simulation tools

Simulation has emerged as a popular tool for performance evaluation of complex TCP/IP algorithms and protocols. We begin this chapter with a discussion on the role of simulation in performance evaluation of TCP/IP networks, followed by some important simulation concepts, including validation, verification, and statistical correctness of simulation results. We then define a classification of simulation tools available to TCP/IP network analysts and present a detailed introduction to two popular simulation tools and their applications in TCP/IP network simulation.

4.1 THE ROLE OF SIMULATION

Simulation is a useful technique for performance evaluation of TCP/IP networks. Some reasons for using simulation are:

1. If the proposed network is not available for measurement, simulation provides a convenient way to predict the performance.
2. Even if a network is available for measurement, simulation may still be preferred because it allows the evaluation of performance under a wide variety of workload and network conditions.
3. Simulation allows a performance analyst to compare several alternative TCP/IP architectures under identical and repeatable network conditions.
4. Simulations can incorporate more details than analytical modeling; thus, more often results can be produced that are closer to reality.

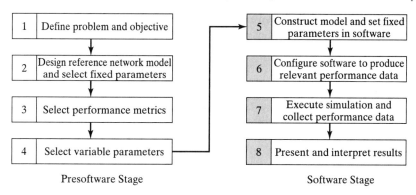

FIGURE 4.1: Steps of a systematic simulation study.

5. Researchers often use results from more detailed simulations to validate analytical results. A "match" between analytical results and simulation results give confidence to the user.

4.2 STEPS OF A SYSTEMATIC SIMULATION STUDY

For any performance evaluation task, it helps to define the task in several steps. For example, Jain [186] divides a performance evaluation project into 10 steps to help new researchers avoid common mistakes. These steps can be adapted to simulation projects as well. In this section, we show the steps that can be useful in a systematic simulation study. Similar discussion of steps can be found in other sources [63, 215].

Before describing the individual steps, we first discuss the issue of using software in simulation studies. TCP/IP network simulation involves use of a simulation software. The software is required to run the simulation on a computer to produce the simulation results. In the literature several synonymous terms, such as *simulation tool*, *simulation program*, and *simulation package*, are used to refer to this software. Many analysts, especially new students, rush to the use of a simulation software without giving much thought to the actual modeling problem at hand. Such a premature start to software use often leads to costly redevelopments and reexecutions of the simulation program to produce the required results.

Before "touching" the simulation software, one has to complete a number of important steps. For this purpose, the entire simulation study can be broken into two stages, *presoftware stage* and *software stage*. Given the simulation task at hand, the exact steps involved in each of these stages will vary. Nevertheless, each stage could have a set of steps (as shown in Figure 4.1) common to any simulation task. These steps are:

1. **Define the objective of the study.** State the goals and objectives of the simulation very clearly at the start of the study. Subsequent steps attempt to meet these objectives. One must consult all relevant people during the formulation of the problem statement. If the problem is defined entirely by the analyst, it may not be well understood by management.

2. **Design reference network model and select fixed parameters.** TCP/IP simulations usually involve some sort of network involving routers, servers, links, and so on. Also, some applications, for example, FTP and WWW, are associated to some hosts. The task in this step would be to design the reference network (topology) on a piece of paper and then select the network parameters, such as the link bandwidth, buffer size, traffic model, traffic load, and so on. The values of these parameters remain fixed for all simulation executions. The traffic model must be selected very carefully to simulate a real system as closely as possible. An incorrect selection of traffic model can render simulation results useless even if the network modeling is accurate. For example, if the traffic in a real system shows burstiness over many time scales, a self-similar traffic model must be selected. Selecting a Poisson traffic model yields incorrect results.

3. **Select performance metrics.** Determine the metrics to be used for the performance study. The usual metrics are TCP throughput, packet delay, jitter, and so on. Chapter 1 provides a comprehensive list of performance metrics for TCP/IP networks. These performance metrics, sometimes referred to as output or response variables [63], are observed at the end of simulation. Sometimes it may not be possible to directly measure a user metric, but it can be derived from two or more response variables.

4. **Select variable parameters.** In most TCP/IP simulations, the objective of the simulation is to assess the impact of certain variables on the performance metrics. For example, for a wireless IP network, one may be interested in studying the impact of bit error rate (BER) of the wireless link on TCP throughput. In this case, BER is a variable parameter and TCP throughput is a performance metric. These variable parameters are sometimes referred to as input or control parameters [63]. The analyst must select the variables carefully to achieve fruitful performance results. If important variables that may have significant impact on the overall performance are left out, the study will not be very useful. However, at this stage, it may not be possible to guess which variables will have the highest impact. Hence, one should select a large set of variables to start with and discard some of them later if necessary. In some cases, the variable may not be a "parameter" as such, but it may be an algorithm or a scheme in which different simulation executions have different versions of the algorithm. Up until now, we did not have to work with the simulation software at all. The next four steps involve the use of a simulation software and constitute the software stage.

5. **Construct the network model and set fixed parameters in simulation software.** Build the reference network model designed in Step 2 into the software. Also set the values of the fixed parameters in the software model. This step may require some coding, unless everything can be done via user menus. The actual programming language to be used for the coding depends on the software used. For example, *ns*, a popular simulation software for TCP/IP networks, uses C++. See Sections 4.8 and 4.9 for examples of model construction in two popular simulation softwares. While constructing a model, the programmer must verify that there is no bug and the model works properly. The model that is constructed must also be a valid model, that is, it should accurately represent

the real system that is being modeled. Model verification and validation is discussed in Section 4.4.

6. **Configure simulation software to produce relevant performance data.** The software must be configured or programmed to record the values of the performance metrics selected in Step 3. Again, some coding may be necessary.

7. **Execute simulation program and collect performance data.** Finally, we execute the simulation program. These executions are known as "simulation runs." When the simulation runs complete, the performance metrics data are collected in disk files. We must make sure that the output data collected are valid and do not contain "large" statistical errors. Validation and error analysis of output data are discussed later in the chapter.

8. **Present and interpret results.** The data collected in the previous step are usually in raw form. These data must be converted into "knowledge" through clever presentations. Typically, raw data are processed further to produce visual graphs. The performance metrics are plotted on the y axis, and the variables are plotted on the x axis to show the impact of variables on the performance metrics. Sometimes useful tables are created from these raw data to show certain performance results. After presenting the results in graphs and tables, the analyst must interpret them to make useful conclusions. Presentation and interpretation of results require some art. Given the same data, two different analysts may choose to highlight two different results and make two different conclusions. Sometimes it is useful to share the results with another expert to seek any possible new ideas for presentation or a "second opinion." At this stage, it may be necessary to go back and run a few more simulations to collect data for some additional performance metrics or for some new values of the variables.

Breaking down the entire simulation study into the preceding steps has several benefits. One obvious benefit is the better management of the simulation project, as the whole project can be approached one step at a time. The other benefit is the possible grouping of the steps with an objective to distribute the entire simulation task among multiple individuals, especially when the simulation study is a large project employing several people. Steps 5 to 7 are software-specific and can be done independently by a research assistant having expertise in a particular software tool, such as OPNET. Another person, maybe the supervisor or the chief investigator of the project, can work on Steps 1 to 4 and later on Step 8 once the data are collected. Other breakdowns may also be possible depending on the task at hand, project budget, and the nature of people's expertise.

4.3 TYPES OF SIMULATIONS

In this section, different types of simulations are introduced.

4.3.1 Continuous versus Discrete Event

The state of the system modeled can be continuous (e.g., concentration of substance in a chemical system) or discrete (e.g., queues of packets in a packet switching network). A simulation using continuous-state model is called continuous-event simulation. In contrast, a discrete-event simulation (DES) uses a discrete-state model of the system. The main component of a DES is a linked list of events waiting to happen. Each event has an associated time value indicating the time to execute the event. As the simulation progresses, new events are added to the list, and waiting events are popped up whenever their times come. A global simulation clock is maintained, which is updated to the next event time. Readers interested in details of DES structure are referred to [215].

4.3.2 Terminating versus Steady State

Based on the terminating criteria, simulations can be classified into two categories, *terminating* simulations and *steady-state* simulations. In this section, we discuss the context and usefulness of these types of simulations.

A terminating simulation is used to study the behavior of a network system for a well-defined period of time or number of events. For example, one may be interested in evaluating the performance of a new TCP protocol stack only during the office (peak) hours, 9 AM to 5 PM. In this case, traffic representing peak hour activities is simulated and the simulation is terminated exactly after 8 hours of simulated time. Instead of time duration, one could also be interested in evaluating the performance of a new scheme for downloading, say, 100 specific objects from a popular web site. In the latter case, the simulation terminates as soon as the last of the 100 objects is downloaded.

If we are interested in investigating the steady-state behaviors of a network system, we cannot use terminating simulations. For example, if we need to measure the long-term packet loss rate in a congested router, we must continue to simulate the system until the system reaches steady state. Before the steady state, mean packet loss rate fluctuates as the system goes through a transient phase. This phenomenon is illustrated in Figure 4.2. It is clear from Figure 4.2 that the experimenter must be very careful when reporting results from steady-state simulations; if the simulation is terminated before the system reaches steady state, the obtained result can be significantly higher or lower than the expected value.

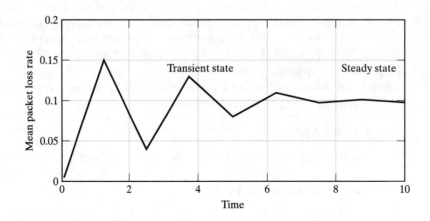

FIGURE 4.2: The transient phase in a steady-state simulation.

4.3.3   Synthetic versus Trace-Driven Simulation

To evaluate the performance of a given TCP/IP network using simulation, we need some input traffic pattern. The performance results obtained are then valid for the specific input traffic pattern. In many simulations, input traffic is *synthetically* generated using random traffic generators. For such randomly generated traffic, the traffic pattern is chosen from a set of predefined traffic models, such as Poisson or exponential, ON-OFF, and self-similar, to match the traffic pattern of a real system as closely as possible. The primary advantage of using such traffic generators within a simulation is ease of operation (traffic is generated automatically on-the-fly).

Although random traffic generation remains a popular choice for TCP/IP network simulation, the input traffic for this method never matches 100% with the actual traffic observed on a given practical network. To achieve more credibility, many performance analysts use *trace-driven* simulation to evaluate the performance of a new algorithm. The steps in a trace-driven simulation are shown in Figure 4.3. Traces of packet arrival events (arrival time, packet size, and so on) are first captured from an operational network using a performance measurement tool (e.g., tcpdump). These traces, after some processing, are then used as input traffic for the simulation. There are no random traffic generators. Using the same trace, the performance of several algorithms and schemes can be evaluated for comparison purposes. We will discuss an example of trace-driven simulation later in the chapter.

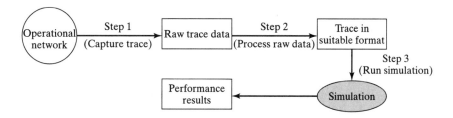

FIGURE 4.3: The steps of trace-driven simulation.

TABLE 4.1: TCP/IP traces available on the Internet (http://ita.ee.lbl.gov).

Trace File	Trace Description
lbl-pkt	2-hour trace of TCP/IP packet arrivals between LBL and the rest of the world
lbl-conn	30-day trace of TCP connections between LBL and the rest of the world
worldcup98	1.3 billion web requests at 1998 world cup servers
nasa-http	2-month trace of HTTP requests at NASA server
npd-routes	Internet route measurement data

Nowadays, there are many traces freely available from the Internet. These traces range from simple packet arrival times on an Ethernet LAN to more sophisticated HTTP logs. Table 4.1 lists some of the traces available from the official Internet trace archive (http://ita.ee.lbl.gov). These traces were collected at the Lawrence Berkeley Laboratory (LBL). Some of these traces are captured using specialized hardware for greater resolution and accuracy, while others are obtained using simple monitoring tools, such as `tcpdump`. Availability of such traces enables the performance analysts to focus on the simulation techniques without having to worry about capturing the trace.

The traces shown in Table 4.1 are several years old. There are other sites that provide more recent traces [8, 9, 20, 24].

4.4 SIMULATION VALIDATION AND VERIFICATION

During the construction of a simulation model of a TCP/IP network, a number of assumptions about the behavior of the network system are made. There are two important steps for ensuring the quality of a simulation study. *Validation* is the first step that makes sure that the assumptions are realistic. The second step, called *verification*, is to make sure that the model implements those assumptions correctly. It may be possible that a model is valid but is not implemented correctly and vice versa.

It is very difficult or even may not be possible to create a simulation model that is 100% valid and verified for all possible combinations of input parameters and scenarios. This is especially true for large, complex networks with many simulated elements. Nevertheless, there are some guidelines to follow to validate and verify the simulations, at least for some important scenarios. One such guideline is to look for "surprise" in the output. It is easier to detect such surprises in the trends of the output rather than in the absolute values. If the output does not follow an intuitive trend, such as the throughput does not increase when the bottleneck link bandwidth is increased slightly, the model should be inspected carefully for any possible bug in the code.

Analytical modeling is another tool often used for validating simulation results. If known analytical models are available, such as a simple queuing model, results from the simulation are compared with the analytical values. Any significant discrepancy is a source of possible error in the model.

Finally, comparison with real network data is the most preferred way to validate simulations; however, a real system may not exist or be available for measurement. Sometimes measurement data are available on the Internet from another source. Some sort of comparison with such data, therefore, is recommended. Simulation results are often considered with skepticism unless some evidence of validation can be shown. A more in-depth discussion of validation and verification techniques can be found in [63].

4.5 CONFIDENCE LEVEL OF SIMULATION RESULTS

It is not enough to have a valid simulation model. Most TCP/IP simulations use some sort of random numbers to generate various random events such as packet arrival times, packet sizes, file sizes, and so on. Because of such randomness, the results obtained from a simulation also exhibit random phenomena. If a terminating simulation is replicated 10 times, each with a different random seed, 10 (slightly) different outputs are produced. The question is then, how can we trust the simulation results?

We must remember that the simulation output is only an estimate of the actual value. We should, therefore, establish, through statistical analysis, some level of confidence on the simulation outcome. Without such a confidence level, the whole simulation exercise, in some cases, can be as good as tossing a coin.

4.5.1   Confidence Level Formula

The goal of simulation is to obtain the mean value, μ, of a particular output variable (e.g., packet loss rate). Since it is not possible to obtain the exact value, stochastic simulations try to estimate μ from a number of observations obtained under a number of different random input sequences. Let us denote the sequence of observations (samples) for an output variable from a simulation experiment as $x_1, x_2, \ldots, x_n$. The actual value of the output variable is estimated by calculating the mean of the individual observations as:

$$\overline{X}(n) = \frac{1}{n} \sum_{i=1}^{n} x_i \tag{4.1}$$

The estimator $\overline{X}(n)$ itself is a random value that depends on the sequence of observed values. The question that naturally arises is: what is the accuracy of this estimator? In other words, what is the magnitude of $|\overline{X}(n) - \mu|$? μ is an unknown quantity that is approximated by the observations from simulation experiments.

The confidence in an estimate can be measured by the following probability [263]:

$$P(|\overline{X}(n) - \mu| < \delta) = 1 - \alpha, \quad 0 < \alpha < 1 \tag{4.2}$$

or

$$P(\overline{X}(n) - \delta \leq \mu \leq \overline{X}(n) + \delta) = 1 - \alpha, \quad 0 < \alpha < 1 \tag{4.3}$$

where $(1 - \alpha)$ is the *confidence level* of the estimator $\overline{X}(n)$ and δ is the *half-width* of the confidence interval. In other words, one is $100(1 - \alpha)\%$ confident that the true average of the output variable lies in the interval $(\overline{X}(n) - \delta, \overline{X}(n) + \delta)$. Equation (4.3) is based on the assumption that the probability distribution of the estimator is well behaving (i.e., not long-range-dependent) and symmetric. Some possible tests to check the validity of this assumption are to look at autocorrelation and variance reduction.

The next step is to calculate δ for a desired α. If the observations $x_1, x_2, \ldots, x_n$ can be regarded as the realizations of independent and identically distributed (i.i.d.) random variables, then δ can be calculated as [263]:

$$\delta = t_{n-1,1-\frac{\alpha}{2}} \sigma[\overline{X}(n)] \tag{4.4}$$

where

$$\sigma^2[\overline{X}(n)] = \sum_{i=1}^{n} \frac{(x_i - \overline{X}(n))^2}{n(n-1)} \tag{4.5}$$

For $n > 30$ (large number of observations or samples), the t-distribution in Eq. (4.4) can be replaced by the standard normal distribution. In that case, $t_{n-1,1-\frac{\alpha}{2}}$ is replaced by $z_{1-\frac{\alpha}{2}}$, which is the upper $(1 - \frac{\alpha}{2})$ of the critical point obtained from the standard normal distribution.

In most cases, a confidence level of 95% ($\alpha = 0.05$) is desired, which yields $z_{0.975} = 1.96$ (from Table A3.5.1 in [283]). Therefore, the half-width δ of the confidence interval is calculated as:

$$\delta = 1.96 \times \sigma[\overline{X}(n)] \tag{4.6}$$

Once the δ is calculated for 95% confidence level, the *relative precision* ε of the simulation results is obtained as:

$$\varepsilon = \frac{\delta}{\overline{X}(n)} \tag{4.7}$$

or

$$\varepsilon = \frac{1.96 \times \sigma[\overline{X}(n)]}{\overline{X}(n)} \tag{4.8}$$

Usually, the *relative-precision* of the estimators is chosen to be 0.05 or 5% of the estimated values. This means that simulation experiments should be continued (more observations continued to be collected) until a 5% relative precision is achieved with 95% confidence.

If the observed samples are not i.i.d., Eq. (4.5) will provide a biased result that might provide either an excessively optimistic confidence level, in the case of positively correlated observations, or an excessively pessimistic confidence level, in the case of negatively correlated observations. Therefore, it is useful to test the observations for any possible correlation, both negative and positive, before calculating the confidence level. A number of methods to test the correlation among a set of samples can be found in [263].

4.5.2 Terminating Simulation

To implement the confidence level process for terminating simulations, the entire simulation is repeated many times with different random numbers (seeds). Each repetition is called an independent replication (IR) of the same simulation. The purpose of using different seeds is to make sure that each replication uses different (statistically independent) sequences of pseudorandom numbers. With the IRs, the output from each replication can be considered i.i.d. The simulation is repeated until the desired confidence level and precision are reached.

Figure 4.4 illustrates the process of achieving the desired confidence level with satisfactory precision for terminating simulations. Using different seeds does not guarantee *nonoverlapping* random number sequences in different replications. The simplest way to make sure that the sequences are nonoverlapping is to start the next replication from the last number used in the current replication.

4.5.3 Steady-State Simulation

Unlike terminating simulations, there is no well-defined terminating point for *steady-state* simulations; hence, replications of the same simulation are not appropriate with

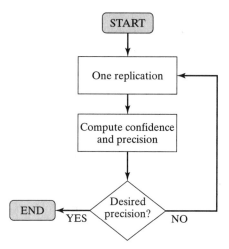

FIGURE 4.4: Flow chart for implementing confidence interval with terminating simulations.

steady-state simulations. Instead, many samples are collected from a single run and these samples are analyzed for calculating the precision and the confidence level.

A system initially remains in a nonstationary period, also referred to as a *warm-up* period, when the sample values fluctuate a lot. After the warm-up period, the system becomes stable and the sample values asymptotically reach a steady state (statistical equilibrium). The sample values during the warm-up period are discarded to remove any bias in the estimation. The confidence interval is calculated from samples collected during the stable period only.

The major challenge with steady-state simulations is to determine how long to run the simulation to complete the warm-up period and finally achieve the desired precision in the post–warm-up period. Two different techniques used to control the length of a steady-state simulation are described next.

Fixed-Length Simulation.   With fixed-length simulation, the duration of simulation, measured in simulation time or number of samples collected, is decided in advance and the confidence level is calculated after the simulation is completed. Graphical representation of data (e.g., Figure 4.2) may also be used to detect the end of the warm-up period.

The major disadvantage with fixed-length simulations is the difficulty in predicting the length that will allow the system to reach steady state and provide the desired precision. If the predicted length is too short, the results are discarded and a new simulation is run with longer duration. If the length is too long, time and resources are wasted unnecessarily. Many trials and errors are necessary before one can find the correct length of the simulation.

This inherent difficulty in predicting the correct length of the steady-state simulation has led to numerous publications without providing any confidence level and precision of the simulation results. In such publications, the authors merely run the simulation for a "long" time hoping to achieve an adequate accuracy.

Running a simulation for a "long" time, however, does not necessarily guarantee a good confidence level and precision. What is sufficiently long for one set of parameters may not be long enough when some input parameter (e.g., buffer size) values are changed. Fixed-length simulations, therefore, may lead to erroneous conclusions.

Adaptive-Length Simulation.   Because of the complexities mentioned in the previous section and difficulties with a fixed-length approach in steady-state simulation, techniques have been developed to control adaptively the length of a simulation by conducting *on-line* statistical analysis of the samples as they are collected during the simulation. The simulation is stopped automatically when the desired confidence level and precision are reached. Such methods of analysis are also referred to as *sequential* techniques. With sequential techniques, the experimenter completely avoids the need for predicting the length of the simulation in advance and saves time and computer resources that would have been wasted in trials and errors.

The flow chart for implementing adaptive length simulation is shown in Figure 4.5. The simulation process goes through two different stages. In Stage 1, the end of the warm-up period is detected. Stage 2 simulates the steady-state behavior of the reference network, collects observations for certain output variables, performs statistical analysis on the collected observations at some specific checkpoints, and stops the simulation when the desired confidence level and precision are reached for the estimated variables. At either stage, the simulation is stopped if a maximum number of samples have been collected.

Several methods can be implemented to reduce the correlation among the observed samples. *Nonoverlapping batch means* is one such method that can be implemented quite easily [263]. According to this method, a number of successive samples are grouped into a batch and the batch mean is considered as a single sample. Long batches are expected to reduce the correlation among the observations

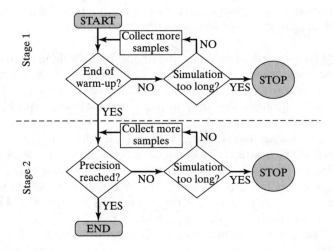

FIGURE 4.5: Flowchart for implementing confidence interval with steady-state simulations.

significantly and the batch means are more likely to become realizations of i.i.d. Equations (4.4) and (4.5) can now be applied to the batch means to more effectively compute the confidence interval.

Detection of the end of the warm-up period (Stage 1 in Figure 4.5) is a complex task. A number of heuristic rules have been suggested by various authors for determining the duration of the initial transient period [263]. One rule differs from another in complexity and performance. According to one rule, which is easy to implement and performs "reasonably" well, the initial transient period is over after n_0 observations if k consecutive batch means collected after observation n_0 all fall within a small interval of width Δ. Appropriate values for k and Δ are selected through a few pilot simulations of the system under evaluation. For more accurate determination of the warm-up period, one can also use a statistical test to determine the time-stationarity of simulation output data. One can assume that a given simulation has entered its steady state, when the time-stationarity of the output data is confirmed.

The analysis in Stage 2 is preceded by the detection of the warm-up period in Stage 1. All batch means in the warm-up period are discarded before entering Stage 2. The analysis and the collection of batch means in Stage 2 are as follows.

At first, 31 batch means are collected once the system enters the steady state. The relative precision ε is computed using Eq. (4.8) on these 31 batch means. The simulation is stopped if 5% relative precision is achieved with 95% confidence, otherwise one more batch mean is collected and the process is repeated until either the required precision is achieved or the limit of *maximum* samples (the condition of "simulation too long" in Figure 4.5) is reached.

4.5.4 Common Simulation Mistakes

Many commercial software packages do not provide any built-in facility to calculate the confidence level and the relative precision of the simulation output. However, one can save the individual observations in a file and later process the file using statistical packages (e.g., Matlab, or even Excel).

Some user-friendly simulators (e.g., OPNET) have a built-in facility to save the sequence of observations and provide the confidence level and interval of the mean (of the observed sequence) after the simulation is stopped. The user of such packages, however, must exercise caution in accepting the provided confidence level, as such packages do not perform any correlation test on the sequence of observations.

Usually, the observations (such as packet-loss rate in TCP/IP networks) of a simulation of a communication network are highly correlated. The user, therefore, must perform a correlation test and accept the confidence level and interval of the output only if the correlation is negligible (below a certain threshold).

One of the consequences of not implementing good confidence-level analysis of the simulation output is the possibility of observing an anomalous behavior of the simulated network system. An anomalous behavior could be an inconsistent output of an observed variable when an input parameter is varied from one end to the other of a given range. For example, in a packet-loss rate versus buffer-size simulation, the packet loss rate should never increase if buffer size is increased (when everything else in the simulation remains the same). An experimenter, however, may actually find out that the packet-loss rate with a larger buffer is higher than that with a smaller buffer. Such inconsistencies may result from large error margins in the simulation output.

Pawlikowski and colleagues provide an excellent case for making confidence-level analysis an integral part of any simulation study and warn the network research community that failing to enforce this on students and next-generation researchers can lead to a deep *credibility crisis* in network simulation [264]. The warning is prompted by the shocking revelation of lack of proper analysis of simulation output in hundreds of research articles published in leading networking journals and conferences, including *IEEE Transactions of Communications* and IEEE INFOCOM.

4.6   SIMULATION WITH SELF-SIMILAR TRAFFIC

It is now well established that the Poisson model cannot adequately capture the burstiness demonstrated in TCP/IP traffic [217, 267]. The model that can be successfully applied for realistically modeling TCP/IP traffic is called *self-similar* traffic. This section presents techniques to generate self-similar traffic without going into details of the self-similar model. For interested readers, a good definition of the self-similar model can be found in [301].

Willinger et al. [320] describes a straightforward way to generate self-similar traffic by superimposing many ON-OFF sources with Pareto distribution for the lengths of their ON-OFF periods. By definition, an ON-OFF source transmits traffic at a constant rate during the ON period and does not send any traffic during the OFF period. The only difference between this method of generating self-similar traffic and the traditional ON-OFF models is in the distributions of the ON-OFF periods. Traditional ON-OFF models use exponential or geometric distributions for mathematical tractability, but it has been established that traditional models do not demonstrate the properties of self-similar traffic [320].

Using the Pareto distribution, self-similar traffic with a specific Hurst parameter H can be generated in two steps:

- Generate a uniformly distributed random variable, x, between 0 and 1,

- Determine the length of an ON-OFF period as $K(x^{-1/a} - 1)$ where $a = 3 - 2H$ and $K = m(a - 1)$ with m being the mean length of ON-OFF period.

The above steps are performed (in a loop) each time the traffic generator enters an ON-OFF state. Once the mean length of ON-OFF periods is known, the values of a and K can be easily computed to achieve a desired Hurst parameter. As an example, Table 4.2 shows the values of a and K to achieve different Hurst parameters for a mean ON-OFF period of two time units ($m = 2$).

The superposition of many ON-OFF sources is illustrated in Figure 4.6, where a single network queue is simulated under self-similar traffic arrival. Each ON-OFF source is modeled as described above, and it is the aggregated traffic at the entry of the queue that is self-similar.

Up until now, we have discussed some of the fundamental concepts and techniques for network simulation without worrying about the details of a specific

TABLE 4.2: Parameter values to generate self-similar traffic with mean ON/OFF period of two time units.

Hurst Parameter (H)	a	K
0.5	2.0	2.0
0.6	1.8	1.6
0.7	1.6	1.2
0.8	1.4	0.8
0.9	1.2	0.4

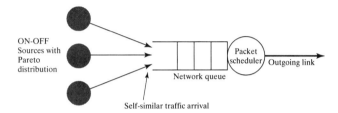

FIGURE 4.6: Generation of self-similar traffic.

simulation software. As mentioned in Section 4.2, we must ultimately use a specific software to carry out the simulation. In the remainder of this chapter, we provide a classification of available simulation softwares and take an in-depth look at two popular simulation softwares widely used for simulating TCP/IP networks.

4.7 CLASSIFICATION OF SIMULATION TOOLS

There are several tools available for simulating TCP/IP networks. In this section, we classify these tools into three basic categories (see Figure 4.7), general-purpose programming languages (GPPL), "plain" simulation languages (PSL), and simulation packages (SP). Each category has its advantages and disadvantages.

There are three major advantages for using GPPLs for TCP/IP simulation. First, GPPLs such as C and Java are ubiquitous tools already available and installed in almost all computer systems and platforms. Second, almost all networking students and researchers know at least one GPPL very well. Third, GPPLs provide total control over the software development process, making it possible to simulate a model in any level of detail. Because of these advantages, GPPL remains an attractive choice for many researchers, despite the proliferation of sophisticated simulation packages. The downside to GPPL is lack of support for DES. For example, the user of GPPL has to spend considerable time and effort writing routines for event handling and random number generation. In addition, routines have to be written to simulate basic TCP functions, such as acknowledgment and retransmission, if TCP is to be simulated. Consequently, model constructions in GPPL take a very long time.

PSLs have basic support for DES. As such, they can significantly cut down model construction time. Examples of PSLs are SIMSCRIPT II.5 [82], SIMULA

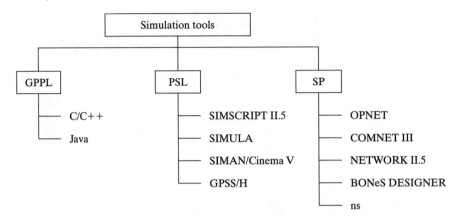

FIGURE 4.7: Classification of simulation tools.

[116], SIMAN/Cinema V [304], and GPSS/H [80]. The drawback of these tools is the lack of ubiquity (one has to procure and install) and the need of programming expertise in a new language. The other limitation of PSLs is lack of built-in libraries for TCP/IP networks; therefore, a researcher interested in TCP simulation must write his or her own routine for TCP.

SPs are the highest level of simulation tools. They provide basic support for DES as well as built-in libraries for TCP/IP networks. Some of them also provide graphical interfaces for users to construct models. Model construction time is generally shorter (in comparison with GPPL and PSL) with SPs. Examples of commercial SPs are OPNET [242], COMNET III [79], NETWORK II.5 [81], and BONeS DESIGNER [111]. By far, OPNET has the most comprehensive libraries for TCP/IP simulation. A public domain SP, called *ns* (developed at UC Berkeley) [310], has become very popular among the CS and EE students worldwide. Later in the chapter, we provide detailed introductions to *ns* and OPNET and their applications in TCP/IP simulation.

4.8 THE "ns" NETWORK SIMULATOR

The network simulator *ns* [310] is a very popular software for simulating advanced TCP/IP algorithms and protocols. *ns* is an object-oriented simulator that can simulate realistic network topologies and characteristics. Network components such as routers, links, transport end points (e.g., TCP, UDP), and network characteristics such as delays are represented by various classes. *ns* is written in C++ and object-oriented tcl (OTcl) scripts that are interpreted. In this section, we present an overview of *ns*, show how the generic steps of the software stage discussed in the beginning of this chapter can be implemented in *ns*, and finally present a few examples of TCP/IP simulations using *ns*.

4.8.1 Model Construction and Parameter Setting

A network model in *ns* is constructed by interconnecting several components, called *ns* objects. These objects include nodes, classifiers, links, queues, and many more.

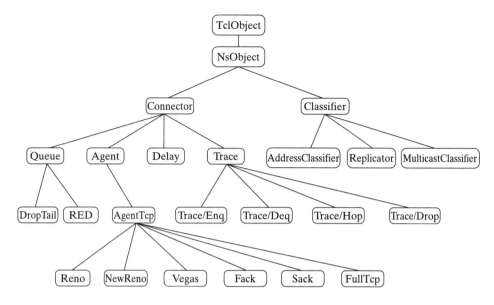

FIGURE 4.8: "ns" class hierarchy.

Objects are built from a hierarchical C++ class structure illustrated in Figure 4.8 (not all available classes are shown in the figure).

All objects are derived from class `NsObject`, which is the base for all classes. `NsObject` includes a method `handle` to handle events and a method `recv` to process received packets. Typically, derived classes override the `recv` method to perform relevant processing. A `Connector` is an `NsObject` from which the objects that constitute links like `Queue` and `Delay` and those that constitute nodes like `Agents` are derived. `Trace` is a subclass of `Connector` that is used to collect data about packets in the network during a simulation. `Classifiers` examine packets and forward them to the appropriate destination by passing the packet object to the `recv` method of the object that represents the destination. ns provides a unicast address classifier, a multicast address classifier, and a replicator that delivers copies of the packet to multiple destinations. Some of the most frequently used objects are described below.

Nodes. Nodes represent clients, hosts, routers, or switches. A node, called s1, can be created by the following command:

```
set s1 [$ns node]
```

Classifiers. Classifiers perform the task of determining the outgoing interface object, depending on the packet destination address and, on occasion, its source address. There are several types of classifiers:

- Address Classifiers, which support unicast packet forwarding.

- Multicast Classifiers, which classify packets based on both source and destination group address.

- Multipath Classifiers, which support equal cost multipath forwarding.

- Replicators, which deliver copies of the same packet to multiple receivers that are stored in an internal table.

Links. Links are used to connect nodes to form a network topology. *ns* offers simulation support for a variety of links ranging from simple links to wireless links. The characteristics that define the link are its head, which is the entry point, a reference to the main queue element, and a queue, which processes the packets dropped at the link. For example:

```
$ns simplex-link <node1> <node2> <bandwidth> <delay> <queue-type>
```

creates a link between the two specified nodes with the specified bandwidth, delay, and queue type. The field simplex-link can be replaced with the desired link type such as *duplex-link* or *duplex-intserv-link*. Queues can be of type DropTail, Fair Queuing (FQ), Stochastic Fair Queuing (SFQ), Deficit Round Robin scheduling (DRR), Random Early Detect (RED), or Class Based Queuing (CBQ). For example, the following command creates a duplex link with a drop-tail queue from node s1 to r1 with a bandwidth of 8 Mbps and a propagation delay of 5 ms:

```
$ns duplex-link $s1 $r1 8Mb 5ms DropTail
```

Agents. Agents are the transport end points, where protocol packets originate or are destined. The class *Agent* has the fields source address, destination address, packet size, IP flow identifier, IP priority field, flags, and the default time to live field to construct the appropriate packet. Agent fields can be set using the *set* command. Once an agent is created and the fields are set, it can be mounted onto a node using the *attach-agent* command. There are mainly two types of agents, UDP and TCP.

- **UDP agents** are used to model UDP at the transport layer and transmit data based on the rate at which the application sends data to it. It does not perform flow or error control. UDP agents are created as follows:

  ```
  set udp_agent [new Agent/UDP]
  $ns attach-agent <node> $udp_agent
  $udp_agent set <field> <field-value>
  ```

  UDP agents are commonly used as transport end points when rate-based traffic generators such as CBR or Pareto are used at the application level. The parameters of UDP agents such as flow identifier, packet size, destination address, destination port, and time to live can be set by using the appropriate variable in place of *field* in the *set* command shown above.

- **TCP agents** are used where flow control and congestion control are required. One-way TCP receivers are commonly known as sinks. TCP agents are created using the command:

  ```
  set tcp_agent [new Agent/<tcp-agent-type>]
  ```

TABLE 4.3: TCP agent types in *ns*.

Agent Type	Description
TCP	A TCP Tahoe sender
TCP/Reno	A TCP Reno sender
TCP/NewReno	A TCP New Reno sender
TCP/Sack1	A TCP sender with selective acknowledgments
TCP/Vegas	A TCP Vegas sender
TCP/Fack	A TCP Reno sender with forward acknowledgments
TCPSink	A TCP receiver that sends one ACK per packet
TCPSink/DelAck	A TCP receiver with a configurable delay for every ACK
TCPSink/Sack1	A TCP receiver with selective ACKs
TCPSink/Sack1/DelAck	A TCP receiver with Sack1 and DelAck
TCP/FullTcp	A two-way Reno sender and receiver

where *tcp-agent-type* can be any of the TCP variants described in Table 4.3.

A TCP connection between two agents is created by:

```
$ns connect <source agent> <destination agent>
```

As with UDP agents, TCP agents are attached to a node using the *attach-agent* command and parameters can be set using the *set* command. Parameters of TCP agents include window settings (e.g., window_), ECN bit specification (ecn_), timer granularity (tcpTick_), congestion window, and ssthresh settings. The most commonly modified TCP parameters are the window parameter that binds the window size that TCP uses, packet size that limits the TCP Maximum Segment Size (MSS), and timer granularity that is used in the RTT and RTO computation algorithms. For example, to change the window size to 15 and set ECN on, use:

```
$tcp_agent set window_ 15
$tcp_agent set ecn_ 1
```

Applications. Applications sit on top of the transport layer and produce data that model the simulation features desired. The main types of applications that *ns* supports are traffic generators and simulated applications. Traffic generators usually use UDP as the transport layer because they are rate-based and do not require congestion management and reliability. Simulated applications usually use TCP as the transport layer.

Applications are attached to the transport end points by the `attach-agent` command. Applications should be made to start (and subsequently stop) sending data at specified times using the start (and stop) commands. An example configuration is given below where a TCP agent is used as the transport layer and an FTP application runs on top of it:

```
set tcp_agent [new Agent/TCP]
$ns attach-agent $source $tcp_agent
```

```
set ftp_app [new Application/FTP]
$ftp_app attach-agent $tcp_agent

$ns at 10.0 "$ftp_app start"
$ns at 20.0 "$ftp_app stop"
```

The main applications currently supported by *ns* include FTP and Telnet (a WWW model is also included in the latest releases):

- File Transfer Protocol (FTP): This is used to simulate file transfer between two end points. FTP transmits an infinite file between the start and stop times. The traffic is controlled by TCP, which performs the appropriate congestion control and transmits the data reliably. A limit on the number of packets can be specified using the produce command.

- Telnet: This generates traffic produced by a Telnet session over a TCP connection. The interpacket intervals can be set by giving a nonzero value to the parameter interval. The following command creates a Telnet application:

  ```
  set telapp [new Application/Telnet]
  $telapp set interval_ 1
  ```

Traffic Generators. Traffic generators are needed to automate generation of traffic according to a desired pattern and load. There are various types of traffic generators available in *ns*, including:

- **Exponential ON-OFF:** Generates packets at a fixed rate during the ON periods, while no packets are sent during the OFF periods. Both ON and OFF periods are derived from an exponential distribution. The size of packets being generated, average ON time, average OFF time, and sending rate can be defined using the set command as follows:

  ```
  set expapp [new Application/Traffic/Exponential]
  $expapp set packetsize_ 1000
  $expapp set rate_ 500k
  $expapp set burst_time_ 100ms
  $expapp set idle_time_ 30ms
  ```

- **Pareto ON-OFF:** This is the same as the Exponential except that the ON and OFF periods are derived from a Pareto distribution. Self-similar traffic can be generated by aggregating several such Pareto ON-OFF sources, as explained in Section 4.6. The shape of the Pareto distribution can be set as follows:

  ```
  set parapp [new Application/Traffic/Pareto]
  $parapp set shape 1.0
  ```

- **Constant Bit Rate (CBR):** Generates packets at a constant rate. Random noise can be introduced to vary the time between sending of packets. Packets are of constant size. The parameters that can be varied are sending rate, interval between packets, size of packets, a flag to specify introduction of random noise, and the maximum number of packets that can be sent, for example:

```
set cbrapp [new Application/Traffic/CBR]
$cbrapp set maxpkts_ 10000
$cbrapp set packetsize_ 5000
$cbrapp set rate_ 16kb
$cbrapp set interval_ 1ms
$cbrapp set random 1
```

4.8.2 Data Collection

In *ns*, there are two different methods of data collection, *tracing* and *monitoring*.

Tracing. Tracing records each packet as it arrives at a node, departs a node, or is dropped at a link or queue. Tracing is useful in debugging or verification of the simulation code. Trace data can be processed later to retrieve data on specific performance metrics. The trace produces output that consists of the following fields:

- Type of operation performed on the packet: enqueue (represented by +), dequeue (−), drop (d), receive (r)

- Time of the operation

- Source node of the trace

- Destination node of the trace

- Packet type

- IP packet size

- Flags

- IP flow identifier

- Source IP address

- Destination IP address

- Sequence number

- Unique packet identifier

An example of a trace output for six trace entries is given below:

```
+ 53.306943 0 1 tcp 1000 ---A--- 2 0.2 2.1 50 40142
r 53.307133 0 1 tcp 1000 ------- 0 0.0 2.0 7479 40051
+ 53.307133 1 2 tcp 1000 ------- 0 0.0 2.0 7479 40051
- 53.307133 1 2 tcp 1000 ------- 0 0.0 2.0 7479 40051
- 53.307467 0 1 tcp 1000 ------- 0 0.0 2.0 7482 40057
r 53.307627 1 0 ack 40 ------- 0 2.0 0.0 7473 40135
```

In the above trace, there are two packet arrivals (indicated by the + sign), two departures (− sign), and two receive events (r). Each trace entry (row) has 12 columns for the 12 fields described. The following command is used to collect the trace record of every packet for the entire length of the simulation.

```
$ns trace-all <tracefile>
```

Tracing has some drawbacks when it comes to collecting data for specific performance metrics. All traces are dumped into a single trace file that requires filtering of output data that are of interest into separate output files. The filtering process requires writing of additional codes in script languages like awk or perl. The complexity of such script programming increases as the scale and complexity of the simulation increase. As we will see later, monitoring is much more efficient for collecting data for specific performance metrics.

Monitoring.   Monitoring can monitor counts, such as number of packets dropped, for all traffic in the network, for specific links, or for specific flows. Separate trace objects are created for such monitoring. These monitoring objects are then inserted into the network topology at specific places. For example, the following code would create a trace object between a src node and a dest node.

```
$ns create-trace <type> <tracefile> <src> <dest>
```

The parameter type can be Enqueue, Deque, Drop, or Recv. For example, for the type Drop, all packets dropped for traffic between src and dest are recorded in the tracefile. The following commands can be used to add a trace agent to trace the TCP congestion window variable:

```
$ns add-agent-trace $tcp_agent tcp_agent
$ns monitor-agent-trace $tcp_agent
$tcp_agent tracevar cwnd_
```

where cwnd defines congestion window size.

Monitoring agents can also be written in C++ code and inserted in source's or sink's send and receive functions. The advantage of writing the monitoring agents in C++ is to have more control over the data collection process. *ns* users proficient in C++, but not so in OTcl, actually prefer to use this method over the trace-based monitoring method. C++ coding has three steps. First, insert an output variable in the source agent's send function. For the sink agent, this will be inserted in the agent's receive function. Second, bind the required output variable to oTCL. The final step is to call the output variable in the *simulation script* and record its value to an output data file. The tracing and monitoring are further illustrated later using an example simulation.

4.8.3   Simulation Execution

After a network model is constructed, parameters are set, and the software is configured to produce the relevant performance data; the next step is to instantiate and execute a simulation. To achieve this in *ns*, an object of class *Simulator* must be created as follows:

```
set ns [new Simulator]
```

The at command can be used to start an application at a specified time as follows:

```
$ns at <time> "<command>"
```

For example, an FTP source can be started at time 0.0 as follows:

```
$ns at 0.0 "$ftp_app start"
```

The simulation can be terminated by calling the finish procedure as follows:

```
$ns at 2.0 "finish"
```

where all the clean-up code is placed in procedure "finish." Finally, the simulation is executed by the following command:

```
$ns run
```

4.8.4 Presentation of Results

ns does not have any built-in support for creating sophisticated graphical presentations of collected data. The raw data must be processed using script languages like awk or perl to produce data in a suitable format for tools like Xgraph or Gnuplot. If monitoring agents are created using C++ codes, the programmer can actually produce data that are in a format ready for Gnuplot to create graphs.

4.8.5 Examples of TCP/IP Simulation Using *ns*

In this section, we illustrate the use of *ns* with two examples.

EXAMPLE 4.1   Evaluating TCP Performance Without Background Traffic

The objective of this simulation is to evaluate the performance of TCP in a simple network without any background traffic and to see if TCP is capable of utilizing the entire link capacity. The simulation process is described in several steps:

- **Step 1: Design Reference Network Model.** The reference network model to be simulated and the associated parameters are shown in Figure 4.9. There is a simple network consisting of two routers, R1 and R2. There is one FTP source connected to R1 and sending a large file to a destination (FTP Sink) connected to R2. The FTP source and the sink are connected to the routers using 10 Mbps links with a propagation delay of 1 ms. The link between the routers has a capacity of 1 Mbps and a propagation delay of 3 ms.

- **Step 2: Select Performance Metrics.** Steady-state *throughput* of the FTP connection is the main performance metric selected to observe the performance of

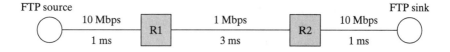

FIGURE 4.9: Reference network for TCP simulation without background traffic.

TCP in this simple network without any background traffic. We also monitor the rate of sequence number increase over time.

- **Step 3: Select Variables.** Buffer size at R1 for the router-to-router link is selected as the variable parameter to examine the effect of buffer size on the TCP throughput.

- **Step 4: Construct Model and Set Parameters in *ns*.**

  #Create the four nodes in Figure 4.9

  ```
  set n0 [$ns node]
  set R1 [$ns node]
  set R2 [$ns node]
  set n1 [$ns node]
  ```

  #Connect nodes with link

  ```
  $ns duplex-link $n0 $R1 10Mb 1ms DropTail
  $ns duplex-link $R1 $R2 1Mb 3ms DropTail
  $ns duplex-link $R2 $n1 10Mb 1ms DropTail
  ```

  #Create TCP source and sink agent

  ```
  set tcp0 [new Agent/TCP]
  $ns attach-agent $n0 $tcp0
  set tcpsink0 [new Agent/TCPSink]
  $ns attach-agent $n1 $tcpsink0
  ```

  #Connect source to sink

  ```
  $ns connect $tcp0 $tcpsink0
  ```

  #Attach FTP application to TCP transport protocol

  ```
  set ftp0 [new Application/FTP]
  $ftp0 attach-agent $tcp0
  ```

- **Step 5: Data Collection.** We show examples of both tracing and monitoring. Tracing is used for collecting the sequence numbers, and monitoring is used for collecting the throughput data. The following statement traces all the packets throughout the length of the simulation and writes the output to the file out.tr.

  ```
  $ns trace-all [open out.tr w]
  ```

  The monitoring of TCP throughput is achieved as follows. #Define "bytes_" and insert the variable in TCP sink agent (tcp-sink.cc) to record TCP throughput.

```
void TcpSink::recv(Packet* pkt, Handler*)

{
... some lines before
bytes_ += hdr_cmn::access(pkt) -> size();
double now = Scheduler::instance().clock();
... some lines after
}
```

#Bind variables in agent's constructor

```
TcpAgent::TcpAgent() : Agent(PT_TCP), ...
{
... some lines before
bind("seqno_", & seqno_);
... some lines after
}

TcpSink::TcpSink(Acker* acker) : Agent(PT_ACK), acker_(acker),
 save_(NULL)
{
... some lines before
bind("bytes_", & bytes_);
... some lines after
}
```

#Initialize variables in *ns-default.tcl* to be linked to oTcl

```
Agent/TCP set seqno_ 0
Agent/TCPSink set bytes_ 0
```

#Open output file for writing data (in Tcl simulation script)

```
set f1 [open seq.dat w]
set f2 [open thruput.dat w]
set f3 [open delay.dat w]
```

#Call output variable in Tcl and write data to output file

```
set seq [$tcp0 set seqno_]
set bw [$tcpsink0 set bytes_]
set delay [$tcpsink0 set e2e_delay_]
puts $f1 "$now $seq"
puts $f2 "$now [expr $bw/$time*8/1000]"
puts $f3 "$now [expr $delay*1000]"
```

#Now recompile *ns* make depend make

- **Step 6: Simulation Execution.** A few pilot runs have revealed that for such a simple reference network, 10 seconds of simulation is quite sufficient for collecting steady-state results.

  #Set simulation time, run FTP sources for 10 seconds.

  $ns at 0.0 "$ftp0 start"

  $ns at 10.0 "$ftp0 stop"

  $ns at 0.0 "record"

  $ns at 10.0 "finish"

  $ns run

  Another script is written to repetitively run the simulation with increasing buffer size.

- **Step 7: Presentation and Analysis of Simulation Results.** If data in the tracefile out.tr are to be used for creating the graphs, then we use *awk* on the tracefile as follows:

```
exec awk {
            {
                if (($1 == "r") && ($4 == "0") && ($5 == "ack"))
                    print $2, $11
            }
    } out.tr > datafile
```

The aforementioned script extracts the time and sequence number of the ACKed packets at node 0 and places the output in *datafile*. Using data thus generated, plots of sequence numbers over time can be obtained using Xgraph (see Figure 4.10). The sequence number graph in Figure 4.10 shows that in the absence of any dynamic background traffic, TCP continues to receive acknowledgments at a constant rate.

For data collected using the monitoring agents, we can directly use Gnuplot to generate the throughput graph shown in Figure 4.11. From the graph we can conclude that TCP cannot perform well with extremely small buffers. In this particular situation, TCP needs a buffer size of at least five packets to function properly. For a buffer of about 20 packets, TCP can almost fully utilize the 10 Mbps available bandwidth in the network; therefore, in this example, a buffer size of 20 is sufficient. Larger buffers will not gain any significant benefit.

EXAMPLE 4.2   TCP Performance in the Presence of Background Traffic

The objective of this simulation is to observe the performance of TCP when the bottleneck link is shared by a variable bit rate (VBR) video source.

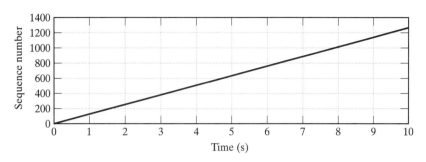

FIGURE 4.10: Sequence number as a function of time.

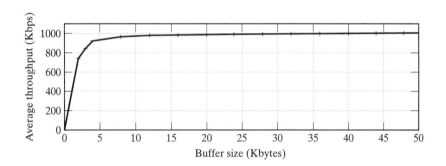

FIGURE 4.11: Average throughput as a function of buffer size.

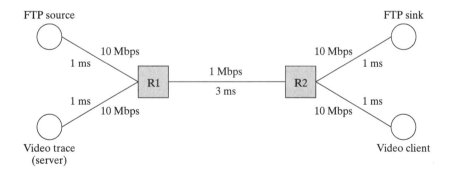

FIGURE 4.12: Single FTP with trace-driven "Star Wars Movie" Internet traffic.

- **Step 1: Design Reference Network Model.** The network model of the previous
  example is augmented with a background *video server* and a *video client* as
  shown in Figure 4.12. This is a trace-driven simulation. A trace of packet
  arrivals for the movie called *Star Wars* is stored in the server. When the client
  downloads the movie over the network, the available bandwidth (to the FTP
  source) varies according to the bandwidth consumption of the video traffic.

- **Step 2: Select Performance Metrics.** Instantaneous throughput of the FTP connection and the packet delay at R1 is monitored for this simulation. The instantaneous throughput indicates how well TCP adjusts its throughput in the presence of background traffic, and the packet delay allows us to observe the variation in the queuing delay caused by the variable bit rate video traffic in the background.

- **Step 3: Construct Model and Set Parameters.**

  #Create two nodes for the video server and the client

  set n2 [$ns node]
  set n3 [$ns node]

  #Connect nodes with links

  $ns duplex-link $n2 $R1 10Mb 1ms DropTail
  $ns duplex-link $R2 $n3 10Mb 1ms DropTail

  #Create UDP source and sink agents

  set udp0 [new Agent/UDP]
  $ns attach-agent $n2 $udp0
  set udpsink0 [new Agent/Dest]
  $ns attach-agent $n3 $udpsink0
  $ns connect $udp0 $udpsink0

  #Create new tracefile object and attach file to Trace application

  set tfile [new Tracefile]
  $tfile filename starwars.nsformat
  set trace0 [new Application/Traffic/Trace]
  $trace0 attach-tracefile $tfile
  $trace0 attach-agent $udp0

- **Step 4: Simulation Execution.** The FTP is started first followed by the video transfer after 10 seconds. This time we run the simulation for 200 seconds, the length of the video clip (180 seconds) plus the initial 10 seconds. These execution settings can be achieved by the following codes:

  #Set simulation time

  $ns at 0.0 "$ftp0 start"
  $ns at 10.0 "$trace0 start"
  $ns at 200.0 "$ftp0 stop"
  $ns at 200.0 "$trace0 stop"
  $ns at 0.0 "record"
  $ns at 200.0 "finish"

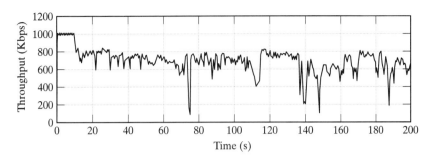

FIGURE 4.13: TCP throughput as a function of time.

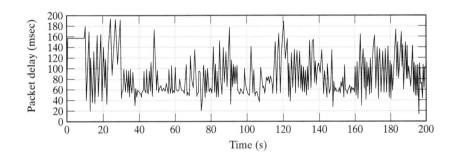

FIGURE 4.14: TCP packet delay as a function of time.

- **Step 5: Presentation of Results.** Throughput and delay are shown in Figures 4.13
  and 4.14. The graphs show that because of the variable bit-rate video traffic in
  the background starting after 10 seconds, the throughput and delay start to vary
  after 10 seconds.

4.9 OPNET

OPNET [242], developed by OPNET Technologies Inc. (formerly called Mil3 Inc.),
is a very popular commercial tool used by many researchers and practitioners for
TCP/IP network simulation. Like *ns*, OPNET is also an object-oriented simulation
tool. However, unlike *ns*, OPNET is a totally menu-driven package with many user-
friendly Graphical User Interface (GUI) interfaces for model construction, data
collection, and other simulation tasks. OPNET's built-in model libraries contain
most popular TCP/IP protocols and applications, including Multiprotocol Label
Switching (MPLS), IP Quality of Service (QoS), and Resource Reservation Protocol
(RSVP). OPNET also models a wide range of network equipment (e.g., routers,
switches, links, etc.) manufactured by leading network equipment vendors including
Cisco, Bay Networks (acquired by Nortel), and Fore Systems (acquired by Marconi).
OPNET can be run on either Unix (e.g., Solaris, HP) or Windows NT/Windows
2000. It supports concurrent users. In this section, we provide an overview of
OPNET, show how the steps of the *software stage* of a simulation experiment can

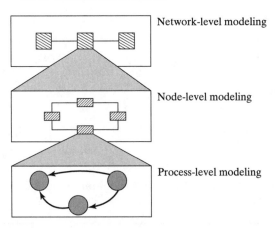

Network-level modeling

Node-level modeling

Process-level modeling

FIGURE 4.15: Modeling hierarchy in OPNET.

be implemented in OPNET, and illustrate the usefulness of OPNET through some example simulations of TCP/IP networks.

4.9.1 Model Construction

Modeling in OPNET is structured in three hierarchical levels, *network*, *node*, and *process*. Network is the highest modeling level used to construct a network by interconnecting network nodes, such as routers and hosts, with communication links. The next level in the hierarchy, the node level, allows us to model the internal architecture of a given network node by using node-level objects, such as *transmitters*, *receivers*, and *queues*. Finally, process-level modeling is used to precisely describe the functional behavior of a given node-level object using finite state machines (FSM) and writing the necessary source codes to describe the states. Figure 4.15 illustrates the modeling hierarchy in OPNET.

With the hierarchy in place, the detailed operation of a given modeling level is hidden from its adjacent higher level, making it easier to use the tool at any level. For example, an ISP interested in resource planning of its TCP/IP networks may choose to work only at the network modeling level without worrying about the detailed operation of protocols and algorithms implemented inside the routers. On the contrary, a TCP/IP protocol designer may need to dive into the process level to make necessary modifications to an existing protocol or design a new algorithm from scratch. The GUI interfaces used in OPNET for modeling at these three levels are described next.

Network-Level Modeling.   The interface for network-level modeling is activated by opening the Project Editor from OPNET's main menu. A network can be constructed by "dragging and dropping" objects from an object palette. Figure 4.16 shows the snapshot of a workspace in the Project Editor, in which an IP network is constructed by interconnecting two RSVP clients with their corresponding servers via two routers. Network models can also be created automatically by using the *Rapid Configuration* facility, which supports numerous network topologies, such as

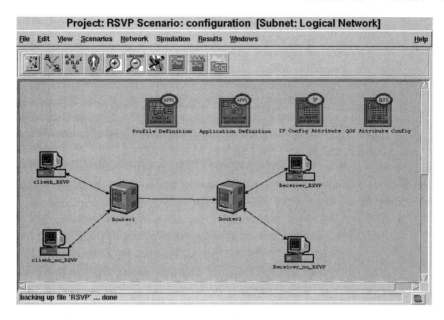

FIGURE 4.16: Screen shot of a network-level modeling in OPNET.

star, bus, ring, mesh, and so on. In addition to the manual and autoconfiguration of the network topology, the network model can also be constructed by importing network topology information collected from a real network.

Node-Level Modeling.   Node modeling is used to model the internal structure of a network node (e.g., workstation, router, switch, etc.). A node model is composed of a number of *modules*, which are the fundamental "building blocks" of a node model. At node modeling level, each module models some aspect of the behavior of a network node (e.g., data transmission, data reception, routing, etc.). The modeling tool at node level is Node Editor, which is used to create and edit node models. Node Editor is opened by selecting the Open submenu from the File menu. A node model can also be opened by double clicking on a network object in the Project Editor. Either way, a Node Editor workspace pops up. Figure 4.17 shows a workspace of the Node Editor, in which the node model structure of Router1 of Figure 4.16 is illustrated.

There are five different types of modules, processor, generator, queue, transmitter, and receiver. A processor represents a generic process. A generator is used to model packet generation and can generate packets as specified by *Probability Density Function* (PDF) and packet format. The queue models a queuing process and may consist of any number of subqueues. The transmitter and the receiver are used to model packet transmission and packet reception, respectively.

Another type of node object is "streams," which is generally used to connect modules (e.g., generator, queue, Tx/Rx modules, etc.). OPNET defines three different types of streams, *packet stream*, *statistic stream*, and *association stream*. A packet

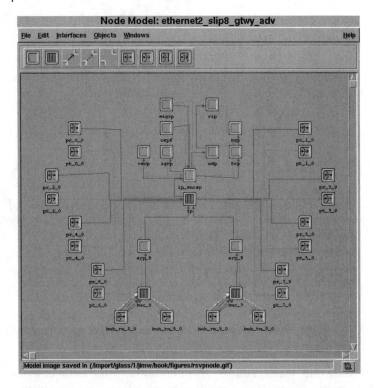

FIGURE 4.17: Screen shot of a node-level modeling in OPNET.

stream represents packet flow between two modules. Statistic streams, also called "statistic wire," do not carry data packets; they are used to convey statistics from module to module. Association streams do not carry any information at all. An association stream is used to *logically* associate a transmitter with a receiver to form a "transceiver." A transceiver is used to send packets to a link and receive packets from the link.

Process-Level Modeling. At the process modeling level, the Process Editor is used to create and edit process models. OPNET graphically depicts a process in the form of a Finite State Machine (FSM). An FSM consists of a number of *states* and the *transitions* between them. Figure 4.18 depicts the process model of the IP module (ip_rte_v4) of Figure 4.17. A process model can be opened by selecting the Open operation from the File menu or by double clicking on the module where the process resides in the Node Editor.

As shown in Figure 4.18, a process is represented by a collection of states, transitions, and the conditions that control the transitions between the states. States are mutually exclusive, which means that a process can be in only one state at any given time. Actions taken in a state are called *executives* in OPNET's terminology. Executives of a state are split into two parts—*enter executives* and *exit executives*. The enter executives of a state are executed when a process enters the state, and the exit executives are executed when the process leaves the state.

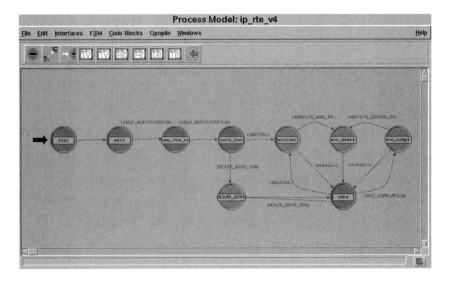

FIGURE 4.18: Screen shot of a process-level modeling in OPNET.

Enter executives and exit executives are described by statements of Proto-C, a proprietary language developed by OPNET. Proto-C inherits the full computational capability of C and $C++$ languages. The built-in Proto-C compiler recognizes all statements written in $C/C++$. In addition, Proto-C provides a powerful and efficient method for describing the behavior of a discrete event system. Executives can be composed in an *editing pad*. For example, double clicking on the top half of a state brings up the editing pad for the enter executives of the state. Similarly, double clicking on the bottom half of a state causes the editing pad for the exit executives to appear. Figure 4.19 shows the enter executives of State arrival of Figure 4.18.

FSM diagrams can be created from the FSM pull-down menu or by using action buttons on the main menu bar in the Process Editor (see Figure 4.18). The Code Blocks pull-down menu contains operations that can be used to specify Proto-C code blocks. Apart from executives code blocks, the following code blocks are also defined in the Process Editor:

- State Variables (SV)

- Temporary Variables (TV)

- Header Block (HB)

- Function Block (FB)

- Diagnostic Block (DB)

- Termination Block (TB)

State Variable block is used to declare *state variables*, which represent information maintained by a process. *State variables* retain their values from one

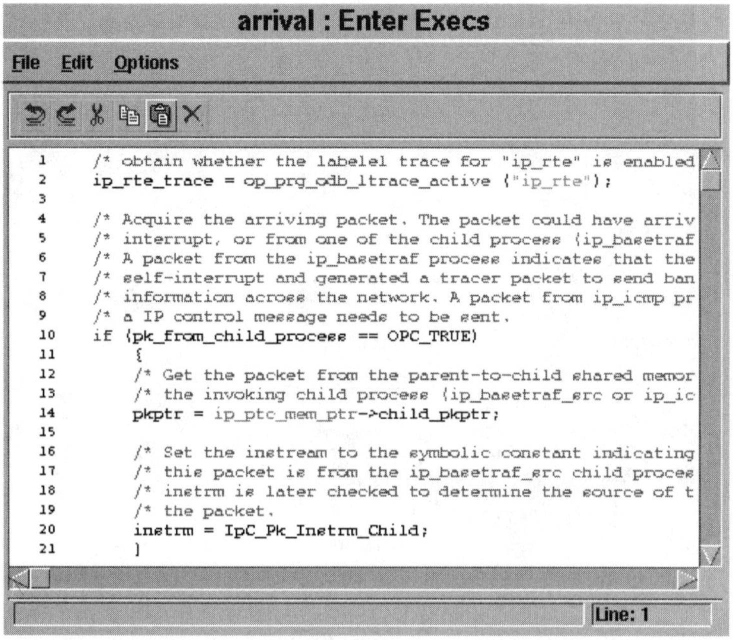

```
                           arrival : Enter Execs

File   Edit   Options

 ⤺ ⤻ ✂ ▣ ▣ ✕

  1      /* obtain whether the labelel trace for "ip_rte" is enabled
  2      ip_rte_trace = op_prg_odb_ltrace_active ("ip_rte");
  3
  4      /* Acquire the arriving packet. The packet could have arriv
  5      /* interrupt, or from one of the child process (ip_basetraf
  6      /* A packet from the ip_basetraf process indicates that the
  7      /* self-interrupt and generated a tracer packet to send ban
  8      /* information across the network. A packet from ip_icmp pr
  9      /* a IP control message needs to be sent.
 10      if (pk_from_child_process == OPC_TRUE)
 11         {
 12         /* Get the packet from the parent-to-child shared memor
 13         /* the invoking child process (ip_basetraf_src or ip_ic
 14         pkptr = ip_ptc_mem_ptr->child_pkptr;
 15
 16         /* Set the instream to the symbolic constant indicating
 17         /* this packet is from the ip_basetraf_src child proces
 18         /* instrm is later checked to determine the source of t
 19         /* the packet.
 20         instrm = IpC_Pk_Instrm_Child;
 21         }

                                                         Line: 1
```

FIGURE 4.19: Editing pad of state executives for process modeling in OPNET.

invocation of the process to the next. They are usually used to store statistical information and other process-wide information users want to monitor. Temporary Variables block is used to declare *temporary variables*. As opposed to state variables, temporary variables do not retain their values from one invocation to the other. They are usually used as "scratch" storage to hold information temporarily. Header Block is used to define symbolic constants, macros, and data types. It contains statements such as #include, #define, struct, typedef, and so on. Function Block allows users to define their own macros, although a wide variety of macros for describing network protocols and algorithms have been defined in Proto-C (Proto-C macros are collectively called *Kernel Procedures* or KP for short). Diagnostic Block is used to define codes that will print diagnostic information when simulation is run in debugger mode. Termination Block allows users to define Proto-C statements that will be executed just before a process is destroyed. It is usually used to free memory space allocated by a process (e.g. data structure, lists, etc.).

The advantage of dividing a program into a number of code blocks is obvious. First, it provides a convenient way to describe a complex system. Second, it facilitates effective debugging in an efficient way. The Compile Code operation from the Compile menu assembles all code blocks into a single $C/C++$ source code file, and then generates object code for the source file using $C/C++$ compiler. Compilation of a process model can also be done by clicking the Compile action button on the main menu. Another operation called List Code can be used to list the source code for the entire process.

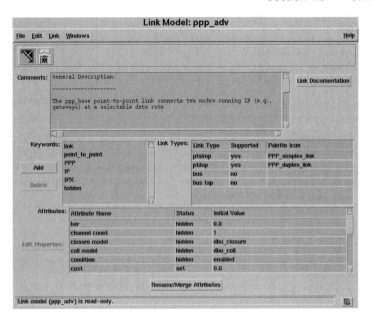

FIGURE 4.20: Link Editor dialog box to set parameters of a point-to-point link object.

4.9.2   Parameter Setting

In OPNET, the parameters of an object are configured using the *parameter editors*. All configurable parameters are grouped in four *parameter models*, each having its own parameter editor:

Link model is used to model the parameters of link objects. It specifies a particular type of communication link (e.g., PPP, bus, etc.). Link model can be created and edited in the Link Editor. Figure 4.20 shows the Link Editor dialog box, which is used to configure the parameters (shown as *Attributes*) of a link. Attributes of a link model can be set in advance, promoted to the higher level, or hidden from the high-level models if necessary.

Packet format model defines the structure of data packets. A packet format model specifies the format of packets (e.g., TCP, IP, ATM, etc.) that are generated by a generator module. Packet format models can be created and edited using the Packet Editor. Figure 4.21 shows the packet format model of TCP. Packet Editor allows users to specify the name, length, and data type for each field in a packet. A packet field can be edited in the `Attributes` dialog box by right clicking on the field.

ICI model specifies the format of a data structure that is used to support interrupt-based communications between processes. For example, an ICI can be associated with an interrupt at an interrupt source. The ICI may contain a pointer to a packet. When there is packet stream interrupt at the destination (simulating packet delivery), the destination can extract the packet pointer from the ICI and pick up the packet. Typically, ICIs are used to exchange

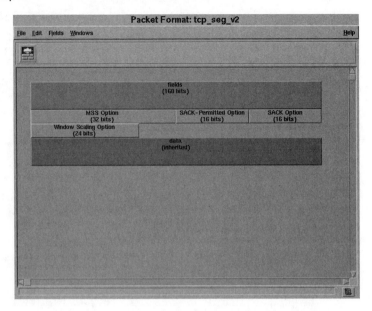

FIGURE 4.21: Packet Editor to specify or edit details of TCP header fields.

control information between protocol layers. ICI models are composed by the ICI Editor, which allows various ICI fields to be defined.

Probability Density Function (PDF) model defines statistical distribution. It is used to define the parameters of the traffic generators. PDF is usually used to specify the traffic profile, for example, the distribution of interpacket generation time, the distribution of packet length, and so on. PDF models can be created and edited by the PDF Editor.

4.9.3   Data Collection

In OPNET, advanced data collection is supported by the Probe Editor, which is activated by selecting Choose Statistics (Advanced) operation from the Simulation pull-down menu (see Figure 4.16). The Probe Editor is used to create *probe* objects that specify where to collect statistics and what statistics to be collected. Like other OPNET objects, a probe object also has a set of attributes that can be configured to specify the name of the probe, statistic, the precise location of data collection, and so on. Figure 4.22 shows a workspace of the Probe Editor.

As we can see in Figure 4.22, there are seven action buttons on the main menu bar of the Probe Editor. Each action button can be used to create a specific type of probe object on subnets, nodes, links, and modules. Probe objects created in the Probe Editor are saved in a *probe file*, which can be used as an attribute of a simulation object. The following probe objects can be created in the Probe Editor:

- Node statistic

- Link statistic

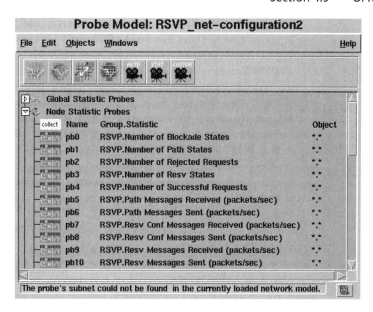

FIGURE 4.22: Probe Editor to collect seven different types of statistics.

- Global statistic

- Simulation attribute

- Automatic animation

- Custom animation

- Statistic animation

4.9.4 Simulation Execution

With OPNET, users can define their own *simulation sequences* and control the execution of simulation. A simulation sequence may consist of any number of *simulation objects*, each containing a set of configurable attributes. A simulation object may define one or more simulation runs, depending on the values of some application-specific attributes. A simulation sequence can be saved in a file for later use. The Simulation Tool in OPNET provides the following capabilities:

- Definition of simulation sequences

- Collection of both vector and scalar statistics

- Control of simulation execution

The Simulation Tool is activated by selecting Configure Simulation (Advanced) from the Simulation pull-down menu (see Figure 4.16). A pop-up window appears as a result of the operation. Figure 4.23 depicts a workspace of the simulation tool. Action buttons on the menu bar provide facilities to create and run

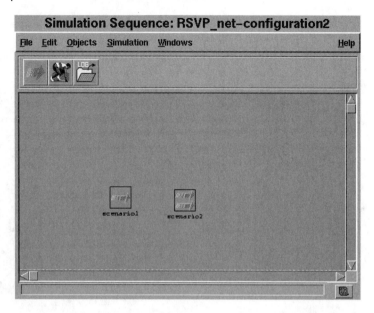

FIGURE 4.23: Simulation Tool showing two different simulation sequences.

simulation sequences. The simulation sequence shown in Figure 4.23 consists of two simulation objects. The first object (scenario1) contains a single simulation run (represented by a single-arrow icon), and the second object (scenario2) contains more than one simulation run (represented by a two-arrow icon).

Multiple values for an application-specific attribute result in multiple simulation runs. For example, we can enter multiple values {0.1, 0.2, 0.3, 0.4, 0.5} for the attribute offered_load, assuming the attribute has been declared in the process model. This results in five simulation runs for the simulated network model, each under a different load. Suppose we have created a probe object to collect "throughput" statistics before simulation execution. Each simulation run generates a scalar throughput statistic (which is saved in the output scalar file). We can then use the Analysis Tool to view the simulation result, in which throughput is plotted against offered_load.

It is possible to specify more than one simulation object in a simulation sequence. Each simulation object may even have a different set of attributes (e.g., different network models, probe files, durations, etc.). The simulation sequence can be executed unattended.

A simulation sequence can be executed as a shell command. This is realized by the OPNET utility program op_runsim. When running simulation in a shell, the only required argument is the name of the network model. Simulation sequences can also be defined via shell scripts (or batch files for Windows NT), just like other shell commands.

In OPNET, simulation can also be run in the *debugger mode*. This is supported by the OPNET Simulation Debugger (ODB). ODB enables users to interactively control the simulation execution and track down any modeling problems quickly

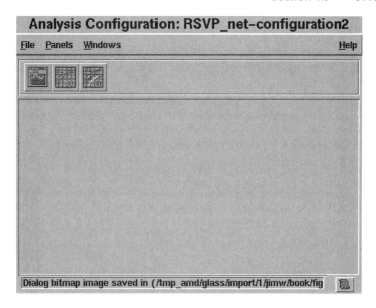

FIGURE 4.24: Main menu of Analysis Tool.

and efficiently. Numerous ODB commands have been developed to allow users to set breakpoints, access state variables, and modify object attributes, and so on.

4.9.5 Presentation of Results

Unlike *ns*, OPNET has built-in facility for visual presentation of simulation results. The Analysis Tool in OPNET provides the capability to manipulate and present the simulation results graphically. Simulation results are saved in the *output vector file* or *output scalar file* during the simulation execution. Analysis Tool extracts data from output vector/scalar files and displays them in the *analysis panels*. The Analysis Tool is usually used to process statistics specified in the probe objects created in the Probe Editor. It is activated by selecting the `View Results (Advanced)` operation from the `Results` pull-down menu. Figure 4.24 shows a workspace of the Analysis Tool.

Action buttons on the menu bar in the Analysis Tool support operations to create vector panels and scalar panels, which are used to display vector statistics and scalar statistics, respectively. Other services provided by the Analysis Tool include:

- Apply numerical processing to statistics

- Edit trace color, style, and thickness, etc.

- Make graph template

- Export data to spreadsheet

4.9.6 Examples of TCP/IP Simulation Using OPNET

In this section we present two practical simulation examples of TCP/IP networks using the OPNET modeling tools and techniques described in the previous sections.

EXAMPLE 4.3 Performance Evaluation of RED

Random early detection (RED) is a new queue management scheme proposed for IP routers to achieve a tighter control on the queue lengths and queuing delays. The **objective** of this simulation is to evaluate the performance of RED and compare it against the traditional queuing scheme known as First In First Out (FIFO) with drop-tail. The step-by-step description of the simulation process is given here:

Step 1. Reference Network and Parameters. The reference network consists of two routers, five clients, and their corresponding servers. The workstations simulate e-mail message senders using TCP Reno. The capacity of the link between the two routers, Router1 and Router2, is 50 Mbits/sec, with a delay of 10 ms. All other links have a capacity of 100 Mbits/sec and a delay of 1 ms. The link between Router1 and Router2 is the bottleneck link in the network, and the buffer at Router1 is the object of scrutiny during the simulation.

Step 2. Performance Metrics. The dynamics of the queue length (or buffer occupancy) is the performance metric chosen for this simulation study.

Step 3. Variables. In this example, the queue management scheme at Router1 is the single variable. We first simulate with FIFO, and then replace FIFO with RED.

Step 4. Model Construction and Parameter Setting in OPNET. In this example, we construct the model at the *network level*, the highest modeling level in OPNET. To construct the reference network designed in Step 1, we first open a new project from the File pull-down menu. A workspace appears. Because the pop-up workspace represents subnet level, we need to place a subnet object in the workspace. To do this, we open the object palette by clicking on the Network Palette action button. Because the network we want to construct is an IP network, we select the internet palette from the palette menu. We then drag a subnet object into the subnet workspace. Now we are ready to go down to the network level to compose an IP network. This is done by double clicking on the subnet object. As a result of this operation, a blank workspace appears. This workspace represents the network level in which we can compose our network model. We can then drag the required network objects from the internet palette. We then connect network nodes using the link model ppp_adv, which is also available in the internet palette. The attributes of each network object are specified in its Attributes dialog box (right click on an object and select Edit Attributes operation). The constructed network model is shown in Figure 4.25.

After the network model is built, we need a few utility objects to define configuration parameters. We drag these objects from the object palette. The Application Definition object is used to define applications, and the Profile Definition object is used to define user profile. The QOS Attribute Config object is used to specify queue management scheme and set related parameters. E-mail traffic parameters are set as shown in Table 4.4. With these parameters, the average traffic generation rate for each TCP source is 16 Mbits/sec, yielding a total traffic generation rate of 80 Mbits/sec, large enough

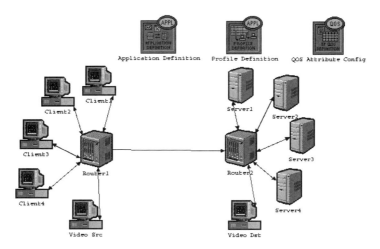

FIGURE 4.25: Network model for RED gateway.

TABLE 4.4: Traffic parameters for simulations.

Parameters	Values	Distribution
Send interval	0.01 sec	Exponential
Group of messages	10	Constant
Message size	2000 bytes	Exponential
Application start time	10 sec	Exponential

to congest the bottleneck link. Instead of a deterministic start time for the sources, we have chosen the exponential distribution to randomize the start of each application for more realistic operating environment. The buffer size of the output interface of Router1 is set to 100 packets. We then configure Router1 to support the FIFO scheme.

Step 5. Simulation Execution and Data Collection. After the network is correctly configured, we can select the desired statistics and run a simulation. We choose the Buffer Usage (packets) statistic for Router1 (right click on Router1 and select Choose Statistics (Advanced) operation). The Probe Editor is opened automatically. In OPNET, all statistics probes are preset with default, bucket capture mode. A statistic is generated in the output vector file for every 100 statistic values collected during simulation. Because we want to see the instant queue size of Router1, we need to change the capture mode for the statistic (Buffer Usage (packets)) to All Values. This can be done by editing the attributes of the probe object. We configure a simulation with a duration of 20 seconds and run the simulation. We save the scenario as **FIFO**.

Now we need to create another scenario called **RED** for comparison purposes. We select Duplicate Scenario operation from the Scenarios pull-down menu. We edit the QoS Information attribute of Router1 (available

TABLE 4.5: RED parameters used
in the simulation.

Parameters	Values
min_{th}	20 packets
max_{th}	80 packets
max_p	0.1
w_q	0.002

in the IP Address Information compound attribute). We enable RED in
Router1 and set the RED parameters as shown in Table 4.5. We save the
scenario as **RED** and run another simulation.

Step 6. Presentation of Results. We can now select Compare Results operation
from the Results pull-down menu to compare the buffer occupancy under the
two different scenarios. The results are shown in the *queue length versus time*
graph in Figure 4.26. Until about 16 seconds have passed, not all sources are
turned on. During this time, link utilization remains low and, therefore, the
queue lengths for both FIFO and RED remain the same. After 16 seconds,
the link utilization jumps to almost 100% and the congestion at the bottleneck
link builds up. During the congestion we should compare the performance
of RED in terms of queue length. As we can see in Figure 4.26, the buffer

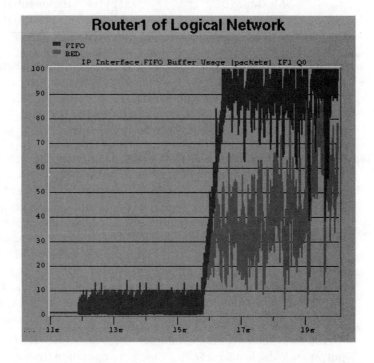

FIGURE 4.26: Evolution of buffer occupancy under FIFO and RED.

occupancy of RED is much smaller than that of FIFO during the congestion period (after 16 seconds).

EXAMPLE 4.4   Fairness Analysis of RED and WFQ.

The **objective** of this simulation is to explore the *fairness* problem in TCP/IP networks when traditional TCP-based data applications and the emerging UDP-based multimedia applications compete head-to-head for link bandwidth at a congested router. The choice of queuing schemes at the routers can play significant roles in achieving fairness in such situations. We will evaluate three different queue management schemes, FIFO with drop-tail, RED, and Weighted Fair Queuing (WFQ). Here are the steps we follow to conduct the simulation using OPNET:

Step 1. Reference Network and Parameters. We reuse the network model designed and constructed in the previous example as much as possible. We need to add a UDP-based source to our model.

Step 2. Performance Metrics. We are interested in the *throughput* achieved by individual TCP/UDP senders to assess the fairness of the queuing schemes.

Step 3. Variables. As in the previous example, the queuing scheme at Router1 is the single variable. We simulate three different schemes, FIFO, RED, and WFQ.

Step 4. Model Construction and Parameter Setting. We make the following changes to our previous network model. Client5 is now configured as a constant bit rate (CBR) video source, which sends video packets to its destination using UDP as the transport protocol. The rest of the model remains the same. The network model is shown in Figure 4.27.

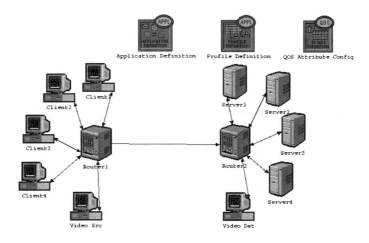

FIGURE 4.27: Network model for fairness evaluation.

We configure the video source with a bit rate of 280 Kbits/sec. The link capacity for all links is set to 1 Mbits/sec. The buffer size of Router1 remains 100 packets.

Step 5. Simulation Execution and Data Collection. We collect individual throughput at each destination. We configure a simulation with a duration of 10 minutes and save the scenario as **FIFO**. To compare the performance of FIFO with RED and WFQ, we create two more scenarios, RED and WFQ, using the same techniques explained in the previous example. We then run a simulation for each scenario.

Step 6. Presentation of Results. Throughput graphs achieved under FIFO, RED, and WFQ are shown in Figures 4.28, 4.29, and 4.30, respectively. The white curve shows the throughput of the video source, and the rest of the curves represent the TCP sources. As we can see, both FIFO and RED have a fairness problem in the sense that the UDP source gets unfairly larger throughput than those achieved by the TCP sources. With WFQ, however, the average throughput achieved by each TCP and UDP source is almost the same. The simulation results suggest that WFQ can enforce fairness among both adaptive (e.g., TCP) and nonadaptive (e.g., UDP) sources.

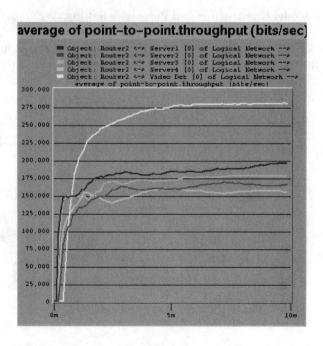

FIGURE 4.28: Average TCP/UDP throughput under FIFO.

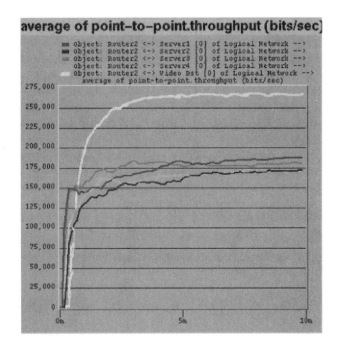

FIGURE 4.29: Average TCP/UDP throughput under RED.

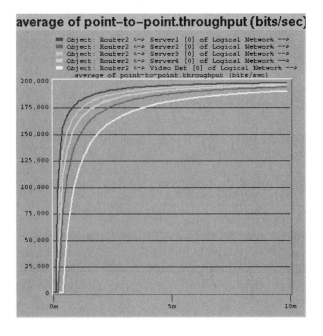

FIGURE 4.30: Average TCP/UDP throughput under WFQ.

TABLE 4.6: A comparison of ns and OPNET.

Criteria	*ns*	OPNET
Built-in library set	Large (wireline), small (wireless)	Large (wireline), large (wireless)
Credibility	Good	Good
User-friendliness	Command-oriented	GUI interface
Technical support	Via mailing list	Professional
Level of details	Less	More
Resource consumption	Large disk space	Large disk space
Cost	Totally free	Very expensive

4.10   SELECTING THE RIGHT TOOL

Despite the fact that there exist a large number of simulation tools, *ns* and OPNET have emerged as *de facto* "standards" for simulating TCP/IP networks. Therefore, in this section, we compare these two tools based on the following criteria (see Table 4.6 for a summary). Although selecting the right simulation tool for a particular need is not an easy decision, Table 4.6 can be used as an aid to this decision-making process.

Built-in libraries.   Built-in libraries for standard networking objects can significantly reduce model construction time. Both OPNET and *ns* have large sets of built-in libraries. However, for TCP/IP over wireless, mobile, satellite, and optical networks, OPNET provides more libraries than *ns*.

Credibility.   Both tools are used by a large number of users worldwide. Many journal and major conference papers cite these tools; therefore, the users do not have to worry about the verification of a library object (e.g., TCP Tahoe, Reno, etc.) that comes with the standard distribution.

User-friendliness.   *ns* is command-oriented; all simulations are written using scripts. OPNET has user-friendly GUI interfaces for most simulation needs. The only time an OPNET user has to write codes is when a new protocol has to be defined or some advanced statistics must be collected in a nonstandard way.

Technical support.   *ns* has mailing lists for the *ns* users. The mailing list, however, is useful only when someone responds quickly enough with good answers. OPNET has professional technical support, for a hefty price tag though, to help users solve their modeling problems.

Level of details.   OPNET objects generally allow a larger set of configuration parameters for the standard simulation objects allowing a more detailed simulation if needed. However, more details do not necessarily mean "better" simulation, as many research-oriented studies need simulations at a much higher level of abstraction.

Resource consumption.   OPNET consumes a lot of disk space to store raw data known as "vector files." Actual disk space requirements depend on the level and extent of the simulation tasks; but, in general, an OPNET user should have one or more gigabytes of space allocated for complex TCP/IP simulations[1]. *ns* also requires large disk space if a tracing method is used to collect data. Both OPNET and *ns* can put a heavy demand on the CPU, depending on the complexity of the simulation; therefore, one should allocate separate machines for simulation. *ns* is usually run on personal machines. OPNET is typically run on a shared machine, which may be a performance problem if there are many concurrent users or other tasks running in the background.

Cost. Cost is a major factor for many trying to decide whether to select *ns* or OPNET. Interestingly, *ns* and OPNET lie on the two extremes of the cost scale. *ns* is *totally free*, and OPNET is *very expensive*. At the time of writing this book, OPNET educational licenses cost U.S. $2,000 per year for the basic version (no advanced wireless simulation) for a single user and more for multiple users. OPNET licenses cannot be shared between two departments in the same university; each department has to purchase a separate license, even if the departments are located in the same building. If technical support is desired, it costs another U.S. $2,000 per year. If advanced wireless networks are simulated, the Radio Modeler must be purchased for another U.S. $2,000 per year. OPNET has some promotional "free usage programs" available for some U.S. universities, but universities outside the United States are excluded from such programs. Industry licenses cost much more (nearly U.S. $60,000). It is no wonder that for most TCP/IP simulations carried out in the universities as part of advanced courses or research degrees, *ns* remains the tool of the day.

4.11   FURTHER READING

Several techniques for simulation validation and verification are described in [186]. A comprehensive survey of techniques for steady-state simulations can be found in [263]. The article describes many heuristics for detecting the end of transient periods. The *ns* distribution [310] includes a large number of examples and test suites that can be run and compared with published results to validate that the simulator is running correctly. OPNET [242] has a comprehensive on-line user manual, but one first has to buy the license to access the manual. A good tutorial on OPNET can be found in [196].

4.12   SUMMARY

Computer simulation is a powerful method for studying the performance of complex and large-scale TCP/IP networks. A systematic simulation study has many steps. These steps are grouped into two stages, the design and planning stage and the software stage. Simulation software is needed in the software stage to conduct the simulations. Two widely used simulation applications, *ns* and OPNET, are described briefly in this chapter. There are several types of simulations. A *terminating* simulation is used to study the behavior of a network system for a well-defined period of time or number of events. On the contrary, *steady-state* simulations are required to observe the network performance when the system reaches a stable operating point. *Trace-driven* simulations are used to simulate a network model under realistic

---

[1]The recommended system and working file space is 550 MB.

traffic traced from an operational network. In most simulations, random numbers and sequences are used to generate various events and input to the simulated environment. Researchers, therefore, must conduct proper statistical analysis of the simulation output to achieve the desired precision and confidence level.

4.13 REVIEW QUESTIONS

1. Describe the steps of a systematic simulation study of TCP/IP networks.
2. What is the significance of the *presoftware stage* in a large simulation study?
3. What is the difference between *terminating* and *steady-state* simulations? Give two examples of each.
4. What is *trace-driven* simulation? What is the benefit of trace-driven simulation? Give one example where trace-driven simulation would be highly recommended.
5. What are simulation *validation* and *verification*? What risks do we run if we skip these two tasks in a simulation study? Explain with one example.
6. What is the *confidence level* of simulation results? What risks do we run if we do not perform confidence-level analysis.
7. What is fixed-length simulation? Why is it difficult to predict the length of a simulation for a desired confidence level?
8. What is adaptive-length simulation? Explain how adaptive-length simulation avoids the need for predicting simulation length in advance.
9. Explain how self-similar traffic can be generated using ON-OFF sources. Table 4.2 shows the values of two parameters, a and K, to achieve different Hurst parameters for a mean ON-OFF period of two time units. Derive the same table for an ON-OFF period of 0.5 time units.
10. Compare *ns* and OPNET in terms of model construction and parameter setting. In your opinion, which one is more user-friendly and why?

4.14 HANDS-ON PROJECTS

1. CSFQ, FRED, and WFQ are three different packet scheduling algorithms proposed for IP routers to achieve fairness among competing flows. Following the steps discussed in Section 4.2, conduct a systematic simulation study to compare these three algorithms. Use either *ns* or OPNET as your simulation software. Use traffic generators for the input traffic for this simulation.
2. Repeat the above project with trace traffic replacing the traffic generators. Use the trace traffic collected from your local network. You can reuse the traces you collected for your tcpdump project in the previous chapter.

4.15 CASE STUDY: WCORP USES MEASUREMENT, ANALYSIS, AND SIMULATION TO DIMENSION SYDNEY–MELBOURNE LINK CAPACITY

Since the opening of the second office in Melbourne, TCP/IP traffic on the interoffice link continued to grow steadily. The 256 Kbps leased line, which was quite adequate at the time of opening the office, is no longer adequate. The application that is affected most is videoconferencing. For quality conferencing, mean packet delay must not exceed 50 ms. However, because of increased queueing at the interoffice link, mean packet delay significantly exceeds 50 ms, severely deteriorating the quality of videoconferencing. This called for a performance study to determine the amount of capacity upgrade required for the leased line.

As a first step, the network administrator used simple network monitoring and queuing theory analysis to estimate required link capacity. In this case, it is a well-defined network problem in which all traffic from the LAN passes through a router and a long-distance link. For a given packet arrival rate of λ packets per second (pps), a link capacity of C (bps), and a mean packet length of L (bits), one can obtain the mean service rate $\mu = \frac{C}{L}$ and server load $\rho = \frac{L\lambda}{C}$ (see Appendix A for M/M/1 queueing formulas). The mean packet delay (in seconds) then obtained as:

$$W_s = \frac{\frac{L}{C}}{1 - \frac{L\lambda}{C}} \tag{4.9}$$

Simple network monitoring reveals that in the peak period, mean packet arrival rate is 120 pps and mean packet length is 256 octets. For these parameters, Eq. (4.9) suggests that the link capacity be upgraded to 286 Kbps (an increase of 30 Kbps) to keep mean packet delay below the 50 ms mark. Based on this queuing analysis, the administrator upgraded the Sydney–Melbourne link to 286 Kbps. After the upgrade, users of videoconferencing reported that performance was slightly improved, but it is still not perfect. To diagnose the problem, traffic was monitored once again. An interesting problem was detected. Although the monitoring data show that mean packet arrival rate and mean packet length remain approximately the same

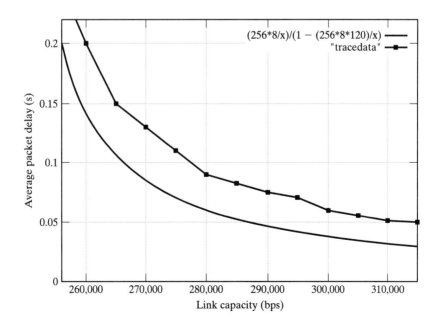

FIGURE 4.31: Packet delay as a function of link capacity.

as before, the mean packet delay was 80 ms, much higher than predicted by the queueing analysis. The administrator realized that this could be the result of self-similar nature of packet arrival, which is known to have a more deleterious effect on queue delay.

This time, the network administrator decided to perform a trace-driven simulation to work out more accurately the required link capacity. First `tcpdump` was used to capture all traffic going from the Sydney office to the Melbourne office during the peak period. The trace will be later used to drive the simulation model. After considering several simulation tools, the administrator selected *ns*, as it was freely available and known to be capable of performing this type of simulation. Using Tcl script, a simulation model was constructed with one exponential traffic generator and one bottleneck link. Several simulations were run, each time with a different link capacity. Figure 4.31 compares queuing analysis results with simulation. Delay was significantly higher for trace-driven simulation. This can be explained by the fact that actual network traffic shows self-similarity that is not captured by the $M/M/1$ model. Simulation results suggest an upgrade to 315 Kbps to keep the delay below the required 50 ms mark. Armed with the trace-driven simulation results, the network administrator recommended the appropriate upgrade of the leased line to the CEO. The CEO was very pleased to see the trace-driven simulation results obtained for the actual corporate traffic and had no hesitation approving the expenditure. The CEO was so pleased with the subsequent improvement in network performance that she eventually gave the network administrator an unexpected salary raise.

CHAPTER 5

TCP Modeling

CHAPTER OBJECTIVES

After completing this chapter, the reader should be able to:

- Appreciate mathematical modeling of TCP for performance optimization of TCP/IP networks

- Understand the fundamental relationship between packet loss probability and TCP performance

- Apply a range of mathematical models to predict TCP performance

In the previous two chapters, we have discussed two important techniques, experimental measurement and computer simulation, for the performance evaluation of TCP/IP networks. The third performance evaluation technique is a mathematical modeling of the TCP algorithms. In the past few years, researchers have developed several models to mathematically analyze and explain the behavior of the TCP. In this chapter, we present the motivation behind the modeling of TCP followed by a discussion of the key models of TCP.

5.1 MOTIVATION FOR MATHEMATICAL MODELING OF TCP

As we commence this chapter on modeling TCP, it is worthwhile considering the reasons why we would be interested in modeling the protocol. For the reader who is more mathematically inclined, this may seem rather obvious and the opportunity of using mathematical models to capture the dynamics of TCP is reason enough. However, for a person who has been involved in developing the current protocol, or writing code that implements TCP, it may seem that mathematicians simply enjoy applying abstract models to fashionable research topics, while at the same time stripping away practical details so that the models are amenable to further analysis. In this case, the reader has an intimate understanding of the mechanisms that define the dynamics of TCP, without needing powerful mathematical techniques to explain how the protocol works. Our desire is to show that in both cases, readers can gain further insight into the behavior of TCP through the use of modeling. The aim of this chapter, therefore, is to present the elegance of models that can be applied to TCP, while at the same time drawing attention to the practical results of these models.

It is very true that every aspect of TCP, including how it starts and the way it responds to network conditions as time progresses, is completely within our control, unlike some other systems that we would be interested in modeling, such as cosmological events or the interactions of particles in the nucleus of an atom. Also, one may conclude that we should simply observe how TCP operates in a given situation. If the situation in which we are interested is difficult to set up within an existing network, there are well-recognized simulation tools that closely mirror software implementations of TCP and can be used to investigate the performance of TCP. As a result, it may seem that we have significant access to the dynamics and performance of the protocol without resorting to using mathematical models.

There are a number of reasons why we would want to move beyond these approaches and start using mathematical machinery to advance our understanding of the control protocol. First, the sheer scale of systems in which we find TCP operating is tremendous. The growth of the Internet from its humble ARPANET beginnings is phenomenal, and TCP is the predominant protocol for transporting data across the Internet. Because of the feedback control mechanisms that TCP incorporates to provide reliable data transfer, the overall system formed by the total number of TCP connections operating across the Internet is one of the largest man-made control systems ever achieved, in terms of both geographic scale and the number of inputs and outputs. To make any attempt to capture a system of this magnitude, we need to resort to mathematical models.

Second, there still remain many unknowns in the environment in which TCP is operating. These include the size of files being transferred by TCP connections and the number of TCP connections currently in existence. In addition, there are other protocols being used to transport data across the Internet, and these may force TCP to respond in ways that we cannot anticipate. The network itself may undergo changes, like routing table updates or even line failures, which result in data being carried through alternate paths in the network. These uncertainties can be effectively represented using stochastic processes that drive the responses of TCP.

TCP is not necessarily the appropriate transport protocol for some applications, such as real-time voice or video connections. These require smooth dynamics in the transmission rates, whereas the response of TCP to packet losses is a drastic reduction in its packet transmission rate. Different transport protocols, therefore, need to be developed for these applications. At the same time, protocols that are designed for transporting real-time data should not adversely affect other traffic that is being carried by TCP. This results in the need to design TCP-friendly algorithms that have a responsiveness like TCP in the long term, and the design of these protocols can be achieved using steady-state models of TCP performance.

Finally, TCP was not designed using optimization. A better way of describing its design process is to say that "protocol patches" have been incorporated into the protocol as difficulties were encountered with either the performance of TCP or how it affected the operation of the Internet. The Fast Retransmission and Fast Recovery algorithms are good examples of "protocol patches." If one is interested in designing transport protocols that achieve optimal system performance, however, mathematical models are required to quantify metrics that define system performance and develop control strategies that result in the optimum being achieved. By modeling the current protocol, we can further determine how close it is to achieving a system optimum, as defined by a specific cost function, and subsequently identify issues that need to be addressed in future control protocols. Robustness of the protocol, however, is as important as optimality, and current protocols are well designed to give robust performance in a wide range of environments, topologies, and levels of congestion.

Having addressed the key reasons for modeling TCP, we can proceed with describing the models themselves. The approach used in this chapter is to begin with the essentials of TCP models—aspects of TCP that appear in all models proposed in networking literature. After laying this cornerstone of TCP modeling, the chapter tours through the major models for TCP, departing from models that simply include TCP essentials, and finally reaching models that allow generalization and optimization of transport control protocols.

5.2 ESSENTIALS OF TCP MODELING

A number of notable models for TCP have been developed, which either shed light on a particular aspect of the protocol or add a new level of generality to the process of modeling transport control within the Internet. It is very useful, however, to consider the similarities of all these models before focusing our attention on any one particular model, as this allows us to keep the key features of the model in mind and not get lost in the details of a specific model. One point to note at this stage is that the models we are considering mainly refer to the Reno flavor of TCP and its modifications, notably NewReno and SACK. This is because interest in TCP modeling work coincided with the significant growth of the Internet and the parallel widespread use of TCP as the dominant transport protocol, and TCP NewReno and SACK have particular features that have contributed to the widespread use of TCP. Earlier versions of the protocol do exist, which may not necessarily contain the features that are classed here as essential for proceeding with TCP modeling. Future TCP flavors may also depart from these essentials. In addition, there are some important dynamics of TCP, such as its slow-start procedure, and other phenomena, such as loss or "compression" of acknowledgment packets in queues, which are not generally included in mathematical models. All TCP connections commence in slow-start and many spend their entire lives in slow-start, because only a few kilobytes of data are being transferred. Thus, it is important to understand that models do have their limitations in reflecting reality. However, the essential features that are listed here form the foundation of TCP as we know it and provide a starting point from which other models can be developed.

There are two key processes that a model of TCP needs to include: (1) the dynamics of the window that defines the number of packets that a TCP source can transmit into the network, and (2) the packet loss process that indicates current traffic loads or congestion within the network. These form the major "blocks" in the resulting control system. One thing to notice about these processes is that they are both "observed" from the reference point of the TCP source. This is obvious for the window size, which is controlled by an algorithm within the source itself. The packet loss process, however, is also observed by the source. The loss process does not arise from any one particular node in the network but can be triggered by any node along the path of the TCP connection, with the source node observing the loss process as an aggregation of information being generated along the connection path.

5.2.1 Window Dynamics

The typical symbol for the current window size is $W(t)$. As discussed in Chapter 2, the essential dynamics of this window size are its linear increase and multiplicative decrease. During the interval in which TCP receives information that packets are not being lost in the network, TCP increases its window linearly. When the source deduces that a packet has been lost, it reduces its window by a factor of the current window size (i.e., multiplicatively). Implementations of TCP normally increase the window by one packet each round-trip (in the linear increase phase) and reduce the window size by half in the event of a packet loss, although these parameters can be generalized in mathematical models of TCP.

Some models have been developed using the packet transmission rate $X(t)$, as this can ease the analysis that follows the development of the model. The standard assumption in this case is that the window size is related to transmission rate by the round-trip time RTT:

$$X(t) = \frac{W(t)}{RTT} \tag{5.1}$$

This does assume that increasing the transmission rate of packets has negligible effect on queueing delays at nodes within the network, so that the round-trip time is effectively constant. Regardless of whether a model uses the state variable of window size or transmission rate, however, all models incorporate the linear increase and multiplicative decrease dynamics of TCP.

5.2.2 Packet-Loss Process

The other main component of a TCP model is a packet-loss process, which triggers the TCP source to reduce its window size. As previously mentioned, this process aggregates information regarding network conditions at all nodes along the path of the TCP connection. The particular TCP connection being considered is competing for network resources, along its path, with other TCP connections that have routes intersecting with this path. It is also competing for network bandwidth with other network traffic in general. These variations in traffic load introduce uncertainty into the arrival of packet-loss information at the TCP source. This is typically modeled as a stochastic process, either with regard to the probability p of losing a particular packet in the network or the intervals between instances when lost packets are detected. The key point is that models incorporate the arrival of packet-loss information, with the TCP source responding by decreasing its window.

In fact, we do not necessarily need to consider the information being returned from the network as confirmation that packets have not been lost. Network information can take the form of explicit notification regarding congestion within the network, although individual congestion messages are most likely to still be coded as binary information. Regardless of whether the information is packet loss or explicit congestion information, TCP models must respond to the stream of network load information that is aggregated along the connection path. This constitutes the other essential component of a TCP model.

5.3 GALLERY OF TCP MODELS

We are now in an excellent position to begin considering TCP models, together with the conclusions that can be drawn with regard to the performance of TCP and other system implications. The specific sequence in which we study these models has been chosen so that greater levels of understanding of the performance of TCP, and generalization to the broader subject of distributed control of elastic traffic, is gained as each model is introduced. This will build a solid understanding of TCP modeling by the end of the chapter.

5.3.1 Periodic Model

The simplest model for TCP that one can devise considers a periodic pattern in the dynamics of the congestion window and the packet-loss process in steady state [237]. No specific version of TCP is assumed. Instead, the TCP window evolves according to generic dynamics common to all TCP versions, with each periodic loss event triggering a single, multiplicative window reduction. Because the steady-state situation is being considered, a maximum window size W is always achieved by the time a packet is lost, which results in the window being reduced to $W/2$. Furthermore, the operation of the system in steady state means that packet losses occur with constant probability p, so that, on average, $1/p$ packets are transmitted into the network between each packet loss (and simultaneous reduction in window size). Also note that, since we are considering TCP in steady state, transients (like *slow start*) do not appear in our representation of the dynamics of the TCP window. Steady state means that we consider the window dynamics to have reached a regular pattern that continues for all time, such that, when considering the long-term performance achieved by the TCP flow control, we can ignore any transients that occurred during the start-up period.

A trace of the window size results in a periodic sawtooth plot (Figure 5.1). If packet losses occur randomly, however, (which is more realistic for TCP), a trace of the window size will not have this perfectly periodic form (the reader can refer to Figure 5.5, which shows a more typical plot of the transmission rate of a TCP source). Despite the fact that a periodic model is less realistic, however, it allows us to derive a fundamental property with regard to the performance of TCP, which is referred to as the *inverse square-root p* law.

Because of the periodic form of the window dynamics in steady state, the performance of a TCP connection in this situation can be derived by determining the

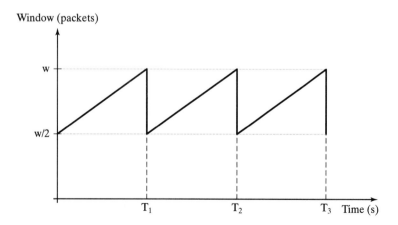

FIGURE 5.1: A periodic model of TCP window dynamics in steady state.

number of packets transmitted in one period and the length of the period. Because of the constant packet-loss probability of p, the number of packets is given by $1/p$, as noted previously, because we have to transfer this number of packets before one packet is lost. An alternative way of finding the total number of packets transferred in a period is to find the area underneath the trace of the window size, which is reasonably straightforward because of the trapezoidal shape of the period:

$$\text{Number of Pkts} = \frac{1}{2}\frac{T}{RTT}\left(\frac{W}{2} + W\right) \quad (5.2)$$

where T is the period between detecting packet losses. Time must be scaled by the round-trip time, as the TCP source is not sending packets continually, and time must advance by a round-trip period before a totally new set of packets, contained by the window size, contributes to the overall number of packets transmitted. Because we know that TCP increases its window at the rate of one packet per round-trip time during its linear increase phase, the time taken to increase its window from $W/2$ to W is $T = RTT \cdot W/2$. Hence, by equating the total number of packets transferred during this period, we have:

$$\frac{W}{4} \cdot \left(\frac{W}{2} + W\right) = 1/p$$

$$\Rightarrow W = \sqrt{\frac{8}{3p}} \quad (5.3)$$

We can now find the average sending rate $\overline{X}(p)$ of the TCP source, which is the number of packets transmitted during each period:

$$\overline{X}(p) = \frac{1/p}{RTT \cdot W/2}$$

$$= \frac{1}{RTT}\sqrt{\frac{3}{2p}} \quad (5.4)$$

This result is referred to as the *inverse square-root p law*, and it is an important and well-known relationship governing the performance of TCP. In particular, it shows that the transmission rate of a TCP source is inversely related to the round-trip time and the square root of the average packet loss probability.

EXAMPLE 5.1

If a TCP connection has an average RTT of 200 ms, and packets are lost along the connection with probability 0.05, the average sending rate of the TCP source is estimated to be:

$$\overline{X} = \frac{1}{0.2}\sqrt{\frac{3}{2 \times 0.05}}$$

$$= 27.4 \text{ pkts/s}$$

using the inverse square-root p law.

5.3.2 Detailed Packet Loss Model

It is rather satisfying that we can use a simple periodic model of TCP to achieve a fundamental result regarding the steady-state performance of the protocol. However, for a person who knows that current implementations of TCP include additional features, such as limits on the window size enforced by the receiver, and has also observed that timeouts are not infrequent in TCP window size traces, the simplicity of the periodic model in Section 5.3.1 may appear a little misleading. In this section, we consider a more detailed model of TCP that incorporates the essential elements modeled in Section 5.3.1, while adding more realistic aspects to represent the protocol more fully. Not surprisingly, we find that the inverse square-root p law does appear again in the performance analysis, although it can be masked if the packet loss probability is high or by limits on the window size.

Duplicate ACKs. Let us first consider a stochastic model of TCP, where information regarding packet losses are solely given by triple-duplicate acknowledgments (ACKs). This means that packet losses only result in the current window size W_i being halved (i.e., the source does not reenter the *slow-start* phase). Our approach follows that of Section 5.3.1, where we calculate the number of packets Y_i transferred in the period of length A_i between packet losses. As we are interested in the steady-state send rate of the source, our goal is to find:

$$\overline{X} = \frac{E[Y]}{E[A]} \tag{5.5}$$

If α_i is the number of the lost packet in the ith period (Figure 5.2), we have $Y_i = \alpha_i + W_i - 1$ as the total number of packets sent in this period. We assume that

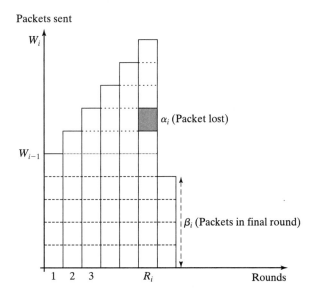

FIGURE 5.2: Detailed analysis of the packets sent during each round of window increase.

packet losses occur independently with probability p, so that the probability that $k-1$ packets are sent before a packet is lost is given by:

$$P[\alpha = k] = (1-p)^{k-1}p \tag{5.6}$$

Thus, the expected number of packets that are lost is:

$$
\begin{aligned}
E[\alpha] &= \sum_{k=1}^{\infty} k \cdot (1-p)^{k-1}p \\
&= \frac{1}{p}
\end{aligned}
\tag{5.7}
$$

We can use this result to simplify the expression for the expected number of packets transmitted by the source:

$$
\begin{aligned}
E[Y] &= E[\alpha] + E[W] - 1 \\
&= \frac{1-p}{p} + E[W]
\end{aligned}
\tag{5.8}
$$

This is our first expression for $E[Y]$. To find our second expression for the expected number of packets, we can determine the number of packets that are sent as the window itself is increased as ACKs return to the source. To do so, we need to introduce the concept of "rounds." The first round is the packets that are encompassed by the initial window size, and a new round begins when the trailing edge of the window borders a packet that has not been counted by previous rounds. Because each round marks a unit increment to the window size, the final window size W_i is given by

$$W_i = \frac{W_{i-1}}{2} + R_i \tag{5.9}$$

where R_i is the total number of rounds in the ith period. Taking the expectation of both sides, we have the result that

$$E[W] = 2E[R] \tag{5.10}$$

Considering the packets counted by each round, we are able to find a second expression for the total number of packets transmitted,

$$
\begin{aligned}
Y_i &= \sum_{k=0}^{R_i-1} \left(\frac{W_{i-1}}{2} + k \right) + \beta_i \\
&= \frac{R_i W_{i-1}}{2} + \frac{R_i}{2}(R_i - 1) + \beta_i \\
&= \frac{R_i}{2}\left(\frac{W_{i-1}}{2} + W_i - 1 \right) + \beta_i
\end{aligned}
\tag{5.11}
$$

where β_i is the number of packets sent in the last round. If we assume that the number of rounds in a period is independent of the window size, we can take the expected value of each quantity in Eq. (5.11) individually, so that we have:

$$E[Y] = \frac{E[R]}{2}\left(\frac{E[W]}{2} + E[W] - 1 \right) + E[\beta] \tag{5.12}$$

Using the simplifying assumption that the number of packets sent in the last round is uniformly distributed between 1 and $W_i - 1$, we have $E[\beta] = E[W]/2$. Finally, by equating the two expressions for the expected number of packets transmitted, we can solve for the expected window size at the end of each period:

$$\frac{1-p}{p} + E[W] = \frac{E[W]}{4}\left(\frac{E[W]}{2} + E[W] - 1\right) + \frac{E[W]}{2} \tag{5.13}$$

which results in the quadratic equation:

$$3\left(E[W]\right)^2 - 6E[W] + \frac{8(p-1)}{p} = 0 \tag{5.14}$$

Because $E[W] \geq 0$, we take the positive root:

$$E[W] = 1 + \sqrt{\frac{8}{3p} - \frac{5}{3}} \tag{5.15}$$

As the packet-loss probability approaches zero, we can approximate the expected window size by $E[W] \approx \sqrt{8/3p}$. We can now find the expected number of rounds $E[R]$ per period using Eqs. (5.10) and (5.15):

$$E[R] = \frac{1}{2} + \sqrt{\frac{2}{3p} - \frac{5}{12}} \tag{5.16}$$

Our goal has been to find the sending rate of the TCP source. To do this, we require the expected duration of the period, $E[A]$. In particular, we can observe that time between the start of the jth round (i.e., sending the first packet in round j) and acknowledgment being received for that first packet, is one round-trip time rtt_{ij}. Therefore,

$$A_i = \sum_{j=1}^{X_i+1} rtt_{ij} \tag{5.17}$$

where the extra round-trip time is the time taken to detect the packet loss. By assuming that the round-trip times are independent of the window size, we have, by taking the expectation of (5.17):

$$E[A] = (E[R] + 1)E[rtt]$$

$$= \left(\frac{1}{2} + \sqrt{\frac{2}{3p} - \frac{5}{12}} + 1\right)RTT \tag{5.18}$$

$$= RTT\left(\frac{3}{2} + \sqrt{\frac{2}{3p} - \frac{5}{12}}\right)$$

where RTT is the average round-trip time. Finally, substituting equations (5.15), (5.8), and (5.18) into (5.5), we get:

$$\overline{X}(p) = \frac{E[Y]}{E[A]}$$

$$= \frac{\frac{1-p}{p} + 1 + \sqrt{\frac{8}{3p} - \frac{5}{3}}}{RTT\left(\frac{3}{2} + \sqrt{\frac{2}{3p} - \frac{5}{12}}\right)} \qquad (5.19)$$

$$= \frac{\frac{1}{p} + \sqrt{\frac{8}{3p} - \frac{5}{3}}}{RTT\left(\frac{3}{2} + \sqrt{\frac{2}{3p} - \frac{5}{12}}\right)}$$

where $\overline{X}(p)$ is measured in packets per second. If the packet-loss probability is very small, the send rate can be approximated by:

$$\overline{X}(p) \approx \frac{1}{RTT}\sqrt{\frac{3}{2p}} \qquad (5.20)$$

which is the inverse square-root p law that we found in Section 5.3.1. However, using this model we have a more accurate expression (5.19) for the send rate for moderate loss probabilities. For high loss probabilities, a model has to take into account timeouts and the exponential backoff of the retransmit timer, as described in the next section.

EXAMPLE 5.2

Returning to the situation given in Example 1, where $RTT = 200$ ms and $p = 0.05$, a better estimate for the sending rate of the TCP connection is now:

$$X = \frac{\frac{1}{0.05} + \sqrt{\frac{8}{3 \times 0.05} - \frac{5}{3}}}{0.2 \cdot \left(\frac{3}{2} + \sqrt{\frac{2}{3 \times 0.05} - \frac{5}{12}}\right)}$$

$$= 26.69 \text{ pkts/s}$$

Timeouts. As yet we have not included the effect of timeouts, which, as a number of studies on TCP measurements have shown, can occur reasonably frequently. A fixed number of duplicate acknowledgments are interpreted as meaning that a particular packet is lost, and many TCP implementations halve the window size after receiving three duplicate ACKs. However, if a TCP source does not receive any duplicate ACKs, or receives less than three, a packet is recognized as being lost only when its retransmission timer times out. At this point the window size is reduced to one and the slow-start threshold is set to half the window size before the packet loss occurred. The lost packet is then retransmitted, and the retransmission timer is reset with double the previous timeout period. Together with the fact that

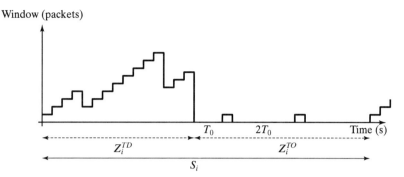

FIGURE 5.3: Intervals that constitute the dynamics of the window in one cycle including a timeout period.

significant delays occur in waiting for the timer to time out, timeouts mean that the sending rate of the TCP source is significantly reduced. We adapt the detailed packet-loss model to demonstrate this consequence.

Figure 5.3 shows a breakdown of the intervals that form the period S_i we are concerned with. Specifically,

$$S_i = Z_i^{TD} + Z_i^{TO}$$

The interval Z_i^{TD} includes all the periods where losses are recovered by duplicate ACKs, while Z_i^{TO} refers to the period when the source is only receiving timeout signals from the retransmission timer. By defining M_i as the total number of packets sent during interval S_i, the expected sending rate of the TCP source is given by:

$$\overline{X} = \frac{E[M]}{E[S]}$$

Using similar notation as the previous section for the triple-duplicate ACK periods (TDPs), in which Y_{ij} is the number of packets sent and A_{ij} represents the duration of each of the periods where losses are detected by duplicate ACKs, and introducing the variable Y_i^{TO} to represent the number of packets sent during the timeouts, the variables M_i and S_i are given by:

$$M_i = \sum_{j=1}^{n_i} Y_{ij} + Y_i^{TO} \tag{5.21}$$

$$S_i = \sum_{j=1}^{n_i} A_{ij} + Z_i^{TO} \tag{5.22}$$

where n_i is the number of TDPs. Assuming that n_i is independent of the number of packets sent in each interval, we have:

$$E[M] = E[n]E[Y] + E[Y^{TO}]$$
$$E[S] = E[n]E[A] + E[Z^{TO}] \tag{5.23}$$

Because only one timeout period occurs for each S_i, the probability Q that a packet loss results in a timeout period is given by $Q = 1/E[n]$; therefore, we can write the sending rate as

$$\overline{X} = \frac{E[Y] + Q \cdot E[R]}{E[A] + Q \cdot E[Z^{TO}]} \tag{5.24}$$

Thus, the quantities Q, $E[Y^{TO}]$, and $E[Z^{TO}]$ are to be determined. According to Padhye et al. [256]:

$$Q(w) \approx \min\left(1, \frac{3}{w}\right)$$

$$E[Y^{TO}] = \frac{1}{1-p} \tag{5.25}$$

$$E[Z^{TO}] = T_0 \frac{f(p)}{1-p}$$

where the expected window size is given by Eq. (5.15) and $f(p) = 1 + p + 2p^2 + 4p^3 + 8p^4 + 16p^5 + 32p^6$. By substituting Eq. (5.25) into Eq. (5.24), our full expression for the send rate of the TCP source is now:

$$\overline{X}(p) = \frac{\frac{1-p}{p} + E[W] + Q(E[W])\frac{1}{1-p}}{RTT(E[X]+1) + Q(E[W])T_0\frac{f(p)}{1-p}} \tag{5.26}$$

Receiver Limitation of Window Size.   Our final modification to the model is to include the practical situation in which the receiver may place limits on the window size. This may occur if a receiver can only process packets up to a maximum receiving rate, in which case the TCP source should not transmit a burst of packets at a rate that overwhelms the receiver. We refer to W_m as the limit that the receiver enforces on the window size and W_u as the window size unconstrained by the receiver. If $E[W_u]$ is less than receiver window limit, that is, $E[W_n] < W_m$, then $E[W_u]$ is given by Eq. (5.15) in the previous section. If, however, $E[W_u] \approx W_m$, the send rate is given by:

$$\overline{X}(p) = \frac{\frac{1-p}{p} + W_m + \min\left(1, \frac{3}{W_m}\right)\frac{1}{1-p}}{RTT(\frac{W_m}{8} + \frac{1-p}{pW_m} + 1) + \min\left(1, \frac{3}{W_m}\right)T_0\frac{f(p)}{1-p}} \tag{5.27}$$

The development of this result follows an approach similar to that used in the previous two sections, and the full derivation is found in [256].

Complete Model.   Combining the results from the previous three sections, we have the complete characterization of the sending rate of a TCP source as follows:

$$\overline{X}(p) = \begin{cases} \dfrac{\frac{1-p}{p} + E[W] + Q(E[W])\frac{1}{1-p}}{RTT(\frac{E[W]}{2}+1) + Q(E[W])T_0\frac{f(p)}{1-p}}, & E[W_u] < W_m \\[4mm] \dfrac{\frac{1-p}{p} + W_m + Q(E[W_m])\frac{1}{1-p}}{RTT(\frac{W_m}{8} + \frac{1-p}{pW_m}+1) + Q(E[W_m])T_0\frac{f(p)}{1-p}}, & E[W_u] \approx W_m \end{cases} \tag{5.28}$$

which can be approximated as

$$\overline{X}(p) \approx \min \left(\frac{W_m}{RTT}, \frac{1}{RTT\sqrt{\frac{2p}{3}} + T_0 \min\left(1, 3\sqrt{\frac{3p}{8}}\right) p(1 + 32p^2)} \right) \tag{5.29}$$

This approximation has been used in the design of TCP-friendly algorithms, which are transport protocols designed for real-time traffic, like video and voice, and provide smoothly varying transmission rates. At the same time, TCP-friendly algorithms respond to long-term packet-loss rates in a similar manner to TCP, so that the real-time flows do not grab bandwidth from TCP connections.

EXAMPLE 5.3

Returning once again to the situation given in Example 1, with $RTT = 200$ ms and $p = 0.05$, if the receiver limits its window size to $W_m = 20$ pkts and the TCP algorithm at the source has a timeout value of $T_0 = 500$ ms, the sending rate of the TCP connection is estimated as:

$$\overline{X} = \min \left(\frac{20}{0.2}, \frac{1}{0.2\sqrt{\frac{2 \times 0.05}{3}} + 0.5 \min\left(1, 3\sqrt{\frac{3 \times 0.05}{8}}\right) 0.05(1 + 32 \cdot 0.05^2)} \right)$$

$$= \min(100, 24.73)$$

$$= 24.73 \text{ pkts/s}$$

The complete model is compared with its approximation and the simple inverse square-root p law in Figure 5.4, where the TCP send rate is plotted as the packet-loss probability is increased for a typical trans-Atlantic connection. Data from *ns-2* simulations are also included in the figure. Figure 5.4 shows that the simple version of the inverse square-root p law estimates the sending rate well for moderately low packet-loss probabilities. However, as the packet-loss probability increases, the simple approximation given by Eq. (5.4) significantly overestimates the send rate as it does not take into account the effect of timeouts. For very low packet-loss probabilities, the effect of the receiver window limit is to enforce a ceiling on the TCP send rate as the packet-loss probability drops. We can conclude from these results that the simple inverse square-root p law is a good approximation only if the average packet loss is small and the receiver does not effectively place any limit on the window size. However, Eq. (5.29) is a good approximation of the sending rate for any loss probability or enforced window limit, as observed from the reasonable match between the curve for the approximation and the *ns-2* simulation data in Figure 5.4.

5.3.3 Stochastic Model with General Loss Process

So far, we have developed both good approximations and detailed expressions for the performance of a TCP source, as measured by the total packet output. However,

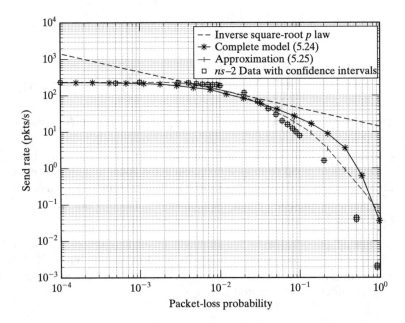

FIGURE 5.4: Estimates of the sending rate of a TCP source, as the packet-loss probability varies, with $RTT = 85$ ms, $T0 = 500$ ms, and $W_m = 20$ pkts.

the intrinsic model for packet losses that we have used until now is an independent and uncorrelated loss process, which may not be the case in the actual Internet. In fact, losses can be quite bursty and dependent on the current window size, as losses increase rapidly when we attempt to transmit a large number of packets across the Internet, although this dependence decreases with increased statistical multiplexing at links. Hence, we are interested in pursuing a model that allows us to include correlations in the losses. All we assume is that the loss process is stationary and ergodic.

At the same time, the detailed packet-loss model in Section 5.3.2 would become rather unwieldy if we introduced a more complicated loss process. A better approach is to simplify our perspective of TCP so that the essential features of TCP are retained, while easing the burden of analysis. This can be achieved by considering the transmission rate X_n at the event of a (or multiple) packet loss, and the intervals S_n between these events (Figure 5.5). Considering the standard response of TCP to these events, the transmission rate [48] is given by:

$$X_{n+1} = \nu X_n + \alpha S_n \tag{5.30}$$

where ν is the multiplicative decrease factor ($\nu = 1/2$, for a typical implementation of TCP). The parameter α is the additive increase factor, per time unit, for the TCP implementation, and is given by $\alpha = 1/(RTT^2)$, as the window size increases by $1/RTT$ for each ACK received. We need to divide the window size by RTT again to get the transmission rate. Figure 5.5 shows the dynamics of the transmission rate of the TCP source, and in this model we can assume that S_n has the general correlation function $R(k) = E[S_n S_{n+k}]$. We also let $\lambda = 1/E[S]$ refer to the frequency of loss events.

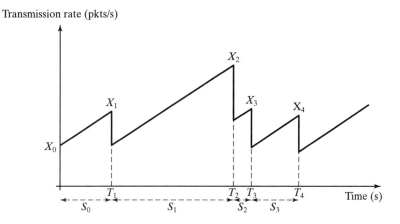

FIGURE 5.5: Dynamics of the TCP transmission rate.

Stationary Solution.   Because (1) the loss process is stationary and ergodic, (2) the estimated interval between loss events is finite, and (3) $v < 1$, Eq. (5.30) has the stationary solution:

$$X^* = \alpha \sum_{k=0}^{\infty} v^k S_{n-1-k} \qquad (5.31)$$

and we can find both the expected value:

$$E[X^*] = \alpha \sum_{k=0}^{\infty} v^k E[S_{n-1-k}]$$

$$= \frac{\alpha}{\lambda} \sum_{k=0}^{\infty} v^k \qquad (5.32)$$

$$= \frac{\alpha}{\lambda(1-v)}$$

and the second moment of the stationary solution:

$$E[(X^*)^2] = E\left[\alpha \sum_{j=0}^{\infty} v^j S_{n-1-j} \alpha \sum_{k=0}^{\infty} v^k S_{n-1-k}\right]$$

$$= \alpha^2 E\left[\sum_{k=0}^{\infty} \sum_{j=0}^{k} v^j S_{n-1-j} v^{k-j} S_{n-1-k+j}\right]$$

$$= \alpha^2 \sum_{k=0}^{\infty} \sum_{j=0}^{k} v^k E[S_{n-1-j} S_{n-1-k+j}] \qquad (5.33)$$

$$= \frac{\alpha^2}{1-v^2}\left[R(0) + 2\sum_{k=1}^{\infty} v^k R(k)\right]$$

Average TCP Sending Rate.   As such, X^* is the stationary solution for the transmission rate just before loss events being detected. However, we are actually interested in the expected sending rate of the TCP source, which is the average transmission rate:

$$\overline{X} = \lim_{T \to \infty} \frac{1}{T} \int_0^T X(t)dt \tag{5.34}$$

To find an expression for $\overline{X}$, we must use the concept of Palm probability, which will not be introduced here, but according to Altman et al. [48]:

$$\overline{X} = \lambda\alpha \left[\frac{1}{2}R(0) + \sum_{k=1}^{\infty} v^k R(k) \right] \tag{5.35}$$

EXAMPLE 5.4

Suppose that packet losses occur, on average, every 1.56 s for a TCP connection that has an average RTT of 200 ms. Further analysis shows that the correlations within the time intervals between packet losses is given by the function $R(k) = 2.44 \cdot 0.21^k$ for $k = 0, 1, 2 \ldots$. This allows us to estimate the TCP sending rate as:

$$\overline{X} = \frac{1}{1.56} \cdot \frac{1}{0.2^2} \left(\frac{1}{2} \cdot 2.44 + \sum_{k=1}^{\infty} 0.5^k \times 2.44 \cdot 0.21^k \right)$$

$$= 0.65 \times 25 \left(1.22 + \frac{2.44 \times 0.105}{1 - 0.105} \right)$$

$$= 24.11 \text{ pkts/s}$$

Conventionally, losses are characterized by the average loss probability p. We can comply with this convention by defining $A(t)$ as the total number of packets transmitted at time t and $L(t)$ as the number of loss events. With this notation, the average loss probability is given by:

$$p = \lim_{t \to \infty} \frac{L(t)}{A(t)}$$

$$= \lim_{t \to \infty} \frac{\lambda t}{\int_0^t X(\tau)d\tau}$$

$$= \frac{\lambda}{\overline{X}} \tag{5.36}$$

$$= \frac{1}{d\overline{X}}$$

where $d = E[S]$. Rearranging the variables in (5.36), we have:

$$\overline{X} = \frac{1}{pd} \tag{5.37}$$

If we normalize the correlation function by d^2, so that $\hat{R}(k) = R(k)/d^2$, and then multiply (5.35) and (5.37) to eliminate d, we have:

$$\overline{X}^2 = \frac{\lambda\alpha}{pd}\left[\frac{1}{2}d^2\hat{R}(0) + \sum_{k=1}^{\infty}v^kd^2\hat{R}(k)\right]$$

$$= \frac{1}{RTT^2p}\left[\frac{1}{2}\hat{R}(0) + \sum_{k=1}^{\infty}v^k\hat{R}(k)\right]$$

Taking the positive square root, the final expression for the sending rate is:

$$\overline{X} = \frac{1}{RTT\sqrt{p}}\sqrt{\frac{1}{2}\hat{R}(0) + \sum_{k=1}^{\infty}v^k\hat{R}(k)} \tag{5.38}$$

which once again reveals the inverse dependence of the average transmission rate on the round-trip time and the square root of the loss probability.

Receiver Rate Limitations. In the situation where the receiver places a limit, M, on the packet rate that it can process, the dynamics of the TCP source transmission rate is now given by:

$$X_{n+1} = \min(M, vX_n + \alpha S_n) \tag{5.39}$$

This is equivalent to limiting the window size to W_m, where $M = W_m/RTT$. By considering an auxiliary process, $\check{X}_{n+1} = \check{X}_n + \min(M/2, \alpha S_n)$ that forms a lower bound to the process X_n in Eq. (5.39), a good approximation for the TCP sending rate [48] is given by:

$$\overline{X} \simeq M - \frac{\lambda M}{8\alpha} \tag{5.40}$$

when the transmission rate is frequently limited by the processing speed of the receiver.

5.3.4 Control System Model

So far, we have implicitly "assumed" that losses occur in the network because of unavoidable congestion conditions when the network is forced to drop a packet, that is, when a node cannot buffer the number of arriving packets. As a result, forced packet drops are not acknowledged by the receiver, so the TCP source deduces that the packets have been lost. However, as we will see in Chapter 12, it is possible for a node in the network to play an active role in controlling TCP connections by deliberately dropping (or marking) packets when the node anticipates the onset of congestion. This approach is known as *active queue management* (AQM). A key proposal for a packet-discarding algorithm, which is under consideration, is known as *Random Early Detection* (RED), and this algorithm probabilistically drops (or marks) packets based on an averaged estimate of the queue length (see Figure 12.5 for the function RED uses to calculate the probability of dropping a packet). When AQM is used by network nodes, a control loop is formed that can be represented

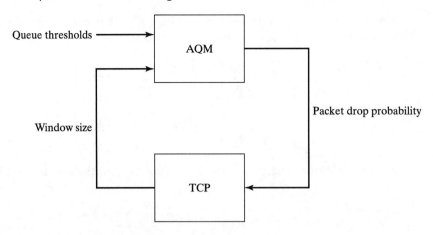

FIGURE 5.6: The control system formed by the TCP source and the active queue management (AQM) algorithm.

by the block diagram in Figure 5.6. Our aim in this section is to develop a model of TCP that can be further used to develop AQM schemes.

Let us consider a single TCP source that has a round-trip delay given by:

$$R(t) = d_p + \frac{q(t)}{C} \tag{5.41}$$

where d_p is the propagation delay along the path of the connection and $q(t)$ denotes the number of packets queued along the path. For simplicity, we assume that all nodes operate with capacity C. The TCP receives notification of packet dropped in the network, and we assume that the number of packet drops is well modeled by a Poisson process $N(t)$, in which packet-loss information arrives at the source at the rate $\lambda(t)$. As a result, the dynamics of the TCP window are given by the differential equation [243]:

$$dW(t) = \frac{dt}{R(q(t))} - \frac{W(t)}{2} dN(t) \tag{5.42}$$

where the window increases linearly when packets are not dropped in the network but experiences multiplicative decreases for each packet loss. Taking the expectation of both sides of (5.42), we have:

$$
\begin{aligned}
E[dW(t)] &= E\left[\frac{dt}{R(q(t))}\right] - \frac{E[W(t)dN(t)]}{2} \\
\Rightarrow dE[W] &= E\left[\frac{dt}{R(q)}\right] - \frac{E[W]\lambda(t)}{2} dt
\end{aligned}
\tag{5.43}
$$

by making the simplifying assumption that the window size is independent of the packet-loss process.

A TCP source only knows that a packet has been dropped in the network after a delay τ. If the total traffic load at a network node is given by $x(t)$ and the node drops packets at a rate of $p(x(t))$, then the average rate of packet drops experienced by a particular connection is given by:

$$\lambda(t) = p\left(\overline{x}(t-\tau)\right) E\left[\frac{W(t-\tau)}{R(q(t-\tau))}\right] \tag{5.44}$$

Hence, we can rewrite Eq. (5.43) as:

$$dE[W] = \frac{dt}{R(\overline{q})} - \frac{\overline{W}}{2} p\left(\overline{x}(t-\tau)\right) \frac{\overline{W}(t-\tau)}{R(\overline{q}(t-\tau))} \tag{5.45}$$

with the final form of the window dynamics being modeled by the differential equation:

$$\frac{d\overline{W}}{dt} = \frac{1}{R(\overline{q})} - \frac{\overline{W}\,\overline{W}(t-\tau)}{2R\left(\overline{q}(t-\tau)\right)} p\left(\overline{x}(t-\tau)\right) \tag{5.46}$$

What remains of the problem is to design the *packet-drop* function $p(\cdot)$ that is deployed at a network node.

While the performance of AQM policies is of considerable interest, this chapter is concerned with modeling TCP dynamics, so we do not proceed with studying algorithms that drop or mark packets (these algorithms are discussed in Chapter 12). The point of developing Eq. (5.46) is to show the interaction between packet discard algorithms and the TCP window size, and the model can be subsequently used in studying the performance of these packet discard algorithms, when they are deployed within the core of the Internet. For example, Misra et al. [243] have analyzed the performance of the RED using Eq. (5.46) and have identified problems with the queue length averaging mechanism in RED. Because of these results, they have considered other mechanisms for AQM, such as proportional and proportional-integral controllers that are commonly used for the control of, for example, mechanical systems. Other mechanisms, however, based on optimal or robust control, can also be formulated. The actual development of more sophisticated AQM algorithms can be pursued as further research.

5.3.5 Network System Model

Our models of TCP have taken the perspective of seeing the network as viewed by the TCP source, and have focused on the dynamics of the window size, or transmission rate, and the losses detected by the source. This is a reasonable perspective to take, because TCP itself is an end-to-end protocol—control of bandwidth resources is distributed to end stations located at the edge of the network. No central bandwidth-manager node is required, and if a central controller were used, it would have an immense computational burden and be vulnerable to failures. However, the perspective of simply focusing on a single TCP source leaves open questions of how bandwidth is shared by TCP connections within the network, and whether the collection of TCP sources can achieve optimal distribution of network bandwidth. If the sources can achieve system optimality, we are further interested to know how fast the system converges and whether the optimum is stable, considering that short-lived connections that transfer only a small amount of data disturb the system from its equilibrium point. These issues are addressed in the following model of the network as a system.

System Model.   In defining a network, let us assume that the network contains L links, each having bandwidth capacity C_l measured in bits/s. Across this network we route a collection of rate-controlled connections, with an individual connection using a particular route r, where r follows a specific path through the set of L links. Furthermore, we can define a routing matrix A with entry $A_{lr} = 1$ if route r uses link l and is zero otherwise. The total collection of routes being used by the TCP connections can be labeled R.

Rate Control Algorithm.   Each rate-controlled connection has a transmission rate x_r, which depends on feedback information μ_l that it receives from the network regarding the traffic load on link l on its route. Let us consider following the system of differential equations [198]:

$$\frac{d}{dt} x_r(t) = \kappa \left(w_r - x_r(t) \sum_{l \in r} \mu_l(t) \right), \tag{5.47}$$

where the feedback information is calculated at each link according to the function:

$$\mu_l(t) = p_l \left(\sum_{r:j \in r} x_r(t) \right). \tag{5.48}$$

The parameter κ is the gain of the differential system and is related to the RTT of the flow. We call the parameter w_r the source's "willingness-to-pay," which describes how aggressive the rate control algorithm is, where this aggressiveness is observed by the amount the source increases its rate when it does not receive feedback to reduce its rate. Notice that, with the combined effect of these two parameters, the dynamics of the transmission rate x_r of a particular connection increases linearly, with parameter κw_r, without any feedback information from the network, but decreases multiplicatively on receiving positive aggregate feedback information. The algorithm, thus, captures the essential features of TCP.

With regard to the function $p_l(\cdot)$ that each link uses to calculate its feedback information, we assume that the function is nonnegative, continuous, and increasing, with a typical function $p_l(\cdot)$ being shown in Figure 5.7. This function, $p_l(\cdot)$, does not directly model packet losses that occur in the network but instead requires some form of explicit congestion notification from the network. However, implementations of TCP that employ this type of feedback information are being developed in which the feedback is provided by AQM algorithms. Modeling the system in this way allows us to investigate the stability of the system optimum and the rate of convergence.

Stability of System Optimum.   To identify the optimal operating point of the system, the net cost (or inversely utility) of operating the system must be formulated. The expression:

$$U(x) = \sum_{r \in R} w_r \log x_r - \sum_{l \in L} \int_0^{\sum_{s:j \in s} x_s} p_l(y) dy \tag{5.49}$$

is a Lyapunov function for the system of differential Eqs. (5.47) and (5.48), which defines the net gain achieved by the system. Specifically, it aggregates the utility

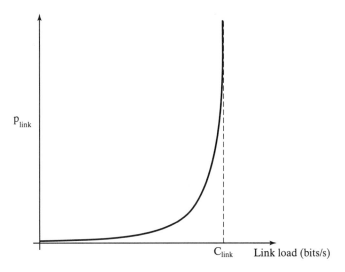

FIGURE 5.7: A graphical example of a function that could be used by a link for calculating the feedback information μ_l.

$U_r = w_r \log x_r$ achieved by each individual source and then subtracts the cost p_l of servicing the resulting bandwidth allocation at each link. By maximizing the Lyapunov function (equivalently the net gain), the performance of the system can be optimized. In particular, if $w_r > 0$ and $p_l(y)$ is nonzero, continuous, and increasing, then $U(x)$ is strictly concave and a unique vector x^*, consisting of the optimal set of transmission rates, exists, and this rate vector maximizes the Lyapunov function. The optimal transmission rates can be found by differentiating the Lyapunov function with respect to each variable x_r:

$$\frac{\partial}{\partial x_r} U(x) = \frac{w_r}{x_r} - \sum_{l \in r} p_l \left(\sum_{s:l \in s} x_s \right) \tag{5.50}$$

and then setting (5.50) to zero for each transmission rate x_r. The optimum point is also stable because:

$$\frac{d}{dt} U(x(t)) = \sum_{r \in R} \frac{\partial}{\partial x_r} U(x) \cdot \frac{d}{dt} x_r(t)$$

$$= \kappa \sum_{r \in R} \frac{1}{x_r(t)} \left(w_r - x_r(t) \sum_{l \in r} p_l \left(\sum_{s:j \in s} x_s(t) \right) \right)^2$$

$$> 0, \text{ when } x_r(t) \neq x^*$$

which implies that the utility of the system is always increasing unless $x(t) = x^*$. In other words, the system converges to the unique maximum of the Lyapunov function (5.49) and is stable about that optimum point.

Rate of Convergence. We are not only interested in the fact that a unique optimum exists and that the system converges to that point—the rate of convergence is important, with regard to the performance of the system. To find the speed of convergence, we need to linearize the system about the optimum point, which we can do by setting $x_r(t) = x_r^* + \sqrt{x_r^*} y_r(t)$. Using the standard notation of representing the derivative of p_l as p_l', the linearized system becomes:

$$\frac{d}{dt} y_r(t) = -\kappa \left(y_r(t) \sum_{l \in r} \mu_l + x_r^{*1/2} \sum_{l \in r} p_l' \sum_{s:l \in s} x_s^{*1/2} y_s(t) \right)$$

$$= -\kappa \left(\frac{w_r}{x_r^*} y_r(t) + x_r^{*1/2} \sum_l \sum_s p_l' A_{jr} A_{js} x_s^{*1/2} y_s(t) \right)$$

Collecting all of these equations into a vector, we have:

$$\frac{d}{dt} y(t) = -\kappa \left(WX^{-1} + X^{1/2} A^T P' A X^{1/2} \right) y(t) \tag{5.51}$$

where X, W, and P' are diagonal matrices with entries x_r^*, w_r, and p_l', respectively, along the diagonals. The rate of convergence is now given by the smallest eigenvalue of matrix Λ:

$$\Lambda = WX^{-1} + X^{1/2} A^T P' A X^{1/2}$$
$$= \Gamma^T \Phi \Gamma \tag{5.52}$$

where Φ is the diagonal matrix of eigenvalues.

For a given network topology, when the routing matrix A is known and the diagonal matrix W, of all the connections' "willingness-to-pay" parameters w_r, is given, we can solve for the optimal rates x_r^*, giving us the diagonal matrix X. We can furthermore find the derivatives p_l' at this optimal point. This allows us to determine how fast the system returns to the optimal operating point, using the diagonal matrix Φ of eigenvalues, after the system has been forced away from its optimal point. This is because the smallest eigenvalue determines the exponential decay of the transient, as the system returns from its temporarily suboptimal performance level back to its optimal operating point. If the magnitude of the smallest eigenvalue is close to zero, then the transient decays very slowly from the system response, resulting in poor system performance for a long period of time. However, if the smallest eigenvalue is rather large, then the transient will decay very rapidly and the system will return to its optimal performance rather quickly.

Let us consider this from a networking perspective, and the smallest eigenvalue of Φ is related to the maximum RTT within the set of connections, or the connection with the largest hop-count. Let us also imagine that an event occurs within the network that forces all the connections to reduce their rates temporarily. For example, a malicious user may attempt to transfer a very large file across the network without using any rate control protocol. Thus, if the maximum hop-count is quite large, then it will take some time for the connection with maximum RTT to return to its original transmission rate. Conversely, if the maximum RTT is reasonably low, then the connection increases its rate to the original level fairly quickly. One could argue that the capacity within the network can be adequately utilized by connections with smaller RTTs while the connection with maximum RTT is increasing its transmission rate. However, we consider the optimal operating point for the network to be the one in which all the connections achieve their optimal transmission rates. Thus, the objective is to maximize the overall utility achieved by all the connections, and not simply high utilization of network capacity. This is related to the concept of fairness between connections.

EXAMPLE 5.5

Consider the simple example shown in Figure 5.8, in which three rate-controlled flows are using a network that consists of two links, which have capacity 10 and 5, respectively. The routing matrix is given by:

$$A = \begin{bmatrix} 1 & 1 & 0 \\ 1 & 0 & 1 \end{bmatrix} \tag{5.53}$$

The flows have "willingness-to-pay" parameters $w_r = [0.5, 1.5, 1.0]$, and the links have price functions $p_{l1}(y) = 0.2/(10 - y)$ and $p_{l2}(y) = 0.5/(5 - y)$. By setting the system of equations given in Eq. (5.50) to zero, we have:

$$\frac{w_1}{x_1} - \frac{0.2}{10 - (x_1 + x_2)} - \frac{0.5}{5 - (x_1 + x_3)} = 0$$

$$\frac{w_2}{x_2} - \frac{0.2}{10 - (x_1 + x_2)} = 0 \tag{5.54}$$

$$\frac{w_3}{x_3} - \frac{0.5}{5 - (x_1 + x_3)} = 0$$

and by using a suitable method for solving the set of nonlinear Eqs. (5.54), such as the Newton-Raphson method, the optimum rates for this system can be found to be $x^* = [0.9, 8.0, 2.7]$. The capacity constraints of the links have been met. Taking the derivative of the price functions at the optimal operating point of the network, we can determine the matrix $\Phi = \mathrm{diag}(0.47, 1.90, 1.27)$; therefore, the convergence of the network shown in Figure 5.8 is determined by the eigenvalue $\phi_{\min} = 0.47$. This eigenvalue is associated with Flow 1, which traverses two hops in the network and, therefore, has the largest RTT among the flows.

Fairness.   Our final interest is in the way bandwidth is shared between connections. If we chose the functions $p_j(y)$ appropriately, we can come close to

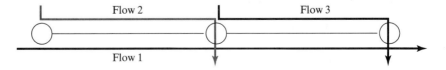

FIGURE 5.8: A simple network with three rate-controlled connections.

achieving the optimum aggregate utility, which is $\sum w_r \log x_r$, for all the connections, by maximizing the Lyapunov function $U(x)$ in Eq. (5.49). In particular, because the aggregate utility is maximized, the system achieves proportional fairness, where

$$\sum_{r \in R} \frac{x_r - x_r^*}{x_r^*} \leq 0 \qquad (5.55)$$

for any other vector of transmission rates x that is different from the optimal solution x^*. Proportional fairness states that the aggregate of the proportional changes for using the nonoptimal solution x is nonpositive, thus indicating that there is no net gain (in terms of total proportional change) from using the alternative solution. More intuitively, proportional fairness says that a connection achieves a transmission rate in proportion to the number of network links that it requires.

Further Congestion Control Algorithms.   The concept of optimizing an entire network, where each source has a utility function U_r which the source uses to evaluate its own benefit from achieving a transmission rate x_r, is a general formulation that allows us to consider many other congestion control algorithms that have dynamics that differ from that of TCP NewReno or SACK [220, 244]. For example, Vegas is another version of TCP, which monitors the round-trip time and adjusts the window size so that only a small number of packets are buffered by nodes along the path of the TCP connection. TCP Vegas optimizes the aggregate utility in which individual sources have utility functions $U_r^V = \alpha_r d_r \log x_r$, where α_r is a threshold parameter used by Vegas and d_r is the round-trip propagation delay of the TCP connection [221]. Experimental results have shown that Vegas achieves higher throughput than TCP NewReno or SACK, while at the same time experiencing lower losses. Analysis of a system of TCP Vegas connections shows that the protocol achieves weighted proportional fairness. This shows that the system optimization approach can be used to give qualitative results on the performance of future congestion control protocols.

5.4 FURTHER READING

Further understanding of the models described in this chapter can be gained from the following references:

- Periodic model [237]

- Detailed packet loss model [256]

- Stochastic model with general loss process [48]

- Control system model [243]

- Network system model [198]

- Markov chain (not discussed in this chapter) analysis of TCP can be found in

    - TCP Tahoe (without Fast Retransmit) [336]
    - TCP Reno (with Fast Retransmit/Fast Recovery) [337]

- TCP Tahoe, OldTahoe, Reno, OldReno [338]

- TCP SACK, Vegas [339]

Existing congestion control algorithms in TCP are not optimized. An exposition on optimization of TCP using feedback control theory can be found in [159, 295, 296]. The objectives of this optimization are to minimize the oscillations in buffer occupancy and maximize the utilization of available bandwidth.

Development of congestion control models for networks providing differentiated services is an active research area. Yeom and Reddy [328] extend the detailed packet-loss model presented in Section 5.3.2 [256] to model the performance of TCP operating within the context of Differentiated Services (DiffServ) networks. These models estimate TCP throughput in terms of the contract rate in a service-level agreement, the packet-drop rate and the round-trip time. Details on DiffServ and other control mechanisms to guarantee quality of service in TCP/IP networks can be found in [187].

The rationale and development of TCP-friendly congestion control algorithms are described in [144].

Web sites that contain further material on TCP modeling include:

- Frank Kelly's page on a self-managed Internet:

  `http://www.statslab.cam.ac.uk/~frank/int/`

- Sally Floyd's page on TCP development:

  `http://www.icir.org/floyd/tcp_small.html`

- Jitendra Padhye's collection of TCP modeling references:

  `http://www.icir.org/padhye/tcp-model.html`

- Mark Allman's collection of TCP/IP research papers:

  `http://tcpsat.lerc.nasa.gov/tcpsat/papers.html`

- The TCP page from DMOZ, the Open Directory Project:

  `http://dmoz.org/Computers/Internet/Protocols/Transmission_Protocols/TCP/`

- The TCP-friendly web site:

  `http://www.psc.edu/networking/tcp_friendly.html` (has a number of direct and indirect links to many publications on TCP modeling and variations of the original TCP-friendly algorithm).

5.5 SUMMARY

This completes our tour of TCP models. In this chapter, we have considered a number of TCP models with varying degrees of complexity and generality. In particular, all models have included the essential dynamics of current TCP implementations; however, each model has revealed a different aspect with regard to the performance of the protocol. While we progressed from model to model in such a way as to learn more about TCP, each model has its place and the choice of a particular model depends on the application at hand. What this chapter has shown is that modeling TCP can be achieved without much analytical difficulty and is an interesting subject to pursue.

5.6 REVIEW QUESTIONS

1. What can we achieve with TCP modeling that cannot be achieved with measurement and simulation? Give examples.
2. This chapter stated that TCP was not designed using optimization. What were the objectives in developing the suite of TCP protocols? What would be the key steps if TCP were designed based on a process of optimization, and what possible difference would be observed with the resulting protocol?
3. What are the essential features of TCP that models of the protocol need to include?
4. What is the *inverse square-root p* law?
5. In the periodic model described in Section 5.3.1, Eq. (5.4) was derived based on a multiplicative decrease factor of 2. Derive the average sending rate formula assuming a multiplicative decrease factor of 4.
6. A TCP connection between Paris and Melbourne has an average round-trip time of 330 ms and a timeout period of 500 ms, and the receiving station limits the window size to 32 pkts. What is a good estimate of the sending rate for the TCP source, if:

   (a) the packet loss probability is 0.005?
   (b) the packet loss probability drops to 10^{-4}?
   (c) the packet loss probability increases to 0.2?

7. Show that a good approximation to the sending rate of a TCP source with round-trip time RTT, initial timeout period $T0$, and packet loss probability p is

$$\overline{X}(p) \approx \frac{1}{RTT\sqrt{\frac{2p}{3}} + T0\min\left(1, 3\sqrt{\frac{3p}{8}}\right)p(1 + 32p^2)}$$

   when the window size is not limited by the receiver.

8. Using Eq. (5.35) for the TCP sending rate with a general loss process, show that with deterministic losses, where $R(k) = d^2$ for all k, the average sending rate is given by:

$$\overline{X} = \frac{1}{RTT}\sqrt{\frac{3}{2p}}$$

9. One definition of fairness is *max-min* fairness, where the aim is to maximize the bandwidth allocation to the user with the smallest bandwidth allocation. Instead, TCP can be well approximated as achieving proportional fairness, rather than max-min fairness. After considering the way max-main fairness is

defined, in what sense is TCP fair? Why is proportional fairness an appropriate definition for achieving an optimum network solution?

10. In weighted proportional fairness, fairness can be observed when the proportional change, $(x_r^* - x_r)/x_r$, for each connection is multiplied by a weight w_r. Explain how TCP Vegas achieves weighted proportional fairness. What is the weight w_r for TCP Vegas? (Hint: refer to [221]).

5.7 HANDS-ON PROJECTS

1. Using the *ns* simulator, develop a simulation model of a single TCP NewReno source attempting to transmit packets through a lossy link. Compare the throughput achieved by the source in the simulations with that predicted by the models described in this chapter. What effect do timeouts and receiver window limits have on the throughput?

2. Download a number of files, with a variety of file sizes, from web servers located around the globe and use tcpdump to determine the total number of losses experienced during the downloads and the average round-trip times of the connections. Calculate the throughput and compare it with theoretical throughput that would be achieved by the models described in this chapter. When is the throughput predicted most accurately by theory?

5.8 CASE STUDY: UNDERSTANDING FACTORS INFLUENCING TCP THROUGHPUT

The network administrator of WCORP has noticed that TCP achieves quite low throughput through the leased line between the Sydney and Melbourne offices—a concern that has also been raised by a number of the employees. Often, the throughput is as low as 38 Kb/s even when the network is lightly loaded, when people are used to throughputs on the order of 120 Kb/s. As a result, the network administrator has been considering what the cause of this low throughput might be.

Based on his theoretical understanding of TCP performance, the network administrator has identified three factors with regard to the performance of TCP: losses in the network, timeout values in the TCP implementation, and receiver window limits. Modifying TCP is not possible on Windows-based machines, but it is possible to modify the kernel on Linux machines. With regard to losses in the network, the network administrator can increase the RAM on the router located at each end of the leased line and allocate more memory to the transmission buffer. This has the side effect of increasing the round-trip time, though, when the buffer is close to being full.

Without necessarily taking the time to either simulate the network or adjust network parameters through trial and error, the network administrator compares the throughput predicted by inverse square-root p law in Eq. (5.4) and the complete model in Eq. (5.29) with the actual throughput achieved by TCP. He obtained the experimental data using tcpdump. After performing this comparison, the network administrator concludes that the losses occurring at the routers, when the transmission buffer overflows, are dominating the performance, and he increases the RAM on these machines from 64 MB to 256 MB. Most of the complaints subside, although the administrator now predicts that the receiver window limit of 20 packets will now dominate the throughput based on theoretical predictions. He modifies the Linux kernel on his machine so that the receiver window limit and the associated buffers in the TCP stack can now handle 30 packets, which further increases the throughput that his TCP connections achieve. This gives him a temporary solution if any particular Linux user finds that he or she is spending much time transferring large files and need to reduce the file transfer times.

C H A P T E R   6

TCP/IP Performance over Wireless Networks

CHAPTER OBJECTIVES

After completing this chapter, the reader should be able to:

- Gain a high-level overview of the most widely used wireless networks

- Understand how characteristics of wireless links adversely impact TCP performance

- Learn techniques to enhance TCP/IP performance over wireless networks

The current strong drive toward Internet access via mobile terminals makes the inclusion of wireless systems such as *Cellular Communications* (CC) and *Wireless Local Area Networks* (WLAN) into the mainstream Internet very desirable. CC and WLAN systems, however, raise a multitude of performance issues, because environmental conditions and terrestrial obstructions and reflections lead to high and unpredictable error rates. CC and WLAN systems mostly share the characteristics of traditional wireless systems (satellite and terrestrial microwave), such as high error rates. They also share some of the characteristics of wired systems, such as low physical layer propagation delays. As a result, to improve their performance, a synthesis of techniques for enhancing the performance of both wired and wireless links is required that also takes into account the requirements of the TCP/IP suite. In this chapter, we present the characteristics and performance limitations of various existing and emerging wireless systems and survey a wide range of approaches for enhancing TCP/IP performance over such links. Although mobility is inherently associated with CC systems, the additional problems that it causes, such as communication pauses whenever mobile devices move between cells, are covered in Chapter 7.

6.1 WIRELESS NETWORKS

In this section, we first review some of the generic characteristics of CC and WLAN systems and follow with a discussion of some specific wireless networking technologies.

6.1.1 Generic Characteristics

The *delivery delay* for a link-layer frame consists of *transmission delay*, that is, frame size divided by link speed; *propagation delay*, that is, the time the signal takes to cross the link; and *processing delay* at the sender and receiver. WLAN and CC links

---

Based on "TCP Performance Issues over Wireless Links" by George Xylomenos and George C. Polyzos, which appeared in *IEEE Communications Magazine*, April 2001. © 2001 IEEE.

have similar propagation delays to wired ones, which are much lower than those of satellite links. Unlike wired links, though, WLAN and CC links suffer from high error rates. In addition to active sources of interference, CC links are affected by atmospheric conditions and multipath fading caused by terrestrial obstructions such as buildings. CC and WLAN links also suffer from indoor multipath fading caused by furniture and people. Therefore, even without considering mobility, WLAN and CC error behavior can vary in a faster and more unpredictable manner than that of satellite links. Mitigating the adverse effects of interference is a complex task at the physical design level, and, in general, the trade-offs made reflect a system's usage requirements. In CC systems, considerable processing is required to reduce the high native error rate of the link, leading to significant processing delays. In WLAN systems, however, the native error rate is much lower, therefore, error recovery is usually left to higher protocol layers.

Depending on the intended application of a system, its link layer may offer either a private switched circuit service, typical in CC systems, or a shared, best-effort, connectionless service, typical in WLANs. To support TCP/IP, the link layer must (at least) encapsulate IP datagrams into link frames. If the native frame size is too small, then the link layer must also *transparently* fragment and reassemble IP datagrams. While minimalistic link layers are sufficient to isolate higher layers from low-level details in wired links, they may be insufficient for wireless links because of their meager performance. In voice telephony, random frame losses of 1% to 2% are considered reasonable as they do not cause audible speech degradation [192]. Because physical layer errors are usually clustered, randomization is achieved by interleaving and coding across several frames. Most Internet applications are not error-tolerant to that extent though; therefore, wireless losses impose additional error recovery requirements for higher protocol layers.

The traditional Internet approach is to delegate error control to higher (end-to-end) layers to allow each application to decide if it needs to incur the corresponding error recovery overhead. This is adequate for traditional links where losses due to errors are very rare. For error-prone wireless links, however, local (link-layer) error recovery can be faster and more adaptable to link characteristics. For this reason, voice-oriented CC systems offer a *nontransparent mode* that incorporates link-layer error recovery, in addition to their native *transparent mode*. Some packet-oriented WLAN systems similarly provide (optional) error recovery to reduce their error rates. Nontransparent services are not a panacea, however, because each error-intolerant application may require a different level of reliability. Furthermore, Internet protocols and applications that implement their own error recovery schemes may interact adversely with *link-layer* mechanisms. For example, the transport layer may retransmit delayed packets in parallel with the link layer, thus, wasting wireless link bandwidth [122].

6.1.2 Wireless Local Area Networks

A characteristic example of WLAN systems is the Lucent (originally NCR) Wave-LAN. The original system employed either direct sequence or frequency hopping, spread spectrum radios at the 900-MHz or 2.4-GHz frequency bands, offering a raw bit rate of 2 Mbps. A receive threshold mechanism was offered to isolate adjacent

WaveLAN networks, but no power control was provided [126]. Later versions of the WaveLAN supported multiple frequency bands to avoid interference between adjacent networks. The success of such WLAN systems prompted the *IEEE* to create the 802.11 standard for WLANs [115], which is basically an enhancement of the WaveLAN. Both the WaveLAN and the IEEE 802.11 offer an Ethernet-compatible interface to higher layers, that is, the same headers, checksums, and frame sizes are used, and a connectionless best-effort service is provided. These networks are broadcast-based, so native multicasting and broadcasting are available. The channel is shared using *Carrier Sense Multiple Access* (CSMA) for access control, that is, a potential transmitter *senses* the medium and waits for it to become silent before attempting transmission. Ethernet complements CSMA with *Collision Detection* (CD), where, if multiple transmitters start simultaneously, they detect the collision, abort their transmissions, and retry later. In wireless networks, collision detection is difficult to implement, as it requires simultaneous transmission and reception in the same band. Hence, the WaveLAN uses *Collision Avoidance* (CA), where transmitters wait for a random interval after the medium becomes idle before starting transmission. The transmitter that starts first seizes the medium and all others back off, thereby reducing the chance of collisions. If, however, a collision occurs, it is not detected and the corrupted frames are not retransmitted by CSMA/CA, thus appearing as losses to higher layers.

The 802.11 standard provides various enhancements over the original WaveLAN. To recover from wireless losses, including undetected collisions, transmitters may optionally ask for acknowledgments to retransmit transparently unacknowledged frames at the link layer. Acknowledgments are transmitted in a contention-free manner by using a reserved interval during which regular transmissions are prohibited. To reduce further contention delay, an operating mode is supported where a master host provides WLAN coordination, deciding who will transmit next. The original 802.11 standard specified radios working in the 2.4-GHz frequency band with 1- or 2-Mbps bit rates. Subsequently, two additional standardization projects were initiated to provide higher speeds. The 802.11a standard uses an entirely new physical layer in the 5-GHz frequency band, providing bit rates ranging between 6 and 54 Mbps. In contrast, the 802.11b standard was developed to increase bit rates over the existing physical layer and frequency band. Commercial 802.11b solutions provide either 5.5-Mbps or 11-Mbps bit rates, using the 2.4-GHz frequency band. WLAN systems can be interconnected with wired networks by using either a router equipped with both wired and wireless interfaces or a transparent bridge, thereby providing connectivity at the network or at the link layer, respectively.

The transmission and propagation delays for WLANs are low because of the short range and high bandwidth of these systems. Total delivery delay, however, is unpredictable because of contention, as in wired Ethernet. The WaveLAN system in particular is robust in the presence of narrowband interference and obstructions within its operating range (up to 500 feet) [124]. Typical frame loss rates are less than 2.5% using maximum-sized frames (1500 bytes). Interference problems can be caused by other spread spectrum devices and wireless networks operating nearby [126]. Because of timing differences in the firmware and hardware of desktop and laptop interfaces, their throughput is not symmetric [253]. Host processing power also affects throughput and frame loss rates between heterogeneous hosts.

Synchronization may lead to excessive collisions during bidirectional communication, which, as they go undetected, must be recovered at higher layers [321].

6.1.3   Cellular Communications Networks

Second-generation CC systems are digital, unlike first-generation systems, which were analog. They are characterized by modest bit rates and circuit mode operation, using either time division (GSM and IS-136) or code division (IS-95) multiple access to share the medium. Digital CC links carry small frames that may contain either encoded voice or data. Compared to WLANs, CC systems exhibit higher transmission and propagation delays because of the lower bit rates and longer distances involved. The outdoor CC environment is also harsher, with multipath fading caused by buildings and hills, leading to high error rates. Because of the real-time requirements of voice telephony, *Forward Error Correction* (FEC) information is added to each frame, allowing damaged frames to be recovered without retransmissions. Bit errors caused by fading are usually bursty; therefore, bits from multiple consecutive frames are interleaved before transmission to evenly spread the error bursts and increase the probability of successful recovery. Interleaving increases the processing delay for each frame but manages to reduce the frame loss rate to a level of 1% to 2% [192], which is not detrimental to voice quality as long as it appears to be random.

Digital CC systems are interconnected to other networks using an *Interworking Function* (IWF) [31], located at the boundary of the CC system. To interface with analog telephony networks, the IWF converts analog waveforms to digital data and vice versa. To interface with digital telephony networks, the IWF performs rate adaptations and frame conversions, because even though both networks are digital, their implementations differ. To directly interoperate with packet data networks such as the Internet, the IWF may also serve as a gateway, as shown in Figure 6.1. In this configuration, the wireless host and the IWF communicate via a base station, which simply relays frames between the two. A *Radio Link Protocol* (RLP) is used between the wireless host and the IWF, offering IP datagram segmentation and reassembly [192]. As a result, the wireless host may exchange IP datagrams with any host on the Internet, using the IWF for routing purposes. The RLP may also provide error recovery to hide wireless losses from the Internet [251].

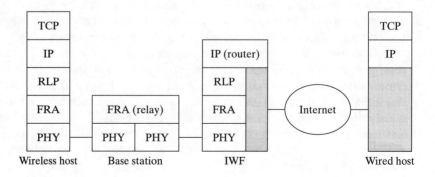

FIGURE 6.1: Connectivity between CC systems and the Internet.

TABLE 6.1: Summary of CC system characteristics.

System	Data Rate	Radio Link Protocol Scheme	Access Scheme
GSM	9.6 Kbps	Selective Repeat ARQ	TDMA
IS-136	9.6 Kbps	Frame Transmission Order ARQ	TDMA
IS-95	8.6 Kbps	Limited Retransmission ARQ	CDMA

GSM offers 9.6 Kbps full-rate channels. The nontransparent mode RLP uses an *Automatic Repeat reQuest* (ARQ) scheme with 240 bit frames. It is a standard sliding window scheme with Selective Repeat, that is, only frames that are actually lost are retransmitted. The RLP causes the native bit error rate of 10^{-3} to be reduced to 10^{-8} at the expense of variable throughput and delay caused by retransmissions [31]. GSM extensions, discussed later in this chapter, provide higher bandwidth services over the same air interface. IS-136 supports 9.6 Kbps full-rate channels. The nontransparent mode RLP uses an advanced ARQ scheme with 256 bit frames. Each frame separately acknowledges multiple consecutive frames by using a bit map to show which frames have been received. Because the link preserves the frame transmission sequence, when a frame is acknowledged we can safely assume that all unacknowledged frames transmitted before it must have been lost. The problem is that because of retransmissions the actual frame transmission order may differ from the original frame sequence. In the IS-136 RLP, the sender keeps track of the exact order of original frame transmissions and retransmissions; therefore, it can correctly determine which unacknowledged frames are lost when a new acknowledgment arrives [251].

IS-95 supports 8.6 Kbps full-rate channels. The nontransparent mode RLP uses 172 bit frames [192]. Network layer packets are first encapsulated into variable size frames with separate error detection checksums and then segmented into *fixed-size* RLP frames. This combines the convenience of variable-sized packets with the efficient error recovery of fixed-size frames. Only negative acknowledgments are used to reduce control overhead. Frames not received after a few retransmissions are dropped; therefore, this scheme trades reliability for limited-delay variance. The residual packet loss rate is 10^{-4}. A higher layer protocol can provide additional recovery if required. RLP recovery delay in CC systems is added to the delay caused by interleaving and FEC coding. Table 6.1 summarizes the main characteristics of second-generation digital CC systems.

6.2   TCP PERFORMANCE ISSUES OVER WIRELESS LINKS

In this section, we discuss the TCP performance issues raised by the high transmission error rates in wireless links. We first explain the fundamental problem caused by transmission errors, followed by detailed discussions of TCP performance in WLAN and CC systems.

6.2.1   Inappropriate Reduction of Congestion Window

Transmission errors are the primary source of performance problems for TCP applications in wireless networks. While a few errors per packet may be corrected by low-level FEC codes, more errors may lead to packet corruption. Corrupted packets are discarded without being handed over to TCP, which assumes that these packets were lost. Because TCP takes packet loss as a sign of network congestion, it reacts to these losses by reducing its congestion window. In most cases, wireless transmission errors are not related to network congestion; thus, these inappropriate reductions of the congestion window lead to unnecessary throughput losses for TCP applications. The resulting throughput degradation can be very severe, depending on factors such as the distance between the sender and the receiver and the bandwidth of the communication path. In the following subsections, we discuss TCP throughput losses in the WLAN and CC environments.

6.2.2   Throughput Loss in WLANs

The WaveLAN suffers from a *Frame Error Rate* (FER) of 1.55% with clustered losses when transmitting 1400-byte frames over an 85-foot distance [253]. Reducing the frame size by 300 bytes halves the measured FER but causes framing overhead to consume a larger fraction of the bandwidth. In shared medium WLANs, forward TCP traffic (data) contends with reverse traffic (acknowledgments). In the WaveLAN, this can lead to undetected collisions that significantly increase the FER visible to higher layers [321]. File transfer tests over a WaveLAN with a nominal bandwidth of 1.6 Mbps achieved a throughput of only 1.25 Mbps [253]. This 22% throughput reduction caused by a FER of only 1.55% is caused by the frequent invocations of congestion control mechanisms which repeatedly reduce TCP's transmission rate. If errors were uniformly distributed rather than clustered, throughput would increase to 1.51 Mbps [253]. This is consistent with other experiments showing that TCP performs worse with clustered losses, as multiple losses within the same transmission window may cause TCP to resort to (slow) timeout initiated recovery [139].

To illustrate the deterioration of TCP performance caused by wireless errors, Table 6.2 shows TCP throughput over a LAN path, consisting of a single WLAN, versus a WAN path, consisting of a single WLAN plus 15 wired links [58]. We show throughput in the absence of any losses, the actual throughput achieved when the WLAN suffers from independent frame losses at a FER of 2.3% for 1400-byte frames, and the percentage of the nominal bandwidth that was achieved. In the WAN case, this percentage is half of that in the LAN case. Because TCP recovers from errors via end-to-end retransmissions, recovery is slower in high delay paths. Table 6.3 shows the nominal bandwidth and actual TCP throughput measured over a single link path, using either an IEEE 802.11 WLAN or an IEEE 802.11b WLAN. The percentages here show that the high-speed link is affected more by losses. Because TCP drastically reduces its throughput after each loss, it takes longer to reach the peak throughput supported by higher speed links.

TABLE 6.2: TCP throughput over LAN and WAN connections.

Connection	Nominal Bandwidth	Actual TCP Throughput	% Achieved
LAN	1.5 Mbps	0.70 Mbps	46.66
WAN	1.35 Mbps	0.31 Mbps	22.96

TABLE 6.3: TCP throughput over IEEE 802.11 LAN connections.

LAN Type	Nominal Bandwidth	Actual TCP Throughput	% Achieved
IEEE 802.11	2 Mbps	0.98 Mbps	49
IEEE 802.11b	11 Mbps	4.3 Mbps	39.1

6.2.3 Throughput Loss in Cellular Communication Systems

CC links in transparent (voice) mode suffer from a residual FER of 1% to 2%, after low-level error recovery, despite their short frames [192]. For example, a full-rate IS-95 link would segment a 1400-byte IP datagram into 68 frames. Assuming independent frame errors, the probability of a successful packet transmission is 50.49% at a FER of 1%. Frame errors are less bursty than bit errors, because multiple frames are bit interleaved before transmission. Although this process reduces the loss rate and randomizes frame errors, thus avoiding audible speech degradation, it considerably increases processing delay because of interleaving before transmission and deinterleaving after reception. If we reduce the size of IP datagrams to reduce the packet-loss probability, user data throughput also decreases because of the higher TCP/IP header overhead. TCP/IP header compression may be used over slow CC links, shrinking TCP/IP headers to 3 to 5 bytes [180]. Header compression, however, may adversely interact with TCP error recovery and link-layer resets, leading to a loss of synchronization between the compressor and the decompressor, thus causing entire windows of TCP data to be dropped [226].

Although the RLP used in the nontransparent mode of GSM usually manages to recover from wireless losses before TCP timers expire [226], it exhibits high and widely varying RTT values. Measurements using ping over a GSM network in San Francisco showed that 95% of the RTT values were around 600 ms with a standard deviation equivalent to 20 ms [225]. Our measurements with ping over GSM networks in Oulu, Helsinki, and Berlin produced similar results but with higher standard deviations. Large file transfer experiments, however, reveal that RTT can be occasionally much higher with real applications over operational networks, reaching values of up to 12 seconds. Figure 6.2 shows our RTT measurements from a commercial GSM network in a typical urban environment (Oulu, Finland) during a file transfer session. These RTT values consist of processing time, the 2×150 ms delay of the GSM channel, plus 250 to 1250 ms and 35 ms to transmit a packet and its acknowledgment, respectively. Our research confirms the observations of other researchers in that high latency seems to be caused by interleaving, rate adaptation, buffering, and interfacing between GSM network elements [225].

Increasing the size of the TCP *Maximum Transfer Unit* (MTU) not only reduces TCP/IP header overhead, thus improving bulk transfer throughput, but also increases the response time of interactive applications. For example, transmission of a 1500-byte IP datagram over GSM takes around 1.25 seconds, which is unacceptable for interactive applications. Measurements over operational GSM networks show that TCP throughput is optimized for a MTU size of approximately 700 bytes (690 bytes in [224], 720 bytes in our experiments). Our measurements also show that TCP over GSM suffers from occasional interruptions lasting for 6 to 12 seconds,

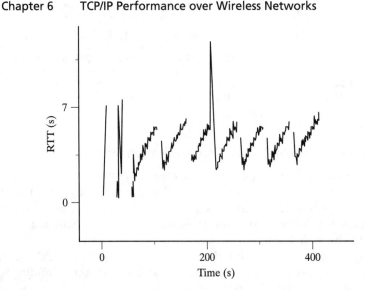

FIGURE 6.2: TCP RTT behavior over GSM.

caused by RLP-level disruptions lasting for a couple of seconds. Analysis of this problem suggests that some IP datagrams are buffered and later released out of sequence, a phenomenon that appears in full-scale, operational GSM networks but is rarely simulated or encountered in small-test networks.

Disruptions are also caused by link resets that occur when a RLP frame cannot be transmitted after a few retries or when a serious protocol violation occurs. This causes the sender and receiver sequence numbers to be reset and flushes all buffers, meaning that in practice the GSM RLP is *not* fully reliable. To reduce the number of resets, the maximum number of retransmissions (by default 6) can be increased during connection setup [226]. Throughput may also be increased by adapting the GSM RLP frame size. Although small, fixed-size frames simplify RLP operation and make it more robust in worst-case conditions, choosing a frame size appropriate for prevailing conditions can provide throughput improvements of 18% to 23%, depending on the radio environment [224].

When the end-to-end path includes multiple wireless links, for example, when two hosts on distinct wireless networks communicate via the Internet, losses accumulate accordingly. This leads to more frequent invocations of TCP congestion-control mechanisms, which, besides further reducing throughput, also cause wireless links to remain idle for prolonged periods of time, an important issue for circuit-switched CC links. Furthermore, when a TCP packet is lost after crossing some wireless links in the path, its retransmission has to cross them again, risking new losses and wasting wireless bandwidth. Losses have more pronounced effects on paths with higher end-to-end delay that require TCP to maintain large transmission windows to keep data flowing. On such paths, TCP also suffers from *spurious timeouts*, that is, timeouts that would be avoided if the sender waited longer for acknowledgments. In addition to the high and unpredictable delays caused by RLP error recovery, CC systems explicitly allow prolonged disconnections during handoffs, causing numerous spurious timeouts. A related problem, *spurious fast retransmits*, occurs when packets are reordered beyond the TCP duplicate acknowledgment threshold, an event that occasionally occurs with the GSM RLP.

6.3 IMPROVING TCP PERFORMANCE OVER WIRELESS LINKS

Many enhancements have been proposed to address TCP throughput problems over wireless links. In this section, we discuss some of the key approaches used by these enhancements.

6.3.1 Splitting TCP Connections

Because end-to-end retransmissions are slow over longer paths, TCP connections can be *split* at the wireless gateways connected to both wireless and wired links, as shown in Figure 6.3. In this manner, when packets are corrupted by transmission errors over the wireless link, they can be retransmitted over the wireless part of the path only. Indirect-TCP [55], also known as I-TCP, is a TCP enhancement scheme based on the split approach. In this scheme, a software agent at the wireless gateway intercepts TCP connection establishment messages and transparently decomposes the end-to-end connection into separate TCP connections for the wired and wireless parts of the path. The agent bridges these connections by forwarding TCP packets between the two. The connection over the wireless part has a lower delay, leading to faster TCP retransmissions, while the connection over the wired part remains unaware of wireless losses. TCP can also be replaced over the wireless part of the path by another transport protocol, providing improved error recovery [326].

The main drawback of the split approach is that it violates end-to-end TCP semantics, because an acknowledgment originating from the wireless gateway may reach the sender before the corresponding data packet reaches its destination. If the gateway crashes after the acknowledgment has been returned to the sender, but before the data packet has reached the receiver, the sender incorrectly assumes that the packet has reached its destination safely. Another issue with split schemes is that wireless gateways face significant overhead as packets must undergo TCP processing twice.

6.3.2 Snooping TCP at Base Stations

The Snoop TCP scheme has the same objective as split TCP, that is, to confine retransmissions over the wireless part of the path only. This is achieved by *snooping*

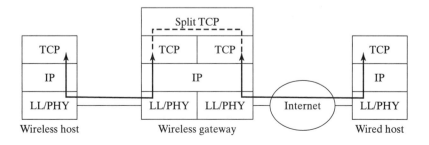

FIGURE 6.3: Operation of split TCP.

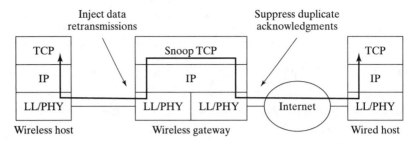

FIGURE 6.4: Operation of Snoop TCP.

inside TCP connections so as to transparently retransmit corrupted packets without breaking end-to-end TCP semantics [60]. In this scheme a Snoop agent maintains state for each TCP connection traversing the wireless gateway (Figure 6.4). TCP data packets sent from the wired to the wireless host are cached locally, until TCP acknowledgments from the wireless host verify that they were received. When duplicate acknowledgments arrive, indicating that a packet was lost, the packet is retransmitted by the agent from its local cache. The duplicate acknowledgments are then suppressed, that is, they are not propagated to the wired host, to avoid triggering end-to-end TCP retransmissions and congestion control. The agent also uses local timers to detect losses when duplicate acknowledgments themselves are lost. The agent *snoops* inside TCP packet headers to gather the state information it needs to avoid generating its own control messages.

Snoop outperforms split TCP schemes [58], without violating TCP semantics, because TCP itself remains unmodified. It also avoids conflicting local and TCP retransmissions [122] by suppressing duplicate TCP acknowledgments whenever it performs local error recovery. With Snoop, however, only the direction of transfer from the wired to the wireless host benefits from local error recovery, as the TCP receiver is implicitly expected to be located next to the wireless gateway. This is because Snoop relies on TCP acknowledgments to detect whether a packet was received or lost, which are returned very fast when the agent and the TCP receiver are on either side of the wireless link. If a wireless host is sending data to a remote receiver though, TCP acknowledgments are returned too late, and they may even signify congestion losses over a wired link. As a result, Snoop is most profitable when nearly all data flow from the wired toward the wireless host.

6.3.3 Notifying the Causes of Packet Loss

As we discussed earlier, the main reason for degraded TCP performance over wireless links is that TCP cannot determine whether a packet was lost because of transmission errors or because of congestion. *Explicit Loss Notification* (ELN) [57] is a scheme that enables TCP to distinguish between corruption- and congestion-induced losses, thus allowing the sender to properly react in each case. Whenever an agent at the wireless gateway, such as the Snoop agent, detects a noncongestion-related loss, it sets an ELN bit in subsequent TCP headers and propagates it to the receiver, which echoes it back to the sender. The agent uses queue-length information to heuristically distinguish congestion from wireless errors. When receiving an ELN notification, the TCP sender at the wireless host retransmits the lost packet without invoking congestion control.

If a significant amount of data originates from the wireless host, as in interactive applications, the ELN scheme can considerably improve performance. This scheme works well in conjunction with Snoop TCP, because both schemes are required to perform local retransmission in both directions over the wireless link. However, because lost packets can only be retransmitted after a round-trip time has elapsed when an acknowledgment with the ELN bit set is returned, error recovery is slow compared to Snoop TCP. Although ELN is applicable to most topologies, it requires modifications to the transport layers of remote wired hosts, in addition to the agents at wireless gateways.

6.3.4   Adding Selective Acknowledgments to TCP

When multiple packets are lost in the same transmission window, the sender can only infer the first packet that was lost from the duplicate acknowledgments returned. After retransmitting the lost packet, the sender must wait for new duplicate acknowledgments to be returned to detect the next lost packet. As a result, TCP can only recover from a single loss per RTT [139]. Wireless links may frequently corrupt multiple packets per window, leading to high-error recovery delays, especially over high-delay paths.

The *Selective Acknowledgment* (SACK) option for TCP allows each acknowledgment to specify, in addition to the last packet received in sequence, up to three contiguous blocks of data that have been received beyond this packet [236]. The sender can, thus, infer which packets have been lost after the last packet acknowledged and retransmit them without waiting for additional duplicate acknowledgments. TCP with the SACK option may be used either end-to-end or only over the wireless part of a split TCP connection, significantly improving throughput in both cases [58]. In the end-to-end case recovery remains quite slow over high-delay paths, because the SACK option cannot speed up individual retransmissions. The TCP SACK option is discussed in more detail in Chapter 11.

6.3.5   Summary and Comparison of Enhancement Schemes

To assess the TCP enhancement schemes discussed here, we must consider the following factors:

- **End-to-end semantics.** A reliable transport protocol must provide true end-to-end semantics, that is, acknowledgments must absolutely certify that data packets have reached their destination safely. It is, therefore, crucial for an enhancement scheme to preserve the end-to-end semantics of TCP.

- **IP payload access.** Schemes that require the wireless gateway to access the payload of IP datagrams violate the layering principle. Furthermore, when IPSEC is used for secure communications, the IP payload is encrypted by the end hosts; thus, it is not visible to intermediate nodes.

- **Wireless gateway overhead.** While TCP enhancement schemes may require cooperation from the wireless gateway, they should keep the corresponding

TABLE 6.4: Comparison of TCP enhancements for wireless links.

Enhancement Scheme	End-to-End Semantics	IP Payload Access	Wireless Gateway Overhead	Ease of Deployment
Split TCP	No	Yes	High	Not easy
Snoop TCP	Yes	Yes	High	Not easy
ELN	Yes	Yes	Low	Not easy
SACK	Yes	No	None	Easy

overhead to a minimum. Schemes that require state maintenance for each TCP connection do not scale well for large networks.

- **Ease of deployment.** Schemes that require modifications to existing infrastructure, for example, wired servers and wireless gateways, are not easy to deploy.

Table 6.4 compares the TCP enhancements discussed previously against these factors. With the exception of the SACK option, which is already being deployed but only provides minor improvements, no enhancement scores well in all areas. This implies that we must always make a trade-off between these factors. Which factor should take precedence over the rest depends on the networking scenario. For example, if a TCP enhancement solution is needed for a private financial transaction network, then modifications in the existing infrastructure may not be a serious obstacle, while preservation of end-to-end semantics may be of prime importance because of high-reliability requirements.

6.4   WIRELESS SYSTEM EVOLUTION AND TCP/IP

As wireless networks continue to evolve, TCP/IP performance will remain an important issue. In this section we briefly describe the evolutionary paths of CC and WLAN systems and discuss the future of TCP/IP in the forthcoming wireless era.

6.4.1   Trends in Cellular Communication Systems

The trend for CC systems is to provide higher bit rates and better support for packet-data services to become more attractive for Internet access. To leverage existing infrastructure, second-generation CC systems (e.g., GSM) will be extended to support higher bit rate applications. In GSM each frequency band is shared via *Time Division Multiple Access* (TDMA), with each TDMA frame consisting of eight slots, that is, each frequency band supports eight GSM circuits. The *High Speed Circuit Switched Data* (HSCSD) system is an extension of GSM providing bit rates of up to 56 Kbps. HSCSD reserves multiple slots per frame, in effect multiplexing several GSM circuits into a high-speed logical circuit. The *General Packet Radio Service* (GPRS) system is a packet-switched extension of GSM [190]. GPRS *dynamically* reserves multiple slots per frame to send data packets at a high speed, thus allowing the channel to be shared by multiple wireless hosts. As a result, GPRS enables wireless hosts to be constantly attached to the Internet, at a fraction of the cost of a dedicated CC circuit. GPRS also supports multiple physical layer encoding schemes, providing user bit rates of up to 160 Kbps, depending on radio conditions. The actual bit rate available also depends on the capabilities of the wireless host, that is, how many slots per frame it can handle. Early experiments and simulations show that Internet packet-loss rates over GPRS are around 2%.

Higher speeds will eventually be offered by the next generation of CC systems. The *Enhanced Data Rates for GSM Evolution* (EDGE) system is an extension of GSM that has also been adopted as an extension of IS-136. The EDGE system provides an evolutionary path to third-generation networks, offering speeds of 384 Kbps or more [150]. The third-generation European CC system, *Universal Mobile Telecommunications Services* (UMTS), is based on *Wideband Code Division Multiple Access* (W-CDMA), supporting both circuit and packet switched modes at various bit rates [117]. Phase one includes services similar to GPRS, providing bit rates of up to 384 Kbps in the wide area. The W-CDMA scheme allows the bit rate to be varied, depending on user requirements and radio conditions, with forthcoming phases promising bit rates of up to 2 Mbps in the local area. By increasing the number of radio cells in a given area, more bandwidth can be allocated to each user, but the cost of the radio infrastructure increases proportionately. As a result, the highest data rates will only be offered within limited areas where the cost of providing these reduced size *microcells* will be justifiable, for example, in densely populated areas. Sparsely populated areas, however, will be covered by terrestrial or satellite systems using very large cells, or *macrocells*.

6.4.2   Trends in Wireless LAN Systems

The trend for WLAN systems is to provide higher speeds and support for mobility between adjacent networks, with each network essentially becoming a microcell. An extensive amount of work has also been performed toward developing more efficient *Medium Access Control* (MAC) protocols for shared access WLANs [93]. A multitude of very short range (in room) systems, or *Personal Area Networks* (PANs), have been designed for low bit rates. The coverage area of a PAN is commonly referred to as a *picocell*. Bluetooth is a spread spectrum system providing bit rates of up to 1 Mbps within its operating range of a few meters [103]. It provides connectivity between diverse wireless devices that may dynamically enter and leave the PAN. Its TCP performance should be similar to low-end WLANs. The IEEE 802.15 project, which specifies a PAN standard based (partially) on Bluetooth, is working on its radio link level interoperability with IEEE 802.11. For very high speeds, the *Local Multipoint Distribution Service* (LMDS) will offer broadband wireless Internet access using the 28 or 40 GHz frequency bands, with an operating range of 1 to 3 kilometers. LMDS is a Wireless Local Loop system providing 1 to 2 GHz of bandwidth to *fixed* hosts. LMDS uses powerful link layer coding schemes, and investigations show that it can reliably carry TCP traffic [230].

6.4.3   TCP/IP over Heterogeneous Wireless Systems

The design of each wireless system reflects specific trade-offs between infrastructure cost, data rate, and coverage area. Because of the diversity of existing and future application requirements, we expect that, at least for the foreseeable future, multiple such systems will coexist. The key characteristic underlying both existing and emerging wireless systems is support for the TCP/IP protocol suite, which will allow them to communicate with each other by becoming part of the Internet. The next step is to provide direct interoperability between wireless systems by allowing users to transparently move not only between cells within the same system but also from one system to another. This would enable users to dynamically select the system best suited to their requirements, among those available in their present location. The result could be unified *hierarchical* cellular systems, with large cells being overlaid by multiple smaller cells in areas with high user densities [195].

Hierarchical cellular systems must be carefully designed to avoid increasing the gravity of handoff-induced problems. The small size of microcells will lead to more frequent handoffs, while their high data rates may potentially lead to increased losses during each handoff. Furthermore, handoffs between overlaid cells may also dramatically change the performance of underlying wireless links, leading to considerable variations in the characteristics of end-to-end paths. While the performance difference between a microcell and a macrocell cannot be masked by either link or transport layer mechanisms, cooperation between layers could enable higher layers to better adapt their behavior to lower layer capabilities. The emerging concept of *software radios* that allow the configuration of physical and link layer parameters in real time [172] is expected to further promote link adaptivity; hence, protocol adaptivity will become even more critical in the future.

Intensive research has been directed toward adaptive link layers that provide information to higher layers in an orderly fashion to support network-independent adaptivity mechanisms at higher layers. The *Multi Service Link Layer* (MSLL) approach provides multiple link services to higher layers, with each one serving the requirements of a particular class of applications [322]. The *Wireless Internet NEtwork* (WINE) project is also studying protocol adaptivity and link-dependent configuration to optimize IP performance over wireless links without exposing lower layer details to TCP. A protocol enhancing proxy approach has been developed, the *Wireless Adaptation Layer* (WAL), to handle automatic adaptivity. Both schemes export standardized link performance metrics to facilitate the operation of adaptive higher layer protocols.

6.5 FURTHER READING

A good coverage of wireless network architectures can be found in [219, 285]. End-to-end TCP semantics can be preserved in Split TCP schemes by synchronizing the acknowledgments between the two connections [231]. This, however, exposes the recovery delays of the wireless part of the path to the other side, which adapts its transmission rate accordingly, thus reducing throughput.

During periods of persistent losses, TCP timeouts can be avoided if an agent at the wireless gateway *chokes* the TCP sender by transparently closing the receiver's advertised window [75]. The sender then freezes all pending timers and enters the *persist* mode, where it periodically probes the receiver's window without reducing its transmission rate.

The spurious timeouts and fast retransmissions caused by delayed lower layer retransmissions and packet reordering in wireless links can be avoided by using the TCP timestamp option in outgoing packets and echoing these timestamps in the corresponding acknowledgments. This allows spurious timeouts and fast retransmissions to be easily avoided without changing TCP semantics [223].

Many link layer schemes have been proposed to improve TCP performance over wireless links [127, 224, 226]. These schemes provide a more reliable link to higher protocol layers. Xylomenos and Polyzos [322] have shown that TCP unaware link-layer schemes can considerably outperform Snoop TCP when both communicating hosts are wireless or when most data flow from a wireless to a wired host.

6.6   SUMMARY

The performance of the TCP/IP protocol suite over Cellular Communications and Wireless Local Area Network systems is far from satisfactory because of their relatively high error rates. TCP throughput decreases dramatically even at modest error rates because of its assumption that all losses are caused by congestion that leads to drastic reductions of its transmission rate after wireless losses. These performance problems are more pronounced with higher speed wireless links and longer end-to-end paths. There exist a wide variety of performance enhancement schemes that either modify TCP to recover better from wireless losses or provide link-layer error recovery to hide these losses from TCP. Wireless system evolution is headed toward higher data rates and the coexistence of heterogeneous systems. It seems that to tackle the challenges of emerging wireless architectures we need improved cooperation between protocol layers that will enable each layer to adapt better to the fast changing wireless environment of the future.

6.7   REVIEW QUESTIONS

1. The IEEE 802.11 WLAN standard and most CC system RLPs support link-layer acknowledgments and retransmissions for error recovery. Are there any applications with you that would not want to use these options?

2. The CSMA/CA access protocol does not detect collisions as CSMA/CD does. How does this limitation affect link-layer and transport-layer performance?

3. The IS-136 RLP assumes that if a frame is acknowledged, all frames that were transmitted earlier but are still unacknowledged must have been lost. Why TCP cannot do the same?

4. Why is TCP performance more affected by losses over high-delay and high-speed network paths?

5. Which are the main factors leading to TCP throughput degradations over wireless links?

6. With some Split TCP schemes, a data packet can be acknowledged without first reaching its destination. Why is this a problem?

7. Why can TCP without Selective Acknowledgments only recover from a single packet loss per round trip time?

8. Why does Snoop suppress the duplicate TCP acknowledgments it receives after retransmitting lost packets?

6.8 HANDS-ON PROJECTS

1. Implement Snoop TCP, I-TCP, and TCP with ELN in the freely available *ns*-2 simulator. Conduct simulation experiments to measure and compare TCP performance using these three schemes. Write a report describing your results.

2. Implement Snoop TCP, I-TCP, and TCP with ELN in the freely available FreeBSD operating system. Build a wireless test bed, and conduct experiments to measure and compare TCP performance using these three schemes. Write a report comparing your experimental results with those you obtained using the *ns*-2 simulator.

3. Explain how ELN helps TCP distinguish corruption from congestion-induced losses. What sort of modifications are required at the TCP level to implement ELN?

4. Table 6.4 compares four approaches addressing TCP performance problems over wireless networks. Present application scenarios where some approaches are considered more suitable than the others.

6.9 CASE STUDY: WCORP INSTALLS WIRELESS LANS

To support indoor mobility, WCORP installed wireless LANs (WLANs) in its Sydney office. While the wireless access greatly facilitated Internet access in seminar and meeting rooms, users of WLANs complained about network performance. In particular, the users noticed that file downloads took much longer when a WLAN was used. The network administrator measured the file download times for three typical file sizes over both wired Ethernet and wireless LANs during peak traffic hours. The 15 Kb file represents HTML Web pages, the 150 Kb file represents compressed image objects, and the 1.5 Mb file represents compressed video objects. Table 6.5 shows the average file download times derived from 10 experiments. It was really interesting to see that for large files, download time was 50% higher with a WLAN.

After considering several options from Table 6.4, the administrator decided to use TCP with Selective Acknowledgments (SACK) to combat the file download problem over WLANs. TCP SACK is known to speed up TCP recovery when multiple segments in the same transmission window are lost, a case commonly observed over wireless links. Another reason for selecting TCP SACK was its availability in the existing TCP/IP infrastructure at WCORP. The only action needed

TABLE 6.5: Comparison of file download times between wired Ethernet and WLAN.

File Size	Download Time (sec)	
	Wired Ethernet	**WLAN**
15 Kb	3	5
150 Kb	25	40
1.5 Mb	120	239

TABLE 6.6: Improvement on file download times with TCP SACK.

| File Size | Download Time with WLAN (sec) | |
	Traditional TCP	TCP SACK
15 Kb	5	4
150 Kb	40	32
1.5 Mb	239	170

to implement this solution was to turn the SACK option on in the TCP/IP stacks. After configuring TCP with the SACK option, another round of measurements was conducted to assess the impact of this change on performance. Table 6.6 compares file download times before and after the SACK option was configured. Although file download times are still higher than those in a wired network, the administrator was delighted to see a considerable improvement over the past WLAN results. The users now seem to be happy to pay a small performance price for the mobility and ease of use they enjoy with the wireless LANs.

C H A P T E R 7

TCP/IP Performance over Mobile Networks

CHAPTER OBJECTIVES

After completing this chapter, the reader should be able to:

- Explain the characteristics of mobile networks

- Understand specific issues concerning TCP performance degradation caused by mobility

- Learn techniques to address TCP performance problems caused by mobility

While the ability to remain connected to the Internet even when mobile is obviously attractive to an Internet user, it also severely exposes the limitations at the different layers of the current Internet's TCP/IP suite, which was designed for a primarily static environment. In this chapter, we illustrate the key impacts of mobility on the TCP and discuss several approaches that have been proposed to improve TCP's performance.

7.1 CELLULAR AND AD HOC NETWORKS

We use two models, cellular and ad hoc, to explain the mobile networks. These two models exhibit different characteristics and, hence, have an impact on TCP in different ways. Figure 7.1 illustrates these two networking models. A cellular network consists of a collection of mobile hosts served by a central coordinating entity called the base station. The base station arbitrates the channel allocation between the mobile hosts. Mobile hosts communicate directly and only with the base station. If the source and destination are within the same cell, the base station acts as a one-hop relay between the two end nodes. However, if the destination is not within the same cell as the source (or vice versa), the base station forwards packets from the source to a backbone distribution network (or vice versa), which then routes the packets to the destination.

In ad hoc networks, mobile hosts establish a network without the aid of a backbone infrastructure. Sources and destinations communicate with each other through multi hop paths consisting of peer stations in the network; thus, the mobile hosts play the additional role of routers in the ad hoc network model. Ad hoc networks typically employ distributed protocols for medium access control (MAC) (e.g., IEEE 802.11 [121], MACA [191], MACAW [66], etc.) and routing (e.g., DSR [73], AODV [269], ZRP [156], etc.).

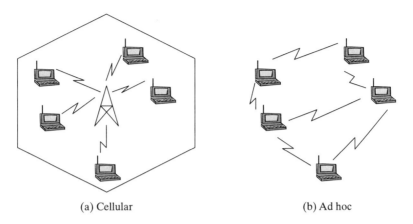

(a) Cellular   (b) Ad hoc

FIGURE 7.1: Cellular and ad hoc networks.

7.2 TCP PERFORMANCE IN CELLULAR NETWORKS

In this section, we analyze the key TCP performance issues in the cellular environments. Before we do so, we provide a brief introduction to the Mobile IP scheme, which extends the traditional IP to support user mobility in cellular environment.

7.2.1 Mobile IP

Mobile IP is the Internet Engineering Task Force (IETF) standard to support mobility in the IP-based Internet [78]. While there have been several other approaches proposed thereafter, most of the approaches are mere extensions of the basic Mobile IP model. Because Mobile IP is the standard used to support mobility of Internet users, its mechanisms have a direct impact on the performance of TCP connections when users migrate from one part of the Internet to another.

Entities. The basic entities involved in the Mobile IP operations are the mobile host (MH), the home network or the default network to which the mobile host is connected, the foreign network or the network to which the mobile host has migrated, and the static corresponding host (SH) with which the mobile host communicates. The Mobile IP aware entities in this setup include a home agent (HA) in the home network, and a foreign agent (FA) in the foreign network. The key requirements for the home agent and the foreign agent are that they should be fixed hosts and cannot be mobile. Figure 7.2 illustrates the aforementioned entities. We now present the basic set of operations in Mobile IP:

Operations.

1. When the MH moves from its home network to the foreign network, it first gets a foreign address in the foreign network. The MH registers with the HA in its home network, providing the HA with the foreign address. The HA maintains a table of the mappings between the home addresses of the different MH and their current foreign addresses. To prevent a malicious host from hijacking a

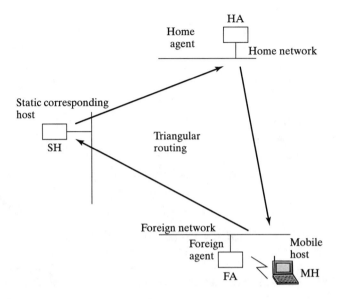

FIGURE 7.2: Mobile IP.

connection belonging to another host, Mobile IP uses a secure authentication protocol to verify each new registration request that comes in at the HA.

2. When an IP packet destined for MH arrives at the home network, the HA in the network receives the packet on behalf of the MH. The HA uses the address resolution protocol (ARP) to receive packets addressed to the MH. Specifically, when an ARP request is issued by the gateway in the network for the home address of the MH, the HA replies to the ARP request with its own MAC address. The gateway, on receiving the ARP reply, uses the HA's MAC address while forwarding the packet resulting in the HA receiving the packet.

3. Once the HA receives the IP packet on behalf of the MH, it then encapsulates the packet in another IP packet addressed to the foreign address of the MH and sends the packet over to the foreign address. The MH then receives the packet in its foreign network.

4. In the reverse direction, when the MH replies to the SH, the MH can directly send a packet across to the SH instead of tunneling it back through the HA. Thus, packets from the SH to the MH take the SH to HA to MH path, while packets from the MH to the SH take the MH to SH direct path. For this reason, Mobile IP routing is also referred to as the triangular routing approach.

5. An optimization to the triangular routing approach in IPv4 (and also incorporated in the IPv6 standard) involves the MH informing the static host about the new foreign address of the MH. Thereafter, the static host uses the foreign address to send packets to the mobility host directly. This precludes the need for packets to be first sent to the HA and then tunneled back to the MH, thus reducing the latency in the communication.

6. If and when the MH migrates to a new foreign network, all it does is register with the HA its new foreign address and the triangular routing (and the

optimization thereafter) ensures that packets addressed to the MH's home address are routed to it correctly.

7.2.2 Impact of Mobility on TCP Performance

Although Mobile IP does support user mobility in the Internet, it suffers from several drawbacks as far as ongoing connections are concerned that degrade the throughput of such connections. This is especially true for TCP connections, and we elaborate on some of the reasons below:

1. **Blackouts.** While Mobile IP allows users to migrate from one network to another, user mobility within the same cell does not in any way involve the Mobile IP mechanisms. For example, in a wide-area wireless network, the user can potentially be moving at pedestrian or automobile speeds and still stay within the cell of the same base station (typically with a coverage of 2 to 5 miles) for an extended period of time. This mobility, however, is not without its drawbacks. Sinha et al. [293], through real field experiments, show that mobile hosts can experience what they call *blackouts* during the mobility. Blackouts are periods during which the mobile host is not connected to the base station. Such blackouts can occur either because of the specific location that the user is passing through or fading, and so on, and are shown to last anywhere from a few seconds up to a few tens of seconds. When TCP experiences these blackouts and its retransmission timer expires, it wrongly infers that the network is suffering from a high degree of congestion and, hence, resets its congestion window to one and goes into the slow-start mode. Thus, if the blackouts occur frequently, the throughput of the TCP connection is degraded severely.

2. **Handoff latency.** When the mobile host moves from one cell to another, it takes a finite amount of time for Mobile IP to react to the handoff by updating the home agent to reroute packets to the new cell. In the meantime, the packets sent to the old cell of the MH typically are dropped by the old base station. When TCP experiences such bursty losses (typically resulting in a retransmission timeout), TCP resets its window size to one and goes into the slow-start mode, thus experiencing throughput degradation when handoffs occur frequently. This problem is particularly exacerbated when the MH is roaming far away from its home network. This is because of the fact that the update time is proportional to the distance from the MH to its home network.

3. **Triangular routing and large RTT.** When the triangular routing of Mobile IP is performed to handle the host mobility, the path from the static corresponding host to the MH is artificially long because of the two-stage tunneling from the corresponding host to the HA, and then from the HA to the MH. This in turn results in increased round-trip time (RTT) for the connection. Because TCP's throughput is inversely proportional to the RTT of its connection (see Chapter 5), the triangular routing performed by Mobile IP results in lesser throughput for the connection. This problem can be further exacerbated because of certain security mechanisms in the current Internet that prevent edge networks from forwarding packets that do not have a source address from that network, thus requiring even the reverse path from the MH to the static host to go through the HA. Even in the case where route shortening is performed, the connection

still spends a period of time in the triangular routing phase of Mobile IP until such an optimization can be performed; therefore, for this duration the connection does suffer from poor throughput.

7.2.3 Approaches to Improve TCP Performance

In this section, we present a summary of three approaches that have been proposed either as improvements to the basic TCP or as an alternative to TCP. For each of the approaches, we identify the fundamental ideas behind the protocol and discuss why the ideas contribute to improved performance when the transport protocol is used over a mobile cellular network.

Wireless Transmission Control Protocol. Wireless Transmission Control Protocol (WTCP) is a transport protocol proposed by Sinha et al. as an alternative to TCP over wide-area wireless networks [293]. The fundamental properties of WTCP are:

1. It uses rate-based transmissions instead of window-based transmissions of TCP. Using rate-based transmissions avoids the pitfalls that TCP experiences because of its window-based transmissions. Specifically, given the typical low bandwidths of wide-area wireless networks, TCP's window-based transmission results in a bursty behavior, which in turn leads to high variability in the round-trip times (because the transmission times of previous packets in a window significantly affect the round-trip time of subsequent packets), resulting in extremely high retransmission timer values.

2. It does not use retransmission timers. Instead, it uses a combination of Selective Acknowledgment (SACK) and probing to recover from errors and support reliability. While using just a SACK mechanism would be sufficient from most losses, the probing mechanism in WTCP handles suffix losses, that is, losses of packets transmitted at the end of any transmission period, because the receiver does not send back any SACK information for such losses.

3. It uses interpacket separation as the congestion metric instead of using losses as the congestion indication mechanism. By monitoring the interpacket separation times, WTCP detects congestion when the average interpacket separation increases. This allows WTCP to predict congestion in advance, while TCP waits for congestion to occur before reacting to it.

4. It takes into account only the forward path characteristics when performing congestion control. This is in contrast to TCP, which relies on both the forward path and the reverse path characteristics to perform congestion control. In wide-area wireless networks where path asymmetry can be high, this property helps WTCP exclude the reverse path characteristics in the throughput equation.

5. It uses a "packet-pair" based bandwidth estimation approach to estimate rate during the start-up phase and when recovering from blackouts. This allows a WTCP connection to ramp up to the available bandwidth in the span of a round-trip time instead of TCP's slow-start phase, which can potentially take a few round-trip times to reach the available capacity.

While readers are encouraged to see [293] for a detailed exposition on the properties of WTCP, we discuss here only the property of WTCP that is germane to the focus of this chapter, namely, blackout recovery. Blackouts are extended periods of time when the mobile host remains disconnected from the base station. They occur because of the mobile host moving into "black spots," areas where there is no channel connectivity, during its mobility. For example, a mobile user might experience a blackout if he or she is passing through a tunnel or steps inside a building for a short amount of time. Blackouts can also occur because of the channel state being bad at a particular location because of fading.

While blackouts are a typical characteristic of wide-area wireless networks, TCP does not recognize such phenomena primarily because the environment for which TCP was designed—a static wireline network—does not exhibit them. Hence, when a blackout occurs, TCP assumes that the network is badly congested, and, depending on the length of the blackout, might react wrongly in one of several ways. From the initial RTO value for the TCP connection, TCP continues attempting retransmissions for a threshold amount of time before it resets the connection. The TCP standard recommends a threshold of only 100 seconds before the reset is done [274]. Therefore, if a blackout exists for more than 100 seconds, the TCP connection could potentially be reset[1]. In addition, even if the connection is not reset, when TCP comes out of the blackout, it goes back to a window size of one and performs slow start. Hence, after every blackout the TCP connection would experience severe rate reduction, and it would take at least a few RTTs before it can use up the available capacity.

WTCP, however, treats blackouts differently. WTCP does not use retransmission timers and does the following when it does not receive an ACK from the receiver for a threshold amount of time: It enters its blackout handling phase and periodically sends probes to the receiver (akin to the TCP keep-alive or window-zero probes). The periodicity at which the probes are sent is increased exponentially until it reaches a maximum threshold. Finally, when the connection comes out of the blackout, WTCP uses a packet-pair–based, bandwidth estimation scheme to estimate the available bandwidth along the path of the connection, and sets its rate to the estimated available bandwidth. Hence, WTCP does not suffer from the throughput degradation of TCP when it comes out of blackouts.

Fast Handoffs. Seshan et al. [194] propose a new handoff scheme that improves on the Mobile IP to improve the performance of TCP during frequent handoffs. As presented earlier in the section, Mobile IP incurs a certain delay between the time the MH moves to a new base station cell and the time the new location of the MH is registered with the home network (and packets start getting rerouted to the new cell). All packets sent to the MH during this period are lost, typically resulting in TCP experiencing a retransmission timeout and the consequent window cut-down to one and the slow-start phase. The new handoff scheme proposed under this work attempts to solve this problem and has the following basic properties:

---

[1]Although TCP recommends values of only about 100 seconds, the actual value depends on the implementation. For example, the BSD implementation of TCP uses a value of around 420 seconds.

1. While the foreign address of the MH under the Mobile IP is a unicast address, under the new scheme, each MH is allocated a temporary multicast address. Thus, in contrast to Mobile IP where the home agent tunnels packets to the MH's new unicast address, in the new scheme the HA uses the multicast address allocated to that MH to forward packets.

2. The base station of the cell in which the MH is currently present is a member of the multicast group identified by the multicast address allocated to that MH. Therefore, when the HA forwards packets to the multicast group, the packets are automatically routed through the underlying IP multicast routing infrastructure to the base station, which then forwards the packets to the MH. Note that although the multicast address is allocated to the MH, the host does not join the multicast group.

3. When the MH receives a beacon (i.e., it is in proximity to the cell of another base station) from another base station, based on the signal strength received and its mobility pattern, it predicts whether it will enter the cell of that base station in the future. Upon predicting yes, the base station issues a request to the new base station to join the same multicast group as the current base station. When the new base station joins the multicast group, it starts receiving packets meant for the mobile host. However, at this stage, the new base station is still not chosen as the primary base station of the mobile host and, therefore, does not forward the packets to the MH. Instead, the new base station buffers a certain number of the last few packets received for the MH.

4. When the MH finally decides (based on signal strength, etc.) that the new base station should become its primary base station, it issues an appropriate message to its current and the new base stations. The message to the new base station includes information about the last few packets received by the MH. The new base station then starts forwarding packets from its buffer to the MH after synchronizing its buffer with the information about which packets have already been delivered to the MH. The current base station meanwhile leaves the multicast group associated with the MH.

The combination of properties presented above result in very minimal packet losses occurring because of the handoffs of the MH. Specifically, the advantages stem from two factors: (1) the predictive buffering at the new base station that prevents the MH from experiencing any period of disconnectivity in terms of the TCP packet stream it is receiving, and (2) the use of the multicast address that precludes the need for the HA to perform any routing updates when the MH moves to the new cell.

End-to-End Approach to Host Mobility.   Snoeren and Balakrishnan [299] propose a new end-to-end approach to support host mobility that improves on TCP performance in the presence of user mobility. The key difference between the proposed approach and Mobile IP is that the former relies solely on end-to-end mechanisms and therefore does not require any network upgrades. The key aspects of the approach are as follows:

1. Upon moving into a new network, the MH securely updates the Domain Name Server (DNS) nearest to its home network with its new location. Given that applications typically perform a DNS lookup before attempting to connect to any Internet host, this allows corresponding hosts that attempt to connect to the MH after its movement to learn its new address in a seamless manner. Note that if the MH is the one that is to initiate a connection, there is no issue in the first place as the MH issues the connection request with its new IP address. To prevent DNS caching from interfering with the above scheme, DNS servers are precluded from caching bindings belonging to MH.

2. In addition to performing the secure DNS update, for each active TCP connection, a special SYN packet that signifies a change of IP address is sent to the corresponding host. The special packet includes authentication information and can potentially include new connection setup parameters based on the MH's new location. This provides for an efficient way to migrate all TCP connections at the MH to the new location of the MH.

The key advantage of this approach is the fact that it does not incur the overheads of the triangular routing that Mobile IP incurs. In other words, while Mobile IP's triangular routing would perform the two-stage routing (corresponding host to HA, and HA to MH), this would in turn degrade TCP performance as the throughput of a TCP connection is inversely proportional to its round-trip timer. However, in the end-to-end approach proposed, the connection always traverses a direct path from the corresponding host to TCP, thus not incurring any additional overhead. The savings observed further increase if the Mobile IP scheme is constrained to route packets through the HA on the reverse path also (see Section 7.2.1).

The second advantage of the proposed scheme over Mobile IP is the fact that the overheads incurred caused by mobility are independent of the distance of the MH's new location from its home network. Recall from the previous section that the update overhead in Mobile IP is proportional to the distance between the home network and the foreign network. However, the overheads incurred under the proposed approach are always proportional only to the distance between the MH and the corresponding host. Finally, other than the TCP improvements discussed, the proposed approach is also beneficial from a deployment standpoint because end-system upgrades are easier to realize than network upgrades. For example, TCP SACK implementations are currently supported by most network protocol stacks, while IPv6 is still to be deployed ubiquitously.

7.3 TCP PERFORMANCE IN AD HOC NETWORKS

In this section, we analyze the key TCP performance issues in the ad hoc networking environment. Before we analyze the performance issues, we provide a brief introduction to a new routing protocol, called Dynamic Source Routing, which replaces the traditional routing protocols to support user mobility in ad hoc environment.

7.3.1   Dynamic Source Routing

The Dynamic Source Routing (DSR) protocol proposed by Broch et al. [73] is a simple but robust approach to routing in ad hoc networks. Experimental results [74] have shown that DSR (and more generically reactive routing protocols) provides significantly better performance than traditional proactive routing protocols in a variety of scenarios. We use DSR as a representative ad hoc routing protocol for the rest of our discussions. We hasten to add that although we assume DSR as the underlying routing protocol, the discussions presented remain valid as long as the underlying routing protocol is a reactive one. Another good example of a reactive protocol is the Ad Hoc On-Demand Distance Vector (AODV) protocol [269].

DSR is an on-demand routing protocol that makes use of source routing and an aggressive caching policy. Each node maintains a hop-by-hop route to other nodes in the network. When a route to a desired destination is not available in the cache, a route request (RREQ) flood is initiated by the source. If a node receiving an RREQ is not the destination or does not have a cached route to the destination, it forwards the RREQ using a local broadcast after stamping the packet with its ID. Otherwise, it sends a route reply (RREP), containing the complete discovered route, as a unicast message to the source by reversing[2] the path traversed by the RREQ.

On a link failure, a route error (RERR) message is unicast to the source. Upon receipt of the RERR message, the source initiates a route recomputation. The nodes that forward or snoop out the RERR packet also learn of the failed link and accordingly flush their caches. Cache purging in DSR heavily relies on the RERR packets. Several features of DSR, including on-demand route requests, source routing, and aggressive caching, are desirable in ad hoc networks because: (1) on-demand routing optimizes the routing traffic by performing route computation only when necessary; (2) source routing precludes the need for route-loop detection mechanisms; and (3) the aggressive caching policy is useful for limiting the number of nodes to which a route request propagates.

7.3.2   Impact of Mobility on TCP Performance

As in the case of Mobile IP, notwithstanding the fact that DSR supports effective routing, TCP suffers from severe throughput degradation because of mobility in ad hoc networks. We now list some of the mobility-related reasons for TCP's performance degradation:

1. **Route failures.** One of the key characteristics of a mobile ad hoc network is frequent route failures[3]. When there is a route failure, a TCP connection that is using the route can potentially lose a congestion window worth of packets. When TCP detects the bursty losses, because it has no way of distinguishing between congestion losses and route-failure losses, it resets its congestion window to one and enters into the slow-start phase. Because a TCP connection goes back to a window size of one for every route failure and takes a few round-trip times to climb up to the available capacity, it observes severe throughput degradation during mobility. A problem that exacerbates the

---

[2] Assuming bidirectional links.

[3] At this stage we refer only to route failures between source destination pairs that otherwise have a valid path in the network.

problem even more is the high round-trip time variations in ad hoc networks. Because the underlying MAC can be unfair [204] and because transmission delays are a significant fraction of the end-to-end delay, TCP experiences large variations in its round-trip time resulting in the mean deviation of the round-trip time being high. Recall that the retransmission timeout of TCP is set to the average (smoothed) round-trip time value plus four times the mean deviation. Therefore, the timeout value can be wrongly inflated, resulting in TCP detecting a loss only after a large amount of time, further degrading the throughput of the connection.

2. **Route recomputations.** Once the route error message reaches the source of the connection, the routing protocol at the source would then begin its route recomputation process. The TCP connection at the source is not able to send any more packets out into the network until the route is recomputed. The problem is worsened during heavy network loads when the route recomputation time can be high. TCP perceives the route computation time as increased round-trip times, resulting in a more inflated retransmission timeout.

3. **Network partitions.** While we have discussed route failures between source destination pairs that have a valid route in the network, this category includes route failures where the source and destination of a TCP connection belong to different partitioned components of the network. In this case, TCP can potentially reset the connection if the partition lasts for more than 100 seconds (see Section 7.1). Even if the network is connected again, TCP enters its slow-start phase after cutting down its window size to one. While this behavior is warranted in the presence of congestion, it severely degrades TCP's performance during mobility.

7.3.3   Approaches to Improve TCP Performance

In this section, we present two approaches to improve TCP performance over ad hoc networks. Both approaches use a generic *explicit link failure notification* (ELFN) scheme, although they differ in their specific mechanisms. We elaborate on the differences as we discuss the approaches.

TCP-Feedback and TCP-ELFN.   Chandran et al. [95] propose a TCP-feedback scheme that uses an explicit link failure notification (ELFN) from the node upstream of the link failure on the path to improve TCP performance. More recently, Holland et al. [334] revisit the properties of a TCP-ELFN scheme and have provided valuable insight into how an explicit, link-failure notification scheme can improve upon TCP's performance. The following are some of the salient aspects of a feedback-based or ELFN-based approach.

1. When a link failure occurs, the node just upstream of the link sends back an explicit link failure notification to the source of every TCP connection that passes through that link. Recall from Section 7.3.1 that the routing protocol already furnishes such an error message (in the form of the RERR message) to the source. However, the RERR message was sent back only to the source of that particular packet that could not be delivered. While link failure can potentially be detected when a node cannot hear any beacons (periodic *Hello*

messages) from the corresponding adjacent node, most routing protocols abstain from using such a beaconing to save precious bandwidth. Hence, a link failure is typically detected when a data packet cannot be successfully delivered over a link even after retransmissions are attempted for some threshold number of times.

2. Once a source node receives a link failure notification, it first issues a route recomputation request. In addition, it sends a message to the transport layer that essentially freezes the transport layer state including, entities like window size, timers, and so on. Most protocols that fall under this category of approaches add a new sleep state (SNOOZE [95]) to the TCP state diagram that reflects this state of TCP. When a new route is computed, the TCP connection comes out of the sleep state and starts functioning as normal. When the connection is first put to the sleep state, an associated sleep timer is started. If the sleep timer expires before a new route is computed, the connection is brought out of the sleep, state resulting in its experiencing losses (as in the case without ELFN) and, thus, reducing its window size to one.

3. A scenario not addressed by the sleep state is one in which the network is partitioned when the initial route recomputation message is sent and later becomes connected. In this case, even as the connection is in the sleep state the transport protocol has to periodically probe the network to determine whether the network is reconnected. Although this responsibility can be left to the routing layer, this is sufficient because the routing layer cannot attempt an unbounded number of transmissions, whereas the transport layer can perform retransmissions until it decides to reset the connection.

4. One modification to the basic ELFN approach discussed here is to reset the TCP congestion window to half its size when a connection is brought out of the sleep state. This would ensure that the existing flows (if they exist) along the new path do not experience severe congestion suddenly.

The key advantage of ELFN-based approaches is that they hide the latency of route recomputations on path failures from the TCP layer. Specifically, the performance gains are obtained from the following factors: (1) stopping any more transmissions until a new route is computed, thereby preventing those packets from being lost along the broken route; and (2) freezing the state of the TCP connection, thereby preventing it from cutting down its window size to one and entering the slow-start phase.

Although the ELFN-based approaches have been demonstrated to perform much better than regular TCP in mobile scenarios, it has also been demonstrated that ELFN-based approaches might suffer from lower throughput in static network scenarios [294]. This observation is a result of the MAC-layer–based, link-failure detection mechanism described earlier. Because the MAC layer determines link failure when it fails to deliver a packet across a link, it is possible for the MAC layer to infer wrongly link failure when the link is merely experiencing a high degree of contention. Hence, in static but heavily loaded scenarios, ELFN messages are generated even if there are no route failures. Because the source freezes and waits for a new route computation before it can come out of the sleep state, the connection unnecessarily experiences throughput degradation.

Hop-by-Hop Rate Control. Sinha et al. [293] have recently proposed hop-by-hop rate control that would enhance TCP performance over ad hoc networks. The basic approach proposed is relatively simple: each router (MH) performs rate control on each of its outgoing links based on feedback from the downstream routers. However, the benefits achieved by performing the hop-by-hop rate control are multifold. We list a few of them here:

- Sinha et al. [293] demonstrate that one of the primary reasons for TCP-throughput degradation is queue buildups caused by flooding of route request packets during periods of high mobility. During these periods, the data (TCP) packets experience significant queuing delays, resulting in TCP's retransmission, timeout value becoming large. As discussed before, this results in severe throughput degradation because TCP detects and recovers from actual losses in a delayed fashion. By employing a hop-by-hop rate control in the network, the problem of such extreme queue buildups is avoided.

- Several related works have demonstrated the unfair nature of TCP toward long-haul (large number of hops) connections. This effect is exacerbated in ad hoc networks in which the round-trip times can be significantly high for such connections. Specifically, in TCP a long-haul connection experiences congestion as long as any of its links experiences congestion; therefore, the probability of a flow experiencing congestion increases with its path length. Furthermore, the TCP window expansion progresses at the rate of 1/RTT; therefore, long-haul connections progress more slowly than their shorter counter parts, resulting in more unfairness. Hop-by-hop rate control solves both problems. Congestion on one hop is not propagated onto all links as long as the congestion is not persistent *and* the rate progression is dependent on the end-to-end delay (because rate control is happening over a single link).

- Finally, hop-by-hop rate control is more responsive to route failures because the feedback time is minimal. In other words, while in the case of regular TCP the feedback from the point of failure has to traverse all the way back to the source (not to mention the possibility of that message getting lost because of more upstream link failures), the problem does not exist when performing hop-by-hop rate control.

7.4 FURTHER READING

C.K. Toh's book [308] is a good source of ad hoc networking architectures, algorithms, and protocols. A good discussion of specific cellular networking technologies can be found in [219, 285]. Goff et al. [155] have proposed a TCP enhancement, called Freeze-TCP, which is shown to improve TCP performance in a cellular environment. With Freeze-TCP, the mobile host advertises a zero window size to "freeze" the sender temporarily when it detects impending handoff due to changes in signal strength. Freeze-TCP is a true end-to-end solution in the sense that it can be implemented without requiring any modifications in the intermediate base stations or the fixed sender.

7.5 SUMMARY

In this chapter, we have provided an overview of the problems that mobility has on TCP performance. We have assumed two network models, cellular and ad hoc, and identified in each of the cases what the specific issues are concerning TCP-throughput degradation caused by mobility. We have also provided a discussion of a subset of the approaches proposed in related literature that attempt to enhance TCP performance in the presence of mobility.

The key issues regarding mobility in cellular networks that potentially impact TCP performance are (1) occurrence of blackouts because of the mobile host moving to a blind spot in the base station cell, (2) latency for handoffs, (3) overhead of the triangular routing performed by Mobile IP, and (4) latency in updating the HA about the new location of a MH. While (3) results in increased round-trip times and, hence, lower throughput for the TCP connection, all the other factors result in bursty packet losses leading to further throughput degradation.

The three approaches discussed in the chapter include: (1) WTCP, a rate-based transport protocol that uses interpacket separation for detecting congestion and a packet pair–based rate estimation approach for recovering from connection blackout periods; (2) fast handoffs, a multicast-protocol–based handoff scheme that reduces the packet losses caused by handoff; and (3) end-to-end approach to host mobility that avoids the need for triangular routing or any update to the underlying network infrastructure.

In ad hoc networks, the key mobility issues that affect TCP performance are: (1) frequent route failures and the consequent packet losses and TCP window cut-downs, (2) overhead because of frequent route recomputations, (3) varying round-trip times, and (4) network partitions. The main approaches discussed in the chapter include (1) TCP-ELFN and TCP-Feedback, both of which send back an explicit notification to the TCP source about a route failure; the TCP source freezes its state until a new route is computed, resulting in improved throughput performance, and (2) hop-by-hop rate control that performs rate control on a hop-by-hop basis resulting in smaller buffer build-ups even during high mobility, faster reaction to congestion, and fair service to flows regardless of the path length of the flows.

7.6 REVIEW QUESTIONS

1. What are ad hoc networks? How are they different from cellular wireless networks and what is their significance?

2. Do the mechanisms in Mobile IP kick in for all kinds of host mobility? Explain the reasons behind your answer.

3. What are the key factors associated with host mobility in cellular networks that contribute to TCP performance degradation?

4. Outline the mechanisms used by the WTCP protocol with the associated motivation behind them.

5. What are the potential pitfalls of using rate-based transmissions at the transport layer? Why does the WTCP protocol not suffer from these pitfalls?

6. Explain how the fast handoffs mechanism alleviates the impact of host mobility on TCP performance.

7. Why is using an end-to-end approach necessarily better than using Mobile IP? Discuss the pros and cons.

8. What are the fundamental differences in terms of mobility between cellular networks and ad hoc networks?

9. Describe and contrast the approaches in the chapter that attempt to improve TCP performance over ad hoc networks. Give application scenarios in which one is considered more suitable than the others.

10. Discuss briefly the elements of a generic transport protocol necessary to handle host mobility.

7.7 HANDS-ON PROJECTS

1. Using *ns*-2 simulator, compare the performance of the three approaches to improve TCP performance in a Mobile IP environment. You might have to write some C++ code to implement some of these approaches in the *ns*-2 simulator.

2. Implement the three approaches of Project 1 in freely available FreeBSD systems. Build a test bed and conduct experiments to measure and compare the performance of these three schemes using the performance measurement tools discussed in Chapter 3. Now compare your experimental results with the ones you obtained from the *ns*-2 simulator.

3. Repeat Project 1 for the ad hoc networks.

4. Repeat Project 2 for the ad hoc networks.

5. Implement Freeze-TCP [154] in FreeBSD. Measure and compare its performance against WTCP.

7.8 CASE STUDY: WCORP TUNES TCP TO COMBAT BLACKOUTS IN MOBILE NETWORKING

To maintain close interactions with clients, WCORP employees frequently travel to client sites. In the past, networking while on the move was not popular among the WCORP employees because of slow and expensive access cost with cellular operators. After the availability of GPRS, an always-on packet data service, however, many employees find it useful to be on line while on the move. Of particular interest is downloading important files from corporate servers to laptops. These transfers are done in the background while the employees can concentrate on driving or other business.

While there is no major problem faced by employees in Melbourne, Sydney employees started to face a TCP connection reset problem each time they use the 8-Km-long M5 tunnel (longest tunnel in Sydney) that connects Sydney's east to the west. After some investigation, the problem was pinned down to the 300-sec TCP reset threshold implemented in WCORP servers. During peak hours, travelers spend about 500 seconds in the M5 tunnel and experience a total blackout for the entire duration. WCORP TCP keeps retransmitting during the blackouts and resets the connection after 300 seconds. Any file transfer in progress, therefore, ends prematurely, causing user dissatisfaction.

To combat the long blackout and premature connection termination problem, the network administrator considered several options, including alternative transmission control protocols (e.g., WTCP) and simple tuning options (e.g., increasing TCP reset time value in WCORP servers). Finally, it was decided that a replacement of TCP/IP stacks with alternative implementations would be prohibitively expensive. Therefore, as a simple solution to the blackout problem, TCP/IP stacks were configured with a reset value of 550 sec. After this TCP tuning, no premature connection termination was experienced in the M5 tunnel.

CHAPTER 8

TCP/IP Performance over Optical Networks

CHAPTER OBJECTIVES

After completing this chapter, the reader should be able to:

- Gain an overview of optical networks

- Learn transport architectures for carrying TCP/IP traffic over optical networks

- Understand specific performance issues when TCP/IP traffic is transported over optical networks

- Design optical packet switches that maximize TCP performance

Optical networks are being deployed in the Internet backbones paving the way for the next generation high-speed Internet. The introduction of optical technology in the Internet architecture brings in new challenges and performance issues. In this chapter, we review the main proposals for all optical networking with a particular focus on all optical packet switching. We then provide an example of TCP over optical-packet-switching performance analysis to show how the requirements of the optical technology affect TCP in an end-to-end network performance perspective.

8.1 EVOLUTION OF OPTICAL NETWORKS

The dawn of optical communication technology dates back to the early 1970s with the first fiber-optic transmission systems. Since then optical communications have evolved very effectively, leading to very powerful transmission systems, both in terms of channel bit rate and of link length, thanks to the introduction of all-optical amplification in particular. Despite these extraordinary advances, optics has not penetrated much into the switching and management part of the network.

In the last few years issues such as optical switching and transparent optical networking have emerged as the next steps in high-speed networks evolution. As a testimony of this challenge, technical magazines and journals are devoting more and more special issues to these subjects, and journals and conferences devoted to this are born.

The big interest in optical networking is boosted by the advances in coherent optical transmission, leading to Dense Wavelength Division Multiplexing (DWDM) systems able to accommodate up to hundreds of wavelengths per fiber, and in integrated optics for passive and active optical components design. By means of DWDM it is almost effortless to turn the optical fiber into a bunch of high-speed links (the wavelengths) multiplying the overall network capacity and connectivity opportunities by one or two orders of magnitude. With integrated optics the implementation of active network components such as switches and multiplexers is becoming more and more realistic.

The targets of this evolution are the so-called *optical transparent networks*, in which the signal carried within the network never leaves the optical domain. As a matter of fact, at present, signals are converted from optical to electrical in the network nodes for many reasons such as:

- regeneration, which is necessary to amplify the signal, reshape the bit impulse, and retime the whole bit sequence

- processing and control, which are the set of functions used to control the quality of the transmission channel (such as error checking)

- wavelength conversion, to switch a signal from one wavelength on the incoming link to another on the outgoing link

- switching and congestion resolution, which are the most typical functions of a switching matrix, to forward incoming data from one inlet to one outlet while allowing for statistical multiplexing of the available resources.

The optical to electrical conversion is a system bottleneck that limits the overall network throughput and makes the network elements more complex. Nowadays, the aforementioned functions can be performed in optics, for instance, all-optical 3R regenerators are available as well as all-optical switches and wavelength converters. Most of these components are laboratory test beds and are not yet available off-the-shelf, but they will very likely be available in the next few years, at least for the implementation of high-capacity backbone networks.

The compatibility and the integration of optical transparent networks with present-day legacy networks and protocols, of which TCP and IP is definitely one of the most outstanding examples, is a subject of intense debate within the scientific community. In this chapter we address exactly this issue and present some examples of analysis of TCP performance in this scenario.

8.2 IP OVER DWDM

To integrate IP and DWDM one must consider the huge investments of many operators in advanced transmission infrastructure and the resulting need for a gradual and smooth migration. At present, various techniques are widely used to support high-performance data transport, such as ATM and frame relay, so that emerging DWDM networks are initially required to support other protocols than IP. Moreover, most optical networks rely on the SONET/SDH standard to provide point-to-point links at the physical layer. SONET/SDH has the main advantage of being a well-established and developed standard defining data framing, multiplexing scheme, and fault management, all resulting in a reliable and controllable network infrastructure from the operator's point of view.

The most immediate approach to IP over DWDM integration is simply to overlay all these technologies, stacking the existing protocols over the DWDM transmission infrastructure. An example of this overlay architecture is presented

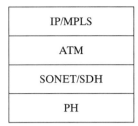

| IP/MPLS |
| ATM |
| SONET/SDH |
| PH |

FIGURE 8.1: Example of the full stack of protocols in the case of an overlay approach involving ATM and SONET in between IP and DWDM.

in Figure 8.1. The drawback of this approach is that it reduces efficiency and has high costs of network management. In practice, many functions are replicated in different layers and a significant protocol overhead is added to the user data through the stack (see [158] for a detailed overhead analysis of IP/AM/SONET).

For this reason, the trend is to investigate network solutions that reduce intermediate layering between IP and DWDM and, at the same time, maintain the required functionalities and even enhance their performance. For instance, the options of carrying IP packets directly over SONET have been proposed [292], and the elimination of the SONET layer itself can be achieved by providing PPP/HDLC framing over optical light paths (the so-called digital wrapper).

Another option is the introduction of a newly defined optical layer below existing layers, accessible through the Optical User Network Interface (O-UNI). This layer is thought to provide enhanced optical connectivity to higher layers and isolate the DWDM resources from higher layer protocols. The main function of the optical layer in this case is wavelength channel provisioning, by appropriately setting switches along the end-to-end path, support for network survivability (protection/recovery mechanisms), data framing, monitoring, and addressing to establish optical channels between the edge nodes of the optical network.

The definition of the optical layer has been pursued mainly by the International Telecommunication Union (ITU) [177] to allow vendors to provide standardized equipment. This approach is an improvement with respect to the multiple layer configuration of Figure 8.1; but, in any case, it requires the definition of an optical layer protocol that implies increased complexity in network management and interworking. A further drawback is represented by the circuit-oriented nature of the optical layer that may limit the flexibility in sharing the bandwidth and could make the introduction of new optical networking technologies, such as optical packet switching, more complex.

All these approaches can be viewed as solutions where the existing IP would overlay a set of transport networks, running their own protocols (whether SONET or ITU optical layer, the basic principle does not change) and controlled separately.

A different and more integrated approach is to ensure an easier evolution toward future optical networking technologies to integrate the IP control plane with the optical control plane. The functions performed by the optical adaptation layer are shifted into higher layers (similar to the approach followed by the Multiprotocol Label Switching (MPLS) paradigm).

In the following sections, we describe the optical networking alternatives in the perspective of integration with Multiprotocol Label Switching (MPLS). We start with a brief review of MPLS and then discuss the case of wavelength-routed networks, that is the Multiprotocol Lambda Switching (MPλS) proposal and of optical burst/packet switching.

8.3 MULTIPROTOCOL LABEL SWITCHING

Multiprotocol Label Switching (MPLS) is a connection-oriented protocol (in contrast to regular IP) setting up unidirectional, end-to-end connections between routers, called Label Switched Paths (LSPs) and identified by an additional label added to the IP datagrams [281]. To better understand the principles behind this proposal, it is worthwhile to recall that, at present, IP routers perform four main tasks:

Routing: Supporting various protocols to maintain network connectivity information stored in the routing tables

Forwarding: Determining the output interface for each incoming packet by using the routing table

Switching: Transporting each packet to the proper output interface as determined by the forwarding process

Buffering: Resolving contention when multiple arrivals occur

The definition of MPLS aims at clearly partitioning the network layer function into two basic components: *control* and *forwarding*. The control component is responsible for routing. It uses standard routing protocols, such as the well-known OSPF and BGP, to exchange information with other routers, and maintains a forwarding table based on the routing algorithms. The forwarding table is based on the concept of forwarding equivalence class (FEC). The entire set of packets that a router can forward is split into a finite number of subsets that are the forwarding equivalence classes. Packets belonging to the same FEC are treated by the router in the same way for forwarding. Packets with different IP headers could belong to the same FEC. In a router each FEC is characterized by the address of the next hop router in the forwarding table. The definition of the FECs and of the relative next hops are performed by the control component.

The forwarding component has the task of processing incoming packets, examining the headers, and making forwarding decisions, based on the forwarding table [118]. In MPLS, the forwarding operation is realized by means of labels, a short, fixed-length entity that is carried by the packet and is used as entry for the information contained in the forwarding table. It identifies the FEC to which a packet belongs. Packets belonging to the same FEC are, from a forwarding point of view, indistinguishable and are forwarded in a connection-oriented fashion from source to destination along an LSP. The label can be encoded in the forwarding protocol header when available, as happens in ATM networks, or as a "shim" label added in between layer-2 encapsulation and layer-3 IP packets. As an example, in Figure 8.2 is shown the use of the shim header added to a PPP layer over SDH/SONET and the MPLS label mapping in the ATM VPI/VCI header.

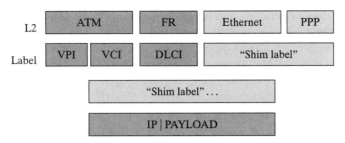

FIGURE 8.2: Example of MPLS shim label insertion in Ethernet frame and of MPLS label mapping into ATM VPI/VCI.

The MPLS proposal does not concern switching and buffering because they are implementation-dependent and do not influence the routing and forwarding decisions.

MPLS has important consequences with respect to traffic engineering in the IP layer. For instance, it is possible to set up explicit routes through the network to optimize the usage of available network resources or to create distinct paths for different classes of quality of service. More importantly, for the subject of this chapter, the concept of label forwarding simplifies the forwarding component of the router, enabling a higher packet processing rate.

8.4 MULTIPROTOCOL LAMBDA SWITCHING

The most significant proposal to integrate MPLS with wavelength routed all-optical networks is MPλS [52]. This approach considers the wavelength as the unit of capacity available in the optical network. End-to-end links are made available by the network as a sequence of wavelengths on different fibers.

In MPλS, LSPs are mapped into wavelengths; therefore, MPλS is a possible approach for the design of control planes for optical cross-connects (OXCs) based on MPLS traffic engineering, and it is eventually supposed to cooperate with DWDM multiplexing capabilities in IP routers. MPλS aims at providing a framework for real-time provisioning, typically several seconds and hopefully milliseconds, of optical channels in switched optical networks. In particular, it allows the dynamic provisioning of optical channels and assists the network survivability through enhanced protection and restoration capabilities in the optical domain.

An OXC is a transparent switching element in an optical transport network that establishes routed paths for optical channels by locally connecting an optical channel from an input port (fiber) to an output port (fiber) on the switch element. Even if in principle an OXC performs the switching function in a purely electrical or optical domain, the latter is assumed. Therefore, the granularity for the switching function is the wavelength, and hence the OXC is also referred to as *wavelength routing switch*. Correspondingly, the problem of setting up an end-to-end optical path is called the routing and wavelength assignment problem.

The definition of an optical, channel-layer network aims at supporting end-to-end networking of optical channel paths between access points. It is supposed to provide the following functions: routing, monitoring, grooming, and protection and restoration of optical channels. In this situation, programmable OXCs, with reconfigurable switch fabrics and relatively smart control planes, are critical to the realization of the optical, channel-layer functions, especially in mesh optical networks.

MPλS creates point-to-point optical channels between access points in the optical transport network, using the same signaling protocols as MPLS. The OXCs become IP-addressable devices capable of performing all MPLS-related functions, such as resource discovery, state information spreading, path selection by means of constraint-based routing, and path management. For instance, some protocols based on the well-known IS-IS or OSPF can be used to disseminate state information, which is then employed to determine the end-to-end optical path; moreover, a signaling protocol such as RSVP can help to instantiate the optical path.

An OXC does not perform packet-level processing in the data plane, which means that the forwarding information cannot be extracted from the packet but must be implied from the wavelength of the optical channel. In an optical transport network with OXCs, a single link is given by a physical fiber between OXCs, and wavelengths play the role of labels. OXCs with MPλS provide optical channels by establishing a relation between an input port-wavelength tuple and an output port-wavelength tuple, locally managed by a proper controller, which cannot be altered by data plane functions.

However, some important differences exist between MPλS with OXCs and MPLS with electrical routers. Label merging is not possible in an optical domain because several wavelengths cannot be merged into one. Furthermore, OXCs can support a coarse granularity only in resource allocation because a small number of optical channels with coarse, discrete bandwidth can be managed, as opposed to electrical routers that in principle do not limit the number of paths and their granularity.

8.5   OPTICAL BURST SWITCHING

The MPλS approach considers the wavelength as the unit of capacity available and maps LSPs into wavelengths. This may not be the most efficient solution for multiplexing, because the incoming flow of information is bursty by nature. The future Internet will need a fast mechanism for wavelength provisioning to set up high-capacity, end-to-end optical connections. To this end, most of the electronics present in the network must be bypassed, and a reduction in wavelength provisioning time-scales is required. The trend is to go from pure circuit-switching, DWDM-based networks to more efficient, that is, statistical multiplexing, and possibly cost-effective optical networks.

Optical burst switching [274] represents a first step in this direction and can be seen as a middle-term solution toward all optical packet switching. The goal of optical burst switching is to improve wavelength utilization and sharing by introducing a more dynamic wavelength management.

The basic idea behind optical burst switching is to set up a wavelength path on the fly when a large data flow (the burst) is identified. The burst is transferred transparently along this path that is reset at the end of the transfer. The aim is to allow for a larger degree of wavelength sharing with processing limited to the call set up and tear down.

A separate control packet precedes each burst by a basic offset time, carrying forwarding information. One relevant degree of freedom in the design of this kind of network is the dimensioning of the offset time interval. Indeed, the offset might also account for an additional contribution that allows differentiation of the performance of various classes of service and granting them different priorities. The principle is that the longer the extra offset, the higher the priority, because the corresponding flow can reserve well in advance of the required resource. For establishing an optical connection, several issues must be studied: optical-burst determination algorithm, routing and wavelength assignment algorithm, resource reservation mechanism, and end-to-end connection setup.

Optical-burst determination is the decision process for setting up an end-to-end optical path or not, depending on the nature of the data stream to be sent. The size of this data stream has to be quite large with respect to the connection setup time and round-trip delay time to have an efficient transmission. For instance, setting up an optical path for electronic mail is not efficient in terms of resource utilization, so that this kind of "short-life" application should use conventional electronic devices. It appears then that some sort of control information must go from the applications layer to the network and/or optical layer to carry the characteristics of the information flow being transmitted. Otherwise, complex mechanisms for traffic aggregation and grooming have to be employed to fully exploit the optical pipes.

Once a decision is made, optimal routing is performed to determine the path and this is combined with an efficient wavelength assignment along the path to the destination. Therefore, multiple algorithms are necessary to properly manage and assign the resources. These resources must now be reserved along the path so that a reservation mechanism is developed to complete the end-to-end connection setup.

The generality of the MPLS architecture makes this proposal suitable for a optical burst switching scenario. Each optical-burst switching (OBS) node can be equipped with an IP/MPLS controller, which makes it similar to a conventional electronic label switch router. These nodes are classified as either core or edge. The former perform burst switching, which means that an incoming burst on a given wavelength is switched across an optical switching system to another wavelength on an output port.

One must observe that wavelengths for data are not terminated; for example, no optical-electronic-optical conversions occur in the core nodes while control information is transmitted on terminated wavelengths because they have to be processed and this can be done in electronics only. This allows an efficient electronic control by the MPLS control plane. Thus, control information such as labels can be sent as IP packets along reserved paths. In burst-switching networks, resources, such as bandwidth, are reserved in a one-way process to improve their utilization, but this implies that data bursts may be blocked somewhere along the transfer to the destination.

When MPλS is adopted, an incoming data flow has a label, stored in the control packet, which identifies the wavelength over which the data burst is traveling. To create an LSP, the control plane preliminary associates a well-defined output label, that is, a wavelength, to this input label. Another possible approach is to employ Labeled Optical Burst Switching (LOBS) [114]. Rather than associating the data burst to an input (fiber, wavelength) pair, the label carried by the control packet identifies the next hop in the LSP. This means that any wavelength within the selected output fiber can be used to transfer the data burst, thus providing a remarkable performance improvement. As a matter of fact, burst blocking can now occur only if all wavelengths within the selected fiber are busy. However, proper traffic engineering is required to make this event very unlikely.

The routes to the destinations can be computed by explicit routing or constraint-based routing, and the signaling for managing end-to-end paths can be done by label distribution or resource reservation protocols. Edge nodes are equipped with electronic devices so that they can perform all functions typical of IP routers. Edge nodes play a fundamental role because this is the place where bursts are formed, and these can consist of several IP packets (assembly function). At the same time a control packet is created for end-to-end resource reservation, a proper label is associated to the data flow and an end-to-end path is computed. Also, control packets can be classified according to the priority of the related data flow to provide differentiated services. However, some MPLS functions cannot be implemented optically because at the moment it is not possible to merge different wavelengths into one, as it is possible in electronics with labels.

8.6   OPTICAL PACKET SWITCHING

As already outlined, the final goal in terms of flexible bandwidth management and data flow multiplexing is optical packet switching. Packet switching aims at optimizing the exploitation of the DWDM channels by their fast and dynamic allocation, overcoming the inefficiency typical of the circuit transfer modes. Packet transfer modes are flexible by nature regarding bandwidth exploitation. The link capacity is then shared in time among packets, and, in principle, all the networks links are better used.

All-optical packet switching is a research topic that has been investigated over the last decade. The target we foresee nowadays is the implementation of transparent optical packet routers to carry TCP/IP traffic. The main problems to overcome are the technology limitations imposed by the lack of optical memories and by the characteristic of optical devices.

In general, routing and forwarding are the functions that impose more severe throughput limitations. The reason is that the algorithms to run, are more complex and require more processing time, thus placing a limit on the overall packet processing rate. With MPLS, the control (routing) component is decoupled from the forwarding component. Optical routers require a further partitioning of the forwarding component into forwarding algorithm, that is, routing tables look up to determine the datagram next hop destination and switching function that is the physical action of transferring a datagram to the output interface properly chosen by the forwarding algorithm. The main goal is to limit the electro-optical conversion to the minimum to achieve better interfacing with DWDM transmission systems. This is achieved using the following techniques:

- the packet label or header is converted from optical to electrical and the execution of the forwarding algorithm is performed in electronics

- the datagram payload is optically switched without conversion to the electrical domain

Therefore, to be effective, the implementation of an optical router requires a full optical switching matrix and a forwarding algorithm able to cope with the speed of optics. The former has been widely investigated, and demonstrators of optical packet switching matrices are available [134, 135], based on the use of Semiconductor Optical Amplifier (SOA) as optical gates [85].

Regarding the latter, considering that core routers may experience heavy traffic conditions in IP backbones, improving the working conditions of forwarding processors is a critical task. As a matter of fact, IP header processing implies the software processing of hundreds of code lines. Investigations into this problem [84] lead to the conclusion that pure IP forwarding is a system bottleneck unless it is possible to guarantee a lower bound to the length of the optical packets. Because the packet payload is optically switched transparently, the time available to perform the forwarding algorithm is related to the average packet length. Therefore, the forwarding algorithm imposes a lower bound to the packet length; otherwise either the packets are artificially spaced, decreasing the link utilization, or some packets must be discarded because the router forwarding does not have time to process them. Callegati et al. provide calculations that suggest the average packet length should be on the order of 10 Kbytes to be compatible with present lookup technology for the IP header [84].

MPLS can improve or bypass the forwarding bottleneck. Optical Edge Devices (OEDs) are responsible for LSP setup, insertion of IP packets into one or more optical packets, insertion of a suitable label into the optical packet header, and forwarding it to the next hop MPLS switch, which processes the label only, without taking care of the IP header (see Figure 8.5). Therefore, MPLS and optical packet switching match very well, and an optical router combining these technologies exploits the best of both electronics and optics. Standard protocols are used in the noncritical, routing component; MPLS labels are used in the forwarding algorithm, where stringent performance limits are present; and, finally, optics are used in switching and transmission, providing very high data rate and throughput.

The general architecture of a DWDM optical packet router is presented in Figure 8.3. The figure outlines the various functional subblocks:

- **Input-output interfaces:** used to demultiplex the wavelengths of a fiber and to perform electro-optical conversion of the datagram label

- **Optical space switch:** the set of space switches used to physically connect the various input-output ports

- **Delay line buffer:** used to solve contention in the time domain if needed (buffering is treated in more detail in Section 8.6.2);

- **Electronic control:** used to perform label processing and forwarding table lookup, as well as to pilot the optical devices to properly set up the switching matrix.

8.6.1 Optical Packet Format

A key issue in optical packet switching is the format of optical packets, which should be built in a way that takes into account the needs of the optical technology. For

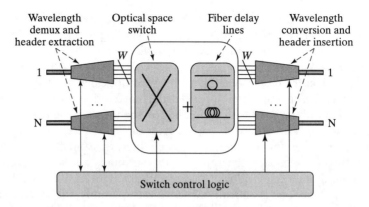

FIGURE 8.3: Functional architecture of an optical packet router.

instance, a suitable time interval, called the guard band, must be introduced between packet header and payload and between packets to guarantee the time needed for optical path setup in the switching matrix [135]. The device switching time may be as short as tens of nanoseconds but still not negligible at very high data rate (1 nanosecond accommodates 10 bits at 10 Gbit/s line speed), and guard bands are necessary to avoid loss of valid data. We may imagine, therefore, the optical packet switched backbone as clouds of optical routers with edge routers that build optical packets from IP datagrams and set up the LSPs.

Again, MPLS offers the means to fulfill the technology requirements. Optical packets are created in the edge routers by adding label and guard bands to the IP datagram. Grooming and/or segmentation of datagrams may also take place here if needed [132]. Regarding the packet format, two proposals have been investigated:

- fixed length packet with slotted network operation [135]

- variable length packets with asynchronous network operation [305]

The former proposal is more appealing as far as optical switching matrix implementation is concerned, but the main drawback is that it requires optical synchronization and it is not very well suited to carry information that is natively of variable size. For instance, the optical packet format defined by the KEOPS project [135] was of fixed duration, with a 14-byte header transmitted at 622 Mbps and a payload with data rates from 622 Mbps to 10 Gbps. The latter does not require synchronization and is more appealing as far as interworking with TCP/IP is concerned, but the optical switch is, at present, more difficult to build and does not perform as well as in the previous case.

In any case, an access interface is necessary in the edge routers that interface with optical routers. An example of how such an interface could be implemented is presented in Figure 8.4, where both fixed length incoming traffic (e.g., ATM) and variable length incoming traffic (IP datagrams) are considered. Because of the lack of optical memories, the two functions of *optical packets generation* and *transmission* must coincide. An optical packet is created and transmitted at the same time; therefore, all the bits to be put in it have to be already available at the

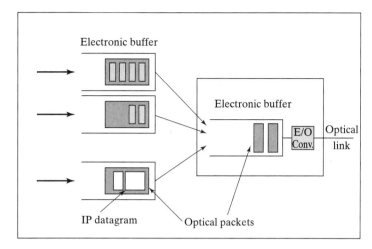

FIGURE 8.4: Example of optical edge device (OED).

interface. For this reason, the buffering is performed in electronics at the interface. A general definition of how the interface works could be:

1. an electronic memory is necessary to store the bits coming from the input link, waiting to fill an optical packet
2. based on a scheduling policy to be decided, optical packets are then taken and transmitted

As usual, the packetization scheme must address the issue of efficiently filling the optical payload under the constraint of a maximum packetization delay. With respect to this issue, the problems are slightly different in the two cases of fixed and variable length incoming packets. In any case, the basic idea is very simple: not only store as many incoming packets as possible before sending the optical packet to fill the payload, but also put a limit on the time a datagram lingers in the interface queue.

8.6.2 Congestion Resolution in Optical Packet Switches

Finally, we address the issues of congestion resolution and service differentiation in optical packet switches, where congestion may arise because of temporary overload of a given output port. Congestion resolution may be achieved in the time domain by means of queuing and in the wavelength domain by means of suitable wavelength multiplexing.

Queuing. Queuing is achieved by delay lines (coils of fibers) that are used to delay packets as if they were placed for some time into memory and then retrieved for transmission. The delay line buffer is similar to a normal queue but not the same. The main difference is that while a packet may be stored as long as needed in an electronic memory, it can stay for an upper limited time (the time necessary to travel the longest fiber delay line) in the optical buffer. Furthermore, in the case of variable length packets, the performance of the buffer is very sensitive to the so-called buffer time scale, that is the length unit of the various delay lines. This problem has been studied and modeled in detail [83]. Callegati argues that a number of delay lines on the order of a few hundred are needed to guarantee performance in terms of packet loss probability below 10^{-3}, which could be considered acceptable for Internet applications. Unfortunately, a buffer with such a number of delay lines is presently beyond the reach of optical technology because of splitting loss and power penalties [85].

Wavelength Multiplexing.   Fortunately, queuing is not the only congestion resolution tool available. Wavelength multiplexing may be used jointly with queuing to greatly improve performance. With the term *wavelength multiplexing*, we address the strategy used to allocate the wavelength to packets on the DWDM links. The alternatives are mainly the following two [132, 133]:

1. **Wavelength circuit (WC)**, in which the elementary path within the network for a given LSP is designated by the wavelength; therefore, packets belonging to the same MPLS connection are all transmitted on the same wavelength
2. **Wavelength packet (WP)**, in which the wavelengths can be used as a shared resource, the traffic load is spread over the whole wavelength set on an availability basis, and packets belonging to the same MPLS connection can be spread over more wavelengths.

Wavelength circuit is easier to manage. Wavelength packet is more complex to control in general but provides superior performance. In this case, should a packet be forwarded to a wavelength that is congested, it can be rerouted toward a less congested wavelength on the same fiber, thus keeping the same network path (same fiber) and exploiting wavelength multiplexing. This scheme has proved effective in the case of a purely connectionless network, in which an intelligent wavelength selection algorithm may lead to a reduction in the packet-loss probability of several orders of magnitudes [86]. For instance, quite a good performance can be reached with just a few tens of fiber delay lines.

Unfortunately, in a connection-oriented network scenario such as MPLS, the wavelength hopping of packets belonging to the same LSP causes, out-of-order arrivals and updates of the forwarding table. The former issue means more complex interfaces at the edge of the optical network for resequencing and the latter a possible overload for the control function of the optical packet switch. Therefore, a trade-off has to be found between wavelength hopping for congestion resolution and forwarding of packets of the same LSP on the same wavelength as long as possible. Research regarding wavelength multiplexing in a connection-oriented network, such as with MPLS, has been started in recent investigations, proving that a performance improvement of several orders of magnitudes in terms of packet loss may be achieved with wavelength multiplexing. In a 4×4 switch, with 16 wavelengths per fiber, a packet-loss probability as low as 10^{-4} can be reached with just eight fiber delay lines per buffer. Furthermore, by using intelligent wavelength selection algorithms, aiming at reducing the wavelength hopping of LSPs, it is possible to limit the out-of-order packet to about 10% of the total.

8.7 PERFORMANCE OF TCP/IP OVER OPTICAL NETWORKS

As previously explained, the overlay solution of IP over optical offers to the TCP user an end-to-end transparent channel (one or more wavelengths) that is provided and managed at the optical level but can be considered as a point-to-point link at the IP level. Similarly, MPλS over wavelength-routed networks provides IP with label switched paths in the optical network characterized by a latency that is fixed and well known once the path is established.

In these cases, TCP performance is related to the performance of the optical connections that do not vary during the lifetime of the TCP session. The latency in particular is the parameter that influences the TCP behavior and in particular the TCP window evolution. In the aforementioned scenario, congestion does not arise once the optical path is established. Therefore, the end-to-end latency of the path is the main parameter to influence TCP performance.

The situation is different for optical burst or packet switching. In these cases, and in particular in optical packet switching, the IP datagrams experience a delay and a loss that may randomly vary according to network load conditions and path setup. Therefore, a more detailed analysis of TCP behavior is necessary. In the remainder of this section, we present an example of such an analysis with reference to optical packet switching. In particular, we consider the network architecture proposed in [132]. The scenario is that of an optical packet switched backbone, with optical packet switched routers able to process fixed length packets on a per label basis (Figure 8.5). We assume that datagrams are inserted into optical packets that are labeled according to the datagrams' FECs and then forwarded to their destination through the optical packet switched network.

Because of the packet switched nature of this network, packet loss and delay may arise as a consequence of congestion, and their values are a function of the nodes behavior. In the following, we briefly review some results regarding the end-to-end performance analysis of such networks and then apply these results to an analysis of the behavior of TCP.

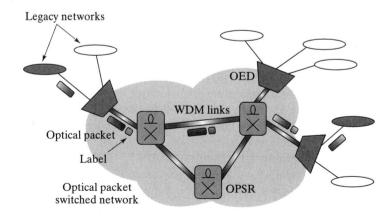

FIGURE 8.5: Example architecture of the optical packet switched network.

8.7.1 Optical Packet Network End-to-End Performance

In a DWDM optical-packet-switched network, despite the limitations on optical buffer capacity, node architecture and wavelength multiplexing techniques can be defined to achieve very low optical packet-loss probabilities. We can then assume that congestion within the optical network is a rare event. As a consequence, the end-to-end delay becomes the main parameter to influence the TCP/IP performance.

The main characteristic of the optical network is that the packets are generally delayed for short amounts of time in the nodes, while there is an additional delay at the network edges, where optical packets are built. Therefore, because of this architecture, the end-to-end delay is typically made of the following main contributions:

1. delay in the access interface (incoming and outgoing)
2. delay in the network nodes
3. propagation delay on the fibers between the nodes

Interface Delay.   The edge interface can be split logically into two sections. In one, IP datagrams are gathered according to the FEC they belong to and optical packets are assembled. In the other, optical packets are queued to be transmitted on the optical link. Therefore, the delay experienced in the access interface by IP datagrams can be split into two components called packetization delay and transmission delay. The former is the time necessary to form a new optical packet once a datagram is present in the interface. The latter is the queuing time in the FIFO transmission queue plus the transmission time on the output link.

We measure the packetization delay as the amount of time elapsed between the arrival of full datagram (i.e., the time the last bit of the datagram is received) and the time it is sent to the transmission queue. Packetization is accomplished by means of a buffer where IP datagrams are stored until the optical packet is full or until a timeout expires. A timer is indeed used to limit the latency at the access. We also assumed that the header generation takes much less time than the aforementioned delay and can, therefore, be neglected.

An example of evaluation of the packetization delay, performed by simulation by assuming on/off incoming traffic in the cases of both exponential and Pareto distributions, can be found in [87]. The scenario is that of legacy networks at a speed of 100 Mbps and an optical network with 10 Gbps links. Simulations and analysis have been carried out for an optical packet length of $T = 2.8$ μsec. The results obtained lead to an upper bound of the delay experienced by the packet in the various network sections.

The packetization delay results on the order of some hundreds of microseconds with very high probability; therefore, we assume that the timeout to send an optical packet, even if it is not yet full, can be set at 500 μsec. Regarding the transmission delay, a complete analysis is not easy but bounds can be found. Following the approach presented in [87], we assume that its absolute value is about a fraction of a millisecond.

Node Delay.   The delay in the core routers was computed referring to an optical packet switch with output queuing. The delay experienced by the optical packets in crossing the network nodes is made up by header processing, switching matrix setup and queuing delay in the fiber delay lines. Header processing and switching matrix setup should be negligible when MPLS forwarding and fast recon-figurable optical switches, such as Semiconductor Optical Amplifiers (SOA), are used. This delay should sum up to well less than 1 µsec, a value that is negligible when compared with the other values considered in this calculation. The queuing delay is a function of the traffic load. It can be computed as the sum of queuing delays in all the nodes of an end-to-end chain that, in its turn, can be calculated by means of classical analysis. By assuming a chain of switches and by means of an additive approximation, it is possible to find an upper bound of the overall delay when crossing a chain of tens of switches.

Propagation Delay.   Finally, the propagation delay is not peculiar to the network architecture, but it is related to the geographic topology, the transmission media employed and to the resulting distance between the nodes. Typical values are 4 to 5 microseconds per Km and are taken into account for the discussion of TCP/IP mapping over the optical backbone.

Approximate evaluation of overall end-to-end delay by means of a simple additive formula exploiting the results previously summarized leads to values upper bounded an end-to-end delay in the range of a millisecond.

8.7.2   Mapping of TCP in Optical Packets

In this section, the mapping of TCP connections onto optical packets is discussed. Considering the very high data rates made available by the optical network, the bandwidth-delay product has to be carefully evaluated [213]. The delay value is given by the round trip time of the optical network, which has been calculated in the previous section.

As for the contribution of the network, it can be kept to less than 1 millisec-ond, to which the contribution of the propagation delay must be added. With a 1000 kilometer connection, the one-way delay is roughly 5 ms (due to propagation) plus approximately 1 ms so that the overall round trip delay is about 12 ms: at 2.5 Gbps the capacity of the data pipe is then roughly 30 Mbits. This value is by far larger than the maximum allowable TCP advertised window so that this pipe is efficiently used only by multiplexing many TCP connections.

Having shown the need to share an optical pipe among many TCP connections, a policy must be defined to fill the optical packets with TCP segments. This means that the access interface plays a fundamental role because it performs the translation to and from optical packets, and it must take decisions in relation to the policy adopted, for example, how many IP datagrams can be hosted in an optical packet and which of them are put into the same packet. The number of TCP segments that can be mapped onto an optical packet depends on the TCP maximum segment size, on the optical packet length in time, and on the rate at which the optical network operates.

Let us consider, for instance, three different data rates for a land-line connec-tion: 2.5, 10, and 40 Gbps. If the duration of the optical packet is roughly 2 µsec,

TABLE 8.1: Maximum number of segments that can be stored in one optical packet MSS (bytes).

Rate (Gbps)-MSS (bytes)	460	960	Time length (μs)
2.5	1	0	2
10	5	2	2
40	20	5	2
2.5	2	1	4
10	10	5	4
40	13	20	4
2.5	4	1	6
10	16	7	6
40	65	31	6

it can contain 5 Kbit, 20 Kbit, and 80 Kbit, at 2.5, 10, and 40 Gbps, respectively. Thus, depending on the TCP maximum segment size (MSS), different numbers of segments are stored in the same optical packet. Table 8.1 reports how many segments can be put in one optical packet for different data rate values, two MSSs, 460 and 960 bytes (which means IP datagrams of 500 and 1000 bytes, respectively), and three different optical packet durations.

To define the packetization policy, TCP congestion mechanisms have to be taken into account. In the optical network scenario, congestion is a rare event, and it has been shown that packet-loss probability can be reduced to a mere 10^{-10}. Two mechanisms are employed by TCP to detect a loss, expiration of a retransmission timer (timeout), and reception of three duplicate ACKs. If congestion happens, fast retransmit and fast recovery come into play and avoid the negative effects caused by timeouts. Actually, Cohen and Hamo [110] claim that no more that three segments, hopefully two, are allowed to be lost from the same window to avoid timeouts, which mean a slow start. This must be taken into account when mapping TCP segments into optical packets. On the other hand, if an optical packet containing one or more datagrams with ACK messages belonging to different connections gets lost, this is not enough for the related retransmission timer(s) to expire so that, again, fast retransmit and fast recovery are invoked.

This means that to not penalize the end-to-end throughput, multiple segment losses within the same window must be avoided. Thus, when building the optical packet in the edge interface, it is necessary to be able to distinguish to which connection a TCP segment belongs to avoid to put TCP segments belonging to the same connection in the same optical packet. In other words, the edge interface operates in such a way that TCP segments belonging to the same connection are spaced far enough or, at least, are mapped into different optical packets.

Moreover, the edge interface is likely to be equipped with a control component responsible for managing and assigning labels according to FECs. This means that the optical edge device, when building optical packets, has to put into an optical packet segments both belonging to equal priority flows and addressed to the same remote edge device. Also, when possible, two consecutive segments of the same data flow have to be stored in separate optical packets with the same FEC, of course.

The final consideration is the behavior of TCP during the slow-start phase. During this phase, TCP segments are sent with exponential growth, while during congestion avoidance they are sent roughly linearly. In traditional routers, this may lead to congestion because the overall traffic addressed to an output link may temporarily exceed its capacity; therefore, output buffers must be accordingly dimensioned. The edge interface, on the other hand, works with very high speed output links that never get congested, at least with today's operating conditions. So this problem does not at all affect the optical network interface.

8.7.3   Optical Packet Design in the TCP/IP Environment

Following the general discussion of the previous section, here we provide some more detailed results concerning the influence of optical packet switching on TCP performance. In particular, we address the trade-off between the design parameters of optical packetization, such as the optical packet length and the timeout in the edge interface, when the performance is expressed in terms of packetization efficiency, packetization delay, and TCP congestion window behavior. The performance evaluation is carried out using the *ns* simulation tool described in Chapter 4.

To determine relationships between the packetization efficiency, the packet length, and the timeout, IP packet length distribution must be known. A typical behavior that corresponds to reality in many cases is represented by a bimodal distribution that, in this case, consists of packets whose length is between 64 bytes (45%) and 1536 bytes (30%) [107]. The simulation reference environment is represented in Figure 8.6, in which four optical switches are interconnected through 2.5 Gbps links, and each edge interface is loaded with 80 TCP agents, with average load 0.2 per TCP agent, distributed as group of four agents onto 20 links at 100 Mbps. Therefore, the resulting load on the output link of the edge interface at 2.5 Gbps is 0.8. The reference values of timeout are $t = 1.6510^{-6}$ s, $t' = 10t$, and $t'' = 100t$, t being the reference packet time of previously developed studies on optical packet networks [135]. Simulation results are analyzed below.

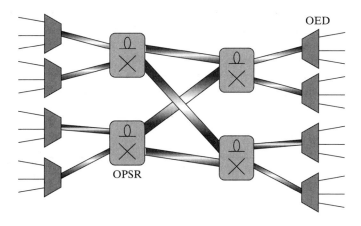

FIGURE 8.6: Network setup used in the simulations with *ns*.

Packetization Efficiency. Figure 8.7 shows the packetization efficiency as a function of the optical packet size for the three different values of the packetization timeout. Except for the case of the highest timeout, which in any case has negative effects on the delay, the packet size should be chosen in the range of, few hundreds of bytes so that the efficiency can reach its maximum. The optimal value of the efficiency increases as the timeout increases.

Packetization Delay. The packetization delay is represented in Figure 8.8 for the same values of the timeout. It shows the increase of the delay corresponding to increase in efficiency. The value of the packetization delay as a component of the end-to-end delay should be kept low so that it does not interfere with the TCP congestion control mechanisms. It is important that the congestion window be always adequately open so that the optical bandwidth can be efficiently used. We can notice a "knee" in the delay graph. It would be a good design choice to select the packet length to keep the delay at the right-hand side of the "knee." This can be achieved by selecting a packet greater than approximately 300 bytes.

Congestion Window. In Figure 8.9, the temporal behavior of the congestion window for two different values of packetization timeout is shown for a packet length of 400 bytes, that, taking into account the packet overhead, approximately corresponds to a packet duration of t at 2.5 Gbps. In the case of high timeout values, the congestion window shows lower values, and it closes to low values much more often. A much better behavior is shown for the lower timeout, where the window dynamic is much higher and congestion window does not close very often.

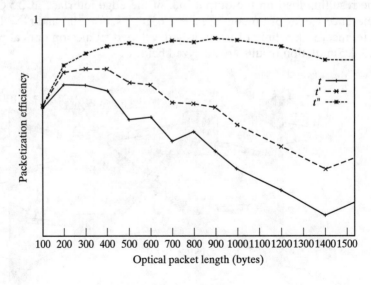

FIGURE 8.7: Packetization efficiency as a function of the optical packet length, for different values of the packetization timeout: $t = 1.65\,e\text{-}6$, $t' = 1.65\,e\text{-}5$, $t'' = 1.65\,e\text{-}4$.

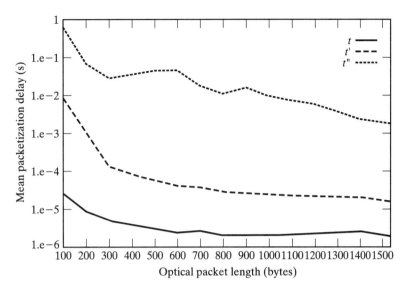

FIGURE 8.8: Packetization delay as a function of the optical packet length, for various values of the packetization timeout: $t = 1.65$ e-6, $t' = 1.65$ e-5, $t'' = 1.65$ e-4.

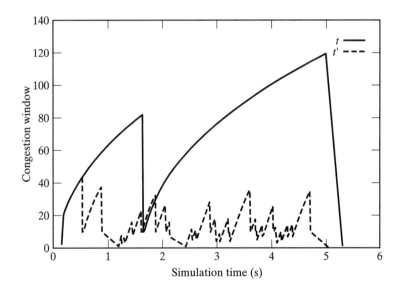

FIGURE 8.9: Example of a temporal behavior of the TCP congestion window for packet length of 400 bytes and different values of the packetization timeout: $t = 1.65$ e-6, $t' = 1.65$ e-5.

Summary of Simulation Results. Based on the preceding simulation results, we can make two important conclusions:

1. For TCP/IP traffic, optical packet length should be chosen around 300 to 500 bytes;
2. Packetization timeout should not be set to "very" large values.

8.8 FURTHER READING

Details of DWDM systems can be found in [214], and details of MPLS can be found in [279].

8.9 SUMMARY

Optical networks are being deployed to build very high speed Internet backbones. In this chapter, the mechanisms to carry TCP/IP traffic over the optical networks have been discussed. Such mechanisms include both optical label-switched and optical packet-switched techniques. Performance of TCP over label-switched paths is not a major issue, as congestion does not arise once an end-to-end wavelength path is established for the lifetime of a TCP session. However, there exist several performance issues for transporting TCP traffic over packet-switched optical networks. The design parameters of optical packetization, such as optical-packet length and packetization timeout, must be optimized to avoid negative impact of optical packet switching on TCP performance.

8.10 REVIEW QUESTIONS

1. What is all-optical networking, and what is the motivation behind it?
2. What is the fundamental difference between MPλS and optical packet switching?
3. In traditional IP routers, packets are buffered in memory queues when a given outgoing port is overloaded or congested. Can we also do the same kind of buffering in optical packet switches? Why or why not?
4. What constraints do we have for buffering optical packets? Explain how buffering can be achieved in optical switches.
5. What is wavelength multiplexing? How can it help manage congestion in optical switches?
6. What is wavelength packet (WP)? Why is WP more effective for connectionless networks than for connection-oriented networks?
7. What are the TCP performance issues in the MPλS over wavelength routed networks?
8. What are the TCP performance issues in the optical-packet switching networks?
9. Describe the delay components in a packet switching optical network. Why is the delay more in the edge devices than in the intermediate nodes?
10. What determines the number of TCP segments that can be packetized into a single optical packet?

11. To minimize the loss of end-to-end TCP throughput, what considerations are to be taken into account during packetizing IP datagrams into optical packet?

8.11 HANDS-ON PROJECTS

1. Repeat the *ns* simulation described in Section 8.7.3 for a reference network with eight optical switches. Now compare your results with those presented in Figures 8.7, 8.8, and 8.9. Do you observe any major difference?
2. Repeat the above simulation with different flavors of TCP (e.g., TCP Vegas and TCP Reno). Do you observe any difference? Write a report explaining your results.

CHAPTER 9

TCP/IP Performance over Satellite Networks

CHAPTER OBJECTIVES

After completing this chapter, the reader should be able to:

- Appreciate the role of satellites in TCP/IP networks

- Gain insight into the fundamental satellite link characteristics affecting TCP performance

- Consider a wide variety of approaches to address TCP performance issues in satellite networks

- Select appropriate tools and techniques to improve TCP/IP performance over satellite networks

The recent evolution of the Internet has been accompanied by new opportunities and market potential for multimedia applications and services. The emerging applications, for example, broadband access, IP multicast, media streaming, and content delivery distribution, require larger bandwidths and quality of service (QoS) guarantees as opposed to the "best effort" service in the traditional Internet. Satellite plays a significant role in developing a hybrid (satellite/terrestrial) network infrastructure that can support these emerging applications because of its number of advantages, including global coverage, bandwidth flexibility, reliability, and multicast capability. Annual satellite revenues globally will likely grow to over $100 billion by the end of year 2010 [267]; however, satellite network characteristics, for example, long propagation delay, channel impairment, and bandwidth asymmetry, pose new threats to TCP/IP performance. A number of TCP enhancements have been proposed and implemented to address these satellite-specific challenges. We begin this chapter with an introduction to satellite systems and architectures, followed by the TCP performance issues over satellite networks. We then discuss several key techniques and protocol implementations to enhance TCP performance over satellite networks.

9.1 A BRIEF HISTORY OF DATA SATELLITES

Historically, the first satellite network accessing the Internet, called SATNET, was initiated in mid-1975. The network was sponsored by the Advanced Research Projects Agency (ARPA), the Defense Communications Agency, the British Post Office, and the Norwegian Telecommunications Administrations [152]. The network consists of four ground stations (two in the Washington, D.C., area at Etam and Clarksburg; one in Goonhilly, England; and one in Tanum, Sweden) interconnected by a simplex, 64-Kbps Intelsat IV-A SPADE channel. The ground station sites were equipped with satellite Internet message processors (SIMPs), which were extensions of the ARPANET IMPs and which implemented channel access and network access protocols. Gateway computers, implemented with PDP-11 hardware, connected SATNET and ARPANET to permit internetwork communications. One of the goals of the SATNET experiments was to test the feasibility and extensibility of different channel access schemes [203, 206, 307] and to gain experience with the implementation, operation, and performance evaluation of packet satellite networks. New generation satellite networks are being developed with requirement of supporting Internet access and multimedia services and applications [27, 207].

9.2   MOTIVATIONS FOR USING SATELLITES

There are many motivations for using satellites. The main advantages of satellite communications are:

- *Ubiquitous coverage.* A single satellite system can reach every potential user across an entire continent regardless of location. Such coverage is particularly useful in areas with low subscriber density and/or in areas that are otherwise impossible or difficult to reach. Current satellites have various antenna types that generate different footprint sizes. The sizes range from coverage of the whole Earth as viewed from space (about 1/3 of the surface) down to a spot beam that covers much of Europe or North America. All these coverage options are usually available on the same satellite. Selection between coverage is made on transparent satellites by the signal frequencies. It is spot-beam coverage that is most relevant for access. Future systems will have very narrow spot beams of a few hundred miles across that have a width of a fraction of a degree.

- *Bandwidth flexibility.* Satellite bandwidth can be configured easily to provide capacity to customers in virtually any combination or configuration required. This includes simplex and duplex circuits from narrowband to wideband and symmetric and asymmetric configurations. Future satellite networks with narrow spot beams should deliver rates of up to 100 Mbps with a 90-cm antenna, and the backplane speed within the satellite switch could be typically in the Gbps range. The uplink rate from a 90-cm user terminal is typically 384 Kbps.

- *Cost.* The cost is independent of distance. The wide area coverage from a satellite means that it costs the same to receive the signal from anywhere within the coverage area.

- *Deployment.* Satellites can initiate service to an entire continent immediately after deployment, with short installation times for customer premise equipment. Once the network is in place, more users can be added easily.

- *Reliability and security.* Satellites are among the most reliable of all communication technologies, with the exception of SONET fault-tolerant designs. Satellite links only require the end stations to be maintained, and they are less prone to disabling through accidental or malicious damage.

- *Disaster recovery*. Satellite provides an alternative to damaged fiber-optic networks for disaster recovery options and provides emergency communications.

- *Connectivity*. Satellite networks provide multipoint-to-multipoint communications facilitated by the Internet and broadcasting capability.

9.3 TYPES OF SATELLITES

A satellite communication network system consists of a space segment and a ground segment. The space segment consists of satellites that are classified into geostationary orbit (GEO) and nongeostationary orbit (NGEO) satellites. The NGEO satellites are further divided into medium earth orbit (MEO) and low earth orbit (LEO) satellites according to the orbit altitude above the Earth's surface. Most of the first-generation satellite systems used GEO [25, 26], whereas next-generation satellite networks include MEO and LEO constellations in addition to GEOs. The features and characteristics of GEO, MEO, and LEO satellites are discussed next.

GEO Satellites.   The altitude of GEO satellites is 35,786 km above the surface of the Earth. The orbit period is 24 hours, which gives the advantage of continuous visibility and fixed geometry. This has made GEO satellites one of the principal means of distribution of television, telephone, and data communications throughout the world. Most of the commercial telecommunications satellites currently in operation are in GEO orbit. A GEO satellite can provide service to a very large area. If we restrict the look angle of the ground station to a minimum of 20 degrees above the horizon, the surface area that can be served by one satellite corresponds to about 135 million square kilometers, or 26% of the total surface of the Earth. Only three GEO satellites are required to provide service to all the tropical and temperate zones but not the poles. Because of their positions above the equator, GEO satellites cannot provide service beyond 81 degrees north or south latitudes (76 degrees latitude if we restrict the minimum ground station elevation to 5 degrees above the horizon). The significant problem with GEO is the propagation delay. The typical one-way propagation delay is about 250 to 280 ms, which makes GEO satellites not applicable to real-time applications.

LEO Satellites.   The altitude of LEO satellites is typically between 700 and 2000 km. Altitudes between 2000 and 5000 km are avoided because of the presence of the Van Allen radiation belt, which is capable of damaging satellites. The orbit period is somewhere between 100 and 120 minutes. Providing continuous communications coverage to a given point on Earth using LEO satellites requires the use of 6 to 8 planes with 6 satellites per plane. To avoid interruptions at the end of each pass, data buffering must be employed at the ground station, or the next visible satellite must be acquired and tracked before communications are handed over from the setting satellite. Because of the lower altitude, LEO satellites can provide service to a rather small area at any given time. One-way propagation delay is about 20 to 25 ms. LEO satellites operating in high inclination orbits can provide service to the near-polar regions. Motorola's Iridium and GlobalStar belong to this category [138]. Iridium uses 66 LEO satellite constellation, and GlobalStar uses 48

TABLE 9.1: Comparison between LEO, MEO, and GEO.

Orbit type	Low Earth Orbit (LEO)	Medium Earth Orbit (MEO)	Geostationary Earth Orbit (GEO)
Altitude (km)	700 to 2000	10,000 to 15,000	36,000
Satellites needed for global coverage	> 32	10 to 15	3 to 4[1]
One-way propagation delay	5–20 ms	100–130 ms	250–280 ms
Elevation angle	Low to medium	Medium to high	Low to medium
Capacity per satellite	128 Mbps–10 Gbps	128 Mbps–10 Gbps	1–50 Gbps
Handover	Frequent	Infrequent	Never
Onboard processing	Possible	Possible	Possible
Store and forward	Yes	Yes	Not required
Point to point connections	No	No	Yes
VSATs	Yes[2]	Yes[2]	Yes[3]
Broadcast TV	No	No	Yes
SNG (satellite news gathering)	Yes	Yes	Yes

(1) Coverage only extends to latitudes of 70° N and 70° S
(2) Via a regional gateway
(3) Private and shared hubs possible

LEO satellites. Both these systems were designed to provide telephone services. GlobalStar currently is being used for emergency communications as well.

MEO Satellites. The altitude of MEO satellites has to be selected between the inner and outer Van Allen radiation belts, typically around 10,355 km above the surface of the Earth. The orbit period is 6 hours. The world can be covered by 10 to 12 satellites in 2 to 3 planes, that is, 5 satellites in each of the 2 planes or 4 satellites in each of the 3 planes. The typical propagation delay for a MEO satellite is 110 to 130 ms. An example of MEO satellite system is ICO [64]. Table 9.1 shows a comparison of LEO, MEO, and GEO system characteristics.

9.4 SATELLITE INTERNET ARCHITECTURES

In a broad sense, satellite Internet is classified into two major categories: connectivity networks and access networks.

1. *Connectivity networks.* In connectivity satellite networks, user-to-user connectivity is established via satellite onboard routing. It avoids some degree of ground infrastructure. Bandwidth utilization efficiency can be gained through the use of onboard processing and ATM or fast packet switching or even optical switching in the distant future. As a consequence, the complexity and

TABLE 9.2: Global Broadband Satellite Networks.

Services	Spaceway	Astrolink[1]	EuroSky Way	Teledesic[1]
Data uplink[2]	0.384–6	0.384–2	0.160–2	0.016–2
Data downlink[2]	0.384–20	0.384–155	0.128–640	0.016–64
Number of satellites	8	9	5	30
Satellites	GEO	GEO	GEO	MEO
Frequency band	Ka	Ka	Ka	Ka
On-board processing	Yes	Yes	Yes	Yes
Operation scheduled	2003	2003	2004	2004/5

(1) Program onhold
(2) All bandwidth in Mbps

TABLE 9.3: Satellite Access Systems.

Characteristics	Star Band	Wild Blue	IPStar	Astra BBI	Cyber star	DirectPC (Hughes)
Data uplink[1]	38–153 K	384 K–6 M	2 M	2 M	0.5–6 M	128–256 K
Data downlink[1]	40 M	384 K–20 M	10 M	38 M	Max. 27 M	Max. 3 M
Market	Consumer	Business SME	Consumer business	Business	ISP multicast	Consumer business
Frequency band	Ku	Ka	Ku	Ka	Ku/Ka	Ku, Ka
Satellite	GEO	GEO	GEO	GEO	GEO	Eutelsat Hotbird Galaxy
Operation scheduled	Nov. 2000	Mid 2002[2]	Late 2002	Late 2000	1999–2001	1997–2001

(1) Kbps/Mbps
(2) Delayed

    demand for satellite resources can be much higher than that needed for an access satellite [105, 155, 207, 312].

2. *Access networks.* Access networks, on the other hand, have evolved with the new application of broadband interactive connectivity to the Internet. These networks require a forward link from the network gateway to the user and the return link from the user to the network gateway. These two links are highly asymmetric, and the links may have totally different characteristics. The bandwidth allocation must accommodate two links per user [168]. Frequency reuse is employed, and different frequency bands can be used for the user and gateway links.

Table 9.2 provides some of the new generation Ka-/Ku-band satellite systems comparison. These systems, which are under development at the time of writing this book, are expected to provide global coverage and high bandwidth. Table 9.3 describes different broadband access systems, which provide regional coverage and are less complicated than their global or connectivity counterparts. They are more cost-effective, have less associated technical risk, and have fewer regulatory issues. Currently, StarBand, Cyberstar, and DirectPC are already supporting Internet users as an alternative technology to DSL and cable modem.

The global satellite networks and access systems described in Tables 9.2 and 9.3 require to support broadband Internet access. However, to achieve high data throughput, TCP has to be optimized to accommodate satellite link characteristics such as long propagation delay, high error rates, and bandwidth asymmetry. The main focus of this chapter is the enhancements made to TCP to overcome these impairments. These are discussed further in Sections 9.7, 9.8, 9.9, and 9.10.

9.5   SATELLITE CHARACTERISTICS AFFECTING TCP

Although satellite links have been part of the Internet from its beginning, the rapid expansion and evolution of the Internet have accentuated certain performance limitations imposed by satellite links. In this section, we discuss the link characteristics affecting TCP behavior and performance in satellite communications environment.

9.5.1   Long Feedback Loop

There are three components of end-to-end latency: propagation delay, transmission delay, and queuing delay, of which propagation delay is the dominant part in satellite links. For GEO satellites, one-way propagation delay is typically on the order of 270 ms and may be more when forward error correction (FEC) is used. So, TCP round-trip time (RTT) is more than 500 ms, which is the time it takes for a TCP sender to determine whether a packet has been successfully received at the destination. This long feedback delay has several undesirable effects on TCP.

Slow Start.   TCP uses the Slow Start mechanism to probe the network at the start of connection. The time required by the Slow Start to reach a bit rate B is given by the following formula [28, 29, 153, 261]:

$$Slow\ Start\ Duration = RTT \left(1 + \log_2 \frac{B * RTT}{l}\right)$$

where l is the average packet length expressed in bits. The equation is satisfied if the Delayed ACK Option is not implemented, that is, the receiver sends one acknowledgment (ACK) for each received segment. Simulation results of Figures 9.1 and 9.2 show TCP sequence number growth and TCP throughput, respectively, during Slow Start. In this simulation, a GEO satellite link ($RTT = 560$ ms) of 1.5 Mbps and packet size of 1 KB were used. It is clear that it takes time for TCP to increase the throughput. In the meantime, if there are no other connections, the available bandwidth is wasted. In Table 9.4 [261] are shown the duration of Slow Start phase for different types of satellites, LEO, MEO and GEO, and for different values of B, when $l = 1$ KB, which is a common value for TCP segment size. It

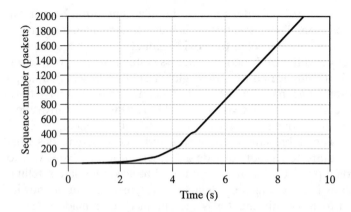

FIGURE 9.1: Sequence number of TCP segments during Slow Start.

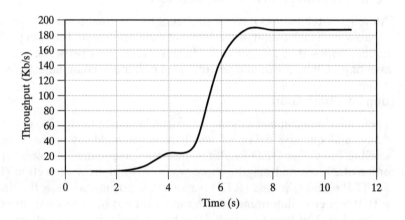

FIGURE 9.2: TCP throughput during Slow Start.

TABLE 9.4: Duration of Slow Start for LEO, MEO, and GEO Satellites.

Satellite Type	RTT (ms)	Slow Start Duration (seconds)		
		B = 1 Mb/s	B = 10 Mb/s	B = 155 Mb/s
LEO	50	0.18	0.35	0.55
MEO	250	1.49	2.32	3.31
GEO	550	3.91	5.73	7.91

is clear that for long-delay satellites, such as GEOs, TCP stays longer on Slow Start, which explains the poor utilization reported in many studies [29, 37, 41, 261]. Figure 9.3 compares simulation results of Slow Start over satellite ($RTT = 500$ ms) and terrestrial ($RTT = 80$ ms) links in terms of data transfer. Slow Start duration in terrestrial links are orders of magnitude shorter than those in satellite links.

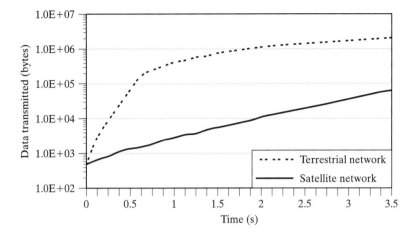

FIGURE 9.3: Slow Start comparison [41]. Simulations of the amount of data sent by TCP over a satellite network ($RTT = 500$ ms) and a terrestrial network ($RTT = 80$ ms) as a function of time. The amount of time shown represents the Slow Start Duration of a TCP connection over the GEO link to reach the advertised window using Slow Start.

If delayed ACK mechanism [70] is implemented, then the time required by the Slow Start to reach the bit rate B is given by the following formula [153]:

$$Slow\ Start\ Duration = RTT \left(1 + \log_{1.5} \frac{B * RTT}{l}\right)$$

That means the Slow Start Duration becomes even longer than what is indicated in Table 9.4. Thus, delayed ACK is another source of wasted capacity during the Slow Start phase.

Many actual TCP flows, like those carrying HTTP, transfer small files. In these cases, the entire transfer could be complete during Slow Start. This means that a TCP connection is not able to utilize all available resources in the network.

Furthermore, when packets are lost, TCP reenters Slow Start or Congestion Avoidance, and the losses could be caused by link errors and not by congestion. When TCP experiences losses early in the Slow Start, it sets its initial estimate of the available bandwidth far too low. Because the probing becomes linear (Congestion Avoidance) rather than exponential, after the initial estimate is set, the time to get to full transmission rate can be very long [261].

Congestion Avoidance.   As in Slow Start, the growth of data rate is a function of bandwidth delay product in Congestion Avoidance, too. In fact, during each RTT the data rate increases by $l/(B * RTT)$. So if a TCP connection is in Congestion Avoidance and some bandwidth becomes available, it will take a long time for this connection to use the available bandwidth. This time will be much longer in the presence of transmission losses. Therefore, the Congestion Avoidance in satellite networks with long RTTs performs worse than in terrestrial networks, as illustrated in Figure 9.4.

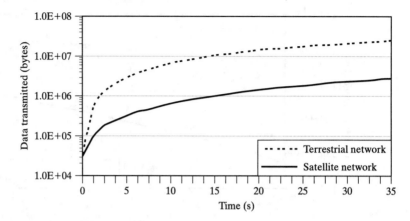

FIGURE 9.4: Congestion Avoidance comparison [41]. Simulations of the amount of data sent by TCP over a satellite network ($RTT = 500$ ms) and a terrestrial network ($RTT = 80$ ms) as a function of time. The amount of time shown represents the Slow Start Duration of a TCP connection over the GEO link to reach the advertised window using Congestion Avoidance.

Fast Retransmit and Fast Recovery.   Fast Retransmit and Fast Recovery, discussed in Chapter 11, are also affected by long RTTs. Satellite connections are able to inject enough new segments into the network during recovery to trigger multiple fast retransmissions per window of data, which may severely damaged TCP performance.

TCP Fairness.   TCP throughput fairness is another issue over satellite links with very long RTTs. Because the TCP algorithm is self-clocking, based on received ACKs, several connections sharing the same bottleneck may see their clocks running at different speeds. A long RTT connection cannot increase its congestion window as quickly as a short RTT connection can. The short RTT connection unfairly captures a larger portion of the network bandwidth as a result. This is particularly true in the presence of congestion and subsequent loss, where the congestion window is opened linearly based on the RTT of the connection. Moreover, the congestion window of long RTT connections has "farther to go" before the optimal value is reached due to the large bandwidth-delay product. This further limits the throughput of long RTT connections through the bottleneck, as compared to shorter RTT connections.

9.5.2   Link Impairment

Satellite systems are subject to various impairment, including multipath, interference, fading, rain attenuation and shadowing. Bit error ratio (BER) using legacy equipment and existing transponder technology is in the range of 10^{-4} to 10^{-7}. Even though advanced modulation and adaptive coding techniques can reduce the BER to the order of 10^{-10}, satellite networks in general experience higher BER than terrestrial networks.

TCP was initially developed for wire-line with low BER, such that the majority of segment losses are due to network congestion. Thus, TCP uses all packet drops

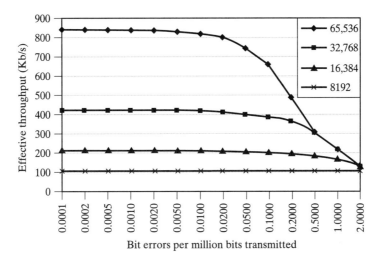

FIGURE 9.5: Impact of bit error rate on TCP throughput for large files with window size as parameter. $RTT = 590$ seconds and B $= 2048$ Kb/s.

as signals of network congestion. So, TCP cannot distinguish between a segment loss caused by congestion and a loss caused by bit errors. Consequently, the sender reduces its transmission rate even when segments are lost because of bit errors. As discussed in Section 9.5.1, losses during Slow Start and Congestion Avoidance lead to lower throughput than the available bandwidth and consequently degrade TCP performance. The combination of high BER and long RTT leads multiple segment to loss within a single window. As explained in Chapter 11, multiple segment loss is a fundamental issue with TCP.

Figure 9.5 shows the effect of BER on TCP throughput for different window sizes. The data are from an experiment [173] over a GEO link with RTT being 590 ms and channel bandwidth 2048 Kbps. It is clear from the figure that TCP performs poorly in the presence of high error rates. Another interesting observation is that TCP is more sensitive to errors for larger window size. It turns out that for very large congestion windows, the BER has to be so low that it is almost impossible with today's technology [262] to achieve this. Note that this is not only a problem of TCP over satellite links. Even in case of TCP over fiber links and bandwidth of several Gb/s, the required BER is too low to be achieved in practice [147]. In response to this problem, a new version of TCP, called HighSpeed TCP, is being proposed [147]. HighSpeed TCP is discussed in Section 9.8.

9.5.3   Bandwidth-Delay Product

The bandwidth-delay product (BDP) defines the amount of data a TCP connection should have "in flight" (data that have been transmitted but not yet acknowledged) at any time to fully utilize the channel available capacity. The delay used in this case is the RTT, and the bandwidth is the capacity of the bottleneck link in the path. Because the RTT for GEO satellites is large and higher bandwidth links are required, TCP needs to keep a large number of packets sent but not yet acknowledged.

TABLE 9.5: Round trip times corresponding to the maximum standard window size of 64 Kb at various rates.

Rate (b/s)	RTT (seconds)
33.6 K	15.6
128 K	4.096
1.55 M	0.340
10 M	0.050
155 M	0.003
622 M	0.0008

In connections with a large bandwidth-delay product, such as GEO satellite networks, TCP senders and receivers with limited congestion/receive windows are not able to take advantage of the available bandwidth. The standard maximum TCP window of 65,535 bytes is not adequate to allow a single TCP connection to utilize the entire bandwidth available on some satellite channels. In a loss-free network, the TCP throughput is limited by the following formula [272]:

$$Max\ throughput = \frac{window\ size}{RTT}$$

Therefore, when using the maximum TCP window size of 65,535 bytes and a GEO satellite link with RTT of 560 ms, the maximum throughput is limited to:

$$Max\ throughput = 65,535\ bytes/560\ ms = 117,027\ bytes/second$$

Therefore, a single standard TCP connection cannot fully utilize even a T1 rate GEO channel. Table 9.5 shows the maximum RTT to be able to use a given bandwidth with a single TCP connection using the maximum window size of 64 KB. In general, multiple TCP flows share the satellite bandwidth. In this case, even though a single flow cannot utilize the channel capacity, the set of flows might be able to.

Another problem related to the high BDP is the stability of TCP congestion control schemes. Analysis in [222] shows that as BDP increases, active queue management schemes (see Chapter 12) including Random Early Detection (RED), Random Early Marking (REM), Proportional Integral (PI) controller, and Virtual Queue, all eventually become prone to instability, which leads to lower performance.

9.5.4 Bandwidth Asymmetry

In broadband satellite access networks, *bandwidth asymmetry*, between forward and return channels, exists on the order of 10:1 or more. Thus, as discussed in Chapter 10, a low bandwidth acknowledgment path can significantly slow down the growth of the TCP sender window during Slow Start, causing poor utilization of expensive satellite channels. Several techniques to improve TCP performance over links exhibiting bandwidth asymmetry are discussed in Chapter 10.

9.5.5 Variable Delays

If LEO and MEO satellites are used, the propagation delay is much less than that for the GEO; however, the problem with LEO and MEO orbits is their variability. Because these satellites are not geostationary, for continuous communications there is the need for intersatellite links, which also adds to the delay and the variability. For example, for LEOs, the delay can vary from a few ms to about 80 ms. This could affect the accuracy of TCP RTT and timeout estimation. Studies (on Teledesic systems) show that delay variation in LEO satellite constellations has insignificant impact on TCP performance [35, 40]. However, more studies are needed to understand better whether this will have an impact on TCP performance.

9.5.6 LEO Handoff

For continuing coverage, a TCP connection may be handed off from one LEO satellite to another. The handoff may cause packet loss. Also, the propagation delay may vary because of changes in the connection path, and the queuing delay and delay variation may be significant. Large variations of RTT may lead to false timeouts and retransmissions. Intersatellite routing could also cause congestion inside future LEO satellite networks.

9.5.7 Spectral Congestion

The radio spectrum is not only limited by nature but also the allocations for commercial communications are regulated by international agreements. With the use of satellites in high-speed Internet, the bottleneck in the system is likely in the links between the Earth and satellites. These links are fundamentally limited by the uplink/downlink spectrum. The internal satellite network should generally be free of heavy congestion, but the gateways between the satellite and the Internet could become congested more easily, particularly if admission control were not efficient [162]. Congestion can lead to packet loss and adversely affect TCP performance.

9.5.8 Security

Satellite communications are especially sensitive to security attacks. Indeed, having a broadcast nature, satellite transmissions can easily be intercepted and corrupted. Eavesdropping on network links is a form of passive attack that could reveal critical traffic control information that would compromise the proper functioning of the network. Eavesdropping could also imperil the privacy of user data. Passive monitoring is easier in wireless and satellite networks, where it can be conducted without detection. However, the resources needed to monitor a satellite link are not trivial [35].

9.6 GOALS FOR TCP PERFORMANCE ENHANCEMENT SOLUTIONS

The impairment and problems that TCP encounters over satellite links degrade its performance considerably in such environments. To mitigate these negative effects, a number of solutions have been proposed by the research community. These proposed performance-enhancing techniques can be broadly categorized into link layer solutions and TCP layer solutions. At the link layer, solutions are introduced to repair and hide link layer impairment from TCP layer. The predominant solution at this layer is forward error correction (FEC) [232, 281] to reduce BER. TCP layer solutions can be further divided into two categories:

End-to-end solutions in which the end-to-end semantic of TCP is maintained. These types of solutions are discussed in Sections 9.7 and 9.8.

Non–end-to-end solutions in which the end-to-end semantic of TCP is violated. These types of solutions are also known as Performance-Enhancing Proxy (PEP) and are discussed in Section 9.10.

It is clear that there is no single perfect solution for all TCP problems over satellite links. The proposed solutions have their strengths and their drawbacks. In some cases, a mitigation for a given problem results in degrading other aspects of TCP performance. In the end, as in all engineering problems, network designers have to select one solution or a combination of them based on the best trade-offs among their features and the system requirements and applications. In this section, we present a number of goals that can be used as guidance when evaluating alternate methods of improving TCP/IP performance over satellite links [300].

Scalability.   The Internet is becoming the universal media of communications and is essential for most social activities; therefore, scalability in terms of the number of users and data rates is the first requirement to be satisfied. That is true for satellite networks as part of the Internet infrastructures. This means that enhancement solutions that lead to congestion aggravation or collapse should be avoided.

Transparency.   Transparency means that the improvement mechanism has no impact on the TCP connections with the exception of improving their performance. The improvement mechanism should be invisible to the end user and should not break the integrity of end-to-end TCP flow. For example, the enhancement should not compromise the security features of the end-to-end communications.

Backward Compatibility.   The enhancement mechanism should work with the existing Internet protocols and infrastructures. Independently of the satellite industry growth, satellite links will remain a small fraction of Internet infrastructure for the foreseeable future; therefore, it is unrealistic to expect the entire Internet community to change their protocols or applications to allow for users who access the network via satellite. Also, the enhancement solutions should be application-independent.

Efficiency.   Satellite resources are typically more expensive and scarcer than terrestrial ones, such as optical fibers. The enhancement solutions, therefore, should make the use of satellite links as efficiently as possible.

Economy.   Finally, the enhancement solution should make the satellite service both competitive with other alternatives and appealing to users and service providers. That means the service should offer a good trade-off between cost and quality of service to users and be profitable for service providers.

9.7 TCP ENHANCEMENTS FOR SATELLITE NETWORKS

In this section, we present TCP enhancement solutions in which the end-to-end semantic of TCP is maintained. These types of solutions are desirable from the point of view of the general Internet architecture and end-to-end principle [148]. Their main drawback, however, is that they require changes to be made in all end and/or intermediate nodes, so in some cases, violating the backward compatibility, scalability, and economic goals. The research community has generated a large number of end-to-end solutions, but IETF has been very careful in recommending just a few of them. Even though an end-to-end solution could perform very well over satellite links, to be recommended it should at least not harm the rest of the Internet traffic.

Fast Retransmit, TCP NewReno, Selective Acknowledgements, and TCP Vegas discussed in Chapters 6 and 11 are helpful in satellite networks too. These ideas are particularly important in satellite networks, where because of their large bandwidth-delay product, a large number of segments are in flight at any given time, causing multiple segment losses within a window. In this section, we consider several other TCP enhancements that appear promising for satellite networks.

9.7.1 Path MTU Discovery

Path Maximum Transmission Unit (MTU) Discovery [246] is used to determine the maximum packet size a connection can use on a given network path without being subjected to IP fragmentation. The sender transmits a packet that is the appropriate size for the local network to which it is connected and sets the IP "Don't Fragment". (DF) bit. If the packet is too large to be forwarded by a given router along the path, this router returns an Internet Control Message Protocol (ICMP) message to the sender. The ICMP message indicates that the original segment could not be transmitted without being fragmented and also contains the size of the largest packet that can be forwarded by the router. More information regarding MTU Discovery can be found in [204].

Path MTU Discovery allows TCP to use the largest possible packet size without the cost of fragmentation and reassembly. TCP congestion window is increased in number of segments, rather than bytes; therefore, larger segments enable TCP sender to increase the congestion window more rapidly in terms of bytes. That means TCP yields better channel utilization [35].

The disadvantage of Path MTU Discovery is that it may cause a delay before TCP is able to determine the maximum allowable packet size in the path between sender and receiver. Satellite delays can aggravate this problem. In practice, however, Path MTU Discovery does not consume a large amount of time due to wide support of common MTU values [35]. Additionally, caching MTU values may be able to eliminate discovery time, although the exact implementation of this and the aging values remains an open issue. Path MTU Discovery is recommended to be used with TCP over satellite links [35].

9.7.2 TCP for Transactions

TCP for Transactions (T/TCP) attempts to reduce the connection handshaking latency from two to one RTT for small transactions [71]. T/TCP achieves this by

TABLE 9.6: TCP delay effects on HTTP transfer for GEO and LEO satellite connections. All delays are in seconds.

TCP Option	GEO RTT = 600 ms		LEO RTT = 80 ms	
	1500 byte	**500 byte**	**1500 byte**	**500 byte**
Standard TCP	1.9	2.5	0.31	0.42
T/TCP	1.2	1.7	0.17	0.25
TCP with "4 MSS"	1.4	1.7	0.18	0.23
T/TCP with "4 MSS"	0.8	1.1	0.10	0.15

allowing the sender (server) to transmit data in the first segment sent (along with SYN). This reduction in latency can be significant for short web traffic over satellite links. In Table 9.6 the HTTP delay experienced with TCP and T/TCP over GEO and LEO links is compared for maximum segment size of 1500 and 500 bytes [162]. The results clearly indicate that HTTP transfers experience shorter delays over T/TCP. The results also indicate that like TCP, T/TCP's Slow Start has problems with large RTTs. In fact, the lowest delays are obtained combining T/TCP with 4MSS, which means starting Slow Start with an initial window of four. A drawback of T/TCP is that it is more vulnerable than TCP against spoofing and SYN flooding attacks [281].

9.7.3 Window Scaling

Small window size can severely limit TCP throughput over long propagation links (Figures 9.6 and 9.7). The standard TCP has a maximum window size of 64 KB, which is too small for high-speed satellite links. The window scale option, recommended in RFC 1323 [181], significantly increases the amount of data that can be outstanding by introducing a scale factor to be applied to the window field. With the scaling, TCP can achieve a window size of 1.1 GB. A satellite connection can now theoretically achieve a throughput upward of 15 Gbps, which is more than adequate for current satellite networks. However, increased window size can also cause sequence number wraparound problems for TCP. To address the wraparound problem, TCP needs to implement two mechanisms, namely, Protection Against Wraparound Sequence (PAWS) Number and Round-Trip Time Measurements (RTTM). PAWS and RTTM work as follows. Based on its clock, TCP sender puts a 32-bit timestamp in the segment header. The receiver echoes this timestamp back to the sender using the acknowledgments, and the sender subtracts this timestamp from the current time to measure the RTT. The timestamp concatenated with the sequence number is used by the PAWS algorithm to avoid wraparound.

Using large windows often requires both client and server applications or TCP stacks to be hand-tuned (see Appendix C) by experts. Furthermore, even if the window scale factor is implemented, it is up to the application layer to take advantage of a large window and most of the applications in use do not. For example, Unix FTP typically advertises windows between 4 and 24 Kbytes.

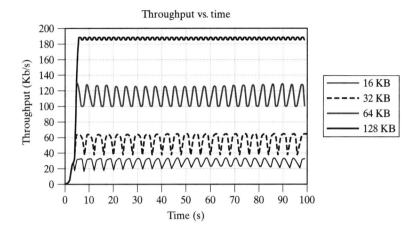

FIGURE 9.6: TCP throughput as a function of time over a 2048 Kb/s GEO link with $RTT = 580$ m.

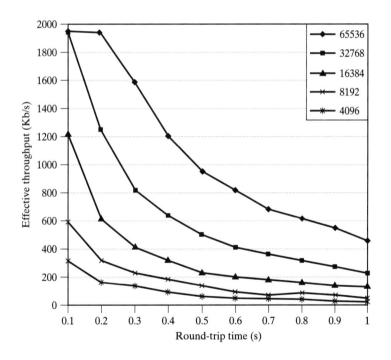

FIGURE 9.7: TCP throughput as a function of RTT over a 2048 Kb/s GEO link with $RTT = 580$ m.

9.7.4 Large Initial Window

Ideally, the sender would like to increase the value of the congestion window (*cwnd*) as quickly as possible to maximize throughput, but in Slow Start this is done slowly to probe the network bandwidth and, therefore, the duration of Slow Start can be a limitation to performance, as seen in Section 9.5.1.

The initial phase of a TCP connection begins with a value of initial congestion window (IW) equal to 1 at the sender's side (although an IW of 2 segments is allowed) [36]. As the Slow Start phase progresses, *cwnd* is increased based on the incoming ACKs. The Large Initial Window proposes to begin with a larger value of *cwnd*, allowing more segments to be transmitted during the first RTT of the connection [34, 36]. This in turn speeds up the number of ACKs received at the sender, allowing the congestion window to increase at a faster rate. The initial value of *cwnd* is defined [34] as follows:

$$IW = min\{4 \text{ MSS}, \ max\{2 \text{ MSS}, \ 4380 \text{ bytes}\}\}$$

where MSS defines the maximum segment size. Equivalently, the upper bound for IW size is based on the MSS, as follows:

```
If (MSS <= 1095 bytes)
    then IW <= 4 * MSS;
If (1095 bytes < MSS < 2190 bytes)
    then IW <= 4380 bytes;
If (2190 bytes <= MSS)
    then IW <= 2 * MSS;
```

The IW only applies to the first RTT of data transmission following the TCP three-way handshake [34].

With this option the duration of Slow Start (reported as Slow Start Duration in Table 9.4) can be reduced by up to three RTTs. Note from Table 9.4 that even after this reduction, Slow Start Duration for GEO satellites can still be very high. When delayed ACKs are used, the increased IW can also save a delayed ACK time out compared to initial *cwnd* of one segment.

For connections transmitting only a small amount of data, a larger IW reduces the transmission time, assuming low segment drop rate. For many e-mail and HTTP transfers [141] that are less than 4K bytes, the larger IW would reduce the data transfer time to a single RTT.

Several research studies have evidenced the advantage of a larger initial window. In [209] a reduction in World Wide Web page transfer over satellite links is shown. Marchese in [233] shows that the advantage of an increased IW is more evident for shorter transfers. The measurements in [162] indicate that the combination of T/TCP and a larger IW yields an improvement up to 50% compared to standard TCP.

Simulation results of Figure 9.8 demonstrate the impact of increasing IW from 1 to 4 to the number of sequences sent in time. For higher IW, TCP can send more segments during the same period of time; therefore, the throughput will increase, as shown by simulations results in Figure 9.9. The impact of using an IW of 4 is shown also in Table 9.6.

Using an IW of three or four segments is not expected to present any danger of congestion collapse [34]; however, it may degrade the performance in some networks. A larger IW is beneficial especially for short transfer over long RTTs at the cost of bursting data into a network with unknown conditions, which could lead

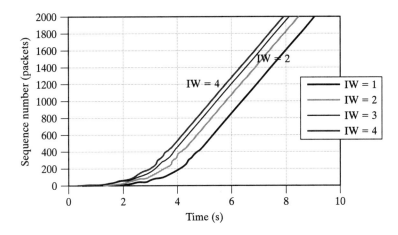

FIGURE 9.8: Sequence number of TCP segments during Slow Start with IW as parameter.

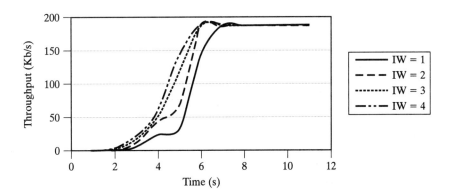

FIGURE 9.9: TCP throughput during Slow Start with IW as parameter.

to congestion and more losses. Reducing the burstiness of traffic, for example by pacing the segments in a burst [311], may make the use of a larger initial window more appropriate.

For cases where IWs larger than four segments are needed, researchers have proposed new solutions such as the Quick-Start mechanism discussed later in Section 9.8.1.

9.7.5 Byte Counting

This enhancement is designed to counter the effects of the delayed ACKs on TCP throughput. As discussed in Section 9.5.1, delayed ACKs increase the time needed by the TCP sender to increment the congestion window during Slow Start. Byte counting proposes to increase the congestion window based on the number of transmitted bytes acknowledged by incoming ACKs, rather than on the number

TABLE 9.7: Throughput improvement
by using byte counting.

File Size	Throughput Improvement (%)
30 KB	9.4
100 KB	16.9
200 KB	15.3
5 MB	9.5

of ACKs received [34, 38]. In this way, the congestion window is opened according to the amount of data transmitted, rather than on the receiver's ACK interval.

Table 9.7 reports the throughput improvement when *cwnd* is increased based on byte counting instead of ACK counting. As shown, the improvement for short transfers is better than for long ones. This indicates that byte counting not only is important in Slow Start but also remains beneficial during Congestion Avoidance.

There are three forms of byte counting presented in [38, 39]. The first is *unlimited byte counting* (UBC) [38]. This mechanism simply uses the number of previously unacknowledged bytes to increase the congestion window for each ACK. UBC has been shown to improve transfer time in limited tests over satellite links [37], but it is also too aggressive during Slow Start–based loss recovery. The second form, called *limited byte counting* (LBC) [38], was designed to fix UBC aggressiveness by limiting the amount of *cwnd* increase to two segments. However, LBC is still slightly more aggressive than the standard algorithm during Slow Start loss recovery [39]. The third form of the mechanism, called *appropriate byte counting* (ABC) [39], applies LBC only during initial Slow-Start period. The reason for such a change is that an ACK for N previously unacknowledged segments during loss recovery does not necessarily indicate that N segments have left the network in the last RTT. For example, suppose segment N is dropped by the network and segments $N+1$ and $N+2$ arrive successfully at the receiver. The TCP sender receives only two duplicate ACKs and, therefore, must rely on the retransmission timer (RTO) to detect the loss. When RTO expires, segment N is retransmitted. The ACK sent in response to this retransmission is for $N+2$. However, this ACK does not indicate that three segments have left the network in the last RTT, but rather only that one segment left the network. Therefore, the appropriate increase of *cwnd* is only one segment.

ABC is shown to increase throughput but still needs to be tested over a wide range of real networks [39]. At the time of writing this book, ABC is being considered by IETF [32].

9.7.6 Delayed ACKs after Slow Start

With Delayed ACK option, receivers do not acknowledge every incoming segment, but rather every other segment. While this can be advantageous on asymmetric links with low bandwidth in the return direction, this strategy slows the growth of the congestion window during Slow Start and can limit throughput, because new transmissions are clocked out based on received ACK. Delayed ACKs after Slow

Start (DAASS) is a strategy designed to counter the effects of delayed ACKs on long delay paths [38]. The receiver acknowledges every incoming segment during the Slow Start phase, and returns to the delayed ACK algorithm during Congestion Avoidance. Thus, the Slow Start phase is shortened because the sender's congestion window reaches its maximum value more quickly. In simulations [38], using DAASS improves transfer time compared to a receiver that always generates delayed ACKs. Using DAASS increases the loss rate slightly because the sender is more aggressively injecting segments into the network.

The major problem with DAASS is in the implementation. It is not clear how the receiver knows when the sender has terminated the Slow-Start phase and, therefore, the implementation of DAASS is an open issue. DAASS has several possible interactions with other proposals made by the research community. DAASS can aggravate the congestion on asymmetric networks by sending more ACKs. So, the interaction between DAASS and the methods proposed to reduce the number of ACKs is an open research question. DAASS also provides some of the same benefits as using a larger initial congestion window, and it, therefore, may not be desirable to use both mechanisms together. Because of these issues, DAASS is not recommended and more research is required in this direction.

9.7.7 Explicit Congestion Notification

Explicit Congestion Notification (ECN) allows routers to inform TCP senders about imminent congestion without dropping segments [143, 278]. In case of congestion, routers mark IP packets with a special Congestion Experienced (CE) codepoint, and the TCP receiver echoes the congestion information back to the sender in an ACK packet. ECN improves the performance of TCP connections. In particular, as shown in the simulation-based comparisons [143], one advantage of ECN is its ability to avoid unnecessary packet drops for short or delay-sensitive TCP connections. A second advantage of ECN is in avoiding some unnecessary retransmit timeouts in TCP. As discussed above, determining whether a segment loss was caused by congestion or corruption is very important for TCP performance over satellite links. ECN mechanism can be used as part of a mechanism to differentiate between congestion losses and error losses in satellite networks. More research work is needed in this direction. The implementation of ECN requires the deployment of Active Queue Management such as RED in routers. ECN is already an IETF standard and is likely to be adopted gradually in the Internet [278].

9.7.8 Multiple Connections

Another way to overcome the TCP's inefficiencies in satellite environment is to use multiple TCP flows to transfer a given file. The use of N TCP connections makes the sender N times more aggressive and, therefore, can improve the throughput in some situations [41–43]. However, with the aggressiveness comes the risk of aggravating congestion in the network [38]. Also, the advantages [33] provided by using multiple TCP connections are now largely provided by TCP extensions such as larger window and SACKS.

9.7.9 Pacing TCP Segments

TCP congestion control is not well matched to large but intermittent bursts of traffic, such as responses from HTTP/1.1, which uses persistent TCP connections to transfer multiple web page elements. When restarting data flow after an idle period, standard TCP either begins Slow Start or uses the prior congestion window. The first approach leads to low performance, while the second optimistically sends bursts of back-to-back segments, risking congestion. Rate-based spacing (RBP) [311] is a technique used in the absence of incoming ACKs, where the TCP sender temporarily paces TCP segments at a given rate until the ACK clock can be restarted. As soon as the first ACK is received, RBP ceases and TCP ACK resumes. The pacing rate may either be derived from recent traffic estimates or may be known through external means.

Pacing data during the first RTT of transfer may allow TCP to make effective use of high bandwidth-delay pipes, such as satellite links, even for short transfers. Simulation studies [311] of RPB for HTTP-like traffic show substantial throughput improvement compared to Slow Start after idle periods and slight improvement compared to burst-full-*cwnd* after idle period. Determining the pace rate and the initial *cwnd* used in this case, remain open for further research. RPB requires some extra mechanisms such as a sender timer for pacing. The overhead of timer-driven data transfer is often considered too high for practical use. Pacing segments may make estimating the available bandwidth more difficult. Although RPB is promising, additional work is required to fully understand its behavior.

9.7.10 TCP/IP Header Compression

The reduction in overhead is especially useful when the link is bandwidth-limited, such as mobile satellite links. With TCP/IPv4 headers of at least 40 bytes and TCP/IPv6 headers of at least 60 bytes, there is a significant amount of overhead found in each TCP segment. Some of this information is constant or slowly changing during a connection and need not be repeated with each transmitted segment. This includes the source and destination addresses, port numbers, and other static information. Header compression typically reduces TCP/IPv4 headers from 40 to 3 to 5 bytes (3 bytes for some common cases, 5 bytes in general) [119, 120, 180]. In its most general form, header compression involves the process of intermittently transmitting a full header, with subsequent compressed headers referencing the contents of the previous full header. A sender may send a full header when one or more of the header fields must be updated. The compression happens at the link layer, so routing is not affected because the header is expanded before being passed to the IP layer. In addition to improving throughput of user data, compression can reduce segment loss caused by bit errors, for uniformly distributed bit errors, because the probability of a header error is reduced. The shorter, compressed packets are less likely to be corrupted, and the reduction in errors increases throughput.

The initial TCP/IP header compression scheme was proposed by Van Jacobson [180]. This scheme encodes the changes in fields that change relatively slowly and sends only their differences from their values in the previous packet instead of their absolute value. Correct decompressed packets refresh the information on the decompressor side, based on which following packets can be recovered. A corrupted packet is dropped and makes the compressor desynchronized. Subsequent packets received by the decompressor can also be dropped if they contain a field which depends on the lost packet even though they are transmitted correctly. This is called *error propagation*. When this happens, no duplicate ACK is generated, and the decompressor can only resynchronize when it receives a packet with an uncompressed header. So, fast retransmit and selective ACK cannot be used, which deteriorates the TCP performance [119]. To solve this problem, the *twice algorithm* [119] was designed to repair the desynchronization. When a packet cannot be decompressed correctly, it is assumed that one or more packets that carry the same delta values are lost. The decompressor applies these values two or more times. If the result can pass the TCP checksum, the packet is considered correctly decompressed. The performance improves if the decompressor can explicitly request a full header from the compressor. Simulation results [119] show that *twice algorithm*, in conjunction with the full header request mechanism, can improve throughput 10% to 15% compared to uncompressed transmissions across a wide range of bit error rates.

A new header compression framework, called Robust Header Compression (ROHC) was developed [128] by IETF to improve the TCP/IP header compression, especially over links with significant error rates and long RTT. Based on this framework, profiles are designed for each protocol. In [129] is proposed a ROHC for TCP. Header compression with ROHC can be characterized as an interaction between two state machines, a compressor and a decompressor. The primary mechanism used by ROHC to detect incorrect decompression is a CRC over the original header. Additional advantages of the new scheme are the ability to compress TCP options such as SACKS, Timestamps, and the headers of handshaking packets (SYNs and FINs).

9.7.11   Security Issues

IPsec [199] protocols are designed to provide authentication, integrity, confidentiality, and nonrepudiations. From the security point of view, the TCP enhancement should not interfere with IPsec. Here we describe some possible implications of TCP enhancement on IPsec.

In IPsec the TCP segment transmitted over IP is encrypted. If the TCP enhancement technique is used between end hosts at the TCP level and does not involve the intermediate routers, however, it can be used with all IPsec security services. Examples of such TCP enhancements are Slow-Start acceleration techniques and ACK filtering (discussed in Chapter 10).

In case the TCP enhancement mechanism involves the intermediate routers but does not require access to the TCP data encapsulated by IP, it can be used again with all IPsec security services. Examples of such enhancements are AQM mechanisms such as RED, discussed in Chapter 12.

If the TCP enhancement technique involves the intermediate routers and requires read access to TCP data encapsulated in IP datagram, the IPsec Encapsulated Security Payload (ESP) security service cannot be used. Therefore, the user should be aware that using these techniques could result in violated confidentiality. Examples of such enhancements are discussed in Section 9.10.

Finally, if the TCP enhancement techniques involve the intermediate routers and require write access to the TCP data encapsulated in IP datagram, the IPsec security services such as confidentiality, authentication, and integrity cannot be used. It is clear that such enhancements are very sensitive to security attacks. Instances of such enhancements are some PEPs solutions, discussed in Section 9.10.

9.7.12 Conclusions for TCP Enhancements

Enormous research work has been dedicated to improve TCP over satellite links using solutions that maintain the end-to-end TCP semantic. These types of solutions fit better with existing Internet architecture and the end-to-end principle [148]. But applying such solutions is not easy at all. As discussed in this section and Section 9.5, not only are there several difficult impairments to mitigate, but in many cases there are interactions between them also. For example, the combination of larger BDP and high BER results in worsening TCP performance, compared to the case when these impairments act alone. Another difficult aspect of improving TCP over satellite links is that trade-off solutions have to be considered among many metrics and features. For example, speeding up Slow Start improves throughput but could lead to congestion. The harder part dealing with solutions that maintain the end-to-end TCP semantic is to make sure that when used in the whole Internet no problems are caused to the rest of users. Because of such difficulties, IETF recommends only a few proposed solutions for TCP over satellites. Table 9.8 summarizes the solutions required and recommended by IETF. The table is built based on RFC 2488 [35]. Those mechanisms denoted as "recommended" are IETF standard track mechanisms for the use of TCP on satellite environments. Those mechanisms marked "required" have been defined by IETF as required for hosts using the Internet.

The extent to which TCP protocol enhancements are able to improve the performance of TCP over a satellite system is shown in Table 9.9.

TABLE 9.8: Summary of IETF Recommendations for TCP over satellites.

Mechanism	Use	Where Applied
Path-MTU discovery	Recommended	Sender
Header compression	Recommended	Satellite link
FEC	Recommended	Satellite link
TCP Congestion Control		
Slow start	Required	Sender
Congestion avoidance	Required	Sender
Fast retransmit	Recommended	Sender
Fast recovery	Recommended	Sender
Increased IW[1]	Recommended	Sender
TCP Large Windows		
Window scaling	Recommended	Sender & receiver
PAWS	Recommended	Sender & receiver
RTTM	Recommended	Sender & receiver
TCP SACKS	Recommended	Sender & receiver

(1) In RFC 3390.

TABLE 9.9: TCP Enhancements Comparison.

TCP over Satellites Limitations	Latency	Large BDP	Link Impairment	Asymmetry
Large IW	X			
DACKs	X			
Byte counting	X			X
TCP NewReno	X	X	X	
TCP SACK	X	X	X	
TCP Vegas	X	X	X	
Windows scaling	X	X		
T/TCP	X			
PMTU Discovery	X			
ECN	X	X		
FEC			X	
Multiple connections	X	X		
TCP pacing	X	X		
Header compression			X	

9.8   ADVANCED ENHANCEMENTS AND NEW VERSIONS OF TCP

Improving TCP over satellite and other high BDP networks has attracted considerable interest from the research community. This section describes some new proposals that require further study before they are considered for application. Such proposed solutions expand over a wide spectrum of improvements. At one end of this spectrum there are simpler, more incremental and more easily deployable changes to the current TCP. Examples of such proposed solutions are HighSpeed TCP and Quick-Start. At the other end of the spectrum there are solutions with more powerful changes that result in new transport protocols with higher performance but with less chance to be deployed in a large scale on the Internet, at least in the immediate future. An example of such solution is Explicit Control Protocol (XCP). Other proposals, such as TCP Westwood and TCP Peach, reside along the simplicity-deployability-power spectrum. In the end, the choice among all these solutions depends on the trade-off between performance and deployability. Because of the size and multidimensional complexity of the Internet, the robustness in heterogeneity is valued over efficiency or performance, which leads to favor evolution compared to revolution of changes. But these evolutionary steps should go in fundamentally correct long-term directions of the Internet. Here we present some of the most promising research proposals to improve TCP over high BDP links.

9.8.1   Quick-Start TCP

Quick-Start TCP [185] introduces a new mechanism for transport protocols to determine an optional allowed initial congestion window at the start of data transmission. The source indicates its initial desired rate in packet per second by sending a Quick-Start Request option in the IP header of the initial TCP SYN or

SYN/ACK packet. Each router along the path could either approve the specified initial rate, reduce it, or indicate that nothing above the default initial rate for that protocol is allowed. The TCP receiver communicates the final rate to TCP sender in a transport level Quick-Start Response in answering SYN/ACK or ACK packet. Quick-Start allows TCP connections to use high initial windows when there is unused bandwidth along the path. Quick-Start is based on the ability of routers to determine whether the output link is significantly underutilized. As discussed in Section 9.7.4, RFC 2414 permits an initial congestion window of up to four segments. Quick-Start would be required for connections using an initial window higher than four segments. Quick-Start could be especially beneficial for moderate-sized connections in well-provisioned environments including high bandwidth satellite links. The main problem with this proposal is that it requires all routers to support Quick-Start protocol and to implement some mechanism for estimating the current link underutilization.

9.8.2   HighSpeed TCP

As discussed earlier, for TCP to utilize high bandwidth links, low error rate is required [261]. Once a TCP flow is in Congestion Avoidance phase, it takes a large number of RTTs for this flow to use extra bandwidth made available on the link [185]. This leads to low utilization of satellite links. Also, for high bandwidth links, where a large congestion window is needed, it takes a large number of RTTs to recover from consecutive timeouts, which lowers the performance. HighSpeed TCP, proposed in [185], improves the performance of TCP in high bandwidth links where TCP operates with a large congestion window. In HighSpeed TCP, the additive increase and multiplicative decrease are functions of the congestion window itself instead of being constant values as in standard TCP. This makes it possible to use high bandwidth links with reasonable error rates and reduces delays to recover from multiple timeouts or to use available bandwidth. Even though not designed specifically for satellite links, HighSpeed TCP would improve the performance on high bandwidth-delay satellite links. HighSpeed TCP requires changes only to the TCP sender.

9.8.3   TCP Peach

TCP Peach is a new TCP congestion control scheme designed for satellite networks [29, 30]. TCP Peach is composed of two new algorithms: Sudden Start and Rapid Recovery, in addition to the two traditional TCP algorithms, Congestion Avoidance and Fast Retransmit. The new algorithms are based on the uses of dummy segments to probe the availability of network sources. Dummy segments are treated as low priority segments. In Sudden Start, the dummy packets are used to estimate the bandwidth of the path, which are used during Congestion Avoidance. In Rapid Recovery, dummy packets help to distinguish between transmission losses and congestion losses. Even though this scheme is shown to outperform standard TCP over satellite links [29], it requires coordination between sender and receiver and most importantly requires all routers in the connection path to apply some sort of priority mechanism. TCP Peach is further enhanced with TCP Peach+ [30].

9.8.4   Explicit Transport Error Notification

Explicit Transport Error Notification (ETEN) [208] was proposed for error-prone wireless and satellite environments. In ETEN the TCP sender is notified when packets get lost because of errors, so the sender can react differently. ETEN assumes that sufficient information about the corrupted packet, such as IP addresses, port numbers, and TCP sequence numbers, is available to intermediate routers or receivers. Another variation of the scheme, Cumulative ETEN (CETEN), uses cumulative error rates detected by intermediate nodes for each link. In [89, 208] are shown simulation results, which confirm the performance improvements achieved using ETEN. ETEN and its variations require changes to intermediate routers, which is the main problem with this solution.

9.8.5   TCP Westwood

The key innovation of TCP Westwood (TCPW) [88] is the use of bandwidth estimation to directly drive *cwnd* and *ssthresh*. The TCP sender continuously monitors ACKs from the receiver and computes its current Eligible Rate Estimate (ERE). ERE is based on the rate of ACKs and their payload. Upon a packet loss indication (3DUPACKs or a timeout), the sender sets the *cwnd* and *ssthresh* based on ERE. For a complete description of TCPW, see [88, 314].

TCPW was enhanced to TCPW Bulk Rate (BK) [324], which differentiates between congestion loss and transmission loss using a combination of RTT measurements and the gap between expected and achieved rates. When it is determined that the losses are due to errors, TCP BK uses three new mechanisms: Bulk Repeat, Fixed Retransmission Timeout, and Intelligent Window Adjustment. In Bulk Repeat, on receiving a new partial ACK, the TCP sender retransmits all outstanding packets in the current congestion window instead of sending only one lost packet as in TCP NewReno. In [323] the authors argue that this could save multiple RTTs needed to recover all lost packets in the window. In Fixed Retransmission Timeout, if consecutive timeouts occur and there is no packet successfully delivered in between, the next timeout interval is kept the same as the previous one instead of being doubled as in NewReno. This change improves the performance when BER is high. In Intelligent Window Adjustment, the *cwnd* is not reduced to *ssthresh* after a loss. The improved performance of TCPW BK over other schemes is confirmed by simulation studies [323]. Besides the performance improvements, another advantage of TCPW and TCPW BK is that modifications are required only at the TCP sender. More information about TCPW and its variations can be found in [17].

9.8.6   XCP

A generalization of Explicit Congestion Notification (ECN) called eXplicit Control Protocol (XCP) is introduced in [193]. Instead of the one-bit congestion indication used by ECN, in XCP routers inform the sender about the degree of congestion at the bottleneck. To control utilization, the new protocol adjusts its aggressiveness according to the spare bandwidth in the network and the feedback delay. This prevents oscillations, provides stability for high bandwidth or large delay, and ensures efficient utilization of network resources. Without keeping per-flow information, routers signal back to sources the needed changes in their congestion windows.

The simulations reported in [193] demonstrate that XCP outperforms previous AQM mechanisms in terms of utilization, fairness, low queuing delay, and losses. XCP is shown to perform very well in high bandwidth-delay paths, where TCP suffers significantly. This makes XCP appealing for use over satellite links. XCP is a new protocol and its deployment requires changes in both end nodes and intermediate nodes.

9.9   NEW TRANSPORT PROTOCOLS FOR SATELLITE LINKS

Another way to resolve the problems of TCP over satellite links is to design new transport layer protocols optimized for such links. This section provides two examples of new proposed transport protocols, STP and SCPS-TP, designed specifically for satellite environments. Deploying such satellite specific transport layer protocols would require changes in most applications and the Internet infrastructure. Conversely, for large, complex, and heterogenous systems such as the Internet, only evolutionary changes seem realistic; therefore, the practical use of these new transport protocols is to take part in PEP architectures discussed in Section 9.10. Some of their features could also be absorbed by TCP.

9.9.1   Satellite Transport Protocol

Satellite Transport Protocol (STP) [163–165] is a transport protocol that was designed to perform well over satellite links. It is a modification of the original SSCOP protocol [161]. The STP sender and receiver use buffer sizes that are on the order of the bandwidth-delay product of the links. Like TCP, STP provides a reliable, byte-oriented, streaming data service to applications. The transmitter sends variable-length packets to the receiver, storing the packets for potential retransmission until the receiver has acknowledged them. STP's automatic repeat request (ARQ) mechanism uses selective negative acknowledgments rather than the positive acknowledgment. Packets are numbered instead of bytes, and the STP transmitter retransmits only those specific packets that have been explicitly requested by the receiver. Unlike TCP, there are no retransmission timers associated with packets. One of the main differences between STP and TCP, which offers an advantage for asymmetric networks, is the way in which the two protocols acknowledge data. TCP acknowledgments are data-driven; TCP receiver typically sends an ACK for every other packet received. While this is beneficial for accelerating window growth on connection startup, it results in a large amount of ACK traffic for large windows. In STP, the transmitter periodically requests the receiver to acknowledge the data that it has successfully received. Losses detected by the receiver are explicitly negatively acknowledged. The combination of these two strategies leads to low reverse channel bandwidth usage when losses are rare and speedy recovery in the event of loss. Positive ACKs are sent in response to periodic polls sent by the transmitter.

In Table 9.10, the performances of TCP, T/TCP, and STP are compared in terms of the average latency and average number of packets, driven by a traffic generator based on HTTP [228] over an emulated GEO system (RTT = 600 ms). Each table entry is the average of 1000 independent runs with the given protocol. The STP's performance is better than TCP's but slightly worse than that of T/TCP. STP's latency is a little bit higher than T/TCP's because of the traffic smoothing mechanism

TABLE 9.10: Comparison of TCP, T/TCP, and
STP performance for HTTP traffic [162].

TCP Variant	Avg. Latency	Avg. Packets
TCP	2.0	12.3
T/TCP	1.4	7.3
STP	1.5	9.1

used in STP, where packets eligible for transmission are not sent immediately but
rather are paced out over the estimated RTT. These data show another trade-off
in protocol design, this time between smoothing bursty traffic (STP) and reducing
latency (T/TCP).

9.9.2 Space Communications Protocol Specifications-Transport Protocol

Space Communications Protocol Specifications-Transport Protocol (SCPS-TP) was
developed by the MITRE corporation and later standardized by Consultative Com-
mittee of Space Data Systems (CCSDS) to account for the "stressed environment,"
that is, space environment with delay and multiple sources of data loss [333]. SCPS-
TP uses a congestion control algorithm that does not depend on packet loss as a way
to signal congestion in the network. SCPS-TP can react to explicit signals of the two
sources of packet loss (congestion and the satellite disappearing over the horizon).
The ability for SCPS-TP to tailor its response to the nature of the loss allows for
better network utilization and better end-to-end performance without harming the
overall network stability. In [125] laboratory and actual satellite tests are presented,
which show that SCPS-TP yields significant improvement over standard TCP on
error-prone links.

Among several experiments conducted to measure and verify the performance
of SCPS-TP were two "bent-pipe" tests and one on-board test in which the spacecraft
hosted the SCPS software. Results proved that SCPS-TP is well suited to the long-
delay, potentially high bit-error rate environment of satellites. Using options such as
Header Compression, Selective Negative Acknowledgement (SNACK), and TCP
Timestamps produces varying effects under different conditions.

9.10 PERFORMANCE ENHANCING PROXY

Performance Enhancing Proxy (PEP) is used to improve the performance of the
Internet protocols on networks paths where native performance suffers because
of characteristics of the links or subnetworks on the path [136]. PEP represent
the "de facto" solution for TCP problems over satellite links. In this section the
motivations, architectures, implementations, advantages, and disadvantages of PEPs
are explained.

9.10.1 Motivations for the Use of PEP on Satellite Networks

Even though PEP solutions are not very "clean" from the point of view of end-to-
end principle [148], which leads to several drawbacks discussed in this section, they
are practically being implemented to mitigate the problems of TCP over satellite

links. As seen in Section 9.7, most TCP enhancements are not recommended for use in shared networks, such as the Internet, because in general such enhancements are more aggressive than standard TCP. This could lead to aggravated congestion and even congestion collapse. However, to apply these enhancements, all end users and in some cases intermediate routers need to be updated. This is impractical for several reasons. First, the satellite part is just a small fraction of the whole Internet, which does not justify changes in all users. Second, in many cases users are not even aware that their connections are using satellite links. Third, nontrivial parameter tunings are needed in end systems in many cases, which requires professional expertise. Most of the proposed TCP enhancements, however, can safely be used in PEP solutions. In this scenario, the end users can continue to use their standard TCP stacks. The Internet remains safe as more aggressive protocols are now applied only inside PEP subnetworks. Also, the complexity of implementation and tuning is taken care of by the satellite service providers who own and operate the PEP subnetworks. Therefore, PEPs represent a good trade-off between the technical model and the business model of satellite Internet.

9.10.2 Types of Performance Enhancing Proxies

There are many types of PEPs and they can be implemented at any protocol layer; but PEPs typically are implemented at the transport or application layer. There are also PEPs that operate at the data link layer, but such implementations are beyond the scope of this chapter. Some PEP implementations operate across several layers by utilizing the information of these layers.

Most transport layer PEPs are the designed to interact with TCP and to mitigate the problems TCP encounters running over satellite links discussed in Section 9.5. Such PEPs are transparent for application protocols, which operate end-to-end. Examples of transport layer PEPs are the TCP spoofing and TCP connection-split proxies discussed later in this section. Examples of application layer PEPs are Web caches and relay Mail Transfer Agents.

PEP implementations could be symmetric or asymmetric. Symmetric PEPs have identical behavior in both directions. That means the actions taken by the PEP are independent from which interface a packet is received. Asymmetric PEPs operate differently in each directions. The direction could be defined in terms of link or in terms of protocol, such as the direction of TCP data flow or TCP ACK flow. An asymmetric PEP is usually used at the point where the characteristics of the links or protocols in each side of the PEP differ.

PEPs can also be classified depending on their degree of transparency. PEP implementations could be totally transparent to end systems, transport end points, and/or applications. In this case the use of PEPs requires no modifications to end systems. PEPs could require modifications to only one or both the end users. In this instance the PEP is nontransparent.

TCP Spoofing. There are two main strategies in PEP design: TCP spoofing and TCP splitting. In both cases the goal is to shield high-latency or lossy satellite network segments from the rest of the network in a transparent way to the applications. The goal is for the end users to be unaware of the intermediate gateway, other than improved performance.

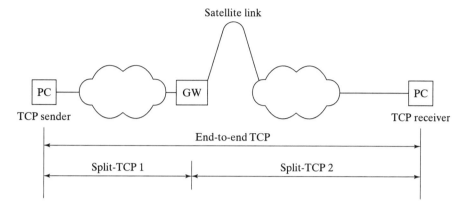

FIGURE 9.10: Two-segment splitting scheme.

The term *TCP spoofing* is sometimes used for TCP PEP functionality. In TCP spoofing a router (gateway) near the source sends back ACKs for TCP segments to give the source the illusion of a short delay path and, therefore, to speed up the sender's data transmission [50, 54, 59, 136]. It then suppresses the true acknowledgment stream from the satellite host and takes responsibility for sending any missing data. Figure 9.10 illustrates the use of a gateway as a "spoofer," which splits the TCP connection. However, unlike a TCP proxy (see next paragraph), spoofing is transparent to both the sender and the receiver. The spoofer takes on the personality of both parties. Details about an implementation of TCP spoofing are in Section 9.10.6.

TCP Splitting.   TCP connection splitting, as discussed in Chapter 6, is particularly applicable to satellite networks even though it violates the end-to-end TCP semantics. In the following paragraphs, examples of two-segment and three-segment TCP splitting over a satellite are discussed [27].

Two-segment splitting. In this method, the end-to-end TCP connection is divided into two segments by inserting a gateway at a sender side as shown in Figure 9.10. Instead of spoofing, the connection is fully split at the gateway on the network side, and a second TCP connection is used from the satellite gateway to the receiver. Logically, there is not much difference between this approach and spoofing, except that the gateway may run different TCP options on the two TCP segments.

This technique is of great use under the following scenarios:

- Networks with star topology consisting of a hub (central) station and many remote stations are widely used for distributing data from the hub station,

- TCP enhancement is usually needed in the outbound direction (hub to remotes) only,

It may not be economically feasible either to introduce the gateway at every terminal or to install new TCP software that supports a window scaling option, etc. into all end terminals.

In this scheme, the TCP sender data rate is improved by separating a satellite segment from the original TCP connection. It also appears for the sender that

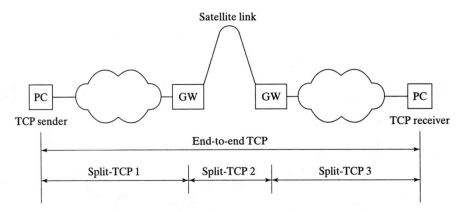

FIGURE 9.11: Three-segment splitting scheme.

RTT is reduced compared with the standard TCP. In the two-segment splitting, the gateway can send data packets regardless of the TCP window size advertised from the receiver. It also employs the optimized congestion control for this segment to improve TCP performance.

Three-segment splitting. In this method, the end-to-end TCP connection is divided into three segments by two gateways (Figure 9.11). The concept is to separate the satellite segment from the terrestrial segments and use an optimized TCP protocol over the satellite link between gateways. As illustrated in Figure 9.11, gateways are located at each earth station and an end-to-end TCP connection is divided into three segments. In the terrestrial segments, a standard TCP is used for communicating between TCP sender/receiver and gateway. The gateway converts TCP to a protocol optimized for satellite links. In some instances the gateways convert simply between versions of TCP. This approach can be used to extend the usefulness of the TCP enhancements outlined in Sections 9.7 and 9.8. Another approach involves using a protocol other than TCP on the satellite segment of the link. By replacing TCP with a protocol specifically tailored for use in satellite environments such as those discussed in Section 9.9, the performance may be enhanced dramatically [270, 300]. Section 9.10.6 describes an implementation of "three-segment splitting technique."

The main advantage of this method is that TCP enhancement is achieved without any modification to the end users while other techniques require installing new TCP software. This scheme is especially suitable for point-to-point networks in which enhancement for both-way is needed such as ISP backbone. Because the gateway analyzes a TCP header, the enhancement becomes unavailable when an encryption is made over TCP segment. This problem also occurs in the two-segment splitting technique.

9.10.3 Mechanisms Used in Performance Enhancing Proxies

The key characteristics of a PEP implementation are the mechanisms used to improve the TCP performance over satellite links. Some examples of PEP mechanisms are described next.

Many TCP PEPs use TCP ACK manipulation. Balakrishnan et al. [61] describe a technique used to smooth out the flow of TCP ACKs to eliminate bursts of TCP segments. Some other PEPs acknowledge TCP segments locally to mitigate the effect of long RTT and it speeds up the Slow Start, which is the main mechanism used in TCP Spoofing. Local negative acknowledgments are also used to trigger local and fast error recovery. Local ACKs are used in PEPs with split connections. When local ACKs are used, and the data are dropped after being acknowledged by the PEP, it is PEPs' responsibility to recover the data. In this case, the PEP has to use local TCP retransmission to the receivers.

Some PEPs perform local retransmissions even when they do not use local ACKs. For example, Snoop caches the received TCP segments and monitors the system for duplicate ACKs from the receiver [59]. When duplicate ACKs are received, Snoop locally transmits the lost TCP segments from its cache.

To mitigate highly asymmetric bandwidth, some PEPs implement TCP ACKs filtering and reconstruction. ACKs are being filtered not to congest the low-speed direction and are reconstructed on the other side of the links. For more information about asymmetry mitigations, please see Chapter 10.

Many PEP implementations support one or more forms of compression. Because compression reduces the number of bits to be sent over a link, it is very useful to be used for bandwidth-limited satellite links. Besides increasing link efficiency, compression reduces latency, improves the interactive responses, and decreases overhead and packet loss.

PEPs can also handle link discontinuities or link outages. During these periods a TCP sender does not receive the expected ACKs and, therefore, closes its connection window on expiration of the retransmit timer. A TCP PEP can send the last ACK, which will make the TCP sender go in the persistent mode and freeze all timers. Using PEP, a period of link outage can be easily hidden from the end hosts, thus keeping the TCP from breaking even for long disconnection times.

9.10.4 Implications of Using Performance Enhancing Proxies

The end-to-end argument is one of the architectural principles of the Internet [53]. This principle requires that certain end-to-end functions can only be performed by the end systems, not by the network. The application of such a principle has been crucial for the success of the Internet. As a consequence of this principle, when one or more routers in a path fail, the end-to-end communications can continue through another path, because no state information is kept in routers for this connection. In contrast, when a switch fails in a telephone network, the connection is terminated. Most of the potential negative implications associated with the use of PEPs are related to the breaking of the end-to-end of connections, with security problems being the most critical.

Fate Sharing.   The ability of a connection to survive network failures depends on how much state information about the connection is kept in the network and whether the state is self-healing. If no connection state is kept in the network or such state is self-healing, as in the case of the Internet, a failure in the network breaks the connection only if there is no alternate path between end systems. That is why for the Internet a connection is more reliable than the intermediate routers.

With the use of PEPs, the connection depends on the state kept in a PEP, and its failure causes the state loss, resulting in the connection termination even though an alternative path might exist. However, satellite links usually are used in cases in which there are no other alternate paths. So for practical purposes, in such cases the use of PEP is not the cause per se of breaking the end-to-end argument. Even when this is not the case, however, one has to compare the advantage in performance improvements brought by PEPs with the risk involved.

End-to-End Reliability. To achieve an end-to-end reliability in data transmission, it is important to have end-to-end acknowledgment at the application level. If PEPs interfere with the application level acknowledgments, for example, a PEP acknowledges application data prematurely, before receiving the ACK from the receiver, end-to-end reliability cannot be guaranteed. TCP PEPs generally do not interfere with application layer ACKs. The application provides end-to-end ACKs; hence, TCP PEPs do not degrade the end-to-end reliability.

End-to-End Diagnostics. The end systems should be able to use diagnostics when problems arise. The existence of PEPs could delay the detection of failures by end systems. In addition, tools used to debug connection failure may be affected by the use of PEPs, for example, PING, which is based on ICMP and not on TCP. It is possible that PING traffic might get routed around the PEP, so PING could indicate the existence of a path when it does not exist for TCP traffic. Traceroute also is affected by the presence of PEPs.

9.10.5 Security with Performance Enhancing Proxies

Application layer security can be used in most of the cases with TCP PEPs; however, only a limited number of applications include support for application layer security. The IP layer security IPsec [199] is very appealing, however, because it can be used transparently by any application.

The most negative effect of using a PEP is that it disables end-to-end use of IPsec. If IPsec is employed, end-to-end PEPs that are implemented in intermediate nodes cannot examine the transport or application headers of IP packets because of the encryption of IP packets. The IPsec's ESP header makes the TCP header and payload unintelligible to the PEPs. Without being able to examine TCP or application header, a PEP may not function at all.

In the case of nontransparent PEPs (and if the users trust them), IPsec can be used separately between each end user and the PEP. This is unfortunately less secure than end-to-end security. For example, security breaches could happen at the PEP during decryption.

Even when a PEP implementation does not break the end-to-end semantic of the connection, the PEP may not be able to function in the presence of IPsec. For example, ACKs manipulations cannot work if the PEP cannot determine the ACKs of interest.

Research for Security Solutions with PEPs. Even though there is no real solution yet in using end-to-end IPsec with PEPs, a considerable research activity exists. One promising approach is the use of multilayer IP security. For example,

TCP headers could be as one layer, with the PEPs being able to decrypt them, while the TCP payload is encrypted end-to-end as a separate layer. This still means trusting the PEP to some extent, but the end-to-end security of the payload is protected. The price to pay for this type of solution is the increased complexity of IPsec. Finding practical solutions for using IPsec with PEPs remains a challenging issue to be addressed.

PEP itself must be protected from attacks. PEP represents a network point where the traffic is somehow exposed. This makes it an ideal platform for launching denial of service or other types of attacks. Taking the PEP out of action is a potential denial of service attack. Therefore, a PEP must be protected (e.g., by a firewall) or must protect itself from improper access by an attacker, just like any other device that resides in the network.

9.10.6 Commercial PEP (SkyX)

SkyX is a commercial product (from MENTAT [14]) implementing a TCP-PEP with splitting solution. A SkyX gateway implementation is shown in Figure 9.12.

SkyX increases the performance of TCP/IP over satellite by transparently replacing TCP for the hop over the satellite link with a protocol optimized for satellite conditions. The SkyX gateway shown in Figure 9.12 works by intercepting the TCP connection from the client and converting the data into the SkyX protocol for transmission over the satellite. The SkyX gateway on the opposite site of the satellite link translates the data back to TCP for communication with the server. No changes are required to the client and server, and the PEP is transparent to applications. The architecture maintains full TCP reliability and end-to-end flow control. The SkyX gateway provides performance enhancement for a variety of satellite networks including point-to-point, point-to-multipoint, and full mesh architectures.

SkyX protocol is optimized to provide maximum throughput over satellite networks and to respond efficiently to satellite latency, bit error, and asymmetric

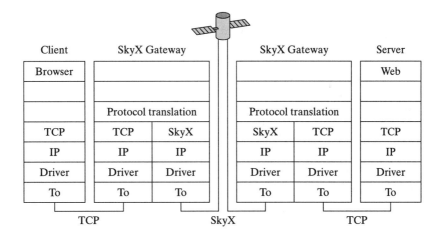

FIGURE 9.12: SkyX Gateway example.

bandwidth conditions. It also takes advantage of optimizations possible on a single-path link with known bandwidth. Major characteristics of SkyX include:

Acknowledgment Algorithm. SkyX uses an efficient selective retransmission algorithm for the acknowledgment of data. Because there is only a single path over the satellite for all packets with no intermediate routing, any gaps in the packet sequence can assumed to be data loss rather than network congestion. The receiving SkyX can immediately request and receive retransmission of the missing data from the transmitting SkyX gateway.

Because SkyX protocol does not use ACKs as the primary means to detect lost data, it requires only infrequent ACKs to confirm data arrival and clear buffers. SkyX, therefore, reduces back channel usage by 75% for Web traffic and up to 99% for file transfer, providing high throughput.

Dynamic Window Sizing. SkyX uses a large window to remove the dependency of TCP on the BDP, allowing high throughput independent of the window size of the end nodes. SkyX dynamically adjusts the window size based on the link bandwidth, delay, and number of simultaneous connections to optimize the utilization of bandwidth.

Rate Control. To avoid the problems of TCP's Slow Start and Congestion Avoidance with large BDP, SkyX protocol uses rate control to set the transmission rate explicitly based on the bandwidth of the link, therefore maximizing the throughput.

FastStart Web Acceleration. SkyX also includes HTTP specific optimizations to further accelerate web downloads. FastStart saves one full round-trip time for each new Web connection by reducing the handshaking required to establish new HTTP connections.

Data Compression. SkyX uses on-the-fly data compression functionality, offering lossless compression ratios up to 5:1, which increases the amount of data that can be sent over the link.

Multicast. SkyX also has multicast functionality, which can convert a TCP unicast connection into a reliable multicast transfer. For example, using standard file transfer applications such as FTP, SkyX can deliver a copy of a file transfer to every remote site with only a single transfer.

End-to-End Reliability and Flow Control. SkyX preserves the end-to-end reliability of TCP so that all data reach the receiver despite any loss on the path. SkyX also preserves TCP's flow control mechanisms to ensure fair utilization of the bandwidth by all users.

SkyX runs over IP and can be used in a gateway to enhance the performance of backbone satellite links, corporate networks, VSAT networks, and satellite links to local area networks. SkyX offers products that can work in 10 Mbps or 45 Mbps and can also be used to enhance the performance of individuals connected to satellite networks.

9.11   FURTHER READING

A good introduction to general issues related to satellite communication can be found in [130, 131, 137, 227, 280]. Good reviews of TCP over satellite communications are provided in [41, 153, 156, 163–165]. Proposed TCP enhancement on satellite networks are covered in [34, 35, 38, 39, 41, 163, 164, 176, 210].

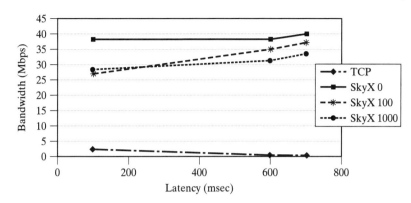

FIGURE 9.13: Throughput: TCP vs. SkyX. Experimental results reported in [319] emulating bulk transfer over a GEO connection with channel bandwidth = 45 Mb/s and with HTTP background traffic. SkyX 0 means there is no background traffic, SkyX 100 means there are 100 concurrent transfers of small files, and SkyX 1000 means there are 1000 concurrent transfers of small files. In TCP throughput the background traffic has almost no effect.

More information on satellite constellations is provided at Lloyd Wood's web page http://www.ee.surrey.ac.uk/Personal/L.Wood/constellations/. More information on TCP over satellite can be found in Mark Allman's web page http://roland.grc.nasa.gov/ mallman/papers/.

9.12 SUMMARY

Satellite communications networks have become an indispensable part of major telecommunication systems. Because of the fundamental satellite system characteristics, such as global coverage, broadcast nature, and bandwidth on demand, satellite system is an excellent candidate for providing high data-rate Internet access and global connectivity for multimedia applications. To meet this goal, the TCP/IP were protocols, which were designed for terrestrial networks, should be optimized to suit the characteristics of satellite links and networks, such as large and changing RTT, high link bandwidth, link asymmetry, and relatively higher BER compared to terrestrial networks.

To improve the TCP performance over satellite networks, a large number of solutions are proposed. These performance enhancing techniques can be categorized into solutions where the end-to-end semantic of TCP is maintained and into solutions where the end-to-end semantic of TCP is violated. Most important solutions of the first type have been discussed. Such solutions expand over a wide spectrum of improvements, from simpler, more incremental to more powerful, new optimized transport protocols. These solutions fit better with existing Internet architecture, but applying them is not an easy task. One problem is that a given solution, while improving one or more performance metrics, could degrade other ones. For example, making TCP more aggressive to better use available bandwidth for large RTTs could lead to congestion collapse. Another implementation problem with end-to-end solutions is that changes might be required in most end users and intermediate routers, which is not realistic. The performance of various alternatives for TCP enhancements are discussed.

Solutions that do not maintain the end-to-end semantic of TCP, also known as Performance Enhancing Proxies (PEPs) are not very "clean" from the point of view of the Internet architecture but are better suited for practical use. PEP's solutions try to isolate the satellite links from the rest of the network. This architecture enables powerful solutions to be applied over satellite segments without interfering with the rest of the network. As shown with examples, PEP solutions can dramatically improve the performance of TCP over satellite networks. Finding practical solutions for using IPsec with PEPs remains an open and challenging issue to be addressed.

9.13   REVIEW QUESTIONS

1. Satellite resources are more expensive than terrestrial ones. Describe the emerging applications that favor satellite solutions over terrestrial ones.
2. What are the main advantages of satellite communications?
3. Discuss the main characteristics of GEO, MEO, and LEO satellite constellations, and report on their relative merits and demerits in terms of throughput, delay, implementation complexity, and cost.
4. What are the satellite link and system characteristics that affect TCP? Show combinations of such characteristics that lead to lower TCP performance.
5. Show by examples that the chosen TCP enhancements can vary depending on which of the enhancement goals are more important in a given scenario.
6. Explain how *delayed ACK after slow start* can improve TCP performance over satellite links.
7. Compare two-segment and three-segment TCP splitting. What are the advantages and disadvantages?
8. How can ECN be used to differentiate between congestion losses and link losses?
9. FEC schemes for satellite links increase the complexity and cost. Why are FECs recommended to be used over satellites?
10. Why is it difficult for a TCP flow over GEO satellite to fully utilize the available bandwidth? Why does this task become even more difficult in the presence of link errors?
11. Why is the advantage of an increased Initial Window more evident for shorter transfer?
12. Explain why using byte counting instead of the number of ACKs received to increase congestion window leads to better TCP throughput.
13. Explain why the mechanism to distinguish congestion losses from link losses should be very reliable?
14. Why are multiple TCP connections for a given applications not recommended? Which other TCP recommended extensions could provide the same TCP performance improvements?
15. Why are Robust Header Compression schemes better suited to be used over links with significant error rates?

16. What is the source of overhead in Quick-Start TCP?

17. In what conditions can HighSpeed TCP better use the available bandwidth then standard TCP?

18. What functionality do TCP Peach and TCP Westwood have in common?

19. XCP improves several aspects of TCP performance; why is it not considered an immediate solution?

20. In what scenarios can satellite optimized transport protocol be used without interfering with the rest of the network, which uses standard TCP?

21. Name two communication scenarios in which PEPs are useful.

22. What is the difference between TCP spoofing and TCP splitting?

23. Describe how end-to-end security is achieved in satellite IP networks. Comment on the security issues related to PEP implementation.

9.14   HANDS-ON PROJECTS

1. Using *ns*-2 simulator, compare the performance of the TCP enhancements discussed in Section 9.7. Write a report describing your results.

2. Using *ns*-2 simulator, compare the performance of the TCP enhancements discussed in Section 9.8. Evaluate the trade-off between performance improvement and complexity of these TCP enhancements.

3. Do some literature search to find details of STP or SCPS-TP. Implement STP or SCPS-TP in *ns*-2 simulator and evaluate its performance over GEO satellite networks under different link conditions with varying bit error rates.

9.15   CASE STUDY: IMPROVING TCP PERFORMANCE OVER SATELLITE USING SKYX

A satellite service provider concluded that to be successful in a competitive market, it should increase the efficiency of its operations. One of the major customer complaints is low data throughput. The problem did not mitigate even after provisioning higher bandwidth for the satellite link, which was a costly exercise. Finally, the service provider turned to WCORP for advice on how to address the throughput problem.

Not long ago, a consultant at WCORP came to know that SkyX is a practical solution for data throughput problem over satellite links. WCORP decided to investigate the effectiveness of SkyX protocol gateways under various loading conditions, TCP connection rates, and error rates for typical satellite link conditions. In addition to simulating satellite conditions, this study also examined the effect of Internet congestion on end-to-end throughput with SkyX protocol gateway [174]. Two types of tests were conducted:

- Single TCP connection throughput for various link bandwidths: High-speed LAN and Internet-2 applications for large data files were simulated comparing the performance with SkyX protocol gateway.

- Multiple TCP connections with fixed per-connection bandwidth: Performance benefit of the protocol gateway for ISP links supporting large numbers of small TCP connections was examined. Tests were run for RTTs of 700 ms

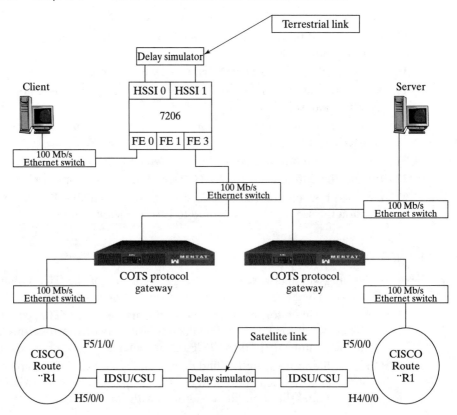

FIGURE 9.14: Network configuration.

to simulate the combination of a 500-ms satellite hop from the user to the Internet backbone and 200-ms delay to reach the server.

Figure 9.14 shows the network test configuration. The network contains two link simulators to simulate the effects of both the satellite link conditions and the terrestrial Internet backbone. The client and server machines were both Sun Enterprise 450 (2 × UltraSPARC-II 296 MHz) with 2048-Mb memory running Solaris 7. A client-server application was used for the load generator.

The performance enhancement provided by the SkyX protocol gateway for a single TCP connection was examined. Without performance enhancement, the maximum throughputs are 320 Kbps for the terrestrial connection and 91 Kbps for the satellite-terrestrial link. These results demonstrate that without performance enhancement, the maximum single-connection TCP throughput rate is approximately equal to the window size (8 Kbyte × 8 bit)/RTT (e.g., 200 ms) = 320 Kbps, even if the link rate is increased. Figure 9.15 shows test results for a RTT of 700 ms with TCP enhancement. The performance using the SkyX protocol gateway is clearly orders of magnitude better than the theoretical TCP maximum as calculated

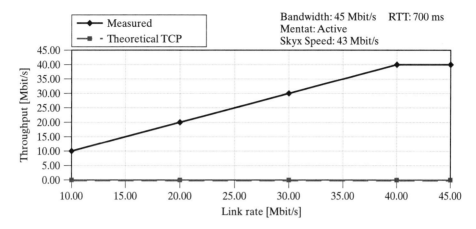

FIGURE 9.15: Single TCP Connection over satellite link with protocol gateway enhancement.

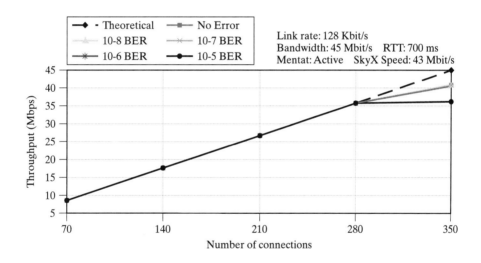

FIGURE 9.16: Multiple TCP connections over satellite link with protocol gateway enhancement.

earlier. Even despite a 700-ms delay, the protocol gateway allows the connection to take advantage of the full bandwidth available.

Rather than a single, large TCP connection, ISPs servicing home users connecting to the Internet support large numbers of small connections on their networks. TCP connection rates are generally limited to the speed of the user's connection to the ISP. The next set of tests were, therefore, designed to examine the performance of TCP with protocol gateway enhancement for large numbers of TCP connections, with each connection limited to 128 Kbps. Various bit error rates were also tested.

Figure 9.16 illustrates the effects of adding the protocol gateway to the network for a delay of 700 ms. It allows the connection to utilize the full bandwidth available.

The performance is essentially identical to the theoretical limit for up to 280 connections. Comparing this graph to the baseline results in Figure 9.15 for the satellite-based network, the protocol gateway provides a substantial increase in aggregate bandwidth at low bit error rates, and at a packet-loss rate of 10%, the aggregate throughput for 350 connections with the gateway is 33 Mbps compared to only 10 Mbps for enhanced TCP.

Armed with the test results, the WCORP consultant advised the satellite service provider to consider SkyX as a viable option to address the throughput problem.

TCP/IP Performance over Asymmetric Networks

CHAPTER OBJECTIVES

After completing this chapter, the reader should be able to:

- Explain types of asymmetry that are present in today's networks

- Comprehend specific performance issues when TCP/IP traffic is transported over asymmetric networks

- Learn techniques to address TCP performance problems in asymmetric environments

The ever-increasing desire of users for high-speed and ubiquitous connectivity has led to the deployment of many new network access technologies. Some of these, such as cable modem, digital subscriber line (DSL), and satellite-based networks, are aimed at alleviating the "last mile" bottleneck, while others, such as wireless, packet radio networks, are motivated by the need to provide users with tetherless access to the Internet, especially to their mobile devices.

These networking technologies often exhibit *asymmetry* in their network characteristics—the network characteristics in one direction may be quite different from those in the opposite direction. For instance, much of the existing cable plant was designed for unidirectional (broadcast) transmission from the head end out to customer premises. As such, the *upstream* bandwidth of the cable plant, from the customer premises out to the Internet, is often limited compared to its *downstream* bandwidth toward the customer premises. In some cases, upstream communication on the same technology may simply be impossible; old cable plants with unidirectional amplifiers and direct broadcast satellite systems such as DirectPC [315] are examples of this. This necessitates the use of a different (and often slower) network technology, such as a dialup modem line, for upstream connectivity. Figure 10.1 depicts such a setup in the context of a "wireless" cable modem network (also known as multichannel multipoint distribution service [MMDS]).

Network asymmetry can adversely impact the performance of feedback-based transport protocols such as TCP. The reason for this is that even if the network path in the direction of data flow is uncongested, congestion in the opposite direction can disrupt the flow of feedback. This disruption can lead to poor performance. This chapter provides an in-depth discussion of the performance problems caused by network asymmetry in the context of TCP. Solutions to achieve near-optimal TCP performance under a variety of asymmetric conditions are described.

Based on "How Network Asymmetry Affects TCP" by Hari Balakrishnan and Venkata Padmanabhan, which appeared in *IEEE Communications Magazine*, April 2001. © 2001 IEEE.

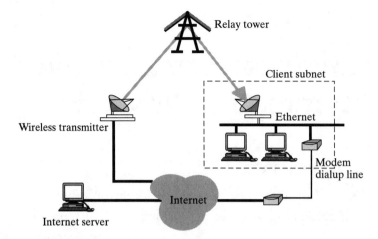

FIGURE 10.1: The network topology of the wireless cable modem network, which illustrates bandwidth asymmetry. Hosts on the client subnet receive data from the Internet via the 10 Mbps wireless cable upstream link and send out data via a low bandwidth (e.g., dialup) downstream link.

10.1   TYPES OF NETWORK ASYMMETRY

Network asymmetry can take several forms. We present a brief classification (Figure 10.2) to help structure our discussion.

10.1.1   Bandwidth Asymmetry

Typically the downstream bandwidth is 10 to 1000 times the upstream bandwidth. Examples include cable modem, ADSL, and satellite-based networks, especially in configurations that depend on a dialup link for upstream connectivity. For example,

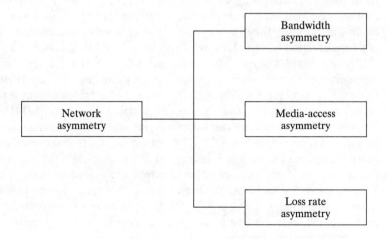

FIGURE 10.2: Different types of network asymmetry.

the DirectPC system utilizes a 400-Kbps satellite link as the forward channel and a dialup line of 14.4 Kbps to 56 Kbps as the reverse channel.

10.1.2   Media-Access Asymmetry

Media-access asymmetry manifests itself in several ways. In a cellular wireless network, a centralized base station incurs a lower medium access control (MAC) overhead in transmitting to distributed mobile hosts than the other way around. In a packet radio network (e.g., the Ricochet Networks [316]), the MAC overhead makes it more expensive to constantly switch the direction of transmission than to transmit steadily in one direction.

10.1.3   Loss Rate Asymmetry

The network may inherently be more lossy in one direction than in the other. If the packet-loss rate in the reverse direction is high, it can considerably degrade the forward link utilization even if there is no data loss in the forward direction. This is a direct result of TCP relying on ACKs to control its congestion window. Because ACKs travel over the reverse channel, high loss rate in the reverse channel would mean high loss rates for the ACKs, preventing the TCP sender from reaching the advertised window.

10.2   IMPACT OF ASYMMETRY ON TCP PERFORMANCE

In this section, we analyze the problems caused by bandwidth asymmetry and media-access asymmetry.

10.2.1   Bandwidth Asymmetry

We first discuss the case in which TCP transfers happen only in the downstream direction and then turn to the bidirectional case.

Unidirectional Data Transfer.   A common example is a user downloading data from a server. For simplicity, we restrict ourselves to the case of a single TCP connection in the downstream direction.

As defined in [211], the *normalized bandwidth ratio*, k, between the downstream and upstream paths is the ratio of the raw bandwidths divided by the ratio of the packet sizes used in the two directions. For example, for a 10-Mbps downstream channel and a 100-Kbps upstream channel, the raw bandwidth ratio is 100. With 1000-byte data packets and 40-byte ACKs, the ratio of the packet sizes is 25. So, k is $100/25 = 4$.

The ratio, k, holds the key to the behavior of TCP in an asymmetric network setting. If the receiver transmits more than one ACK every k data packets, the upstream bottleneck link gets saturated before the downstream one does. This forces the sender to clock out data more slowly than optimal, thus decreasing throughput.

If the upstream bottleneck remains congested for a sustained length of time, the corresponding buffer fills up, causing ACKs to be dropped. On average, only one ACK will get through for every k data packets transmitted by the sender, which can degrade performance in several ways. First, the sender could burst out k packets at a time, which increases the chance of data packet loss, especially when k is large. Second, because conventional TCP senders base congestion window growth on *counting* the number of ACKs and not on how much data is actually acknowledged, infrequent ACKs result in slower growth of the congestion window. Finally, the loss of (the now infrequent) ACKs elsewhere in the network could cause long idle periods while the sender waits for subsequent ACKs to arrive.

Bidirectional Data Transfers.   We now consider the case when both downstream and upstream TCP transfers occur simultaneously. An example of this is a user sending out data (e.g., an e-mail message) while simultaneously receiving other data (e.g., Web pages).

The presence of bidirectional traffic effectively increases the degree of bandwidth asymmetry for the downstream transfer, thereby exacerbating the problems discussed in Section 10.1.1. In addition, there are other effects that arise because of the interaction between data packets of the upstream transfer and ACKs of the downstream transfer. Essentially, the former can quickly fill up the upstream buffer, causing a large delay and a high loss rate for the latter. For instance, a single 1-KB data packet of the upstream transfer can add a whopping 1 second of queuing delay for ACKs of the downstream transfer. The resulting performance problem is illustrated in Figure 10.3 and Figure 10.4, which show that the downstream transfer makes significant progress only when the upstream transfer suffers a hiccup. In these figures, the slope of packet sequence number against time reflects how fast (or slow) data are being transmitted.

In summary, the presence of bidirectional traffic exacerbates the problems due to bandwidth asymmetry and the adverse interaction between data packets of an upstream connection and the ACKs of a downstream connection.

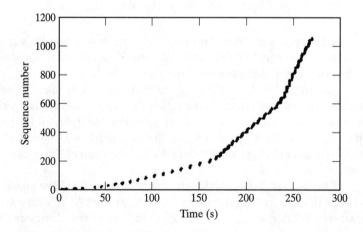

FIGURE 10.3: Measurements of the downstream connection operating over a 10-Mbps wireless cable modem network. The sharp upswings in its data rate occur whenever the upstream connection suffers a loss and slows down (see Figure 10.4).

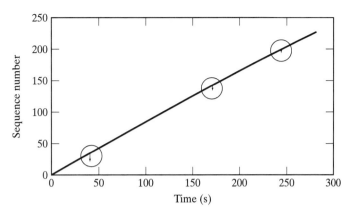

FIGURE 10.4: Measurements of the upstream connection operating over a 9.6-Kbps dialup line. The circles indicate times when the upstream connection retransmits packets.

10.2.2 Media-Access Asymmetry

As discussed earlier, media-access asymmetry manifests itself in several ways; however, the fundamental cause is the same—uneven access to a shared medium by a distributed set of nodes. In a hub-and-spokes model, a central base station has complete knowledge of and control over the downstream traffic; therefore, it suffers a lower MAC overhead than the distributed nodes that contend for the uplink. On the other hand, in a packet radio network, the peer nodes are equals. Nevertheless, the MAC overhead makes it expensive to transmit packets in one direction when there is an ongoing data transfer in the opposite direction. In the remainder of this section, we discuss this issue in detail in the context of a packet radio network. Although we use a network modeled after Ricochet Networks [316], the basic results and conclusions are applicable to all packet radio networks in general. We start by describing the underlying packet radio network technology used in the study.

Topology. The network topology of the packet radio network is shown in Figure 10.5. The maximum link speed between two nodes in the wireless cloud is 100 Kbps. Packets from a fixed host (FH) on the Internet are routed via a gateway (GW) and through the poletop radios (PT), to the mobile host (MH). There are typically between one and three wireless hops before the packet reaches the MH.

Half-Duplex Radios. Because the transmission power drowns incoming receptions in the same frequency band, the radio units in the network are *half-duplex*. This means that they cannot simultaneously transmit and receive data. After transmitting (receiving) a packet, a sender (receiver) wanting to receive (transmit) needs to turn around and change modes. Moving from transmitting to receiving mode takes a nontrivial amount of time, called the transmit-to-receive turnaround time, T_{TR}. Similarly, going from receiving to transmitting mode takes a time equal to the receive-to-transmit turnaround time, T_{RT}.

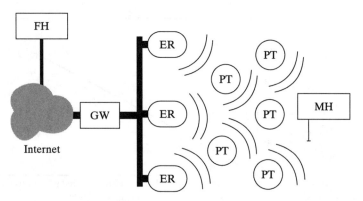

FIGURE 10.5: Topology of a packet radio network. The mobile host (MH) has a modem attached to it, which communicates with fixed host (FH) on the Internet through the poletop (PT), an ethernet radio (ER). The gateway (GW) routes packets between the packet radio network and the Internet.

Media-Access. The radios in the network are frequency-hopping, spread-spectrum units operating in the 915 MHz Industrial Scientific and Medical (ISM) band. The details of the frequency-hopping protocol are not relevant to transport performance, because the predominant reason for poor performance is the interactions between the media-access (MAC) protocol and TCP. The MAC protocol for contention resolution is based on a polling scheme, similar (but not identical) to the RTS/CTS ("Request-To-Send/Clear-To-Send") protocol used in the IEEE 802.11 standard. A station wishing to communicate with another (called the peer) first sends it an RTS message. If the peer is not currently communicating with any other station and is willing to receive this transmission, it sends a CTS message acknowledging the RTS. When this is received by the initiator, the data communication link is established. A data frame can then be sent to the peer. If the peer cannot currently communicate with the sender because it is communicating with another peer, it does not send a CTS, which causes the sender to back off for a random amount of time and schedule the transmission for later. It could also send a NACK-CTS to the sender, which achieves the same effect. In all of this, care is taken by both stations to ensure that messages and data frames are not lost because the peer was in the wrong mode, by waiting enough time for the peer to change modes. To do this, each station maintains the value of the turnaround times of its peers in the network.

Error Control The reliable link-layer protocol used in this network for error control is a simple frame-by-frame protocol with a window size of 1. When a frame is successfully received, the receiver sends a link-level ACK to the sender. If the frame is not received successfully, the sender retransmits it after a timeout period. Such simple link-layer protocols are the norm in several packet radio networks.

The need for the communicating peers to first synchronize via the RTS/CTS protocol and the significant turnaround time for the radios result in a high per-packet overhead. Furthermore, because the RTS/CTS exchange needs to back off when the polled radio is otherwise busy (e.g., engaged in a conversation with a different peer), this overhead is variable. This leads to large and variable communication latencies in such networks. In addition, with an asymmetric workload with most data flowing in one direction to clients, ACKs tend to get queued in certain radio units, such as the client modems.

These variable latencies and queuing of ACKs adversely affect smooth data flow. In particular, TCP ACK traffic interferes with the flow of data and increases the traffic load on the system. Figure 10.6 shows the packet sequence trace of a measured 200-KB TCP transfer over an unloaded wired path and one wireless hop in the packet radio network. This clearly shows the effect of the radio turnarounds and increased variability affecting performance. The connection progresses well for the most part, except for the three timeouts that occur during the transfer. These timeouts last between 9 and 12 seconds each, keeping the connection idle for a total of 35% of the total transfer time! These timeouts clearly underutilize the available bandwidth for the connection.

Why are these timeouts so long in duration? Ideally, the round-trip time estimate (*srtt*) of a TCP data transfer is relatively constant (i.e., has a low linear deviation, *mdev*). Then the TCP retransmission timeout, set to $srtt + 4 * mdev$, tracks the smoothed round-trip time estimate and responds well when multiple losses occur in a window. Unfortunately, this is not true for connections in this

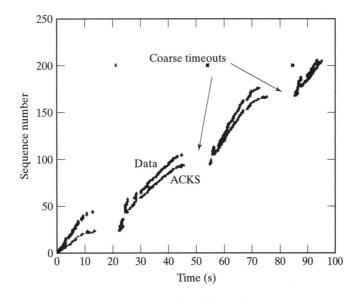

FIGURE 10.6: Packet and ACK sequence trace of a 200-KB TCP bulk transfer measured over one wireless hop in the Ricochet network. The three pauses are sender timeouts, lasting between 9 and 12 s each because large round-trip time variations cause the retransmission timeout estimate to be very long.

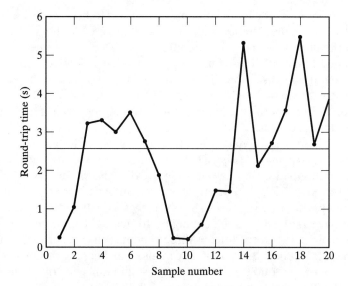

FIGURE 10.7: Twenty round-trip time samples. The samples have a mean of about 2.5 s and a standard deviation of about 1.5 s.

network, as shown in Figure 10.7. This figure plots the individual round-trip time estimates for 20 successive samples during the same connection over the Ricochet network. The mean value of these samples is about 2.5 seconds and the standard deviation is large—about 1.5 seconds. Because of the high variation in the individual samples, the retransmission timer is on the order of 10 seconds, leading to the long idle timeout periods.

In general, it is correct for the retransmission timer to trigger a segment retransmission only after an amount of time that is dependent on both the round-trip time and the linear (or standard) deviation. If only the mean or median round-trip estimates were taken into account, there is a significant potential for spurious retransmissions of segments still in transit. Thus, the challenge is to devise solutions to this problem in which the increased ACK flow and ACK queuing lead to variable latencies and long timeout periods.

An optimization of the link-layer, error-control protocol that piggybacks link-layer ACKs with data frames reduces TCP round-trip variations to some extent. This scheme is motivated by the observation that the radios turn around both for data frames as well as for link-layer ACKs. The presence of traffic in both directions, even when caused by TCP ACKs, already causes turnarounds to happen. So, if link-layer ACKs were piggybacked with data frames, some extra radio turnarounds can be eliminated.

Despite this optimization, the fundamental problem of additional traffic and underlying protocols affecting round-trip time estimates and causing variabilities in performance still persists. Connections traversing multiple hops of the wireless network are more vulnerable to this effect, because it is now more likely that the radio units may already be engaged in conversation with other peers.

10.3 IMPROVING TCP PERFORMANCE OVER ASYMMETRIC NETWORKS

Our discussion thus far makes it clear that there are two key issues that need to be addressed to improve TCP performance over asymmetric networks. The first issue is to manage bandwidth usage on the uplink used by ACKs (and possibly other traffic). Many of these techniques to address this issue work by reducing the number of ACKs that flow over that which has the potential of destroying the (desirable) self-clocking property of the TCP sender where new data transmissions are triggered by incoming ACKs. Thus, the second issue is to avoid any adverse impact of infrequent ACKs.

Each of these issues can be handled by local link-layer solutions and/or by end-to-end techniques. In this section, we discuss solutions of both kinds.

10.3.1 Uplink Bandwidth Management

Uplink bandwidth management may be performed by controlling the degree of compression, the frequency, and the scheduling of upstream ACKs.

TCP Header Compression.   TCP header compression [180] describes TCP header compression for use over low-bandwidth links running SLIP or PPP. Because it greatly reduces the size of ACKs on the uplink when losses are infrequent (a situation that ensures that the state of the compressor and decompressor are synchronized), its use is recommended over low-bandwidth uplinks where possible. However, this alone does not address all of the problems:

1. As discussed in Section 10.4.2, in certain networks there is a significant per-packet MAC overhead that is independent of packet size.
2. A reduction in the size of ACKs does not prevent adverse interaction with large upstream data packets in the presence of bidirectional traffic.

Hence, to effectively address the performance problems caused by asymmetry, there is a need for techniques over and beyond TCP header compression.

ACK Filtering.   ACK filtering (AF) is a TCP-aware, link-layer technique that reduces the number of TCP ACKs sent on the upstream channel. The challenge is to ensure that the sender does not stall waiting for ACKs, which can happen if ACKs are removed indiscriminately on the upstream path. AF removes only certain ACKs without starving the sender by taking advantage of the fact that TCP ACKs are cumulative. As far as the sender's error-control mechanism is concerned, the information contained in an ACK with a later sequence number subsumes the information contained in any earlier ACK[2]. When an ACK from the receiver is about to be queued at the upstream bottleneck router, the router or the end-host's link layer (if the host is directly connected to the constrained link) checks its queues for any older ACKs belonging to the same connection. If any are found, it removes them from the queue, thereby reducing the number of ACKs that go back to the sender. The removal of these "redundant" ACKs frees up buffer space for other

---

[2]Only cumulative ACKs (not selective ACKs) are considered.

data and ACK packets. AF does not remove duplicate or selective ACKs from the queue to avoid causing problems to TCP's data-driven loss recovery mechanisms.

The policy that the filter uses to drop packets is configurable and can be either deterministic or random (similar to a random-drop gateway, but taking the semantics of the items in the queue into consideration). State needs to be maintained only for connections with at least one packet in the queue. However, this state is soft, and if necessary, can easily be reconstructed from the contents of the queue.

ACK Congestion Control.   ACK congestion control (ACC) is an alternative to ACK filtering that operates end-to-end rather than at the upstream bottleneck router. The key idea in ACC is to extend congestion control to TCP ACKs, because they do make nonnegligible demands on resources at the bandwidth-constrained upstream link. ACKs occupy slots in the upstream channel buffer, whose capacity is often limited to a certain number of packets (rather than bytes).

ACC has two parts: (1) a mechanism for the network to indicate to the receiver that the ACK path is congested, and (2) the receiver's response to such an indication. One possibility for the former is the RED (Random Early Detection) algorithm [146] at the upstream bottleneck router. The router detects incipient congestion by tracking the average queue size over a time window in the recent past. If the average exceeds a threshold, the router selects a packet at random and marks it, that is, it sets an Explicit Congestion Notification (ECN) bit in the packet header. This notification is reflected back to the upstream TCP end-host by its downstream peer.

With ACC, both data packets and TCP ACKs are candidates for being marked with an ECN bit. Therefore, upon receiving an ACK packet with the ECN bit set, the TCP receiver reduces the rate at which it sends ACKs. The TCP receiver maintains a dynamically varying delayed-ACK factor, d, and sends one ACK for every d data packets received. When it receives a packet with the ECN bit set, it increases d multiplicatively, thereby decreasing the frequency of ACKs also multiplicatively. Then for each subsequent round-trip time (determined using the TCP timestamp option) during which it does not receive an ECN, it linearly decreases the factor d, thereby increasing the frequency of ACKs. Thus, the receiver mimics the standard congestion control behavior of TCP senders in the manner in which it sends ACKs.

There are bounds on the delayed-ACK factor d. Obviously, the minimum value of d is 1, because at most one ACK should be sent per data packet. The maximum value of d is determined by the sender's window size, which is conveyed to the receiver in a new TCP option. The receiver should send at least one ACK (preferably more) for each window of data from the sender. Otherwise, it could cause the sender to stall until the receiver's delayed-ACK timer (usually set at 200 ms) kicks in and forces an ACK to be sent.

Despite RED + ECN, there may be times when the upstream router queue fills up and it needs to drop a packet. The router can pick a packet to drop in various ways. For instance, it can drop from the tail, or it can drop a packet already in the queue at random.

ACKs-First Scheduling.   In the case of bidirectional transfers, data as well as ACK packets compete for resources in the upstream direction (Section 10.4). In this case, a single FIFO queue for both data packets and ACKs could cause problems.

For example, if the upstream channel is a 28.8 Kbps dialup line, the transmission of a 1-KB-sized data packet would take about 280 ms. So, even if just two such data packets get queued ahead of ACKs (not an uncommon occurrence because data packets are sent out in pairs during slow start), they would shut out ACKs for well over half a second. And if more than two data packets are queued up ahead of an ACK, the ACKs would be delayed by even more.

A possible approach to alleviating this problem is to schedule data and ACKs differently from FIFO. One algorithm, in particular, is *ACKS-first scheduling*, which always accords a higher priority to ACKs over data packets. The motivation for such scheduling is that it minimizes the idle time for the downstream connection by minimizing the amount of time that its ACKs spend queued behind upstream data packets. At the same time, with techniques such as header compression [180], the transmission time of ACKs becomes small enough that its impact on subsequent data packets is minimal. (Networks in which the per-packet overhead of the upstream channel is large, e.g., packet radio networks, are an exception.) As with ACC, this scheduling scheme does not require the gateway to explicitly identify or maintain state for individual TCP connections.

ACKS-first scheduling does not help avoid the delay caused by a data packet in transmission. On a slow uplink, such a delay could be large if the data packet is large in size. One way of reducing the delay is to fragment the data packet into small pieces before transmission [68, 297].

10.3.2   Handling Infrequent ACKs

This can be done either end-to-end or locally at the constrained uplink.

TCP Sender Adaptation.   ACC and AF alleviate the problem of congestion on the upstream bottleneck link by decreasing the frequency of ACKs, with each ACK potentially acknowledging several data packets. As discussed earlier, this can cause problems such as sender burstiness and a slowdown in congestion window growth.

Sender adaptation (SA) is an end-to-end technique for alleviating this problem. A bound is placed on the maximum number of packets the sender can transmit back-to-back, even if the window allows the transmission of more data. If necessary, more bursts of data are scheduled for later points in time computed based on the connection's data rate. The data rate is estimated as the ratio *cwnd/srtt*, where *cwnd* is the TCP congestion window size and *srtt* is the smoothed RTT estimate. Thus, large bursts of data get broken up into smaller bursts spread out over time.

The sender can avoid a slowdown in congestion window growth by simply taking into account the amount of data acknowledged by each ACK, rather than the number of ACKs. So, if an ACK acknowledges s segments, the window is grown as if s separate ACKs had been received. (One could treat the single ACK as being equivalent to $s/2$ instead of s ACKs to mimic the effect of the TCP delayed ACK algorithm.) This policy works because the window growth is only tied to the available bandwidth in the downstream direction, so the number of ACKs is immaterial.

ACK Reconstruction.   ACK reconstruction (AR) is a technique to reconstruct the ACK stream after it has traversed the upstream direction bottleneck link.

AR is a local technique designed to prevent the reduced ACK frequency from adversely affecting the performance of standard TCP sender implementations (i.e., those that do not implement sender adaptation). This enables us to use schemes such as ACK filtering or ACK congestion control without requiring TCP senders to be modified to perform sender adaptation. This solution can be easily deployed by Internet Service Providers (ISPs) of asymmetric access technologies in conjunction with AF to achieve good performance.

AR deploys a soft-state agent called the ACK reconstructor at the upstream end of the constrained ACK bottleneck. The reconstructor does not need to be on the downstream data path. It carefully fills in the gaps in the ACK sequence and introduces ACKs to smooth out the ACK stream seen by the sender. However, it does so without violating the end-to-end semantics of TCP ACKs, as explained below.

Suppose two ACKs, $a1$ and $a2$, arrive at the reconstructor after traversing the constrained upstream link at times $t1$ and $t2$, respectively. Let $a2 - a1 = delta\_a > 1$. If $a2$ were to reach the sender soon after $a1$ with no intervening ACKs, at least $delta\_a$ segments are burst out by the sender (if the flow control window is large enough), and the congestion window increases by at most 1, independent of $delta\_a$. ACK reconstruction remedies this problematic situation by interspersing ACKs to provide the sender with a larger number of ACKs at a consistent rate, which reduces the degree of burstiness and causes the congestion window to increase at a rate governed by the downstream bottleneck.

How is this done? One of the configurable parameters of the reconstructor is ack_thresh, the ACK threshold, which determines the spacing between interspersed ACKs at the output. Typically, ack_thresh is set to 2, which follows TCP's standard delayed-ACK policy. Thus, if successive ACKs arrive at the reconstructor separated by $delta\_a$, it interposes $ceil(delta\_a/ack\_thresh) - 2$ ACKs, where $ceil()$ is the ceiling operator. The other parameter used by the reconstructor is $ack\_interval$, which determines the temporal spacing between the reconstructed ACKs. To do this, it measures the rate at which ACKs arrive at the input to the reconstructor. This rate depends on the output rate from the constrained upstream channel and on the presence of other traffic on that link. The reconstructor uses an exponentially weighted moving average estimator to monitor this rate; the output of the estimator is $delta\_t$, the average temporal spacing at which ACKs are arriving at the reconstructor (and the average rate at which ACKs would reach the sender, if there were no further losses or delays). If the reconstructor sets $ack\_interval$ equal to $delta\_t$, then we would essentially operate at a rate governed by the upstream bottleneck link, and the resulting performance would be determined by the rate at which unfiltered ACKs arrive out of the upstream bottleneck link. If sender adaptation were being done, then the sender behaves as if the rate at which acks arrive is $delta\_a/delta\_t$. Therefore, a good method of deciding the temporal spacing of reconstructed ACKs, $ack\_interval$, is to equate the rates at which increments in the ACK sequence happen in the two cases. That is, the reconstructor sets $ack\_interval$ such that $delta\_a/delta\_t = ack\_thresh/ack\_interval$, which implies that $ack\_interval = (ack\_thresh/delta\_a) * delta\_t$. Therefore, the latest ACK in current sequence, $a2$ is held back for a time roughly equal to $delta\_t$, and $ceil(delta\_a/ack\_thresh) - 2$ ACKs are evenly interposed in this time.

Thus, by carefully controlling the number of and spacing between ACKs, unmodified TCP senders can be made to increase their congestion window at the right rate and avoid bursty behavior. ACK reconstruction can be implemented by maintaining only "soft state" at the reconstructor that can easily be regenerated if lost. Note that the reconstructor generates no spurious ACKs and the end-to-end semantics of the connection are completely preserved. The trade-off in AR is between obtaining less bursty performance, a better rate of congestion window increase, and a reduction in the round-trip variation, versus a modest increase in the round-trip time estimate at the sender. We believe that it is a good trade-off in the asymmetric environments with which we are concerned.

10.4   EXPERIMENTAL EVALUATION OF PERFORMANCE IMPROVEMENT TECHNIQUES

Detailed experiments were carried out [56, 257] to evaluate the effectiveness of the performance improvement techniques discussed in the previous section. In these experiments, TCP Reno was used as the base protocol. Reno was enhanced with ACC, AF, SA, and AR, in various combinations. We briefly discuss some of the key experimental results.

10.4.1   Experiments with Bandwidth Asymmetry

In this setting, there is a 10-Mbps downlink and a 28.8-Kbps uplink with TCP header compression enabled. The maximum window size was set to 120 packets and all queue sizes were set to 10 packets. Table 10.1 shows the performance of a single downstream transfer.

AF/AR and AF/SA perform the best, achieving throughputs between 15% and 21% better than Reno. ACC/SA performs about 5% better than Reno for this configuration. The important point is that the degree of burstiness is reduced significantly, while the upstream router queue is no longer perpetually full because of AF or ACC. This can be seen from Figure 10.8, which shows the time evolution of congestion windows for the different protocols. Table 10.1 shows the time-averaged TCP congestion window and round-trip times for the different protocols. It is clear from the table that reducing the frequency of ACKs alone is not sufficient, and that techniques like SA or AR need to be used as well.

AR results in a larger round-trip time than the other protocols, but this leads to the best performance for this setting of parameters because it reduces the number of losses (because packet transmissions from the source are now spread over a longer duration). For ACC/SA, a RED gateway is used to mark packets (ACKS) and drop packets when the queue is full. It was found that using a random drop policy is

TABLE 10.1: Performance of different protocols in the presence of losses in the downstream direction.

Metric	Reno	ACC/SA	AF/SA	AF/AR	AF Alone
Throughput (Mbps)	6.71	6.95	**7.82**	8.57	**5.16**
Average *cwnd* (pkts)	66.7	62	**65.3**	104.6	**43.8**
Average RTT (ms)	79	70	65	97	65

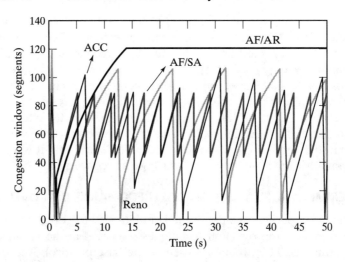

FIGURE 10.8: Congestion window evolution for the different schemes. ACC, AF/SA, and AF/AR do not fluctuate as much as Reno, achieving better performance.

superior to dropping from the tail when an ACK has to be dropped. This is because tail drops sometimes lead to long, consecutive sequences of ACKS being dropped, leading to increased sender burstiness.

In summary, the results show that SA or AR is important to overcome the burstiness that results from a lossy ACK stream, and that a random drop policy at the RED gateway was better for performance.

10.4.2 Experiments with Media-Access Asymmetry

In this experiment, a model of the Ricochet Networks [316] was used. The workload in these experiments consists of a 100-second TCP transfer, with no other competing traffic and a maximum receiver window size of 32 KB. Congestion losses occur as a result of buffer overflow and lead to sender timeouts if multiple packets are lost in a transmission window. The protocols investigated include unmodified TCP Reno, Reno with ACC/SA (i.e., ACC and SA at the sender), and Reno with AF/SA (i.e., AF with SA at the sender).

Figure 10.9 shows the results of these experiments, as a function of the number of wireless hops. The performance of AF and ACC with SA are better than Reno, and AF/SA is better than ACC/SA. The degree of improvement in throughput varies from 25% (one wireless hop) to 41% (three wireless hops).

10.5 FURTHER READING

Lakshman et al. [211] analyzed the problems caused by bandwidth asymmetry and showed that performance degraded if the normalized asymmetry ratio exceeded 1. They also propose the use of the drop-from-front strategy on ACKs in the constrained upstream channel buffer as a way to alleviate the problems that arise.

Kalampoukas et al. [189] studied the problems that arise when bidirectional traffic is present in a bandwidth-asymmetric network, using a combination of analysis

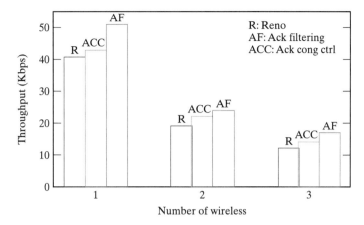

FIGURE 10.9: TCP throughputs from simulations of Reno, ACC, and AF, as a function of the number of wireless hops.

and simulation. They show that *ACK compression* sometimes occurs in these environments causing throughput reduction. To alleviate the effects on throughput, they investigate three approaches: (1) prioritizing ACKs over data on the upstream channel, which results in starvation; (2) using a connection-level, back-pressure mechanism to limit the maximum amount of data buffered in the upstream channel router, which results in unfair bandwidth utilization; and (3) using connection-level bandwidth allocation, which provides flow isolation.

Cohen and Ramanathan [276] studied TCP performance over a hybrid, coaxial cable distribution system using simulations of that network. They conclude that it is important for receivers to tune their socket buffer sizes; use an initial window of two segments as opposed to one; use smaller segment sizes to overcome problems with delayed TCP ACKs and ACK losses; use a finer granularity for TCP timers; and use fast retransmission triggered by a single duplicate ACK for better loss recovery. In general, while some of these techniques improve performance in their network, they are not universally applicable and lead to worse performance in other networks. For example, retransmitting a segment upon the arrival of the first duplicate ACK is not correct in general because of the significant amount of packet reordering in the Internet. The schemes in this paper, in contrast, improve TCP performance in heterogeneous wireless networks without compromising performance in other situations.

Samaraweera [284] presents ACK compaction and expansion that are similar in vein to, but more complicated than, AF and AR. The compacter discards older ACKs in the upstream queue while retaining newer ACKs (just as in AF) but, in addition, conveys the number of discarded ACKs and the total number of bytes they acknowledge to its peer, the expander. The expander can then regenerate the discarded ACKs without having to guess how many ACKs had been discarded. This is an advantage compared to AF/AR; however, it comes at the cost of new protocol machinery to convey the information about discarded ACKs from the compacter to the expander. AF/AR does not require any new protocol machinery.

10.6 SUMMARY

Network asymmetry, in terms of bandwidth, media-access, and loss rate, can severely affect the performance of a feedback-based transport protocol, such as TCP. In this chapter, we have discussed several techniques that provide network designers with solutions for efficient TCP in a variety of asymmetric conditions.

10.7 REVIEW QUESTIONS

1. What is network asymmetry? How many different types of asymmetry do we have?
2. Explain how bandwidth asymmetry causes performance problems for TCP.
3. What is media-access asymmetry? Which networks exhibit this kind of asymmetry? How can media-access asymmetry degrade TCP performance?
4. Explain how loss-rate asymmetry can impair TCP throughput.
5. What is ACK filtering? How can it address the problems caused by bandwidth asymmetry?
6. What is the difference between ACK filtering and ACK congestion control?
7. What is ACK reconstruction? How does it help improve TCP performance over asymmetric links?
8. How practical are ACK filtering, ACK congestion control, and ACK reconstruction? Discuss practical issues associated with these techniques.
9. Would network asymmetry affect the performance of UDP-based applications? Why or why not?
10. One type of asymmetry not discussed in this chapter is packet delay asymmetry. Can you think of a situation when packet delays are asymmetric, despite symmetrical link bandwidth?

10.8 HANDS-ON PROJECTS

1. Design a simulation model to compare the effectiveness of ACK filtering and ACK congestion control in mitigating the effects of bandwidth asymmetry. The simulation model should closely follow the experimental model described in Section 10.4.1. Construct this model in the freely available *ns* software. Use two performance metrics, TCP throughput and average RTT, to evaluate the performance. Collect the simulation results. Based on these results, explain which method performs better under what scenarios. Compare your simulation results against the (experimental) ones presented in Table 10.1.
2. Lakshman et al. [211] proposed the use of the drop-from-front strategy on ACKs in the constrained upstream channel buffer as a way to alleviate the problems that arise because of bandwidth asymmetry. Using simulations, evaluate the performance of this scheme and compare it against ACK filtering.

10.9 CASE STUDY: IMPROVING TCP PERFORMANCE OVER ADSL

Although most WCORP employees work from office, some work from home one or two days a week. Working from home gives more flexibility and makes the job more attractive to some employees. In the past, employees used dialup modems to

TABLE 10.2: Comparison of ADSL, ISDN, and cable modem.

Feature	ADSL	ISDN	Cable Modem
Speed	1.5 Mbps	64 Kbps	1 Mbps
Reliability	Good	Good	Good
Voice/data	Simultaneous	Simultaneous	Simultaneous
Access mode	Always-on	Dialup	Always-on
Installation	No separate line	Separate line	Cable line
Bandwidth sharing	Dedicated	Dedicated	Shared
Cost	Moderate	Expensive	Moderate

access the Internet over the home telephone line. These employees, however, had been experiencing three major problems: (1) long download times, (2) unreliable connections because of an inability to connect or line drop-outs, and (3) inability to make voice calls while using the only telephone line for Internet access. Because of these problems, WCORP has decided to fund for an upgrade of Internet access from home for employees who choose to work from home. Three alternatives were considered: ADSL, ISDN, and cable modem. Although all three alternatives address the three problems associated with dialup modems, they differ in cost, speed, and mode of operation. Table 10.2 compares the basic versions of ADSL, ISDN, and cable modem services available from most ISPs. ISDN was eliminated immediately because of its low speed and dialup access mode. The aspect of bandwidth sharing made cable modem less attractive than ADSL. Another advantage of ADSL over cable modem is that ADSL would not require installation of cables to homes (most homes in Australia do not have cable TV). For these reasons, WCORP has finally opted for ADSL. With the upgrade to ADSL, download speed was expected to be around 1.5 Mbps, around 25 times improvement over dialup modems.

Interestingly, the users of ADSL did not experience 25 times better performance. In fact, it was quite far from that. Measurement of large file download revealed that on average users were able to utilize only 65% of the total download capacity. A more detailed TCP traffic analysis confirmed that the low throughput was caused by ACK congestion in the uplink (from home to Internet). The uplink capacity was measured to only 96 Kbps, 150 times lower than downlink capacity! TCP sender at the server side (Internet) could not pump data faster because of slow arrival of ACK packets from the client side (home).

To address TCP performance problem for home users, WCORP considered three techniques known to mitigate problems arising from bandwidth asymmetry. These techniques are TCP header compression, ACK filtering, and ACK congestion control. Because of ease of deployability, TCP header compression was finally selected as the most appropriate candidate. All home TCP/IP systems were upgraded with TCP header compression to significantly reduce the size of ACK packets. Subsequent measurement showed a dramatic improvement of download time. With header compression in place, home users were able to utilize 95% of the download capacity.

CHAPTER 11

New TCP Standards and Flavors

CHAPTER OBJECTIVES

After completing this chapter, the reader should be able to:

- Discuss and compare the variations in congestion control algorithms of different TCP flavors

- Learn how network simulation can be used to compare the performance of different TCP flavors

In Chapter 2, we presented the basics of the original TCP. Although the original design of TCP was capable of sustaining rapid growth and diversity on the Internet, it had some "flaws" in its congestion control engine. Congestion collapse was first experienced on the Internet in 1986 [179]. An investigation resulted in the design of new congestion control algorithms, now an essential part of TCP. Since the development of the basic TCP congestion control algorithm, known as TCP Tahoe [179, 44] in 1988, a number of variations on the TCP congestion control algorithm have been proposed and studied. These variations modify the slow start phase, the congestion avoidance phase, or the response to losses. In this chapter, we discuss the most prominent variations and present performance comparisons among them using simulations.

11.1 DUPLICATE ACKNOWLEDGMENTS AND FAST RETRANSMIT

A TCP sender detects packet loss when it times out waiting for an ACK. In addition, duplicate ACKs (*dupacks*) can be used to detect losses. As explained in Chapter 2, if a TCP receiver receives an out-of-order segment, it immediately sends back a *dupack* to the sender. The *dupack* indicates the byte number expected (thus, it is easy to infer the last in-order byte that has been successfully received). For example, if segments 0 through 5 have been transmitted and segment 2 is lost, the receiver sends a *dupack* each time it receives an out-of-order segment, that is, when it receives segments 3, 4, and 5. Each of these *dupack*s indicates that the receiver is expecting segment 2 (or expecting byte 1024 assuming segments 0 and 1 are 512 bytes each).

The fast retransmit algorithm uses these *dupack*s to make retransmission decisions. If the sender receives n *dupack*s ($n = 3$ was chosen to prevent spurious retransmissions caused by out-of-order delivery), the sender assumes loss and retransmits the lost segment without waiting for the retransmit timer to go off. TCP then reduces the slow start threshold (*ssthresh*) to half the congestion window (*cwnd*), and resets *cwnd* to one segment. TCP Tahoe (as opposed to Old Tahoe) included fast retransmit in addition to slow start and congestion avoidance.

11.2   FAST RECOVERY AND TCP RENO

TCP Reno retained all the enhancements in TCP Tahoe but incorporated a new algorithm, the fast recovery algorithm. Fast recovery is based on the fact that a *dupack* indicates that a segment has left the network. Hence, when the sender receives three *dupacks*, it retransmits the lost segment, updates *ssthresh*, and reduces *cwnd* as in fast retransmit (by half). Fast recovery, however, keeps track of the number of *dupacks* received and tries to estimate the amount of outstanding data in the network. It inflates *cwnd* (by one segment) for each *dupack* received, thus maintaining the flow of traffic. Thus, fast recovery keeps the TCP self-clocking mechanism alive. The sender comes out of fast recovery when it receives an acknowledgment (ACK) for the segment whose loss resulted in the duplicate ACKs. TCP then deflates the window by returning it to *ssthresh* and enters the congestion avoidance phase.

If multiple segments are lost *in the same window of data*, on most occasions, TCP Reno waits for a retransmission timeout, retransmits the segment, and goes into slow start mode. This happens when, for each segment loss, Reno enters fast recovery, reduces its *cwnd*, and aborts fast recovery on the receipt of a partial ACK. A partial ACK is one that acknowledges some but not all, of the outstanding segments. After multiple such reductions, *cwnd* becomes so small that there are not enough *dupacks* for fast recovery to occur, and a timeout is the only option left.

This scenario is illustrated in Figures 11.1 and 11.2. Figure 11.1 shows the congestion window changes over time, and Figure 11.2 shows the data sequence number (dark line) and ACK number (lighter line) over time for a TCP Reno connection experiencing multiple consecutive losses.

As seen in Figure 11.1, the congestion window grows exponentially (slow start) until some errors to occur start when the congestion window is about 37 KB. The sender receives duplicate acknowledgments, and fast retransmit and recovery trigger. *ssthresh* is set to 18,944 bytes. The sender retransmits the lost packet and

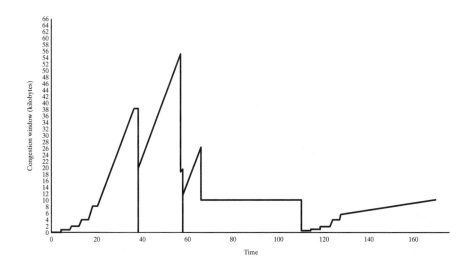

FIGURE 11.1: Reno congestion window with multiple consecutive drops.

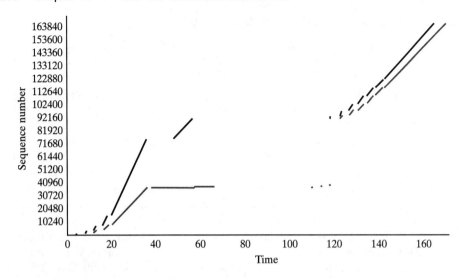

FIGURE 11.2: Reno data and ACK sequence numbers with multiple consecutive drops.

then sets the congestion window to *ssthresh* + 3 segments. On receiving subsequent duplicate ACKs, the congestion window is increased by 512 (the segment size) for every *dupack* (exponential rise). When the first nonduplicate ACK is received, the congestion window is set to *ssthresh*. Another set of *dupacks* is received for a subsequent erroneous packet, and fast retransmit and recovery trigger again. *ssthresh* becomes 9728 bytes. At a certain point, the receiver does not receive any more packets to send *dupacks* for, and the segment it is expecting is in error, so the sender times out (not enough *dupacks* for this segment to trigger fast retransmit and recovery). *ssthresh* is set to half the window size, which is a small number. The sender enters the slow start phase again, starting from a window of one segment. When the window reaches *ssthresh*, the sender enters the congestion avoidance phase.

Figure 11.2 shows that the sequence numbers increase until the losses occur. When fast retransmit and recovery trigger (after the receipt of three *dupacks*), the first lost segment is retransmitted (dark dot in lighter line). More *dupacks* are received (horizontal lighter line). Later, when the window becomes large enough, the sender starts transmitting new segments (the out-of-order segments were cached). Fast retransmit and recovery trigger again, as seen by the *dupacks*. Another retransmission occurs, but the sender times out, as seen by the long time when there is no transmission. Then it sends only one packet, going into slow start.

11.3   TCP NEWRENO

A timeout affects the throughput of a connection in two ways. First, the connection has to wait for a timeout to occur and cannot send data during that period of time. Second, after the retransmission timeout occurs, *cwnd* goes back to one segment. These events adversely affect the performance of the connection.

In Reno, *partial* ACKs bring the sender out of fast recovery, resulting in a timeout in case of multiple segment losses. In NewReno, when a sender receives a partial ACK, it does not come out of fast recovery [139, 145, 167]. Instead, it assumes that the segment immediately after the most recently acknowledged segment has been lost, and hence the lost segment is retransmitted. Thus, in a multiple segment loss scenario, NewReno does not wait for a retransmission timeout and continues to retransmit lost segments every time it receives a partial ACK. Thus, fast recovery in NewReno begins when three duplicate ACKs are received and ends when either a retransmission timeout occurs or an ACK arrives that acknowledges all of the data up to and including the data that were outstanding when the fast recovery procedure began. Partial ACKs deflate the congestion window by the amount of new data acknowledged and then add one segment and reenter fast recovery.

Hoe [167] also suggests two additional algorithms as part of the original NewReno proposal. The first estimates the initial *ssthresh* by using the delay bandwidth product of the TCP connection (which estimates the number of segments that can be in flight). The second sends a new packet for every two duplicate ACKs received during fast recovery. These algorithms are still under investigation and are not part of NewReno as described in RFC 2582 [145].

11.4   TCP WITH SELECTIVE ACKNOWLEDGMENTS

Another way to deal with multiple segment losses is to inform the sender which segments have arrived at the receiver. Selective acknowledgments (SACK) is a version of TCP that adopts this approach. The receiver uses each TCP SACK block to indicate to the sender one contiguous block of data that has been received out of order at the receiver. When SACK blocks are received by the sender, they are used to maintain an image of the receiver queue, that is, which segments are missing and which have arrived at the receiver. Using this information, the sender retransmits only those segments that are missing, without waiting for a retransmission timeout. Only when no segment needs to be retransmitted are new data segments sent out [139, 236].

The SACK implementation can still use the same congestion control algorithms as Reno (or NewReno). It resorts to the retransmission timeout mechanism to deliver a missing segment to the receiver if ACKs are still not received in time. The main difference between SACK and Reno is the behavior in the event of multiple segment losses. In SACK, just like Reno, when the sender receives three *dupacks*, it goes into fast recovery. The sender retransmits the segment and halves *cwnd*. SACK maintains a variable called *pipe* to indicate the number of outstanding segments that are in transit. In SACK, during fast recovery, the sender sends data, new or retransmitted, only when the value of pipe is less than *cwnd*, that is, the number of segments in transit are less than the congestion window value. The value of pipe is incremented by one when the sender sends a segment (new or retransmitted) and is decremented by one when the sender receives a duplicate ACK with SACK showing new data have been received. The sender decrements pipe by two for partial ACKs [139]. As with NewReno, fast recovery is terminated when an ACK arrives that acknowledges *all* of the data up to and including the data that were outstanding when the fast recovery procedure began.

11.5 FORWARD ACKNOWLEDGMENTS

Forward acknowledgments (FACK) also aim at better recovery from multiple losses. The name "forward ACKs" comes from the fact that the algorithm keeps track of the correctly received data with the highest sequence number. In FACK, TCP maintains two additional variables: (1) *fack*, which represents the forward-most segment that has been acknowledged by the receiver through the SACK option, and (2) *retran_data*, which reflects the amount of outstanding retransmitted data in the network. Using these two variables, the amount of outstanding data during recovery can be estimated as forward-most data sent − forward-most data ACKed (*fack* value) + outstanding retransmitted data (*retran_data* value). TCP FACK regulates this value (the amount of outstanding data in the network) to be within one segment of *cwnd*. *cwnd* remains constant during the fast recovery period. The *fack* variable is also used to trigger fast retransmit more promptly [235].

11.6 TCP VEGAS

TCP Vegas [72] was presented in 1994 before NewReno, SACK, and FACK were developed. Vegas is fundamentally different from other TCP variants in that it does not wait for loss to trigger congestion window reductions. In Vegas, the expected throughput of a connection is estimated to be the number of segments in the pipe, that is, the number of bytes traveling from the sender to the receiver. To increase throughput, the congestion window must be increased. If congestion exists in the network, the actual throughput is less than the expected throughput. Vegas uses this idea to decide if it should increase or decrease the window.

Vegas keeps track of the time each segment is sent. When an ACK arrives, it estimates RTT as the difference between the current time and the recorded timestamp for the relevant segment. For each connection, Vegas defines *BaseRTT* to be the minimum RTT seen so far. It calculates the expected throughput as:

$$Expected = WindowSize/BaseRTT$$

where *WindowSize* is the size of the current congestion window. It then calculates the actual throughput (every RTT) by measuring the RTT for a particular segment in the window and the bytes transmitted in between.

The difference between expected and actual throughputs is maintained in the variable *Diff*. If *Diff* is less than a parameter α, a linear increase of *cwnd* takes place in the next RTT; else if *Diff* exceeds parameter β, *cwnd* is linearly decreased in the next RTT. The factors α and β (usually set to 2 and 4) represent too little and too much data in the network, respectively. This is the Vegas congestion avoidance scheme.

Vegas uses a modified slow start algorithm. The original slow start and congestion avoidance need losses to realize the onset of congestion in the network. The modified slow start tries to find the correct window size without incurring a loss. This is done by exponentially increasing its window every *other* RTT and using the other RTT to calculate *Diff*, when there is no change in the congestion window. Vegas shifts from slow start to congestion avoidance when the actual throughput is lower (by some value γ) than the expected throughput. This addition of congestion detection to slow start gives a better estimate of the bandwidth available to the connection.

Vegas also has a new retransmission policy. A segment is retransmitted after one duplicate ACK (without waiting for three *dupacks*) if the RTT estimate is greater than the timeout value. This helps in those cases where the sender will never receive three *dupacks* because lots of segments within this window are lost or the window size is too small. The same strategy is applied for a nonduplicate ACK after a retransmission.

11.7   OVERVIEW OF OTHER FEATURES AND OPTIONS

Table 11.1 summarizes the RFCs describing TCP congestion control. The following is a brief description of some of the new TCP options not discussed in the context of TCP flavors:

- **Idle periods (congestion window validation).** After a long idle period (or application-limited period), the TCP ACK clock is no longer useful and TCP can potentially send a burst of size *cwnd* even though the network conditions have changed. In such cases, RFC 2581 [44] and Jacobson [179] suggest resetting *cwnd* to the initial window size. RFC 2581 [44] suggests an initial window size value of 2 and RFC 2414 suggests min(4 × MSS,max[2 × MSS,4380 Bytes]), where MSS is the maximum segment size. There is currently work in progress on decaying the congestion window *cwnd* by half every RTO interval instead. The value of *ssthresh* maintains the previous *cwnd* value in this case. This feature is discussed in RFC 2861.

TABLE 11.1: Important TCP congestion control–related RFCs.

RFC Number	Describes
2018	selective acknowledgments (SACK)
2309	random early detection (RED)
2414–6	increasing initial window size
2481	explicit congestion notification
2488	TCP over satellite enhancements
2525	known TCP implementation problems
2581	slow start, congestion avoidance, fast retransmit, fast recovery, idle periods, ACK generation
2582	NewReno
2757	long thin networks, e.g., wireless WANs
2760	ongoing TCP satellite research
2861	congestion window validation (decay during idle periods)
2883	SACK extensions (use of SACK for acknowledging duplicate packets)
2884	performance of explicit congestion notification
2923	MTU discovery
2988	retransmission timer (RTO) computation
3042	limited transmit option (recovery with a small window or multiple losses)

- **Number of duplicate ACKs (limited transmit).** As indicated in the TCP Vegas algorithm [72], it may be beneficial to respond to the first or second duplicate ACK. Vegas responded with a retransmission if enough time has elapsed. Other strategies are currently being investigated in the IETF community. One mechanism called "limited transmit" suggests sending a new data segment in response to each of the first two duplicate ACKs received at the sender. Another mechanism is to sometimes reduce the number of duplicate ACKs required to trigger fast retransmission. Limited transmit is discussed in RFC 3042.

- **SACK extensions.** Some work is under way to extend SACK to provide more information on order of packet delivery. This can be effective in improving throughput when packets are reordered or replicated, ACKs are lost, or transmission timeouts trigger unnecessarily. This extension is discussed in RFC 2883. The SACK congestion control algorithm discussed earlier is also being standardized.

11.8   PERFORMANCE COMPARISON OF TCP FLAVORS

In this section, we illustrate the performance of various TCP flavors, varying a number of parameters. We use the *ns* simulator for our simulations. All our simulations use the configuration shown in Figure 11.3, where *Sn* is sending data to *Dn* for $n = 1, 2, 3$. Most of our simulation scenarios consist of two bulk data connections competing with each other. All the traffic is unidirectional and is created by infinite (the source always has data to send) file transfer protocol (FTP) applications running on top of the TCP sources. We also show one simulation with a number of Telnet and FTP sessions.

We use a receiver window size of 128 packets and the packet size is 536 bytes. The timer granularity is 0.5 seconds. The routers have a queue size of 64 packets. For TCP Vegas, we use $\alpha = 2$, $\beta = 4$, and $\gamma = 1$. In most of the simulations, the sources start at the same time and the simulation lasts for 10 seconds.

We measure the commonly used *goodput* metric, which only includes those bytes that are delivered to the receiver application. The goodput is computed by dividing the total amount of data received *at the application level* by receivers during

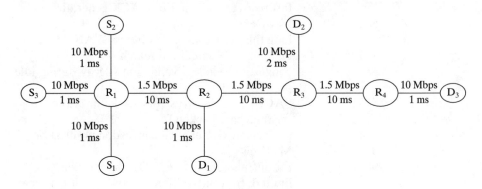

FIGURE 11.3: Network topology used for the simulations.

TABLE 11.2: Interactions of TCP Reno
with other TCP variants.

Flavor/Flavor	Goodput (Kb/s)
Reno/Reno	641.9/569.8
Tahoe/Reno	1050.5/379.4
Vegas/Reno	379.9/1059.1
NewReno/Reno	931.3/394.4
SACK/Reno	1121.7/328.8
FACK/Reno	1273.1/190.82

the simulation time, divided by the simulation time. We also measure the number
of dropped packets, and we plot the congestion window size over time.

Interactions of TCP Reno with Other TCP Flavors.   In this set of simulations,
we have two flows with equal round-trip times sharing a bottleneck link. The first
flow uses Reno, while the second flow varies. We compare all the other flavors with
Reno because Reno is currently widely deployed. Both senders are on node s1 and
both receivers are on node d1 in Figure 11.3.

The goodput values are shown in Table 11.2. We see that the goodput of the
Reno flow suffers in tandem with all the flavors except Vegas. This is because Vegas
is more conservative and responds better to congestion without waiting for packet
loss. This results in a decrease in its overall throughput because Reno is more
aggressive. The NewReno, SACK, and FACK flows perform much better than the
Reno flow because of their better response to packet drops.

Tahoe performs better than Reno because Reno does not react well to burst
drops. As the receiver window size is large, when Tahoe slow starts, it receives
enough *dupack*s to build up its congestion window aggressively. Reno, on the other
hand, goes into fast recovery but only after halving its *ssthresh* and congestion
window. Hence, it builds up its congestion window linearly in comparison to the
exponential window increase of Tahoe.

Round-Trip Times.   Table 11.3 shows the result of simulating two flows of
the same TCP flavor: one between s1 and d1 and the other between s3 and d3
(having more than double the RTT of the other). From Table 11.3, we see that for
all the TCP flavors, the flow having a longer RTT has a lower goodput value. This is
because the longer the RTT, the more time it takes for the ACKs/*dupack*s to come
back, and this limits the rate at which data can be sent (see Chapter 5). Figure 11.4
shows the congestion window versus time for the simulation with two Tahoe sources.
The flow marked Tahoe1 has a longer RTT. We see that during slow start, the *cwnd*
of Tahoe2 increases much faster because it receives ACKs faster. After a while,
the traffic generated by Tahoe2 is enough to cause buffer overflow. Hence, both
the flows lose packets, reduce their *ssthresh*, and go back to slow start. At the time
packet loss occurs, the *cwnd* of Tahoe1 is around 20 in comparison to 128 for Tahoe2.
Hence, when they go back to slow start, Tahoe2 stays in slow start for a much longer
period than Tahoe1 because of its larger new *ssthresh* value. That, coupled with the

TABLE 11.3: Effect of different round trip times.

Flavor/Flavor	Goodput (Kb/s)
Reno/Reno	305.7/899.1
Tahoe/Tahoe	224.6/1194.2
Vegas/Vegas	400.4/1062.5
NewReno/NewReno	406.0/924.0
SACK/SACK	294.5/1165.0
FACK/FACK	508.1/963.0

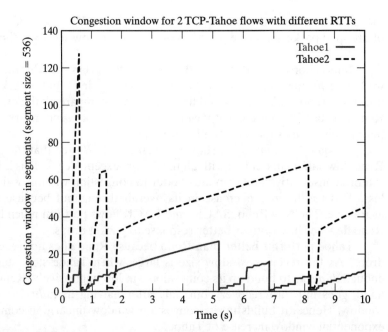

FIGURE 11.4: Congestion window versus time for two Tahoe sources with different RTTs.

fact that Tahoe2 has a shorter RTT, explains why its *cwnd* increases so fast again and also why it manages to take most of the available bandwidth. Similar trends were seen in the congestion window graphs of all the other flavors.

Timer Granularity. Table 11.4 shows the results of simulating two flows, both between s1 and d1 and having the same TCP flavor. The timer granularity was 0.1 seconds for the first flow and 0.5 seconds for the second flow. We see that, in general, for all flavors of TCP, the goodput value is higher for the source with smaller timer granularity. Figure 11.5 illustrates the congestion window graph for the simulation run with two Reno sources. The timer granularity for the flow marked Reno1 is 0.1 seconds and the flow marked Reno2 is 0.5 seconds. We see that both flows

TABLE 11.4: Effect of different timer granularities on goodput.

Flavor/Flavor	Goodput (Kb/s)
Reno/Reno	933.9/437.3
Tahoe/Tahoe	898.3/531.2
Vegas/Vegas	831.8/637.6
NewReno/NewReno	623.9/759.4
SACK/SACK	879.8/589.1
FACK/FACK	767.5/708.8

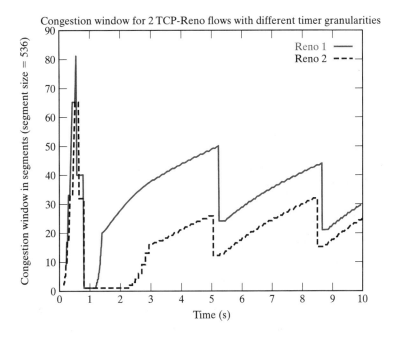

FIGURE 11.5: Congestion window versus time for two Reno sources with different timer granularities.

go through slow start phase where their *cwnd* increases exponentially. This causes buffer overflow and hence both flows lose packets. Notice that both flows have retransmission timeouts around 1 second. While the Reno1 flow recovers from the timeout faster because of its finer grained timer, Reno2 takes much longer and finally resumes its slow start phase around 2.2 seconds. Hence, Reno1 has a much higher goodput value than Reno2.

Active Queue Management and Explicit Congestion Notification.   In this set of simulations, we compare the performance of different TCP flavors in the presence of some router-based active congestion control mechanisms, such as active queue management (see Chapter 12) and explicit congestion notification [277]. Table 11.5

TABLE 11.5: Goodput values and number of packet drops using RED.

Flavor/Flavor	Goodput (Kb/s)	Number of Drops
Reno/Reno	640.1/571.1	48/38
Tahoe/Reno	809.1/608.4	49/38
Vegas/Reno	452.8/986.6	0/68
NewReno/Reno	799.7/523.9	50/38
SACK/Reno	902.1/548.0	50/38
FACK/Reno	956.2/506.8	50/39

shows the goodput values and the number of packet drops that occur when we use RED with router queue size of 64 packets. We simulate two flows, both between s1 and d1. The minimum threshold was set to 20 and maximum threshold was set at 50. The maximum drop probability was 0.1. Comparing Table 11.5 with Table 11.2, we see that using RED resulted in a more fair share for both flows. This can be verified by comparing the goodput of the second flow in the two tables. The goodput of the first flow is reduced because with RED, both flows lose packets in about the same proportion as their bandwidth usage. This is unlike drop-tail, where a flow could lose packets, although it is consuming a small share of the bandwidth, just because its packets reached the router when the queue was full. RED also starts dropping packets much before severe congestion occurs. This results in sources reacting early to congestion. Because the flow having more packets in the network has a higher chance of its packets being dropped at the router, it reacts to congestion more often and reduces its flow and, hence, more fairness results.

From Table 11.5, it is clear that TCP Vegas does not have any packet drops. We noticed this behavior in most of our simulations. This verifies the claim that Vegas reacts well to congestion and takes the necessary precautions before the onset of severe congestion. However, being more conservative reduces the goodput of Vegas (452.8 Kbps) when sharing links with other flavors. Notice that this value is much higher than what Vegas obtained without RED, which shows that RED mitigates the unfairness against Vegas.

Also notice that in the simulation with two Reno flows, the first flow has more packet drops, although both of them start at the same time and both flows have the same RTT. This occurs because in the simulation, the packets of the first flow are sent first and it gets ACKs before the second flow. Hence, its congestion window is larger than that of the second flow, although both of them start at the same time. Figure 11.6 shows a graph of the congestion window versus the time for the two Reno flows. We see that both flows start losing packets around 0.5 s. Because Reno1 has a bigger congestion window, it has more packets in the network and in the router queues; therefore, RED makes it lose more packets. However, the first flow has a larger goodput because, although Reno1 has more packets in the network it does not lose all of them. It just loses more packets than Reno2. Therefore, enough packets still reach the destination to give it higher goodput.

Table 11.6 shows the goodput and the number of packet drops when the experiment is repeated with ECN-aware end systems and routers. The results are

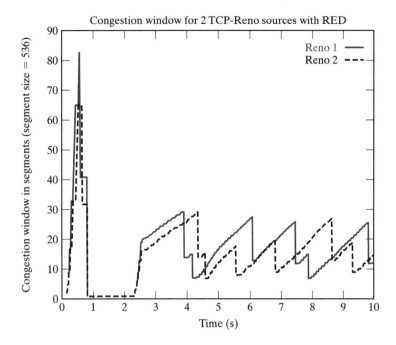

FIGURE 11.6: Congestion window versus time for two Reno sources with RED.

TABLE 11.6: Goodput values and number of packet drops using RED with ECN.

Flavor/Flavor	Goodput (Kb/s)	Number of Drops
Reno/Reno	563.4/647.9	42/32
Tahoe/Reno	802.7/631.6	42/32
Vegas/Reno	451.5/987.9	0/63
NewReno/Reno	683.5/640.1	42/32
SACK/Reno	858.0/592.1	42/32
FACK/Reno	851.1/611.8	42/32

more fair than drop-tail (Table 11.2) and RED without ECN (Table 11.5). The number of packet drops was reduced as expected. Using ECN results in fewer packets being retransmitted and improves overall network conditions as fewer resources are wasted by retransmissions.

Fairness among All TCP Flavors.   We investigate fairness among all flavors by simulating six sources with the six TCP flavors: Tahoe, Reno, NewReno, SACK, FACK, and Vegas. All sources are on node s1 and all the destinations are on node d1. Table 11.7 shows the goodput values achieved by the various flows. As seen in the table, FACK and SACK are the most aggressive, followed by Tahoe, NewReno, Reno, and finally Vegas, the least aggressive.

TABLE 11.7: Goodput achieved when all the flavors share a bottleneck.

Flavor	Goodput Achieved (Kb/s)
Reno	203.6
Tahoe	257.7
Vegas	133.7
NewReno	222.1
SACK	303.1
FACK	347.7

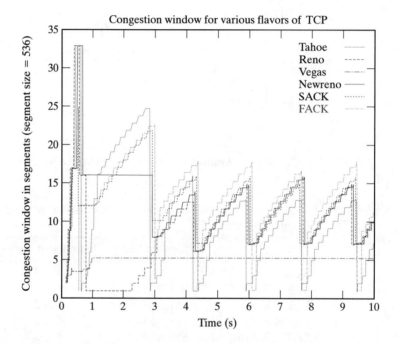

FIGURE 11.7: Congestion window for all flavors running together in the same network.

Figure 11.7 shows the congestion window for all the flows. Notice that Vegas maintains a constant congestion window through most of the simulation time. All the other flavors go through the exponential slow start and eventually their packets get dropped. Notice that Tahoe goes into slow start on packet loss, while Reno times out because it could not go through fast recovery because of the lack of *dupacks*. NewReno, SACK, and FACK do much better in maintaining their congestion window during the period of congestion. This also indicates that these three flavors are more aggressive in holding onto bandwidth that they have acquired. After 3 seconds, we see all the sources constantly increasing their congestion windows in an attempt to probe for available bandwidth until they lose a packet. This results in a sawtooth-like pattern.

Effect of Noninfinite Application Traffic. To test noninfinite application traffic, we performed a simulation with eight sources: five FTP sources and three Telnet sources. The Telnet sources provide bursts of data according to the "tcplib" distribution. All the sources in each simulation use the same TCP flavor. All the sources are located on node s1 and destinations on node d1. We also repeated the same simulations with RED instead of drop-tail. Table 11.8 shows the start and end times of the various flows, and Table 11.9 shows the results for Reno and Vegas (with and without RED).

From Table 11.9, we see that Reno with RED is more fair to Telnet sessions than without RED. When the sources were Vegas, the goodput of all the FTP sources was much higher than that with Reno. The reason Reno has lower goodput is because Reno uses packet loss as an indication of congestion. Hence, Reno goes through sequences of congestion avoidance (when the congestion window is increased and more data are sent) and then packet loss (when the network capacity is eventually reached). On every packet loss, the congestion window is decreased, periodically reducing the data that can be sent, and thus reducing the goodput. Sometimes losses also cause timeouts, pausing transmission and reducing the goodput.

We also notice that for Vegas, using RED did not have any significant effect on bandwidth allocation. This is because of Vegas's more conservative approach to increasing its congestion window. Because Vegas increases its congestion window

TABLE 11.8: Start and finish times of the 8 sources.

Source Number	Start Time (s)	Finish Time (s)
1 (FTP)	0.1	10.0
2 (FTP)	0.1	10.0
3 (FTP)	5.0	8.0
4 (FTP)	5.0	9.0
5 (FTP)	6.0	10.0
6 (Telnet)	0.3	1.3
7 (Telnet)	0.4	10.0
8 (Telnet)	5.2	10.0

TABLE 11.9: Goodput achieved with 8 FTP and telnet sources.

Source	Reno (Kb/s)	Reno/RED (Kb/s)	Vegas (Kb/s)	Vegas/RED (Kb/s)
1	516.7	317.0	556.5	560.9
2	479.4	503.7	450.8	455.2
3	320.1	491.6	314.4	314.4
4	158.6	166.1	319.4	324.8
5	128.6	432.0	608.8	582.0
6	8.5	12.8	4.2	4.2
7	7.5	9.8	5.3	5.3
8	3.5	5.3	1.7	1.7

only if bandwidth is available, long queues do not build up at the routers and, hence, there are no packet drops; therefore, we do not see the benefits of RED.

11.9   FURTHER READING

Fang and Peterson [140] propose mechanisms to be deployed in TCP to achieve better performance in Differentiated Services network. These mechanisms preserve the AIMD principle but change the way some of the TCP congestion variables, like *cwnd* and *ssthresh*, are updated.

A detailed, component by component, simulation-based performance study of TCP Vegas is presented in [165]. TCP Vegas's performance gains are primarily achieved through the innovative slow start and congestion recovery mechanisms. Vegas's congestion avoidance mechanism is shown to have only a minor impact on throughput and a significant negative impact on fairness.

11.10   SUMMARY

Table 11.10 summarizes the different TCP variants. The table shows how slow start, congestion avoidance, and fast recovery differ, as well as the ACK format required. Note that although some flavors appear to improve performance, the gradual deployment of such enhancements into the Internet has to be carefully considered.

11.11   REVIEW QUESTIONS

1. Why are there so many TCP flavors? Do some research and find out which flavors are currently used in practical systems.
2. What is the main motivation behind fast retransmit and fast recovery?
3. Consider a modified version of fast retransmit that waits for four (instead of three) *dupack*s to initiate retransmission and slow start. Discuss performance implications of this modification against the original fast retransmit algorithm.
4. What is the difference between TCP Reno and TCP NewReno?
5. What is the key feature of TCP SACK?
6. Describe the objective of TCP FACK, and explain how it meets this objective.
7. What are the strengths of TCP Vegas?
8. Are there any known performance problems of TCP Vegas? If so, what are they?
9. Explain why we cannot see the benefits of RED with TCP Vegas.
10. What difficulties do we face in deploying new TCP flavors on the Internet?

11.12   HANDS-ON PROJECTS

1. Build a test bed, using the freely available FreeBSD system, to evaluate the performance of TCP for some widely used applications, including Telnet and FTP. Using this test bed, compare the performance of TCP Vegas against TCP Tahoe and TCP Reno in terms of throughput and fairness. Write a report documenting your observations.

TABLE 11.10: TCP Variants.

	Tahoe	Reno	NewReno	SACK	FACK	Vegas
In slow start, cwnd updated with every ACK as	$cwnd+1$	$cwnd+1$	$cwnd+1$	$cwnd+1$	$cwnd+1$	increase every other RTT
In congestion avoidance, cwnd updated with every ACK as	$cwnd+ 1/cwnd$	$cwnd+ 1/cwnd$	$cwnd+ 1/cwnd$	$cwnd+ 1/cwnd$	$cwnd+ 1/cwnd$	linear increase if Diff $< \alpha$; linear decrease if Diff $> \beta$
Change from slow start to congestion avoidance when	$cwnd = ssthresh$	$cwnd = ssthresh$	same, but $ssthresh$ may be estimated	$cwnd = ssthresh$	$cwnd = ssthresh$	Diff $< \gamma$
Fast recovery	none	terminates with partial or full ACK	continues with partial ACK	continues with partial SACKs and sends if pipe$<cwnd$	sends as long as outstanding data $< cwnd$	retransmit with ACK (duplicate or retransmission) if RTT $>$ timeout
ACK format required	ACK	ACK	ACK	SACK	SACK	ACK

2. Read [165] very carefully. TCP Vegas has three modified elements; slow start, congestion, and recovery. According to [165], Vegas's congestion avoidance is the source of its fairness problem. Implement a variant of TCP Vegas with only the slow start and the congestion recovery mechanisms in place; for the congestion avoidance, use the same algorithm used in TCP Reno. Using the test bed of Project 1, assess the performance of this new variant in terms of fairness. What did you find? How do your results compare to the simulation results presented in [165]?

11.13 CASE STUDY: HIGH PERFORMANCE TCP FOR COMPUTATIONAL GRID

WCORP is facing a new problem: *not enough computing power to complete some of the very large scale jobs in time.* The traditional solution would be to acquire a supercomputer and share it among all users executing computationally intensive jobs. However, supercomputers are very expensive to acquire and upgrade. Instead,

WCORP decided to link several servers at the Sydney and Melbourne labs to form a wide area computational grid (WCD). Initially, all WCD servers were equipped with the default TCP flavor, TCP Reno.

WCD provides a much cheaper alternative to supercomputers at comparable performance. A WCD user simply submits a job to one of the servers and waits for its completion. The grid software takes a job and its associated data files from a user and dispatches parts of the job to other (remote) servers, collects results from all servers, and finally presents integrated results to the user. All communication between WCD servers is done over TCP (Reno in this case). Because a part of the job in one server may be waiting for a crucial result from another server, TCP performance becomes a central issue for the successful operation of the WCD.

Many WCORP researchers immediately started to use the WCD as soon as it became available. Unfortunately, the performance experienced by the WCD users was far from satisfactory. The users complained that the time it took to perform a job was too long, even when run at a time when most WCD servers were lightly loaded. Detailed traffic measurement and analysis revealed that the source of the problem was not *server overload* but *packet loss* experienced over the TCP/IP network. Packet loss means that the sending TCP has to detect the loss and retransmit it, blocking the grid application at the other side until the retransmitted packet arrives. Each packet loss thus potentially extends the job completion time, drastically affecting the performance of the WCD.

To address the packet loss problem, the network administrator replaced TCP Reno with TCP Vegas in all WCD servers. The decision to replace Reno with Vegas was motivated by the well-documented result that Vegas reduces packet loss caused by its less aggressive behavior. The administrator was very happy to see that TCP Vegas indeed reduced packet loss over the WCD. Traffic measurements showed that packet loss decreased by a factor of 10. The reduced packet loss has significantly improved job completion times over the WCD.

CHAPTER 12

Active Queue Management in TCP/IP Networks

CHAPTER OBJECTIVES

After completing this chapter, the reader should be able to:

- Explain the role of active queue management in performance optimization of TCP/IP networks

- Learn a range of active queue management algorithms

- Gain insight into performance analysis of active queue management algorithms

Performance of TCP-based applications critically depends on the choice of queue management in the network links. Queue management is defined as the algorithms that manage the length of packet queues by dropping packets when necessary or appropriate [69]. From the point of dropping packets, queue management can be classified into two categories. The first category is *passive queue management* (PQM), which does not employ any preventive packet drop before the router buffer gets full or reaches a specified value. The second category is *active queue management* (AQM), which employs preventive packet drop before the router buffer gets full. Passive queue management (e.g., tail drop) is currently widely deployed in the Internet routers. It introduces several problems (e.g., global synchronization or Internet *melt down*) on the Internet. Active queue management is expected to eliminate global synchronization and improve Quality of Service (QoS) of networks. The expected advantages of AQM are increase in throughput, reduced delay, and avoiding lock-out. This chapter describes the background, objective, and motivation of a number of AQM schemes. For better understanding why AQM was introduced and recommended by the IETF (Internet Engineering Task Force), the currently deployed PQM and the associated problems are discussed first.

12.1 PASSIVE QUEUE MANAGEMENT

The Internet has grown from a small data transfer–oriented network to a large public accessed multiservice network. Various types of real and nonreal time traffic such as FTP, e-mail, HTTP, voice, and even video are transmitted over the Internet. The current implementation of the Internet is based on the TCP/IP protocol stack, which was established in the 1980s when the usage of the Internet was limited to a small group of people with little network congestion. With the growth of the Internet, it has become necessary to deploy AQM to improve the QoS, such as throughput, delay, jitter, and loss on the Internet. RFC 2309 [69] requires low delay service to users as one of the goals of AQM.

Passive queue management is defined as the algorithms having the following two characteristics:

- *No preventive packet drop* is taken for arriving packets until the buffer level reaches some specified value.

- Once the buffer level reaches a specified value, *all arriving packets* are dropped with a *probability of one.*

Passive queue management, therefore, has two states: (1) no packet drop and (2) 100% packet drop. It does not send early congestion warning to senders to decrease their traffic rate with a view to relieving network congestion. A 100% drop causes all senders to back off. The following subsections describe the commonly used PQM schemes.

12.1.1 Tail-Drop

As shown in Figure 12.1, the tail-drop scheme drops packets from the tail of the queue. Once the buffer level reaches a certain threshold, all arriving packets are discarded. Packets already in the queue are not affected.

12.1.2 Drop-From-Front

Drop-from-front discards packets from the front of the queue [212] when the buffer is full or reaches a specified threshold (Figure 12.2). The arriving packet is accepted, while the packet that is buffered at the front of the queue is discarded; therefore, drop-from-front drops the packet in the buffer with the oldest age.

Compared with tail-drop, because drop-from-front drops a packet that is buffered at the front of the queue, it causes the traffic senders to "see" the packet loss one buffer drain time earlier than that in the tail-drop case.

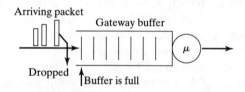

FIGURE 12.1: Tail-drop scheme.

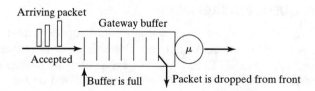

FIGURE 12.2: Drop-from-front scheme.

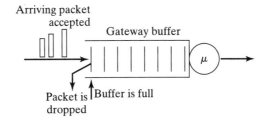

Arriving packet
accepted   Gateway buffer

μ

Packet is | Buffer is full
dropped

FIGURE 12.3: Push-out scheme.

12.1.3 Push-Out

In the push-out scheme, when the buffer reaches a specified threshold, the latest buffered packet is pushed out from the queue to make room for a newly arriving packet (Figure 12.3) [290]. The push-out scheme cannot make the TCP sender "see" packet drop early compared to the drop-from-front scheme. On the other hand, push-out is more complicated than tail-drop and wastes router resources because it discards the latest buffered packet.

12.1.4 Problems with Passive Queue Management

An Internet router normally is attached to a large number of hosts whose total bandwidth requirements, at certain times, exceed the transmission capacity of the gateway. Buffer is used in the routers to absorb the difference between the required and available capacity. There is a trade-off between the buffer size and QoS: a larger buffer size results in a higher throughput but may potentially result in long delays. On the other hand, for a given buffer size, the buffer management scheme affects the QoS of connections.

Regardless of the details of these PQM schemes, all of them meet two characteristics of PQMs as described in the beginning of this section. The following problems however, have been observed when they are used to manage buffers that carry traffic that is controlled by the window-based congestion control algorithms of TCP [69].

- *Lock Out.* In some situations, tail-drop allows a single connection or a few connections to monopolize the buffer space of the router, preventing other connections from getting space in the router queue. This results in unfair sharing of network resources among the connections, thereby giving rise to fairness problems.

- *Full Queue.* Because tail-drop does not drop packets before the queue is full, it results in the router queue being full for a long period of time. This results in long queuing delays.

Because of the inherent problems of passive queue management, IETF recommends AQM for the next generation Internet routers.

12.2   ACTIVE QUEUE MANAGEMENT

Contrary to PQM, AQM provides preventive measures to manage a buffer to eliminate the problems associated with passive buffer management. Active queue management has the following characteristics:

- Preventive random packet drop is performed before the buffer is full.

- The probability of preventive packet drop increases with increasing levels of congestion.

Preventive packet drop provides implicit feedback mechanism to notify senders of the onset of congestion. The feedback is used by the senders to reduce their traffic rate to relieve the level of congestion. Arriving packets from the senders are dropped randomly, which prevents all senders from backing off simultaneously and thereby eliminates *global synchronization*.

RFC 2309 [69] specifies the goals of AQM as follows:

- *Reduce the number of packets dropped in routers* to improve throughput;

- *Provide a low-delay interactive services* by maintaining a small queue size, which reduces the delay seen by flows;

- *Avoid lock-out behavior* by sharing the bandwidth fairly among the competing flows.

After the IETF recommendation on AQM, many AQM algorithms have been proposed in the literature. We do not attempt to provide an exhaustive list of all such proposals. In this section, we discuss some of the well-known AQM algorithms.

12.2.1   Random Early Detection

The default AQM scheme recommended by IETF for the next generation Internet routers is Random Early Detection (RED) [69], which was proposed by Floyd and Jacobson [146] in 1993. Figures 12.4 and 12.5 show the algorithm and drop function of RED. A router implementing RED accepts all packets until the queue reaches Min_{th}, after which it drops a packet with a linear probability distribution function. When the queue length reaches Max_{th}, all packets are dropped with a probability of one.

The basic idea behind RED is that a router detects congestion early by computing the average queue length avg and sets two buffer thresholds Max_{th} and Min_{th} for packet drop as shown in Figure 12.5. The average queue length at time t, defined as $avg(t) = (1 - w)avg(t - 1) + wq(t)$, is used as a control variable to perform active packet drop. The $avg(t)$ is the new value of the average queue length at time t, $q(t)$ is instantaneous queue length at time t, and w is a weight parameter in calculating avg. Normally, w is much less than one. The packet-drop probability, p, is calculated by $p = Max_{drop} \frac{avg - Min_{th}}{Max_{th} - Min_{th}}$. The RED algorithm, therefore, includes two computational parts: computation of the average queue length and calculation of the drop probability.

For each packet arrival

    Calculate the average queue size avg

      If Min_Threshold ≤ avg < Max_Threshold

        Calculate probability p

        with probability p:

          Mark the arriving packet

      else if Max_Threshold ≤ avg

        Mark the arriving packet

FIGURE 12.4: Algorithm of RED.

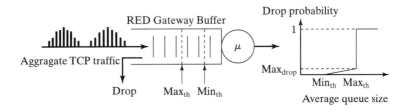

FIGURE 12.5: RED gateway buffer and drop function.

The RED algorithm involves *four* parameters to regulate its performance. Min_{th} and Max_{th} are the queue thresholds to perform packet drop, Max_{drop} is the packet drop probability at Max_{th}, and w is the weight parameter to calculate the average queue size from the instantaneous queue length. The average queue length follows the instantaneous queue length. However, because w is much less than one, avg changes much slower than q. Therefore, avg follows the long-term changes of q, reflecting persistent congestion in networks. By making the packet drop probability a function of the level of congestion, RED gateway has a low packet-drop probability during low congestion, while the drop probability increases as the congestion level increases.

The packet drop probability of RED is small in the interval Min_{th} and Max_{th}. Moreover, the packets to be dropped are chosen randomly from the arriving packets from different hosts. As a result, packets coming from different hosts are not dropped simultaneously. RED gateways, therefore, avoid global synchronization by randomly dropping packets.

The performance of RED significantly depends on the values of its four parameters [97, 240], Max_{drop}, Min_{th}, Max_{th}, and w. In the rest of this section, we discuss the issues that must be considered in setting these parameters.

Selection of Maximum Packet Drop Probability, Max_{drop}.   The selection of the maximum drop probability (Max_{drop}) significantly affects the performance of

RED. If Max_{drop} is too small, then active packet drops are not enough to prevent global synchronization. Too large a value of Max_{drop} decreases the throughput. Although a Max_{drop} value of 0.1 is generally suggested [289], the selection of an optimal value of Max_{drop} according to network and traffic situation is still an open issue [97, 240].

Feng et al. [98] demonstrated that the value of Max_{drop} depends not only on the bandwidth delay product but also on the number of connections. The upper bound of packet drop probability (Max_{drop}) can be expressed as:

$$Max_{drop} \leq \frac{N * SS * C}{B\tau} \tag{12.1}$$

where N is the number of connections, B is the total bandwidth, SS is the segment size, τ is the round-trip time, and C is a constant. From Eq. (12.1), it is not possible to fix a value of Max_{drop} for a dynamically changing network environment, that is, number of connections, round-trip time, etc.

Selection of Buffer Thresholds, Min_{th} and Max_{th}. The selection of buffer thresholds for packet drop can be determined as follows:

- For a RED gateway carrying only TCP traffic, Min_{th} should be around five packets, and Max_{th} should be at least three times Min_{th} [289].

- Non-TCP traffic does not employ the congestion control mechanisms of TCP. A different set of values are, therefore, required for Min_{th} and Max_{th} to protect TCP traffic from non-TCP traffic [49, 260].

Selection of Weight Parameter, w. RED uses the average queue length as a control variable to perform active packet drop. Calculation of the average queue length involves the previous average queue length and the instantaneous queue length modified by a weight parameter w. The average queue length, therefore, works as a low pass filter.

The average queue length is required to track persistent network congestion that occurs over a long time range while, at the same time, filtering out short time congestion. This requirement imposes limitations on the selection of w. If w is too small, the average queue length does not catch up with the long range congestion that may result in the failure of AQM. If w is too large, the average queue length tracks the instantaneous queue, which also degrades the performance of AQM. Therefore, the value of w should be related to the traffic flowing in the queue.

A simple model to calculate w was developed in [146, 289]. However, the assumptions in developing the model of w were too simple to reflect real TCP traffic. Therefore, in certain situations, the values given in [146, 289] may result in nonoptimal performance of the RED queue [329].

A more realistic model for determining w has been proposed in [329], where the aggregate TCP traffic has been taken into consideration. Results have shown that the values (0.05, 0.07) obtained from the model in [329] give better performance than the values (0.001, 0.002) in [146, 289] in certain cases.

Calculating the Average Queue Length to Improve Response Time.   RED uses four parameters and one state variable to regulate its performance. The state variable is the average queue length, which is defined as $avg = (1 - w)avg + wq$ and works as a low pass filter (LPF) [146]. In the above expression, w is a weight parameter and q is the instantaneous queue size of gateway buffer. The average queue length controls the active packet drop in the RED queue. The advantages of using average queue length to control active packet drop are (1) accumulating short-term congestion, and (2) tracing long-term congestion. However, the low pass filter characteristic of average queue is also featured with *slow-time response* to the changes of long-term congestion in networks. This is harmful to the throughput and delay performance of RED gateway. For example, after a long-term congestion, the average queue length stays high even if the instantaneous queue is back to normal or low; RED will, therefore, continue dropping packets even after the end of congestion [240] resulting in low throughput. The slow response of the average queue length will result in the throughput restoring slowly after heavy congestion [106]. A larger value of w can improve the response time, but at the expense of the RED queue tracing *short-term* congestion, which is against the AQM principle.

In [331], a more effective definition and algorithm for calculating avg is proposed. The new algorithm is called *low pass filter/over drop avoidance(LPF/ODA)*, which calculates the average queue length as follows.

- During long-term congestion, calculate the average queue length with an LPF as given in [146]. During this period, the RED queue is in the *active drop phase*;

- If average queue length is high at the end of long-term congestion, halve the average queue length. During this period, the RED queue is in the *over drop avoidance* (ODA) *phase*;

- If the average queue length is below a specific threshold after the end of long-term congestion, renew the value of average queue length using the LPF model.

The LPF/ODA algorithm is shown in Figure 12.6. Results [331] have shown that the LPF/ODA algorithm improves the response time, throughput, and delay of RED queues.

12.2.2   Classifying the RED Variants

The performance of TCP/IP over RED has been widely studied. The studies revealed that although RED can improve TCP performance under certain parameter settings and network conditions, the basic RED algorithm is still susceptible to several problems, such as low throughput, high delay jitter, and bandwidth unfairness. To overcome the limitations of the basic RED algorithm, researchers proposed several variants of RED. Before discussing the different RED variants, we first attempt to classify them based on some key aspects of the algorithm. We then discuss various proposals according to the classifications.

Research on RED and its variants can be classified into two broad categories.

- The first category deals with modifying the *calculation of the control variable and/or drop function*.

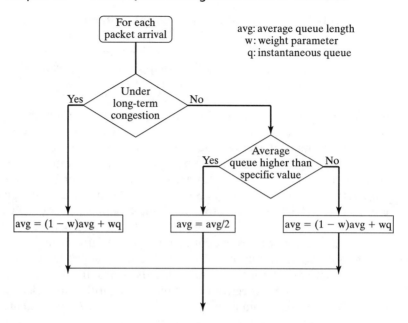

FIGURE 12.6: LPF/ODA algorithm.

- The second category is concerned with *configuring and setting RED's parameters*.

In the first category, called *aggregate control*, the packet-drop probability is nondiscriminative to connections (i.e., all connections have the same drop probability). In the second category, called *per-flow control*, the packet-drop probability applied to arriving packets can be discriminative to different TCP connections (i.e., each connection has its own drop probability). In per-flow control, the thresholds for the gateway buffer to perform packet drop can be set according to the traffic type (TCP vs. UDP) resulting in *class-based threshold*. To improve the performance of the original RED, several variants of RED have been proposed and studied. RED algorithm consists of two parts, as shown in Figure 12.7:

- Calculation of the *drop function* (linear function vs. step function)

- Calculation of the *control variables* (aggregate control vs. per-flow control).

Depending on whether the algorithms modify the drop function or the control variable, the RED variants can be classified as in Figure 12.7. In the following sections, we describe the various RED variants and classify them according to Figure 12.7.

12.2.3   RED Variants with Aggregate Control

RED uses aggregate control to determine the packet discarding probability. However, RED suffers from low throughput when poorly setting parameters, large queuing delay variance (jitter) because of the oscillation of queue level. There

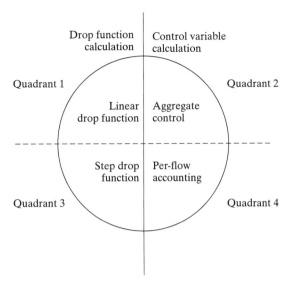

FIGURE 12.7: Classification of RED algorithms.

are several other AQM schemes with aggregate control that address some of the limitations of the basic RED algorithm. In this section, we discuss four such schemes; SRED, DSRED, REM, and BLUE.

Stabilized Random Early Drop.   *Stabilized random early drop (SRED)* has been proposed [255] to make the RED queue stable. Like RED, SRED preemptively discards packets with a load-dependent probability when the buffer in a router is congested. The drop probability, $p(q)$, is divided into three sections as in Eq. (12.2), where B is the buffer capacity, q is the instantaneous queue size, and p_{max} is the maximum packet drop probability.

$$p(q) = \begin{cases} p_{max} & \frac{B}{3} \leq q < B \\ \frac{1}{4} p_{max} & \frac{B}{6} \leq q < \frac{B}{3} \\ 0 & 0 \leq q < \frac{B}{6} \end{cases} \tag{12.2}$$

Instead of calculating the average queue size, SRED drops packets depending on the number of active flows and the instantaneous queue size. By estimating the number of active connections or flows, SRED helps in stabilizing the buffer fill level. Over a wide range of load levels, the router queue is independent of the number of active connections. The final packet drop function p_{sred} in SRED, therefore, is, given by Eq. (12.3) and illustrated in Figure 12.8.

$$p_{sred}(q) = \begin{cases} p(q) & \textit{for a large number of active flows} \\ \frac{p(q)}{65536} (\textit{number of flow})^2 & \textit{for a small number of active flows} \end{cases}$$
$$\tag{12.3}$$

Estimating the number of active flows is obtained without collecting or analyzing state information on individual flows; therefore, SRED overcomes the

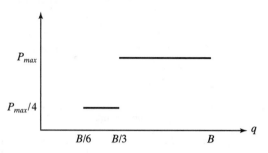

FIGURE 12.8: Drop function of SRED.

scalability problems associated with per-flow management as in [201, 218]. SRED can be classified in quadrants 2 and 3 of Figure 12.7. However, SRED suffers from low throughput. Simulation results show that the normalized throughput of SRED is very low even with a few traffic flows.

An exponential drop function (in contrast to a linear drop function as used in RED) results in a higher throughput [212]. Moreover, the drop function should change according to the level of congestion. As an alternative to a single linear drop function, SRED [255] uses a step drop function.

Double Slope RED.   To improve the throughput and delay of RED, Zheng and Atiquzzaman [328, 330] proposed *double slope RED (DSRED)*, which divides queue between Min_{th} and Max_{th} into two segments. Each segment uses a linear drop function with different slopes, as shown in Figures 12.9 and 12.10. The algorithm for DSRED is shown in Figure 12.11, and the equations governing the drop probabilities of DSRED are given by Eq. (12.4).

$$p_d(avg) = \begin{cases} 0 & avg < K_l \\ \alpha(avg - K_l) & K_l \le avg < K_m \\ 1 - \gamma + \beta(avg - K_m) & K_m \le avg < K_h \\ 1 & K_h \le avg \le N \end{cases} \tag{12.4}$$

α, β, and *avg* are given by:

$$\alpha = \frac{2(1 - \gamma)}{K_h - K_l} \tag{12.5}$$

$$\beta = \frac{2\gamma}{K_h - K_l} \tag{12.6}$$

$$avg = (1 - w)avg + wq \tag{12.7}$$

DSRED adapts to the level of congestion by changing the slope of the drop function. It results in *higher throughput* and *lower queuing delay* compared to the original RED. DSRED uses average queue length as the control variable and, therefore, inherits all the advantages of RED. DSRED can be classified as belonging to quadrants 1 and 2 in Figure 12.7.

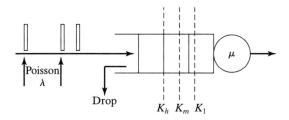

FIGURE 12.9: Model for DSRED buffer at gateway.

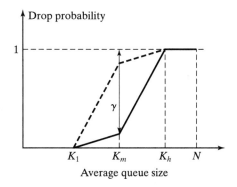

FIGURE 12.10: Drop function of DSRED.

For each packet arrival

    Calculate average queue length avg

    If avg $< K_1$

      No drop

    elseif $K_1 \leq$ avg $< K_m$

      Calculate drop probability based on slope α

      Drop the packet

    elseif $K_m \leq$ avg $< K_h$

      Calculate drop probability based on slope β

      Drop packet

    else

      Drop packet

FIGURE 12.11: Algorithm of DSRED.

Random Exponential Marking.   In the preceding aggregate control algorithms, congestion is measured by collecting queue information and number of active links. In [51], an aggregate control algorithm based on collecting queue and link rate information was proposed that decouples the congestion measure from the performance measure. The proposed algorithm is called Random Exponential Marking (REM), which has the following two features:

- *Match rate clear buffer*. REM attempts to match user rates to the available link capacity and stabilize the gateway queue to a small value.

- *Sum price*. A variable *price* is used to measure the congestion of the link. The end-to-end marking probability depends on the sum of link prices.

Figure 12.12 shows the algorithm of REM, and its marking function is shown in Figure 12.13. In Figure 12.12, *in* is an estimate of the aggregate input rate, *new_in* is current aggregate input rate, p_l is link price to measure the network congestion, *buffer* is the current gateway buffer fill level, and *link_capacity* is the capacity of the link. α and δ are weight parameters to calculate price, γ is the step size in estimating the price, and m_l is the current marking probability.

In REM, the price, p_l, to measure the congestion status of the network is defined as:

$$p_l(t+1) = max(p_l(t) + \gamma(\alpha(b_l(t) - b_t) + x_l(t) - c_l(t)), 0) \qquad (12.8)$$

where $b_l(t)$ is buffer level at time t, b_t is the target buffer level for the AQM, $x_l(t)$ is aggregate input rate for gateway at time t, and $c_l(t)$ is the link capacity at time t.

From Eq. (12.8), when $p_l(0) = 0$ and $x_l(t) \leq c_l(t)$ and/or $b_l(t) \leq b_t$, the network is not congested, $p_l(1) = 0$, and there is no packet marking. Whenever

Periodically

    Update aggregate input rate:

        in ⟵ $(1 - \delta)*in + \delta*new\_in$

    Update marking probability *ml*

        pl ⟵ $max\{pl + \gamma(\alpha*buffer + in\text{-}link\_capacity), 0\}$

        ml ⟵ $1 - \Phi^{-pl}$

Endperiodically

While *buffer* > 0

    marking packet with probability *ml*

Endwhile

FIGURE 12.12: Random exponential marking algorithm.

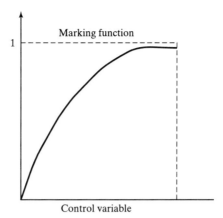

$$1$$ - - - - - - - - - - - - - - - - - -

Marking function

Control variable

FIGURE 12.13: Marking function of REM.

$x_l(t) \leq c_l(t)$ and/or $b_l(t) \leq b_t$ are not satisfied, the price $p_l(t)$ is no longer zero. The packet marking probability is calculated by $1 - \Phi^{-p_l(t)}$. The aggregate input rate and buffer level go down, thereby relieving congestion.

Simulation results have shown that REM maintains a low gateway queue level. As in RED, REM also achieves a high utilization, low packet loss, and queuing delay. REM can help stabilize the gateway queue and reduce packet loss. The most important difference between REM and RED is that REM decouples congestion measure from performance measure.

The REM involves five fixed configuration parameters, δ and α as weight parameters in estimating the input rate and gateway buffer respectively, γ as the step size for updating the price, b_t for maintaining the target buffer level, and Φ for the base in calculating the marking probability. The parameters give rise to two issues: the first is configuring these parameters to ensure the desired performance. The second issue concerns hardware implementation; if REM is going to be implemented in hardware (this is normally required for a high-speed router), only a few values of Φ (e.g., two) are easily implemented.

BLUE. BLUE is an aggregate control active queue management algorithm with only a few configuration parameters [99]. BLUE directly uses packet loss and link utilization to measure network congestion. The BLUE algorithm is shown in Figure 12.14. p_m is the packet marking probability, d_1 is the increase step for p_m, and d_2 is the decrease step for p_m. The minimum time interval between two successive updates of p_m is $freeze\_time$ BLUE, therefore, involves three configuration parameters. BLUE keeps track of the packet loss and link utilization (Figure 12.14).

The basic assumption for BLUE is that the packet loss (or buffer overflow) event is decoupled from the link idle event; therefore, when BLUE detects packet loss caused by buffer overflow, and the update interval is greater than $freeze\_time$, active marking is considered too conservative. BLUE, therefore, increases the packet marking probability, p_m, by a step p_1. In contrast, when it detects link idle and the update interval is greater than $freeze\_time$, active marking is considered

Upon buffer overflow event

    if((current_update – last_update) > freeze_time) then

        $p_m = p_m + p_1$

        last_update = current_update

Upon link idle event

    if((current_update – last_update) > freeze_time) then

        $p_m = p_m - p_2$

        last_update = current_update

FIGURE 12.14: General algorithm of BLUE.

too aggressive and, therefore, decreases the packet marking probability, p_m, by a step p_1. Simulation and test results have shown that BLUE reduces the packet-loss rate and helps to keep the gateway queue stable.

12.2.4   RED Variants with Per-Flow Accounting

In this section, we discuss six AQM schemes, FRED, FB-RED, XRED, CBT-RED, BRED, and SFB, which use per-flow accounting in the network to address some of the limitations (mainly the fairness problem) of RED.

Fair RED.   *Fair RED* (FRED) [218] was proposed to solve the fairness problem among TCP connections. FRED uses per-active-flow accounting to impose, on each flow, a loss rate that depends on the flow's use of buffer space. The loss rate is calculated by using the average queue length for each flow. Different from RED, the averaging in FRED is done at both packet arrivals and departures. As in RED, FRED uses a linear drop function to calculate drop probability. The algorithm for FRED is shown in Figure 12.15. FRED, therefore, belongs to quadrants 1 and 3 in Figure 12.7.

Fair buffering RED.   *Fair buffering RED* (FB-RED) [201] is another per-flow accounting scheme. The main idea of FB-RED is the use of individual bandwidth delay product $\mu\tau$ for each link to modify the packet-drop probability. Two cases have been implemented.

- Using inverse of the bandwidth delay product to calculate *Max_(drop)*.

- Using inverse of the square root of the bandwidth delay product to calculate *Max_(drop)*.

FB-RED uses average queue length as the control variable and, therefore, falls into quadrants 1 and 3 in Figure 12.7.

```
If Min_th <= avg < Max_th
    {
        count=count+1;
        random drop for robust connection

        if qleni >= MAX(minq, avgcq)
            {
                p_b=p_max(avg-Min_th)/(Max_th-Min_th)
                p_a=p_b/(1-count*p_b)
                with probability p_a
                drop arriving packet;
                count=0
                return;
            }
        else if avg < Min_th                    count: number of packet
            {                                            since last drop
                no packet drop;
                count=-1                          avg: average queue size
            }
        else                                      p_max: maximum drop
            {                                            probability
                do tail drop;
                count=0;                          qleni: number of buffered
                drop arriving packet                     packet for ith flow
                return;
            }                                     avgcq: average per-flow
        if qleni=0                                        queue size
                Nonactive++
                calculate average queue length;  Nonactive: number of
                accept arriving packet                   nonactive flow
```

FIGURE 12.15: Random drop algorithm of FRED.

XRED.   RED drops packets without taking into account the context information of the application. For a given application, some packets may be more crucial than the others. For example, let us consider an MPEG video application, which normally has much larger frames segmented into multiple IP packets. The loss of a fragment may render the entire application frame useless at the destination, resulting in a waste of router bandwidth. To reduce bandwidth waste for MPEG video transmission over routers using AQM, XRED was proposed in [170]. The idea of XRED is to describe a packet by three parameters: $FlowID$ for traffic flow, $ADUID$ for specified application data unit, and $Content\ Priority$ for packet content with different priority. A list that records these three parameters is maintained at the router (Figure 12.16).

When MPEG frames are fragmented into IP packets, XRED assigns each packet with $Flow\ ID$, $ADUID$, and $Content\ Priority$. The $Content\ Priority$ depends on the frame itself and its position in an MPEG Group of Pictures (GoP). Therefore, in XRED, I frame has the highest $Content\ Priority$, P frames have middle $Content\ Priority$, while B frames have the lowest $Content\ Priority$. Furthermore, the $Content\ Priority$ of packets corresponding to B frames also depends on its position in a GoP. $ADUID$ is used to label the MPEG GoP. When a packet is dropped, its $Flow\ ID$, $ADUID$, and $Content\ Priority$ are written into the list, and each arriving packet

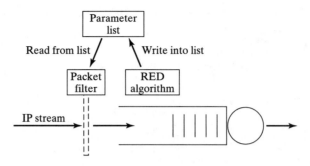

FIGURE 12.16: Model of XRED.

is checked by comparing its parameters with the stored parameters. The packet is discarded if its *Content Priority* is lower than the one in the list.

Although simulation results show that XRED reduces bandwidth waste, XRED has the following disadvantages. First, XRED needs extra fields in the IP header for the three identifiers to perform content-based discarding. Second, it needs to record three parameters for each application flow, potentially giving rise to scalability problems. Third, it needs extra actions to write/read list and compare the three parameters, which might consume a significant amount of computing power at the router.

Class-Based Threshold RED. RED has a fairness problem when TCP traffic competes with UDP traffic. UDP traffic does not employ any congestion avoidance scheme. UDP sources, therefore, do not respond to packets dropped by RED. This results in UDP sources getting more bandwidth than TCP sources, resulting in unfairness between TCP and UDP. To solve the UDP-TCP fairness problem of RED, *Class-Based Threshold RED* (CBT-RED) has been proposed in [260]. CBT-RED sets the queue thresholds according to the traffic type and its priority. UDP traffic is tagged and has its own drop threshold, which is different from other TCP traffic. TCP traffic is, thus, protected from UDP traffic. CBT-RED configures the RED parameters and can, therefore, be classified under the second category as described in Section 12.2.2.

Balanced RED. *Balanced RED* (BRED) [49] is another RED variant that achieves fair bandwidth sharing among TCP and UDP traffic. The basic idea is to regulate the bandwidth of a flow by per-flow accounting based on active flows. As in [255], the buffer is divided into four segments, each having a different drop probability. Therefore, BRED can be considered to fall in quadrants 3 and 4 in Figure 12.7. Although BRED can minimize the differences in the bandwidth obtained by each flow, it needs to maintain the flow states, which means that its implementation complexity is proportional to the router buffer size.

Stochastic Fair Blue. Another interesting AQM to achieve fairness between TCP traffic and nonresponsive traffic (for example, UDP) is Stochastic Fair Blue (SFB) [100]. SFB is realized by combining BLUE [99] with a Bloom filter. The algorithm of SFB is shown in Figures 12.17 and 12.18.

```
B[M][N]: M*N array of bins
enque()
    Calculate hashes h0, h1,...hM-1
    Update bins at each level
    for i=0 to M-1
        if(B[i][hi].qlen>bin_size)
            B[i][hi].pm+=δ
            drop packet
        else if (B[i][hi].qlen==0)
            B[i][hi].qlen-= δ
    pmin=min(B[0][h0].pm,...B[M][hm].pm)
    if(pmin==1)
        ratelimit()
    else
        mark/drop packet with probability pmin
```

FIGURE 12.17: Algorithm of Stochastic Fair Blue (SFB).

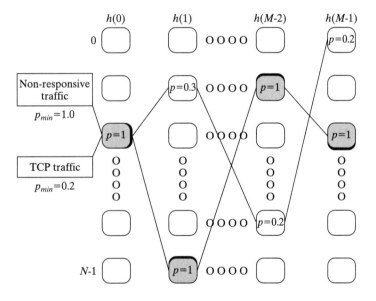

FIGURE 12.18: Bins in Stochastic Fair Blue (SFB). Bins are divided into M level with N bins in each level. Level i with its hash function $h[i]$.

As shown in Figure 12.18, the SFB queue maintains $N * M$ accounting bins, which are organized in M levels with N bins at each level. At level i, the hash function $h[i]$ $(0 \leq i \leq M - 1)$ maps the flow into the jth bin $(0 \leq j \leq N - 1)$ of that level. The accounting bins track the queue occupancy of traffic packets belonging to a particular bin. Therefore, the bins behave like virtual subqueues. Each subqueue has a mark/drop probability, p_m, which increases or decreases by step of δ, depending on whether the subqueue fill level is larger than a given threshold or equal to zero.

Because nonresponsive traffic does not employ any congestion avoidance algorithm, its traffic rate does not respond to packet drops when its corresponding subqueue gets full. Therefore, the corresponding p_m quickly reaches 1 in all the M bins into which it is hashed. For TCP traffic, because of the congestion avoidance, the p_m stays at a normal value that is less than 1. Therefore, the packet at a bin is identified by p_m. At a given bin, if $p_m = 1$, the corresponding packet is classified as belonging to a nonresponsive flow; otherwise it is classified as part of a TCP flow. A nonresponsive traffic flow is driven into the path of bins with $p_m = 1$ at each level. Therefore, the total marking probability for nonresponsive flows is 1 and their rates are limited. For TCP traffic, the total marking probability is less than 1. TCP traffic is, thus, protected from nonresponsive flows.

In summary, the variants of RED, which have been discussed in this section, are based on enhancements made in the drop function, the control variable, and the parameter sets. Table 12.1 summarizes the different RED algorithms according to the preceding criteria. In the next section, we describe the various criteria that are

TABLE 12.1: Summary of features of the variants.

RED Variants	Drop Function	Control Variable	Changes from Original RED
FRED	Single linear	Per-flow queue length	Per-flow queue length, number of active flow
FBRED	Single linear	Average queue length	Per-flow Max_{drop}
SRED	3-segment step	Instantaneous queue length and number of active flow	Step drop function, number of active flows, instantaneous queue
CBT-RED	Single linear	Average queue length	Class-based threshold
XRED	Single linear	Average queue length	Priority-based drop
BRED	4-segment step	Per-flow queue length and number of active flows	Per-flow queue length, number of active flows, step drop function
DSRED	Two linear	Average queue length	Two linear drop functions with different slopes
BLUE	Step function	Link utilization and packet loss	Step increase/decrease function, link rate, packet loss
REM	Exponential function	Link rate mismatch and buffer difference	Exponential function, link rate mismatch and buffer difference
SFB	Step function	Instantaneous queue length	Organize subqueue in Bloom filter

used to evaluate the performance of the RED algorithms that have been discussed in this section and, subsequently, classify the different AQM schemes based on those performance criteria.

12.3   PERFORMANCE EVALUATION AND COMPARISON OF AQM SCHEMES

In this section, we compare and contrast the performance of the RED variants against a number of criteria commonly used to measure the performance of RED algorithms. Both simulation and modeling have been used for performance evaluations. RFC 2309 [69] lists three performance metrics, *throughput*, *delay*, and *fairness*, to evaluate AQM schemes. For interactive applications, such as web browsing, *time response* is another important criteria.

12.3.1   Throughput and Fairness

Throughput is the amount of data that can be transferred by a network from a sender to a receiver during a period of time. Simulation studies on the throughput of RED at a TCP/IP over ATM gateway (Figure 12.19) were carried out in [212]. It was found that RED achieves optimal throughput when Max_{drop} is a function of the bandwidth delay product. Studies proved that an exponential drop function is better than a single linear drop function. However, an exponential drop function needs more *computing power* than the linear drop function; implementation complexity of exponential function is, therefore, more complex than a linear drop function.

The throughput of RED under per-flow queue management was evaluated in [303]. It was found that for a large number of TCP connections, the throughput of RED is generally low. In the presence of a mixture of burst and greedy sources, RED lacks fairness in addition to suffering from low throughput.

Analytical models to evaluate the throughput of RED gateways were developed in [239]. First, a model with a single bursty input traffic was proposed (Figure 12.20). The arriving traffic was modeled by a batch Poisson process, that is, a burst of B packets arriving according to a Poisson process at a rate λ. It was found that the throughput was inversely proportional to the load, which means that RED gateways have low throughput in the case of high load. Second, a model (Figure 12.21) consisting of a mixture of bursty and smooth traffic was proposed.

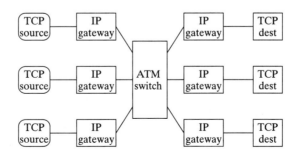

FIGURE 12.19: Simulation configuration for throughput studies of RED for TCP/IP over ATM.

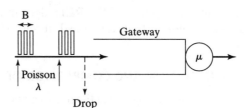

FIGURE 12.20: Single bursty input to RED.

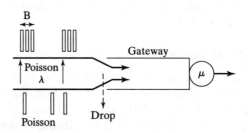

FIGURE 12.21: Analysis model for mixture of burst and smooth traffic in RED.

Bursty traffic was described by a batch Poisson process, and a Poisson process was used to model the smooth traffic. Results confirmed the claim that RED gateways avoid bias against burst traffic.

Fairness deals with the fair allocation of resources when multiple TCP connections share a gateway, and their total demand is greater than the capacity of the gateway. In the case of RED, fairness is concerned with the following two cases:

- Fair bandwidth sharing among TCP flows

- Fair bandwidth sharing between TCP and non-TCP traffic (e.g., UDP traffic)

The first fairness problem of RED for different TCP flows arises from its parameter Max_{drop}, which should be associated with the bandwidth delay product of a connection. Per-flow management has been proposed to solve this fairness problem among TCP connections [201, 218].

The second fairness problem arises from the fact that non-TCP sources do not employ congestion control and congestion avoidance mechanisms. Therefore, when TCP and UDP traffic compete for router buffer space, packets dropped by RED do not affect the sending rate of UDP sources. This results in UDP traffic *stealing* bandwidth from TCP traffic and causing unfairness and degradation of QoS [96]. Class-based management can solve this type of fairness problem [260, 49].

Stochastic Fair Blue (SFB) provides another solution for this type of fairness; however, dependence of SFB on $M*N$ sub-queues and corresponding hash functions to classify the traffic has two limitations. The first is its implementation complexity. For example, to effectively identify a single nonresponsive traffic flow in an N^M aggregate flow requires $O(M*N)$ states.

The second problem is misclassification. Because SFB classifies TCP traffic and nonresponsive flow by the p_m value of the bins, in the case of a large number of nonresponsive flows in an aggregate flow, the number of bins with $p_m > 1$ increases, and the bins for TCP traffic with $p_m < 1$ decrease. There are not enough bins to separate nonresponsive flows from TCP flows. In other words, nonresponsive flows and TCP flows share the same bins. This is called *misclassification* and results in SFB failing to protect TCP flows from nonresponsive flows. In [100], a closed form expression for the probability of a TCP flow being misclassified is given as:

$$p = \left(1 - \left(1 - \frac{1}{N}\right)^K\right)^M \tag{12.9}$$

where K is the number of nonresponsive flows, M is the level of bins, and N is the number of bins in a level. Therefore, there is a trade-off for SFB: N and M are required to be small for low implementation complexity. On the contrary, large N and M are required to minimize misclassification probability.

The fairness of RED for the FIFO (first in first out) and DRR (deficit round robin) scheduling schemes were studied in [157]. RED with FIFO do not provide significant improvement in fairness for TCP Reno. RED with DRR, for the case of TCP Reno, performs better in terms of fairness compared to RED with FIFO. For TCP Vegas, RED queues combined with either FIFO or DRR provide better throughput than TCP Reno.

12.3.2   Delay and Jitter

One of the goals of AQM is to ensure low queuing delay to packets. Because the queue length varies with time, the queuing delay also varies with time. The variance of delay is called *jitter*. Theoretical studies have shown that RED has a large jitter that is also very sensitive to w. The smaller the value of w, the larger is the delay variance [239]. Table 12.2 shows the relationship between w, delay, and jitter.

12.3.3   Time Response

For web browsing under low to medium levels of network congestion, the RED parameters have minimal effect on its response time [106]. Under heavy congestion, RED can be carefully tuned to yield higher throughput than tail-drop at the expense of sacrificing the delay; therefore, for web traffic, RED provides no clear advantage over tail-drop. This is because web browsing is normally characterized by short bursty traffic (compared to FTP), whereas RED is designed for long-lived time. The congestion detection mechanism in RED does not respond well to short-lived traffic.

TABLE 12.2: Delay and jitter of RED queue as a function of w [239].

w	Mean Delay	Jitter
0.1	5.9	40
0.01	7.7	170
0.001	7.2	190

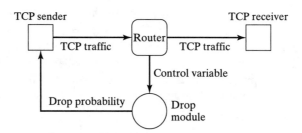

FIGURE 12.22: Feedback model of RED queue.

12.3.4 Traffic Oscillation

RED induces network instability and traffic disruption if not properly configured [142]. Therefore, the optimal configuration of RED has been a problem since its first proposal. In [142], the RED queue was modeled by a feedback control system (Figure 12.22). It was observed that the RED queue varied between zero and full under the commonly used configuration parameters.

In [332], it was shown that the RED queue results in large queue oscillation for two-way traffic in bulk data transfer and weblike traffic. This is because of the tight coupling between the forward and backward TCP traffic, which is caused by TCP's window-based congestion control and RED queue. Experiments have shown that higher bottleneck capacity increases the frequency of oscillation.

12.3.5 Performance Summary of AQM Schemes

A number of variants of RED have been proposed to improve the performance of RED. In Table 12.3, we compare the performance of the RED variants *against the performance of original RED*. For example, CBT-RED has a significantly higher throughput when compared to the performance of original RED. As suggested by IETF [69], we use throughput, delay, and fairness as the performance criteria. An entry of N/A means that the performance of the RED variant for that particular performance criteria is not known. From the table, it is apparent that *it is hard to develop a RED algorithm that improves the performance of all the criteria*.

12.4 AQM AND DIFFERENTIATED SERVICE

RFC 2597 [160] recommends RED with two configuration thresholds (or RED IN/OUT (RIO)) as the AQM in Differentiated Service (DiffServ) routers. Among the services offered by DiffServ, the Assured Forwarding (AF) service has three packet-drop preferences.

Experimental studies of RED queues used in the AF service with two level-drop preferences were carried out in [286]. Results have shown that service discrimination between Assured Service traffic can be achieved by using two levels of drop preference.

Adaptive priority marking for DiffServ in Internet with RED gateway implementation was studied in [97], where reservation of resource for individual

TABLE 12.3: Performance improvement of different AQM schemes over original RED.

RED Variant	Throughput Increase	Decrease in Delay/Jitter	Improvement in Fairness	Shortcoming
FRED	Not significant	N/A	Good for TCP/TCP	Scalability
FBRED	Not significant	N/A	Good for TCP/TCP	Scalability
SRED	Poor	Good	N/A	Low throughput
CBT-RED	Significant	Good	Good for TCP/UDP	Scalability
XRED	Significant	N/A	N/A	Extension header in UDP Additional list files
BRED	Significant	N/A	Good for TCP/UDP	Scalability
DSRED	Good	Good	N/A	
BLUE	Significant	Good	N/A	
REM	Significant	Good	N/A	Implementation complexity
SFB	Significant	N/A	Good	Complexity Misclassification

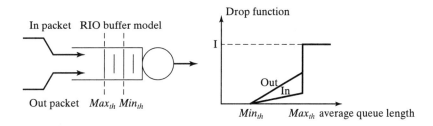

FIGURE 12.23: RIO gateway model and drop function.

connection is not needed. A packet-marking scheme based on measured throughput at the gateway was proposed. Packet-marking probability is calculated based on target bandwidth and observed bandwidth. The authors have evaluated the behavior of their scheme in various network environments. They have shown that their mechanisms have features that make them suitable for use on the Internet.

A performance model to analyze the AF service with RIO was developed in [238]. The gateway buffer model and drop function of RIO are shown in Figure 12.23. It was found that RIO could effectively offer service discrimination.

In [104], *Edge-Based Congestion Management (ECM)* was proposed to improve packet loss in the Differentiated Services (DS) domain as shown in Figure 12.24.

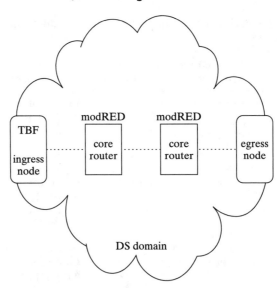

FIGURE 12.24: Edge-based congestion management for the Diffserv (DS) domain.

A RED-like active queue management scheme, called *modRED*, was employed in the core router of the DS domain to provide congestion signal and active packet dropping. A token-bucket-filter (TBF)–based traffic regulator was employed at the ingress node of a DS router.

In addition to an ECN (explicit congestion notification) bit for congestion information in the DS domain, ECM uses an extra LCN (local congestion notification) bit in the packet header to indicate local congestion at a node within the domain. The two congestion bits were used to provide feedback of congestion status to the ingress node. Feedback congestion information and the predicted bandwidth demand was used to decide on the amount of traffic injected into the DS domain.

In the ECM scheme, the bandwidth required at the ingress node was predicted by the average queue length defined in the RED algorithm. Larger average queue lengths inferred a higher bandwidth demand. In the modRED algorithm, an additional threshold, called *FeedbackThreshold*, which takes a value between Min_{th} and Max_{th}, was introduced. When the average queue length is greater than Min_{th} and less than *FeedbackThreshold*, the ECM scheme marks the LCN bit. When average queue length is greater than *FeedbackThreshold* and less than Max_{th}, the ECM scheme probabilistically drops packets and marks ECN bit of all outgoing packets. When the average queue length is greater than Max_{th}, all incoming packets are dropped. Although the ECM scheme can improve the packet loss ratio, ECM needs to introduce an extra LCN bit in the IP packet format.

12.5 FURTHER READING

The behavior of RED and its effect on TCP performance is still under research. Several problems with RED have been reported in the literature:

- Firoiu and Borden [142] observed that RED induces network instability and causes major traffic disruption if the RED parameters are not properly configured.

- May et al. [239] have shown that RED exhibits a large delay variance that is very sensitive to the weight parameter (w).

- Christiansen et al. [106] have discovered that the performance of RED in terms of delay is very poor under certain well-known parameter values of RED.

- The unfairness problem of RED is reported in [96, 157, 201, 218].

- The low throughput problem is reported in [212, 303].

12.6 SUMMARY

In this chapter, PQM and its problems have been presented, followed by definitions, goals, and classification of AQM schemes. The well-known AQM scheme, RED, and its variants are discussed. Although RED can achieve its goals and is easy to implement, its performance under different network circumstances has not yet been thoroughly investigated. The influence of its parameters on its performance is still under research.

To improve the performance of RED, a number of variants of the original RED algorithm have been proposed. In this chapter, the performance of those variants have been compared and contrasted by using a single performance comparison framework. Regarding the use of AQM in the TCP/IP-based Internet, we make the following observations:

- Avoid per-flow management in large networks because it causes scalability issues.

- Although aggregate throughput is important, care should be taken to ensure fairness among connections having different characteristics (e.g., round-trip time).

- The algorithm should be able to distinguish between different types of traffic, such as TCP and non-TCP.

- Because service differentiation is expected in the next generation Internet, the algorithms will also need to provide differentiated treatment to packets with different priority.

The RED variants have improved the performance of RED in various ways. However, these variants have their own advantages and shortcomings. To achieve good performance and minimize the effect of the shortcomings, the RED variants should be used according to the application requirements and network situations at hand. The following could be used as a guideline for selecting the RED variants:

- Per-flow management–based RED algorithms are good choices for applications that are mainly concerned with throughput and fairness among TCP flows, but the scalability is not a main issue (e.g., a small enterprise network).

- Applications interested in fairness between TCP/UDP traffic might find CBT-RED useful.

- For aggregate traffic, emphasizing both throughput and delay, DSRED is one of the good choices.

- SRED could be a good candidate for applications mainly concerned with stability and queuing delay.

12.7 REVIEW QUESTIONS

1. What is queue management? Classify queue management and show the differences.

2. What is congestion? What kind of algorithm is used for congestion control in TCP/IP networks? How does it work?

3. What are the major problems observed in TCP/IP congestion control algorithms associated with the traditional queue management?

4. What is the RED algorithm? How does it work? What are the parameters involved in RED? How is RED's performance affected by its parameters?

5. What are the problems with the RED algorithm? Give an example to explain why and how these problems exist?

6. Describe aggregate control and per-flow accounting as used in active queue management? Compare their benefits and disadvantages?

7. In active queue management algorithms, average or instantaneous queue length is used as one of the indicators of network congestion. Describe the advantages and disadvantages of using the average and instantaneous queue lengths. Give an example to illustrate the situation in which average or instantaneous queue length may fail in indicating network congestion.

8. List the features of multimedia traffic (e.g., MPEG video), HTTP traffic, and FTP traffic.

9. A physical link with a capacity of B Mbps is shared by four connections with different physical link distances of ratios 1:2:4:8. What is the bandwidth that can be fairly shared by each connection? Can this bandwidth sharing be reached with traditional queue management? How is the fair bandwidth sharing achieved with active queue management?

10. Can the Assured Forward service be realized by traditional queue management (e.g., by tail-drop)? If no, explain why. If yes, what are the main differences with the realization by active queue management?

12.8 HANDS-ON PROJECT

Download *ns* simulator from the Internet.

1. Evaluate RED's throughput and queue size performance with $Max_{drop} = 0.1$ and $Max_{drop} = 0.2$; Evaluate RED's jitter performance with $w = 0.01$ and $w = 0.001$.

2. Compare throughput, queue size, and jitter performance for SRED and RED. For parameter settings refer to [255] and [146].

3. Compare time response and throughput performance for LPF/ODA algorithm and LPF algorithm only.

4. Compare throughput performance for BLUE and RED. For parameter settings refer to [99] and [146].

12.9   CASE STUDY: WCORP DEPLOYS ACTIVE QUEUE MANAGEMENT

After the upgrade of the Sydney–Melbourne link capacity, mean packet delay of interoffice traffic settled around the expected 50 ms mark. However, there remained one problem. Although videoconferencing generally performed well, at times the users experienced glitches in their video reception. An extensive study revealed that the glitches were caused by packets arriving at the receiver much later than their expected times. Consequently, these packets had to be discarded at the receiver. The video packets were excessively delayed at the router queue whenever there were large file transfers. This is a direct result of not being able to control the average queue length at the router.

The network administrator decided to deploy active queue management (AQM) at the router to explicitly control the average queue length (and, hence, mean packet delay) at all times, including the times when large file transfers are active. Not all vendors had AQM support in their products. CISCO Systems [3] and Juniper Networks [7] were the two candidate vendors for routers with AQM features. Both vendors had products implementing the basic RED. However, one specific need of WCORP that favored CISCO was the capability of explicitly forcing a high degree of fairness among all flows. CISCO's "flow-based weighted random early detection" forces RED to afford greater fairness to all flows in regard to how packets are dropped. After the deployment and configuration of flow-based RED, measurement showed that packet delay at the router remained within 10% of the mean at all times. As a result of the reduced jitter, videoconferencing users no longer experienced glitches in their reception.

## CHAPTER 13

TCP Implementation

CHAPTER OBJECTIVES

After completing this chapter, the reader should be able to:

- Understand the structure of typical TCP implementations and the data structures and actions to respond to TCP-related events
- Outline the implementation of extended standards for TCP over high performance networks
- Understand the sources of end-system overhead in typical TCP implementations and the techniques to minimize them
- Quantify the effect of end-system overhead and buffering on TCP performance over high-bandwidth networks
- Understand the role of Remote Direct Memory Access (RDMA) extensions and TCP offload technologies for high performance IP networking

On the fastest networks, performance of applications using TCP is often limited by the capability of the end systems to generate, transmit, receive, and process the data at network speeds. For network servers, connection management overheads may also be a limiting factor. End-system performance is determined by a combination of factors relating to the host hardware, interactions between the host and the network adapter, and host system software. In particular, high performance networking involves fundamental structural issues in the end hosts and operating systems: integration of network buffering with operating system memory management, movement of data across the system/application boundary, and division of protocol-related processing between host CPUs and the network adapter—the network interface controller (NIC).

This chapter discusses end-system software implementation issues for TCP, focusing on issues that affect performance of bulk data transfer on high-speed networks. We bypass several aspects of TCP implementation, including urgent data, the PUSH flag, connection resets, options processing, and state transitions for connection setup and shutdown.

Many of the implementation issues and techniques discussed in this chapter concern the relationship between the TCP protocol stack and the surrounding system, rather than the protocol implementation itself. Some do not affect interoperability and, thus, fall outside the scope of the TCP-related RFCs. Even so, they are increasingly important as Ethernet and other IP network technologies advance. As a result of these advances, TCP often serves as a standard transport for storage access and server–server coordination in data center environments, which were previously

Portions reprinted, with permission, from "End System Optimization for High-Speed TCP," by J. S. Chase, A. J. Gallatin, and K. Slocum, which appeared in *IEEE Communications Magazine*, April 2001. © 2001 IEEE.

the domain of more specialized networking technologies such as FibreChannel. This places additional pressure on TCP/IP implementations to deliver competitive end-to-end (application-to-application) performance.

This chapter first gives a structural overview of a typical TCP implementation followed by a discussion of the protocol-related extensions for high performance networks, the sources and impacts of software overhead for TCP/IP, end-system techniques for low-overhead TCP/IP networking, approaches to copy avoidance, and the role of protocol offload. Although described in Chapter 2, some TCP protocol features are revisited in this chapter for explaining the implementation techniques in detail.

13.1 TCP IMPLEMENTATION OVERVIEW

RFC 793 [273] sketches the internal structure of a TCP end system and outlines implementation of basic TCP functions, including reliable data transfer, flow control, connections, and multiplexing. It also outlines a set of primitives for the "TCP/user interface," including *SEND* and *RECEIVE* interface signatures. This interface specifies a minimal set of user functions that must be present in any TCP implementation. The TCP architects conceived that the *TCP user* calling this interface is an application built directly above TCP, but it may also be an upper layer protocol (ULP) such as HTTP or Network File System (NFS).

Figure 13.1 depicts the overall structure of a TCP implementation. The TCP protocol code is divided into a *sender* and a *receiver*; because TCP connections are bidirectional, the sender and receiver are active on both sides of the connection. RFC 793 explicitly assumes that the TCP sender and receiver are implemented in software as operating system modules; however, it does not preclude implementing the TCP/IP protocol modules on the NIC rather than in the host (see Section 13.5).

Figure 13.2 illustrates the data structures of TCP connections. There are three primary data structures associated with each TCP connection endpoint:

- The *transmission control block* (TCB) or *protocol control block* stores the connection state and related variables used by both the sender and the

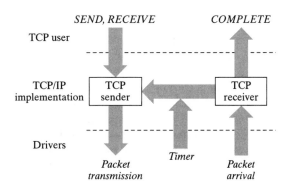

FIGURE 13.1: Overall structure of a TCP implementation.

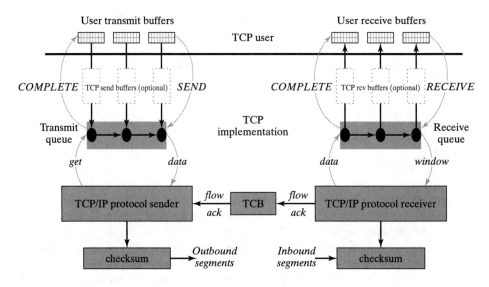

FIGURE 13.2: Data structures of a TCP implementation.

receiver. TCB state variables include various pointers into the send and receive sequence number spaces.

- The *transmit queue* is the sender's list of buffers containing outgoing data that the TCP user has posted for sending (e.g., using *SEND*) but for which acknowledgments have not yet been received.

- The *receive queue* is the receiver's list of buffers for inbound data that have not yet been delivered to the TCP user.

The TCP sender and receiver modules are state machines that initiate actions on the connection in response to external events, based on state information in the shared TCB. The TCP receiver runs asynchronously to process segments (packets) as they arrive. In a typical operating system kernel implementations, the TCP receiver runs in the context of a user process or system network input thread invoked by a wakeup signal from the NIC receive-interrupt service routine or a handler invoked by a software interrupt. The TCP receiver may invoke the TCP sender directly if the received segment requires an acknowledgment (ACK) or if it updates the flow and/or congestion window to allow transmission of new data. The TCP sender may also run in the context of a timer handler or a user process issuing a *SEND* or *RECEIVE* command.

This section summarizes the key aspects of TCP protocol implementation that affect the performance of bulk data transfer. Section 13.1.1 gives an overview of buffering and data movement within each TCP endpoint, and Section 13.1.2 discusses data movement between the protocol implementation and the TCP user. Section 13.1.3 outlines the events that prompt actions from the TCP sender and receiver and the interaction of the two endpoints to allow rate-controlled data exchange, and 13.1.4 deals with the timing of retransmissions. Section 13.1.5 outlines congestion avoidance and control.

13.1.1 Buffering and Data Movement

The role of the transmit and receive queues is to mediate buffering between the protocol implementation and the TCP user. One should view the receive queue and transmit queue as separate from the TCP protocol implementation itself. For example, in Unix implementations derived from the Berkeley (BSD) reference software releases, these buffer queues reside in the protocol-independent socket layer within the operating system kernel. With TCP protocol offload engines the buffers may reside in host memory while the protocol modules reside on the NIC (see Section 13.5).

The TCP sender and receiver may access the buffer queues through a simple interface that is similar to any I/O driver, as illustrated in Figure 13.1. The TCP sender upcalls to the transmit queue to obtain the data for a given sequence range. The TCP receiver notifies the receive queue of correct arrival of incoming data. The TCP receiver may also upcall to the transmit queue to release buffer space when a received segment acknowledges transmitted data. Extraction and merging of segments with specific sequence ranges may take place behind this interface. The BSD TCP receiver maintains the tail of the receive queue internally as a *reorder buffer* to merge segments that arrive out of order.

The mechanisms to coordinate data movement through the buffer queues are paramount for end-system performance. For example, BSD-derived kernels base their buffering and data movement on flexible network buffers called *mbufs*, which incorporate features to move data by reference and reduce the need to copy it. The system constructs packets by stringing together chains of mbufs passed between the levels of the protocol stack. Protocol modules add and remove headers by adding or removing buffers on the chain or by manipulating the mbuf fields to append data, prepend data, or remove data from the buffer regions. Specific mbuf types may reference storage in another system buffer, such as a virtual memory page or a block in the file cache. Each mbuf is reference-counted to allow fast copying of buffer chains by reference. Current network devices are capable of scatter/gather direct memory access (DMA) to send and receive directly from these buffer chains.

A TCP implementation must bound the amount of memory committed to its buffer queues. Most implementations commit buffer space to the queues lazily, so the queues consume memory only when the bandwidth of the network path does not match the rate at which the TCP user produces or consumes the data. For example, Unix systems set buffer bounds as configurable attributes of the socket object associated with each connection. Data build up on the queues as lists of mbuf chains whose aggregate buffer size must not exceed the configured socket buffer maximum. If the transmit queue is full, then *SEND* operations block or fail; if the receive queue is full, then the TCP receiver cannot accept incoming segments. The buffer queue sizes can limit performance, as discussed in Section 13.1.3.

13.1.2 Accessing User Memory

The TCP buffering scheme must provide for movement of data to and from the memory of the TCP user. The mechanisms to accept and deliver data are closely related to the TCP/user interface.

This section deals with data movement for the *SEND* and *RECEIVE* interfaces outlined in RFC 793, which form the basis for the *socket* APIs in Unix/Posix/Linux and other operating systems. In particular, the *SEND* and *RECEIVE* primitives specify a user buffer address and length for the data to be sent or received. Two variants of this basic API are common in TCP/IP implementations.

Copy Semantics.   RFC 793 defines *SEND* and *RECEIVE* with *copy semantics*. The user is free to modify a send buffer after issuing a *SEND*, but TCP must transmit the data that were in the buffer at the time the *SEND* was issued. The definition of *RECEIVE* is less clear, but it does require that TCP place incoming data at the buffer addresses specified by the user. In practice, implementations meet these constraints by copying data between the buffer queues and user memory; these copy operations are often a limiting factor for TCP communication.

To illustrate, BSD-derived systems using typical NICs handle the socket variants of the *SEND* and *RECEIVE* operations as follows. On a send, the socket layer copies data from user memory across the kernel boundary into a freshly allocated *mbuf* buffer chain and appends the data to the connection's transmit queue. The system sends the data by passing the mbufs in this chain through the TCP/IP stack to the network device driver, which initiates device DMA operations on the buffer regions described by the chain. On the receiving side, the network driver allocates buffers for the device to deposit the incoming stream and constructs a chain referencing the buffer regions for each incoming packet header and payload. It passes the chain for each arriving TCP segment through the TCP receiver, which appends the chain to the receive queue for the correct connection. When the TCP user requests data with a *read* system call or other *RECEIVE* equivalent, the kernel copies data from the front of the receive queue into the user-specified buffers, releasing each mbuf after it has copied all of that mbuf's data.

Direct Access.   Another variant of *SEND* and *RECEIVE* allows TCP to access the user buffers directly, bypassing the copy through the optional TCP buffers in Figure 13.1. This approach is common in Unix systems when the TCP user is a kernel-based upper layer protocol (ULP) such as an NFS. If *SEND* passes its buffers by reference, then a buffer chain describing them may be linked directly onto the transmit queue, avoiding the data copy. If, however, the TCP user modifies a buffer with a pending send, then it can cause the TCP sender to transmit inconsistent data (e.g., sending the old data once and then the new data in a retransmission). This may occur even if the TCP implementation itself is correct. The interface must prohibit the TCP user from modifying a buffer until all pending sends on it have completed.

Defining a direct-access *RECEIVE* interface is trickier. RFC 793 explicitly allows an implementation to link user buffers directly into a receive queue. However, most NICs select the target buffer for incoming data based on arrival order; without a mechanism to place incoming data correctly in the user buffers, the system must still copy the data to the locations requested by the TCP user.

To place data correctly, the NIC must recognize the TCP connection associated with the incoming data before moving the data into the connection's receive queue buffers in host memory. This *early demultiplexing* requires special support on the NIC. Even with this support, the system might deposit data in a user buffer before TCP has validated it. While RFC 793 is silent on what it means for TCP to "deliver" data to the user, some have argued that this property violates the fundamental guarantee of reliable, in-order delivery. For correctness, the interface must prohibit the TCP user from interpreting any buffer region as valid unless and until a *RECEIVE* covering that region has successfully completed. We return to this issue in Section 13.4, which discusses techniques and alternative interfaces to enable efficient data movement for high performance TCP.

13.1.3   TCP Data Exchange

The TCP endpoints participating in a connection act as cooperating state machines. The endpoints cooperate by exchanging segments. Each segment contains the sequence number of the first (oldest) byte in the segment (*seg.seq*), the segment data length (*seg.len*), status bits, an acknowledgment sequence number (*seg.ack*) for the last (newest) byte received in order, and an advertised receive window size (*seg.wnd*). Either side may send a segment to transfer data or to induce state changes or actions in its peer at any time.

Segment arrival may prompt a TCP endpoint to take any of several actions. If the segment's data completes a *RECEIVE*, the TCP receiver may deliver the data by notifying the TCP user. If the segment contains a new ACK or window update, the TCP sender may notify the TCP user that a *SEND* has completed or transmit one or more segments containing new data or retransmitted old data. The TCP sender may also send segments as a result of a timer expiration or a new *SEND* or *RECEIVE* command from the TCP user. Any outgoing segments may include new ACKs or window updates.

The TCP sender and receiver at opposite ends of a connection maintain local views of the byte sequence space for a unidirectional data flow. Each endpoint's view is captured in state variables in its TCB. The TCP implementation updates these variables as a side effect of segment exchange or in response to other events such as *SEND* or *RECEIVE* commands. All sequence number arithmetic uses unsigned, 32-bit integers modulo 2^{32}.

Figure 13.3 depicts the active portion of the sequence space—the portion for which local buffer space may exist—and related state variables maintained in each TCB. The transmit queue bound is *snd.bufsize*; the receive queue bound is *rcv.bufsize*. The sender's transmit queue holds at least the bytes in the range [*snd.una, snd.nxt* − 1], which comprise the *retransmission queue*: *snd.una* is the oldest byte that has been sent but not yet acknowledged, and *snd.nxt* is the next byte to send. The transmit queue also includes posted sends for other data beyond *snd.nxt* in the send sequence space; typical kernel implementations maintain this portion of the transmit queue at the socket layer.

Conceptually, the receive queue includes buffer space for all bytes in the range [*rcv.user, rcv.user* + *rcv.bufsize* − 1], where *rcv.user* is the next received byte to deliver to the TCP user. Within this range, *rcv.nxt* is the next byte expected on an incoming segment, and *rcv.last* is the newest byte received in any segment. If data arrive in order then *rcv.last* = *rcv.nxt* − 1. However, if segments arrive out of order, then *rcv.nxt* is the oldest missing byte of a *sequence hole*, and the range [*rcv.nxt, rcv.last*] comprises the receiver's *reorder buffer* for sequencing the

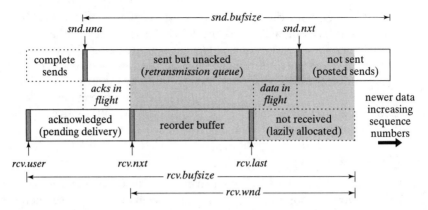

FIGURE 13.3: Sender and receiver views of the sequence space for a unidirectional data flow.

incoming data. The range $[rcv.user, rcv.nxt - 1]$ is received and acknowledged data that the receiver must retain pending delivery to the TCP user; typical kernel implementations maintain this portion of the receive queue at the socket layer.

We now summarize the mandated interactions for efficient TCP communication, focusing on aspects that are essential for bulk data transfer. The following applies to unidirectional data transfer from either sender across the connection to its peer receiver.

Basic Data Transfer.   Each receiver maintains a sliding *window* defining the portions of the sequence space that it will accept. The receiver's flow window size is $rcv.wnd = rcv.bufsize - (rcv.nxt - rcv.user)$, and the window is the sequence range $[rcv.nxt, rcv.nxt + rcv.wnd - 1]$. The gray box in Figure 13.3 depicts the receiver's flow window. The receiver accepts any incoming segment whose sequence range $[seg.seq, seg.seq + seg.len - 1]$ overlaps the window and suppresses duplicates by discarding any segment that does not. If segments arrive in order, each arrival advances $rcv.nxt$ to $seg.seq + seg.len$.

Acknowledgments.   The receiver acknowledges incoming data segments with return segments containing $seg.ack = rcv.nxt - 1$. These segments constitute *cumulative acknowledgments* for all data received in sequence; each ACK subsumes all ACKs sent before it. As each ACK segment arrives, the TCP sender advances its $snd.una$ (if necessary) to $seg.ack + 1$.

Note that cumulative ACKs do not acknowledge any received data in the range $[rcv.nxt, rcv.last]$. If a segment is lost, the sender cannot determine which (if any) newer segments have arrived. Recent protocol extensions support *selective acknowledgments* (SACK) to convey this information; these extensions are discussed in Chapter 11.

Flow Control.   The receiver advertises its flow window size by setting $seg.wnd \leq rcv.wnd$ in return segments. The sender records the window size in $snd.wnd$; The sender's flow window is the range $[snd.una, snd.una + snd.wnd - 1]$.

Each time it becomes active, the TCP sender transmits any unsent data that are ready to send and are within its flow window and congestion window (see Section 13.1.5). Sliding window flow control allows the sender to transmit at the highest possible rate without overflowing the receiver's buffers.

If additional buffer space becomes available on the receiver—for example, if a *RECEIVE* completes with copy semantics (advancing $rcv.user$) or the TCP user posts a new *RECEIVE* with direct-access semantics (advancing $rcv.bufsize$)—then the receiver opens the window and advertises the window update. Although a receiver should never shrink its window unexpectedly, the TCP sender should tolerate this behavior if it occurs.

Segment Size.   To use the network efficiently, TCP implementations should aggressively coalesce data and status information, and piggyback status updates on data transfers. In particular, larger segments are more efficient because they amortize the overhead of header space and protocol processing for each segment across a larger number of bytes. The *maximum segment size* (MSS) is a property of the network path between the sender and the receiver. Each side should advertise its expected MSS—the maximum transmission unit (MTU) of its incoming network interface minus the size of the TCP/IP headers—as a TCP option at connection setup. The MSS for each direction is initially the minimum of the receiver's advertised MSS and the sender's MTU less the TCP/IP header size. The MSS may be constrained further by the network path, as described in Section 13.2.3.

Buffer Size.   For peak bandwidth, $snd.bufsize$ and $rcv.bufsize$ must be larger than the network path's round-trip bandwidth-delay product. If a site's receive buffer queue is smaller than the bandwidth-delay product, then its peer can exhaust the buffer by sending at full bandwidth for less time than it takes for the first returned ACK to arrive. This forces the sender to idle until an ACK arrives with an accompanying window update. A small transmit queue may also have an impact on bandwidth, because it limits the rate at which the TCP user can generate data; this increases the probability that the TCP sender exhausts the transmit queue, forcing it to idle for more data. For good performance each buffer queue size must also be significantly larger than the MSS to allow pipelining of segments in the network.

Delayed Transmission.   If the TCP user produces or consumes data in small units, then TCP must take care to coalesce these units so the connection may continue exchanging data in units of MSS. A TCP receiver should delay ACKs for new data to allow the TCP user to consume the data and free buffer space before the window update, and it must advertise $seg.wnd = 0$ if the new window is smaller than the MSS. This policy helps to avoid the phenomenon of *silly window syndrome* in which the window size degrades to small values, producing a stable pattern of data exchange using small segments. In addition, the *Nagle algorithm* dictates that the TCP sender should delay sending newly posted data until it can send a full segment, unless it can send all of its pending data into the current window and $snd.nxt = snd.una$. If the receiver closes its window, the TCP sender uses a *persist timer* to drive periodic transmission of zero-length segments to probe the window.

Acknowledgment Pacing.   TCP is *self-clocking*; once the sender's flow window or congestion window is exhausted, transmission of new data is driven by arrival of ACKs. Thus, a TCP receiver must not delay ACKs as long as to force the sender to idle the connection and transmit data in bursts. A TCP implementation must impose a time bound on ACK delays, and it must generate at least one ACK for every two full segments worth of data ($2 * MSS$). Failure to do so is an *ack stretch* error. Thus, endpoints must have an accurate notion of the MSS; a common flaw is to stretch ACKs after a change to the MSS as a result of path MTU discovery (Section 13.2.3).

13.1.4   Retransmissions

The TCP sender uses a *retransmission timer* to drive retransmission of unacknowledged data. Failure to receive an ACK may result from a lost data segment or a lost ACK. In either case, the sender must recover by setting a timer to fire after a retransmission timeout (RTO) elapses. The TCP sender sets the timer when it transmits a segment if the timer is not already set. If the timer fires before the expected acknowledgment arrives, then the TCP sender retransmits the segment.

Ideally, the retransmission timer fires immediately after a missing ACK is due to arrive, that is, just over one round-trip time (RTT) after the unacknowledged segment was sent. The difficulty is that network conditions may cause the RTT to vary during the lifetime of the connection. If the timer is too aggressive ($RTO <$ RTT), then the sender retransmits too aggressively, wasting network bandwidth and generating overhead. If the timer is too conservative ($RTO > RTT$), then a lost segment causes the connection to idle until the timer fires. Timer management is critical for performance on network paths that are lossy or that exhibit high RTT variance.

RFC 2988 [265] specifies a procedure for managing an adaptive retransmission timer with backoff, using techniques pioneered by Jacobson [179]. This scheme uses integer arithmetic to compute exponentially weighted moving averages of the RTT and its deviation. The RTO is set to the mean RTT plus a safety margin that is a constant factor of the mean deviation. The exponentially weighted moving averages allow the RTO to adapt to persistent changes in network conditions while preserving stability in the presence of short-term fluctuations in the RTT. Scaling the safety margin causes the TCP sender to be more conservative when the RTT variance is high. This approach has proved to be effective in practice.

To retransmit, most implementations simply send the maximum allowable segment beginning with the oldest unacknowledged byte (*snd.una*). Although this approach may retransmit more data than necessary for interactive applications with small segments, it frees the sender from the need to maintain a history of unacknowledged segments.

13.1.5   Congestion

A retransmission event signals to the TCP sender that congestion may exist in the network. The policies for avoiding congestion and responding to it are critical to the correct functioning of TCP and of the Internet. Congestion management is purely a function of the end systems; the current Internet architecture requires that the network itself respond to congestion merely by dropping packets. While congestion management is beyond the scope of this chapter, we briefly summarize the policies for congestion management using *Additive Increase Multiplicative Decrease* (AIMD), as mandated by RFC 2581 [44] at the time of this writing.

In addition to the receiver-advertised flow window (*snd.wnd*), the TCP sender maintains a *congestion window* (*cwnd*) for each connection, bounding the amount of data it may inject into the network. At any time, the data transmitted must never exceed *min(snd.wnd, cwnd)*. The sender adaptively determines the value of *cwnd* based on the pattern of ACKs.

The sender detects congestion by observing (from a missing ACK) that a segment may have been dropped in the network. To signal congestion early, the receiver immediately responds to each out-of-sequence segment with an ACK segment. Lost or reordered segments are visible to the sender as duplicate ACKs. The *fast retransmit* policy permits the sender to retransmit a segment after receiving three duplicate ACKs, even if the retransmission timer has not fired. The triple-duplicate ACK suggests a high probability of a lost segment, rather than a reordering that does not require retransmission.

In the absence of a congestion signal, the TCP sender ramps up its transmission rate by steadily increasing *cwnd* as ACKs arrive. The purpose is to "probe" the network to converge the data transfer to the available bandwidth of the network path, while adapting to fluctuations in the available bandwidth caused by changes in the competing traffic. Increases in *cwnd* are governed by a dynamic threshold value *ssthresh*. If $cwnd \geq ssthresh$, then the TCP sender increments *cwnd* by at most one segment each RTT; this slow additive growth of *cwnd* is termed *congestion avoidance*. If $cwnd < ssthresh$, then the sender ramps up more aggressively, typically by doubling *cwnd* each RTT; this is confusingly known as *slow start*.

If the sender detects congestion, then it must throttle its sending rate by a multiplicatively decreasing *cwnd* (*congestion control*). Expiration of the retransmission timer suggests severe congestion with multiple segment losses; the sender aggressively throttles back by setting *cwnd* to one segment. If the retransmission is prompted by a triple-duplicate ACK, then the sender reduces *cwnd* by half and sets $ssthresh = cwnd$; the arrival of ACKs for data still in the network drive additive increases to *cwnd* (*fast recovery*).

13.2   HIGH PERFORMANCE TCP

This section introduces protocol features and implementation features for high performance TCP. After discussing these features, subsequent sections focus on reducing overheads by streamlining the TCP implementation and restructuring it to reduce host overheads for data transfer.

13.2.1   High-Bandwidth-Delay Products

High-bandwidth networks and high-latency networks (such as satellite networks discussed in Chapter 9) have large bandwidth-delay products. Such networks are sometimes called "long fat networks" (LFNs). LFNs introduce several performance considerations for TCP implementations.

Most obviously, LFNs require large window sizes, beyond the 16-bit window sizes supported by TCP as originally defined. For this reason, the *window scale option* extends TCP to allow each endpoint to specify a *scale factor* for interpreting its advertised receiver window sizes. An endpoint may use this option to tell its peer that its advertised 16-bit window sizes must be shifted left up to 14 bits. This effectively extends the maximum TCP window size to one gigabyte.

One problem for dealing with large windows is that the window scaling option must be specified at connection setup time. An endpoint may not know in advance that a given network path is an LFN and requires window scaling. Unix-based implementations may select window scaling based on the configured maximum size of the receive socket buffer size ($rcv.bufsize$). This presupposes that the queue sizes are set correctly to exceed the bandwidth-delay product, which is also a property of the network path. One alternative is to set window scaling based on the maximum buffer size supported by the system; the only cost to employing window scaling is that it limits the system to specify window sizes in units of up to 16K. Techniques to automatically tune the window size are discussed in Appendix C.

13.2.2 Round-Trip Estimation

Another potential pitfall with LFNs is that the accuracy of RTT estimation (Section 13.1.4) depends on frequent sample measurements of the RTT. Many implementations record only one transmit time per connection, effectively sampling the RTT once per window. The percentage of segments sampled decreases with larger windows, so this may be insufficient for LFNs. In addition, RTT samples from retransmitted segments must be discarded; in this case, the ACK might have resulted from either the original segment or the retransmitted segment, and these cases are indistinguishable.

To provide for more accurate RTT estimation, RFC 1323 [183] introduces a *timestamp option* enabling the sender to place a transmission timestamp in each segment. With each ACK, the receiver returns the timestamp value from the most recently received in-sequence segment containing the oldest byte that was not previously acknowledged and for which the sender included a timestamp. When this ACK with the echoed timestamp arrives back at the sender, the sender can compute an RTT sample by subtracting the reflected timestamp from the current time. The sampled RTT accounts for delayed ACK, retransmissions, and out-of-sequence data.

RFC 1323 also mandates that the 32-bit timestamp values selected by the sender are monotonically increasing with each window until the timer wraps. The receiver may reject a segment with an out-of-sequence timestamp. This policy is called PAWS: Protection Against Wrapped Sequence numbers. It can provide an important safeguard against accepting out-of-sequence data on high-bandwidth networks, which may wrap sequence numbers at the granularity of seconds. PAWS does not specify the timer tick grain used by the sender, but the timer wrap time must be longer than the maximum segment lifetime in the network.

13.2.3 Path MTU Discovery

TCP is most efficient when it uses the largest MSS accepted by the network path without fragmentation. Using a large MSS may have a cost: it increases the minimum latency through store-and-forward routers. In principle, this could increase the RTT and, therefore, increase the buffering requirements at the end systems. However, a larger MSS reduces the segment overhead per byte of data transmitted, yielding higher throughputs when adequate buffer space is available. It also reduces per-segment overhead on the end systems (see Section 13.6).

As discussed earlier in Section 9.7.1, path MTU discovery (RFC 1191 [246]) enables a TCP sender to automatically discover the largest acceptable MSS for a network path. An initial MSS is established for each connection at setup time, but it may be necessary to reduce the MSS if the MTU of some hop along the network path is too small to accommodate it. Path MTU discovery is increasingly important as new networking standards support larger MTUs to improve performance. For example, standard IEEE 802.3 Ethernet frame sizes impose an MTU of 1500 bytes, but many gigabit Ethernet systems now support "jumbo" frame sizes up to 9000 bytes. While jumbo frames are not widely supported in wide-area transit paths, path MTU discovery enables end systems to use these larger packets when allowable (e.g., in LAN settings) without compromising interoperability.

Dynamic routing may cause the path MTU to change at any time. To discover the maximum MTU of the limiting hop, the TCP sender sets the Don't Fragment (DF) bit in each IP datagram. This forces the router at the limiting hop to drop the packet rather than fragmenting it. The router must generate an ICMP Unreachable error specifying the next-hop MTU. The sender uses this information to reset the MSS before retransmitting. If the MSS is constrained by a limiting hop, the TCP sender periodically probes the network with a segment larger than the MSS to determine if the limitation still exists.

One pitfall for path MTU discovery is that it depends on proper ICMP support along the network path from the TCP sender to the limiting hop. Some routers do not properly generate the ICMP Unreachable error, and some network paths discard ICMP packets because they may act as a vector for denial-of-service attacks. If ICMP Unreachable packets are suppressed for any reason, then TCP connections hang unless the TCP sender reduces the MSS after a sufficiently long sequence of lost segments. The sender must issue a sequence of probes with progressively larger segment sizes to discover the path MTU in this case.

A TCP implementation must correctly handle dynamic changes to the MSS. For example, each endpoint must ensure that it never leaves more than $2 * MSS$ bytes of data unacknowledged to avoid an ACK stretch error. Also, MSS changes may force the TCP sender to resegment data for retransmission if the original segments were dropped just before to an MSS change.

13.3   REDUCING END-SYSTEM OVERHEAD

Data transmission using TCP imposes processing overheads in the host operating system (OS) facilities for memory and process management, as well as the TCP/IP protocol stack and the network device and its driver. This overhead adds directly to latency. More importantly, at high speeds, overhead may consume a significant share of host CPU cycles and memory system bandwidth, siphoning off resources needed for application processing of the data. The end system may ultimately saturate under the combined load of application processing and networking overhead, limiting delivered throughput.

It is tempting to suppose that the advances in CPU power will render communication overhead increasingly irrelevant even with faster networks, but this is not the case. This section explores the effects of overhead using a simple model that assumes the CPU processing cost is linear with the network I/O rate, but in practice memory system limitations may force the CPU to stall as the network I/O rate increases; the larger number of memory cycles per instruction increases the CPU cost. Often the limiting factor is not CPU processing power itself but the ability to move data through the host I/O system and memory. Wider data paths can improve raw hardware bandwidth, but more bandwidth is invariably more expensive for a given level of technology. Advances in network bandwidth follow a step function, but the fastest networks tend to stay close to the limits of the hosts. In particular, optimizations to reduce end-system overhead will be critical for 10 gigabit Ethernet for several years after its introduction. Multiprocessors or multithreading may improve performance to the extent that the system is able to extract parallelism from the network processing; in particular, multiprocessors may yield higher *aggregate* throughputs for servers handling multiple concurrent streams.

This section outlines the factors that affect end-system performance for TCP, gives an overview of optimizations to reduce overhead, and discusses their implications for the network interface and TCP implementation. Some of these approaches to low-overhead networking are now emerging into common practice. The network interface plays a key role for some of these features, and an increasing number of commercial network adapters support them.

13.3.1   Overhead, CPU Utilization, and Bandwidth

We first present a simple model to illustrate the impact of overhead on raw communication bandwidth. Suppose that the CPU on a uniprocessor system incurs a fixed processing, cost, c, per byte of data transferred. The cost, c, is measured in CPU time, for example, cycles. For convenience, we represent c as the fraction of the processing power available in one second. Then network communication at bandwidth B, measured in bytes per second, yields CPU utilization Bc. The CPU saturates at bandwidth $1/c$, causing the system to become *host-limited*; this is the maximum throughput achievable on this system.

Slow networks rarely expose these limitations: if the effective network bandwidth $B < 1/c$, then the system is *network-limited* and overhead does not affect raw throughput. For example, suppose a given TCP system incurs 20 cycles of overhead per byte to receive a network stream. A gigahertz CPU running this software incurs a cost of about 30 µs per 1500-byte Ethernet packet, and saturates at a peak bandwidth of 50 Mbps, or 400 Mbps. The system is network-limited with a 100 Mbps Ethernet network, but upgrading the network to gigabit Ethernet causes it to become host-limited at 400 Mbps rather than delivering the expected order-of-magnitude increase. Because the end system can consume data no faster than 400 Mbps, TCP flow control prevents a sender from transmitting data at a higher rate.

Software structures that reduce end-system overhead are critical to reaching the performance potential of high-speed networks. In a host-limited system, reducing overhead directly improves throughput. Suppose that the processing cost consists of a fixed cost, x, per byte and a variable overhead, y, per byte that may be eliminated through some optimization. The optimization increases the CPU

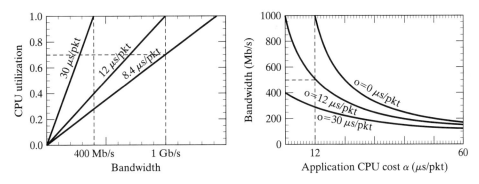

FIGURE 13.4: The effect of communication overhead (o) and application processing cost (a) on CPU utilization and bandwidth. The left-hand graph illustrates a simple linear relationship between bandwidth and CPU utilization. High CPU costs per packet saturate the CPU as bandwidth increases, limiting throughput. The right-hand graph shows the achievable throughput for host-limited systems with varying a and o per 1500-byte packet. The impact of overhead is most significant when the application can process data at high bandwidth.

saturation bandwidth from $B = 1/(x + y)$ to $B = 1/x$, yielding a relative throughput improvement of $(x + y)/x$. In the example, reducing the overhead by 25% to 15 cycles per byte yields a 33% improvement in raw bandwidth.

The left-hand graph of Figure 13.4 illustrates this simple model of the effect of communication overhead. CPU utilization grows linearly with bandwidth, with the slope determined by overhead (given per 1500-byte segment in the figure). An overhead of 30 µs per packet saturates the CPU at 400 Mbps, as in the example. An overhead of roughly 12 µs per packet enables communication at 1 Gbps before the CPU saturates; in this case, a 60% reduction in overhead improves raw bandwidth by a factor of 2.5. With per-packet overhead reduced further to 8.4 µs, the system becomes network-limited on a 1 Gbps network with a CPU utilization of 70%.

13.3.2   The Role of Application Processing

Even if raw communication is not host-limited, reducing overhead can improve application throughput by freeing resources for application processing. The same formula applies: if a is the application's cost to process its data, and o is the communication overhead, then delivered throughput is $1/a + o$ when the system is host-limited. The improvement in application throughput from eliminating overhead grows with the ratio of o to a and is effectively unbounded if $o >> a$. To illustrate, the right-hand graph of Figure 13.4 shows saturation bandwidth as a function of application processing cost, a, per packet for communication overheads, o, of 0, 12, and 30 µs per packet. With $o = 12$ µs, the system achieves a raw bandwidth of 1 Gbps without saturating, but throughput falls off as a increases; eliminating the overhead increases delivered throughput (the $o = 0$ line). In the high-overhead case ($o = 30$ µs), even raw communication is host-limited; eliminating the overhead more than triples bandwidth at $a = 12$ µs.

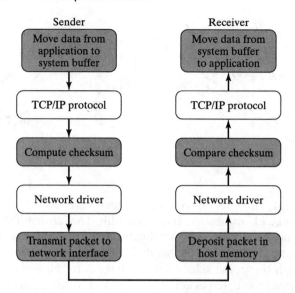

FIGURE 13.5: Sources of end-system overhead for TCP/IP.

Of course, Amdahl's Law dictates that the benefit of reducing overhead o also declines as a grows and the application itself becomes more CPU-intensive. This effect is shown at the far right of Figure 13.4; o has a minimal effect on throughput when $o << a$. Even so, consider the reasonable case in which the network is well matched to the system, allowing raw communication at network speed B ($Bo \leq 1$), and the system is powerful enough to run the application processing at network speed ($Ba \leq 1$). It is easy to see that reducing communication overhead improves application throughput by up to a factor of two in this case. For example, the $o = 12$ line shows throughput of 500 Mbps when $a = o = 12$ μs; eliminating the communication overhead doubles achievable throughput to 1 Gbps.

13.3.3 Sources of Overhead for TCP/IP

Figure 13.5 depicts the key sources of overhead in transmitting data over a TCP connection in a typical system. We can divide overhead into several classes:

- *Per-transfer* overhead includes the cost for each *SEND* or *RECEIVE* operation from the TCP user. These include the costs to initiate each operation—such as kernel system call costs—and the cost to notify the TCP user that it is complete. It also includes the costs to allocate, post, and release buffers for each transfer.

- *Per-packet* or *per-segment* overhead is the cost to process each network packet, segment, or frame. These include the costs to execute the TCP/IP protocol code, allocate and release packet buffers (e.g., mbufs), and field NIC interrupts for packet arrival and transmit completion.

- *Per-byte* overhead includes the cost to copy data within the end system and to compute checksums to detect data corruption in the network. The system incurs these data-touching costs for each byte sent or received at the stages shown in gray in Figure 13.5.

Let o_t, o_s, and o_b denote the per-transfer, per-segment, and per-byte overheads, respectively. Then with transfer size T and segment size S (the MSS), the total overhead o per byte transferred is:

$$o = o_b + o_s/S + o_t/T \tag{13.1}$$

The formula shows that one simple way to reduce overhead is for the TCP user to use the largest possible transfer size T. This can effectively eliminate the impact of transfer overheads for bulk data transfer. Similarly, the sender and receiver can reduce per-segment costs by using path MTU discovery to identify the largest possible segment size S allowable by the underlying network path, as previously discussed. Per-packet and per-transfer costs for buffer management, however, are proportional to the volume of data transferred, given a fixed buffer size. For example, early BSD-based implementations used small mbufs to reduce memory fragmentation and incurred high per-packet overheads to spread packet data across chains of multiple mbufs [197]. Current implementations use larger mbufs as a result of declining memory costs and faster networks. It is common to place packet data in a single mbuf or two mbufs at most, reducing buffer management overhead.

Sections 13.3.4 and 13.3.5 discuss per-packet overheads in more detail. Per-byte data-touching costs—copying and checksumming—tend to dominate per-packet costs and per-buffer costs for bulk data transfer because they are fundamentally limited by the host memory system rather than the CPU. In principle, a well-structured system can entirely eliminate most per-byte overheads. The only unavoidable per-byte costs occur in the application and in moving data between host memory and the NIC. Because copy avoidance is a substantial topic in itself, we leave this issue to the next section. Section 13.3.6 discusses checksum offloading to reduce host data-touching overheads for checksumming.

13.3.4   Per-Packet Overhead

Increasing packet size can mitigate the impact of per-packet and per-segment overheads. Figure 13.6 illustrates the impact of end-system, per-packet or per-segment overheads on delivered bandwidth for host-limited systems on a 1-Gbps network. The left-hand graph shows how increasing segment size S increases achievable bandwidth for varying per-segment overhead, o_s, and per-byte overhead, o_b. We assume that other costs (e.g., per-transfer costs) are held constant and are included in o_b. A per-segment overhead of 1.6 µs has a significant impact on bandwidth for standard 1500-byte Ethernet MTUs. The impact is most pronounced when byte overheads are low enough to allow the system to achieve the full 1 Gbps of raw bandwidth; in this case, $o_s = 1.6$ µs limits the system to about 800 Mbps of raw bandwidth. As packet size grows, the effect of per-packet overhead becomes less significant, and the system converges to bandwidth $1/o_b$. The right-hand graph in Figure 13.6 illustrates the effect of varying the per-packet overhead for packet sizes of 1500 bytes and 9000 bytes (jumbo frames). These basic relationships also apply for per-transfer costs and per-buffer costs and on higher bandwidth networks.

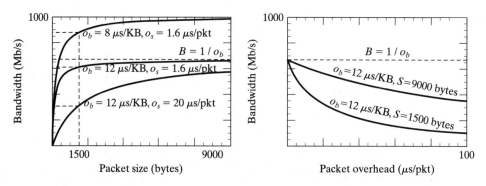

FIGURE 13.6: The relationships between packet size, per-packet overhead, and achievable bandwidth for a host-limited system on a 1 Gbps network.

Because packet sizes are constrained by the properties of the network path, often the most effective way to limit the impact of per-packet overhead is to reduce the overhead itself. TCP/IP protocol processing (header processing) itself is one source of per-segment overhead. While TCP/IP protocol processing has often been cited as a potential bottleneck, several studies have indicated that these costs are typically small relative to data-touching overheads and the cost to interface the TCP/IP stack to the NIC device and the surrounding operating system [102, 108, 182, 197]. Jacobson's scheme for *header prediction* was a significant step in reducing TCP protocol overhead [182, 183]. Header prediction identifies and optimizes common-case code paths in the TCP receiver, yielding a highly efficient code path for the common bottleneck path of data packets arriving in sequence without special needs such as options processing. Mosberger et al. [248] explored related path optimizations to improve cache locality and reduce memory cycles per instruction (mCPI) for protocol processing.

Although TCP/IP protocol processing is efficient, Section 13.5 discusses the alternative of offloading it to the NIC. This allows most per-segment processing to occur on the NIC in parallel with application processing on the host CPU and—more importantly—it introduces new opportunities to reduce per-byte copying costs.

13.3.5 Interrupts

Interrupts are a significant source of per-packet overhead. With 1500-byte packets, a host receiving data at 1 Gbps can incur over 80,000 interrupts per second to signal packet arrival events and another 40,000 interrupts per second to signal transmit completion events on acknowledgment segments. In addition, some systems post a second software interrupt to schedule TCP/IP protocol processing for each incoming segment.

Most high-speed network interfaces support *interrupt coalescing* or *interrupt suppression* to amortize interrupt overheads across multiple packets. This technique selectively delays interrupts if more packets are pending transmission or delivery to the host [123]. This reduces the total number of interrupts delivered; the host interrupt handler may process multiple event notifications from each interrupt. While some interrupt coalescing schemes increase end-to-end latency slightly, they reduce interrupt costs during periods of high bandwidth demand and may deliver better cache performance for processing the notifications.

Another way to reduce TCP overhead is to execute the TCP receiver common-case path (i.e., the header prediction fast path) directly from the NIC receive interrupt handler, rather than scheduling a separate thread or software interrupt handler to process the headers. In addition, some systems disable some or all transmit-complete interrupts, which serve to notify the host that it may release transmit buffers mapped onto the NIC. A TCP sender cannot release buffer space for outgoing data segments until the receiver acknowledges the data.

13.3.6 Checksums

To detect data corruption in the network, TCP/IP generates an end-to-end checksum for each packet covering all protocol headers and data. In most implementations, software running on the host CPU computes these checksums on both sending and receiving sides. This requires the CPU to load all of the data through the memory hierarchy for a sequence of add operations.

One approach to reducing per-byte costs is to coalesce multiple operations that touch the data, completing multiple steps in a single traversal of the packet [109]. For example, some TCP/IP implementations integrate checksumming with the data copy to or from application memory. A similar approach could apply to other processing steps such as compression or encryption. These optimizations are highly processor-dependent and may not yield the expected benefits [102]. Borman [67] demonstrated large reductions in checksum overhead using vector processing in his pioneering work with high-speed TCP on Cray supercomputers.

Another way to eliminate this cost is to compute the checksum in hardware on the network adapter's DMA interface as the packet passes through on its way to or from host memory. The TCP/IP stack and the network device and driver must cooperate in *checksum offloading*. Many high performance NICs support checksum offloading in the host DMA engine, which computes the raw 16-bit one's complement checksum of each DMA transfer as it moves data to and from host memory. This is an effective optimization, although it sacrifices some protection against data corruption in the host I/O system or low-level software.

Changes to the TCP/IP stack to use the hardware checksum are typically minor; simply bypass the software checksum. Three factors, however, complicate hardware checksumming for IP:

- A packet's data may span multiple host buffers; the device accesses each buffer with a separate DMA. A common solution is to combine these partial checksums on the adapter using one's complement addition.

- TCP and UDP actually use two checksums: one for the IP header (including fields overlapping with the TCP or UDP header) and a second end-to-end checksum covering the TCP or UDP header and packet data. In a conventional system, TCP or UDP computes its end-to-end checksum before IP fills in its overlapping IP header fields (e.g., options) on the sender, and after the IP layer restores these fields on the receiver. Checksum offloading involves computing these checksums below the IP stack; thus, the driver or NIC must partially dismantle the IP header to compute a correct checksum.

- Because the checksums are stored in the headers at the front of each IP packet, a sender must complete the checksum before it can transmit the packet headers on the link. If the checksums are computed by the host-NIC DMA engine, then the last byte of the packet must arrive on the NIC before the firmware can determine the complete checksum.

The last issue may require a compromise between host overhead and packet latency, because the adapter must handle large packets in a store-and-forward fashion.

13.3.7 Connection Management

While this section has focused primarily on data transfer, Internet servers are among the most visible performance-critical TCP applications. Many servers manage large numbers of connections for a large user population, although the amount of data transmitted on each connection may be small. This places performance pressure on the mechanisms for connection setup, connection teardown, identifying the connections for incoming segments, buffer allocation across connections, and notifying server applications of connection state. For example, TCB lookup on packet arrival can impose a significant overhead. Mature TCP implementations use variants of hashing [241] for fast TCB lookups with large numbers of connections. Packet streams often show sufficient locality to benefit further from caching the previously accessed TCB. [245].

Also of concern is the mechanism to notify a user process which subset of a large set of open connections is ready to send or receive data. For example, arrival of an ACK may release buffer space in a connection's transmit queue, allowing the TCP user to successfully initiate a new *SEND* operation on that connection. Similarly, data arriving on a connection may allow the user to complete a *RECEIVE* operation on that connection and begin processing the data.

Experiments with Internet servers under load has shown that interfaces that poll the state of a set of connections—such as the Unix *select* operation—are not scalable. Instead, TCP implementations should provide a notification queue mechanism to pass connection-related events to the server application [62, 94].

13.4 COPY AVOIDANCE

In principle, it is possible to eliminate all data copying within the host. Modern network devices access host packet buffers directly in host memory using scatter/gather DMA, eliminating the need for a host CPU to copy data to and from the network interface. The OS can avoid other internal data copying with flexible mechanisms for buffer management, such as the buffer chaining mechanisms discussed in Section 13.1.1. True "zero-copy" implementations are achievable with the right system structure.

Most problematic is the copying of data between the transmit and receive queues and user buffers. Section 13.1.2 outlines the *SEND* and *RECEIVE* interface mandated by RFC 793, which is similar to the socket interface to TCP in many systems. This interface is simple to specify, understand, and use, which has contributed to the success of TCP/IP. However, its copy semantics inhibit high performance data movement because supporting the interface generally requires actually copy-ing the data. On the sender, copying the data protects it from modification if the process reuses the memory before the transmission of the old data completes. On the receiver, copying allows the system to place received data at arbitrary virtual addresses specified by the application.

Avoiding this copying involves complex relationships among the network hardware and software, operating system buffering schemes, and the TCP/user interface. Section 13.1.2 outlines a direct-access variant of the *SEND* and *RECEIVE* interface that allows TCP to directly access the user buffers to avoid copying the data. This example illustrates two key points about copy avoidance: (1) avoiding data copying for a *RECEIVE* interface generally requires specific support on the NIC to process the incoming packet stream and deposit the data in suitable host memory buffers, and (2) the effects on the semantics of TCP user operations are subtle and must be defined carefully. The problem is particularly difficult when moving data into a user process with a protected virtual address space and other receive cases where buffer alignment constraints exist. Copy avoidance is still an active area of research and development, and there are no fully general solutions available.

This section surveys several approaches to copy avoidance for high perfor-mance TCP. We first discuss *page remapping*, a common technique that uses virtual memory to reduce copying across the TCP/user interface. While page remapping preserves copy semantics, it has many limitations. We then present two more general solutions that involve a comprehensive restructuring of the end systems, extending the RFC 793 interface with new variants of the *SEND* and *RECEIVE* primitives to enable fast-path data movement for high performance TCP.

Some TCP experts favor a strict reading of RFC 793 to preclude additional variants of these primitives that do not precisely match the mandated interfaces. However, RFC 793 notes that "considerable freedom is permitted to TCP imple-menters to design interfaces that are appropriate to a particular operating system environment," as long as the "minimum functionality" of the mandated interfaces is present. While the alternative interfaces are more complex to define and use, they are appropriate for upper layer protocols (ULPs) using TCP as a transport and may be exposed directly to performance-critical applications.

13.4.1 Page Remapping

Page remapping—also called *page flipping*—leverages virtual memory management in the operating system to reduce copying in kernel-based TCP implementations. The idea is to use page-grained virtual memory mappings to change buffer access permissions or address bindings without copying the data to a new buffer. On the sender, virtual memory allows the system to protect against modifications to user buffers with pending transmits, even if they are accessible in a user process address space. On the receiver, virtual memory allows the system to deliver data to user buffers under certain conditions by changing the physical page frame mappings for the virtual page addresses covering the user buffers. Research systems have used page remapping for several years [76, 102, 169], and it is now emerging into more common use.

The primary support for page remapping typically resides at the socket layer in the OS kernel. The optimizations trigger only if the data transfer sizes requested by the application are larger than the page size. On the receiver, page remapping requires an MSS matched to the page size, page-aligned application buffers, and a network interface that deposits packet data on a page boundary. In general, this last requirement means that the network interface must split the packet header from its data for common protocols such as TCP.

Page remapping activates when a process requests the kernel to transfer a page or more of data between a network socket and a page-aligned user buffer. Instead of copying data to or from a buffer chain, as described in Section 13.1.2, the system passes the data by reference. For example, in a BSD-derived Unix system using mbufs (Section 13.1.1), *SEND* places the new data on the transmit queue by creating and appending *external mbufs* that reference the page frames backing the application's virtual buffer. The buffer chain and its pages are then passed through the TCP/IP stack to the network driver, which initiates DMA directly from the pages. To preserve copy semantics, the kernel marks any page with a pending transmit as *copy-on-write*, disabling write access. The kernel releases the copy-on-write mapping when the receiver acknowledges the data.

On the receiver, incoming data arrives on the receive queue as buffer chains passed up through the protocol stack. Page remapping can optimize delivery of some subset of the received data under specific conditions. Remapped data must arrive as complete pages; these pages must contain portions of the sequence space that align with virtual page boundaries in the user buffers specified in the *RECEIVE* calls. If these conditions are met, the kernel delivers each page of data by remapping the virtual page of the user's buffer to the physical page frame containing the data, for example, as referenced by an external *mbuf* passed up from the network driver. Copy-on-write is unnecessary because there is no need to retain the kernel buffer after the read; the kernel simply releases the receive queue buffer descriptors, leaving the buffer pages mapped into the application address space. It also releases any user pages whose virtual address mappings were broken by the remapping operations, preserving equilibrium between the process and the kernel buffer pool.

Page remapping is fragile. For example, consider the case in which the TCP user attempts to overwrite a send buffer before the TCP acknowledgment is received. Because the mapping is copy-on-write, the system incurs a page fault, copies the page, and maps the user's virtual buffer to the new copy before allowing the write to proceed. This is necessary to preserve emulated virtual copy semantics, but it destroys any benefit from page remapping. In general, the sending application must allocate enough virtual address space to map the entire transmit queue to benefit fully from page remapping. This effectively means that the virtual memory allocated to the application's send buffers must scale with the window size. The window size depends on the network path and may grow very large for LFNs (Section 13.2.1) and in any case is unknown to the application.

Virtual copies with page remapping are also fragile on the receiver without special support on the NIC. At minimum, the NIC must separate incoming packet headers from their payloads (*header splitting*) and deposit the payloads into buffers aligned to system virtual memory page boundaries. If the MSS is smaller than a page, as is commonly the case, then the NIC must recognize the TCP connection for each incoming packet and process the transport headers (see Section 13.5) to "pack" payloads into contiguous page-size buffers for each connection. These packets may arrive at the receiver out of order and/or interspersed with packets from other flows. Even when the received data are properly packed into page frames, the system may deliver the pages by remapping only when the application's *RECEIVE* buffers are virtually contiguous and suitably page-aligned with the data stream.

Moreover, consider the difficulty with using page remapping for a ULP such as a TCP-based storage protocol (e.g., NFS). In this case, the TCP payloads include ULP headers that affect the data alignment. The actual data (e.g., file blocks) must be page-aligned to deliver to a user process using page remapping; most systems also require aligned data to link into the system I/O cache. This means that the NIC must separate not only the TCP headers from the data but also the ULP headers; thus, the NIC must incorporate specific support for each ULP that benefits from page remapping, as well as support for TCP itself. The NIC processing may be complex for ULPs such as NFS that use variable-length headers or that require ULP-level state to decode the incoming headers.

A final disadvantage is that page remapping requires a TLB invalidation after any change to a virtual physical mapping and after any page access restriction (e.g., copy-on-write). This is expensive on most architectures, and it inhibits scalability on shared memory multiprocessors.

13.4.2 Scatter/Gather I/O

A more general alternative is to introduce a variant of the *SEND* and *RECEIVE* interfaces that do not require copy semantics. One approach is to use *scatter/gather I/O* to allow *SEND* and *RECEIVE* from arbitrary buffer locations, with the system rather than the TCP user selecting the addresses for incoming data. For example, the receiving NIC may deposit incoming data from each packet at any convenient location. The data are described internally by a buffer chain. Scatter/gather I/O defines a new API to allow the system to exchange these buffer chains directly with the TCP user or application.

IO-Lite [258] proposes a general form of scatter/gather I/O between an operating system kernel and user processes. IO-Lite allows more flexible data placement and reduces copying for interprocess communication and storage access as well as network communication. To allow application access to scatter/gather buffers, the application address space is given read-only access to blocks of memory containing portions of the system buffer pool. The system delivers data by passing references to locations in this pool. Buffers are immutable as long as they are referenced, allowing free exchange of buffer chains among processes and system components. IO-Lite introduces a redesigned system I/O cache to use scatter/gather buffering in other OS subsystems. To write or send data, applications may create new buffer chains containing references to received data as well as new data created by the applications. Modifications are handled by manipulating the buffer chains to insert references to new locations for the updated data, to avoid modifying the original copy.

Scatter-gather I/O as proposed in IO-Lite entails a comprehensive restructuring of the operating system and I/O interfaces. One pitfall with this approach is that data are not necessarily contiguous in memory or aligned in a useful way. For example, the application cannot in general overlay programming language data structures on the received data without copying some or all of it. Also, because received data are not page-aligned, received data cannot in general be delivered securely to user-level processes without copying it. Mapping the pages containing the received data into a user process address space exposes the containing pages in their entirety, not just the portions occupied by the received data. This may expose data that are private to other applications, unless the NIC supports early demultiplexing to isolate data arriving on different connections. While this places less stringent demands on the NIC than general support for page remapping, it undermines a potential benefit of scatter/gather I/O.

13.4.3   Remote Direct Memory Access

Another approach to copy avoidance is based on the direct-access TCP/user interface outlined in Section 13.1.2, coupled with NIC support to "steer" incoming data directly into user-specified buffers. This approach is directly applicable to TCP offload NICs that implement the full TCP/IP protocol on the network adapter (Section 13.5).

One proposal, termed *Remote Direct Memory Access* (RDMA), is based on a messaging protocol layered above the transport, in conjunction with NIC support to recognize this protocol. The software registers buffer regions with the NIC driver, and obtains protected buffer reference tokens called *region IDs*. It may then exchange these region IDs with the connection peer by inserting them into RDMA messages sent over the connection. Special RDMA message directives enable one end system to read or write remote memory regions named by the region IDs. The receiving NIC recognizes and interprets these directives, validates the region IDs, and performs protected data transfers to the named buffer regions, for example, to place received data payloads directly into the receive buffers registered for the TCP user. The name RDMA suggests that each end system may be viewed as a remote device that initiates direct memory transfers to and from the memory of its connection peer.

RDMA requires new facilities and interfaces for buffer management, including buffer registration and buffer protection. Limits on the number of registered buffers may complicate application buffer management. Buffer registration and deregistration are protected operations and, therefore, may be unsuitable if many small buffer transfers are required.

The idea of RDMA has been around by various names for many years. It is an important component of the Virtual Interface (VI) and Infiniband network architectures, and of small area network (SAN) systems based on these and related host interface standards. RDMA is also related to *sender-based memory management* [77]. RDMA has been used successfully for performance-critical applications in many settings. It handles arbitrary MTUs and buffer alignments, and supports ULP protocols structured to use it, for example, for network storage access. The Direct Access File System (DAFS) protocol is one important ULP designed for use with RDMA. The popular NFS can also run over a Remote Procedure Call (RPC) protocol extended for RDMA. It is also straightforward to isolate the RDMA complexity within the kernel behind a sockets-like interface based on RFC 793 for use by unmodified applications. Microsoft's Winsock Direct is one example of such a system.

At the time of this writing, RDMA implementations exist primarily in NICs for network link technologies (e.g., SANs) that are proprietary or supplied by a single vendor. While the concepts of RDMA are compatible with standard technologies for IP networking, RDMA requires a new protocol and cooperation between the NICs at either end of the connection. This protocol and the programming interfaces for RDMA buffer management must be standardized so that system and application software can interoperate with multiple RDMA implementations. The VI architecture is one example of a complete interface specification for RDMA.

RDMA for TCP has been controversial. To reduce the impact on the TCP transport itself, RDMA may be defined as a new request/response ULP layered as a "shim" above TCP, and, thus, it cannot be viewed as a general solution for all TCP/IP communication. A key point of contention is whether it is "legal" for an RDMA NIC to act on RDMA directives in out-of-sequence segments to perform reassembly of the incoming data stream directly in the user buffers. This would significantly reduce the cost and complexity of RDMA NICs. However, some TCP experts view this as a violation of TCP ordering properties. One argument is that the direct-access interface is itself a violation of established ordering guarantees if resequencing of out-of-order data takes place directly in the user buffers (see Section 13.1.2). This view precludes any possibility of a general zero-copy receive interface for TCP, and it is not supported by RFC 793 or any other RFC. A more serious argument holds that out-of-sequence RDMA is a technical layer violation if it exposes the contents of out-of-order segments as a "hint" to the ULP protocol implementation (RDMA) itself. This is a conceptual problem rather than a practical one, because in-order delivery to the end application is preserved. Even so, the RDMA model does not fit naturally with the rigid sequenced byte stream model of TCP; it is better suited to new advanced IP transports such as Stream Control Transport Protocol (SCTP).

Work is under way within the IETF to define RDMA protocol standards for TCP and other IP transports. An RDMA Consortium has proposed draft standards for RDMA over TCP, and initial implementations of the standard are in progress. This standardization is necessary to ensure safe interoperability among NICs from different vendors and their associated software. Some NICs supporting TCP RDMA are already on the market, driven by commercially important applications, primarily IP network storage protocols such as DAFS and NFS/RDMA. One example of an early RDMA/TCP implementation is the Emulex GN9000 network adapter for gigabit Ethernet, which supports a VI host interface.

13.5 TCP OFFLOAD

With increasing network speeds—including 10 gigabit Ethernet—there is a rebirth of interest in supporting TCP/IP protocol functions directly on the adapter. NICs with direct support for general TCP/IP communication are often referred to as a *TCP Offload Engines* or TOE NICs. TOE NICs support TCP/IP protocol processing, generalizing the relatively simple and common support for TCP checksum offloading in advanced NICs (see Section 13.3.6). In addition, several NIC models now act as Host Bus Adapters (HBAs) for TCP-based ULPs that encapsulate device protocols—primarily network storage protocols such as iSCSI—over TCP/IP. These HBA NICs also incorporate full support for TCP offload.

TCP offload significantly reduces per-packet overheads for TCP/IP protocol processing on the host CPUs. While TCP/IP protocol processing itself is not a primary bottleneck on well-implemented systems (see Section 13.3.4), it can consume a significant share of the system resources. In one recent experiment with a BSD-derived implementation, TCP/IP protocol overhead alone could consume 30% of CPU time on a 500 MHz Alpha 21264 receiver using standard Ethernet frames (1500-byte MTU) at 1 Gbps [102]. In addition, TOE NICs and HBAs independently coalesce data arriving in multiple small segments, naturally obtaining the benefits of interrupt coalescing discussed in Section 13.3.5.

More importantly, we have seen in the previous section how protocol offload can help to avoid expensive copy operations within the host. A TCP-capable NIC can "pack" data in separate host buffers for each connection, with the TCP headers stripped off. These buffers can be page-sized and aligned, even if the MTU and MSS are small, enabling more general page remapping optimizations. Because a TCP NIC can determine the sequence range of each segment, it can also deposit data directly in user buffers, enabling a direct-access *RECEIVE* interface. On the sending side, a TCP-capable NIC can schedule the movement of data directly from user buffers down to the NIC, as appropriate for pacing each connection. TCP offload alone does not provide general support for ULPs, which intermix ULP headers into the data as described previously. However, TCP offload NICs provide the foundation for RDMA support to handle copy avoidance for ULPs in a general way. Copy avoidance may well prove to be a compelling benefit of TCP offload.

The host/NIC interface for TCP protocol offload presents difficult architectural choices. Because a TOE NIC performs TCP's demultiplexing functions directly on the adapter, the host/NIC interface must explicitly name connections, with separate buffer queues for each connection. In effect, the TCP implementation accesses its per-connection transmit and receive queues in host memory across the device DMA interface. To be fully general, this approach requires new device interface standards to bypass software TCP/IP support in standard operating systems. One alternative is to base this interface on the VI architecture, as in the Emulex GN9000 NICs. One advantage of this approach is that it incorporates support for RDMA using an accepted interface and so supports important RDMA-based ULPs such as DAFS in a general way.

The host interface problem is simplified for ULP-specific TCP offload NICs (HBAs). For example, an iSCSI NIC might appear to the host as any other SCSI storage controller, completely insulating the host from the TCP/IP functions. In addition to terminating TCP endpoints, the NIC can also handle ULP headers to steer ULP payloads to the correct application buffers. This enables the system to avoid copying payload data from the ULP, without the need for general RDMA support. This is similar to FibreChannel NICs (or HBAs), which implement an I/O block transport on the NIC. While this approach is simple and effective, it restricts the NIC to act as a single-function device.

While host CPU speeds may keep pace with increasing network bandwidths, offloading TCP/IP functions to the NIC device can free up a significant share of CPU resources for application-level processing. However, the TOE approach will be effective only if the TOE NIC can handle TCP communication and its host interface at wire speed for common usage patterns. Connection setup and teardown are particularly difficult to handle efficiently, and today's Internet server loads often involve many short connections. Even so, given the maturity of the TCP/IP protocol, some elements of protocol processing can be accelerated with specialized hardware.

13.6   FURTHER READING

Comer's second volume of *Internetworking with TCP/IP* [112] is a great source for understanding the implementation details of TCP/IP. This volume presents a "C" code implementation of TCP/IP, along with detailed explanations of what the code accomplishes. Mosberger et al. [247] describe several techniques that can be applied to network code to improve protocol latency. The report presents experimental results to show TCP/IP performance improvement on a modern RISC processor. Shi et al. [291] present a TCP/IP implementation model that provides throughput guarantees, prioritized bandwidth sharing among multiple connections, and low request-response time even in the presence of heavy system background load. RFC2525 [266] lists some known TCP implementation problems and their solutions. Some of these problems are related to protocol correctness, others to protocol performance.

13.7   SUMMARY

For high-speed networks, the end-system implementation of TCP can become the performance bottleneck. In fact, most traditional implementations, such as BSD implementation, cannot cope with the emerging high-speed networks (e.g., 10 Gbps Ethernet) at line speed. This chapter summarizes critical performance issues for TCP implementation in end systems and surveys solutions for improving bulk transfer performance.

13.8   REVIEW QUESTIONS

1. Why is TCP implementation an important factor in high performance TCP/IP networking?

2. Discuss the protocol and implementation features in a typical TCP implementation that affect TCP performance.

3. What are the sources of end-system overheads in a typical TCP implementation?

4. Discuss three techniques to reduce end-system overheads.

5. What is a long fat network (LFN)? What specific performance issues are introduced by LFNs for TCP implementations.

6. Explain *data copying* in a typical TCP implementation. What is the effect of copying on TCP and application performance?

7. What is Page Remapping? Under what conditions can copying be avoided using Page Remapping? What are the limitations of Page Remapping? What support does it require from the NIC?

8. Explain how Scatter/Gather can avoid data copying across the TCP/user interface. What are the limitations and pitfalls of this approach?

9. What is RDMA? Discuss how RDMA helps avoid data copying. What are the limitations of RDMA?

10. What is TCP offload? How can TCP offload improve application performance?

13.9 HANDS-ON PROJECTS

1. Implement the overhead-reducing techniques discussed in Section 13.3 on a freely available FreeBSD system. Run some experimental tests and report any TCP performance improvements that you observe.

2. Mosberger et al. [247] describe three techniques, *outlining*, *path-inlining*, and *cloning*, to improve protocol latency. Implement these three techniques on a freely available Linux test bed and report any observed TCP performance improvement.

APPENDIX A

M/M/1 Queues

M/M/1 queue is a popular analytical tool frequently used to predict performance of a wide range of systems, including communication networks. In this book, M/M/1 queueing analysis was used in the case study described at the end of Chapter 4. This appendix presents a set of formulas used to derive the M/M/1 queueing performance measures, followed by several examples to illustrate the application of the formulas in performance analysis of TCP/IP networks. As such, we limit our discussion to the key elements of M/M/1 queue. A more complete exposition of M/M/1 and other queues (e.g., M/G/1, M/D/1, etc.) can be found in [65, 186, 202, 313].

A generic system that can be modeled using M/M/1 queue is shown in Figure A.1. There is a single-server serving customers from a waiting queue. The service discipline is strictly first-come-first-served (FCFS). Customer interarrival and the service times of customers are exponentially distributed. The queue is infinite, that is, all arriving customers enter the system and wait there until serviced. The only input parameters used in the analysis are the mean arrival rate, λ, and the mean service rate, μ.

There are a number of performance measures that can be obtained from M/M/1 queue. The most important performance measures, in the context of TCP/IP network analysis, are defined below. Table A.1 lists the formulas that are used to derive these measures.

Server load (ρ). This performance measure defines the load created on the server. For the formulas showed in Table A.1, the load is expected to be a fraction less than 1.0.

Mean time spent in the queue (W_q). The time spent in the queue is the time spent from the moment a customer enters the system to the moment it starts receiving service. W_q is the delay experienced by a customer *on average* while waiting for service.

Mean time spent in the system (W_s). The time spent in the system is the time spent from the moment a customer enters the system to the moment it departs the system. It is basically the time spent in the queue plus the service time. W_s is the time a customer spends in the system *on average*.

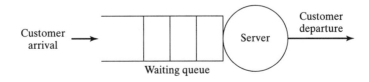

FIGURE A.1: A generic system model for M/M/1 queue.

TABLE A.1:   Formulas
for M/M/1 queue.

$$
\begin{aligned}
\rho &= \frac{\lambda}{\mu} \\
W_q &= \rho \frac{1/\mu}{1-\rho} \\
W_s &= \frac{1/\mu}{1-\rho} \\
N_q &= \frac{\rho^2}{1-\rho} \\
N_s &= \frac{\rho}{1-\rho} \\
P\{N_s \ge x\} &= \rho^x
\end{aligned}
$$

Mean number of customers in the queue (N_q). Number of customers waiting in the queue varies over time. N_q defines the average number of customers waiting in the queue over a period of time.

Mean number of customers in the system (N_s). N_s defines the average number of customers, waiting or being serviced, in the system over a period of time.

Probability of x or more customers in the system ($P\{N_s \ge x\}$). This is the probability that there will be x or more customers in the system at any given instant.

Now we turn to several examples to illustrate the application of M/M/1 performance measures and formulas in TCP/IP networks.

EXAMPLE A.1   Predicting packet delay in LAN router.

Question. Two LANs are often interconnected via one or more routers. Consider a campus network with two LANs, one for the Computer Science (CS) department and the other for the Electrical Engineering (EE) department, interconnected via a router. We are interested in predicting packet delays for CS-EE traffic. All packets from CS LAN to EE LAN must pass through this router. Now let us assume that packets arrive with a mean arrival rate of 1250 per second. The average packet length is 800 bytes, and packet length is assumed to be exponentially distributed. The router to EE LAN interface has a speed of 10 Mbps. The questions we have to answer are what is the mean packet delay in the router and how many packets are there in the router on average.

Answer. To answer these performance questions, we can use the W_s and N_s formulas in Table A.1. We have $\lambda = 1250$, $\mu = 10{,}000{,}000/(800 \times 8) = 1562.5$, and $\rho = 1250/1562.5 = 0.8$.

Mean packet delay in router is obtained as:

$$
W_s = \frac{1/\mu}{1-\rho} = 0.0032 \text{ or } 3.2 \text{ milliseconds.}
$$

Mean number of packets in router:

$$
N_s = \frac{\rho}{1-\rho} = 4 \text{ packets.}
$$

EXAMPLE A.2   Predicting packet loss rate in WAN gateway.

Question. Consider a multisite corporation with two sites interconnected via a WAN. In each site, a gateway connects the site LAN to the WAN. Measurements show that in the first site gateway, packets from LAN arrive at a mean rate of 125 packets per second, and the gateway takes 2 milliseconds on average to forward a packet to the WAN. Using an M/M/1 model, analyze the gateway to predict the number of buffers needed at the gateway to keep packet loss below one packet per million.

Answer. We have $\lambda = 125$, $\mu = 1/0.002 = 500$, and $\rho = 125/500 = 0.25$. Let us assume that x number of buffers keep packet loss rate below one packet per million. Applying the $P\{N_s \geq x\}$ formula from Table A.1,

$$\rho^x \leq 10^-6$$

or

$$x > log(10^-6)/log(0.25) = 9.96.$$

Therefore, we need about 10 buffers to keep the packet loss rate below the required threshold. This result is an approximation only. For true loss rates, one should use models with finite queues (not discussed in this appendix, but can be found in [65, 186, 202, 313]).

APPENDIX B

FreeBSD

TCP/IP was first introduced in FreeBSD [5], an advanced operating system for x86 compatible, DEC Alpha, and PC-98 architectures. It offers many features like advanced networking, performance, security, and compatibility. Moreover, FreeBSD and all of its source code are available free of charge. FreeBSD, therefore, provides an ideal platform for students to implement and experiment with new features of TCP/IP protocol stack. Also, because you will have total control over the operating system, you will be able to run all the freely available performance measurement tools discussed in Chapter 3, including the ones that require root access. This appendix provides a brief introduction to the installation of FreeBSD and discusses kernel modification and configuration through example.

B.1 INSTALLATION

FreeBSD can be installed from a variety of storage media including CD-ROM, DVD-ROM, floppy disk, and magnetic tape, or you can install it directly over an Internet connection. Compared to the installation of other operation systems such as MS-DOS or Windows, the installation process of FreeBSD is relatively complicated. It includes creating the boot floppy image, preinstallation configuration, committing the installation, and postinstallation configuration. The predefined options range from installing the smallest possible configuration to everything. FreeBSD is bundled with a rich collection of system tools as part of the base system. To use system tools provided by FreeBSD in your system, you should make sure that FreeBSD Ports Collection is chosen and installed. If a graphical user interface is desired, then an options set that is preceded by an X should be chosen. The latest version of FreeBSD can be found on the *FreeBSD Website* [5] and many mirror sites. The detailed, step-by-step installation instruction can be found in *FreeBSD Handbook* [4].

B.2 CONFIGURATION

Configuration of FreeBSD is very important. Correct system configuration prevents headaches and saves you valuable time in the future. The system configuration information is kept on the directory /etc and its subdirectories. In this section, the network card and network service configuration are discussed.

B.2.1 Network Card Configuration

To check the configuration for the network interfaces on your system, enter the following command:

```
% ifconfig
```

If the output shows something like:

```
dc0: flags=8843<UP,BROADCAST,RUNNING,SIMPLEX,MULTICAST> mtu 1500
inet 192.168.1.3 netmask 0xffffff00 broadcast 192.168.1.255
ether 00:a0:cc:da:da:da
media: Ethernet autoselect (100baseTX <full-duplex>)
status: active
```

it means the network card is configured and ready. The card has an Internet address 192.168.1.3. It has a valid subnet mask 0xffffff00 (255.255.255.0). It has a valid broadcast address 192.168.1.255. The Ethernet MAC address of the card is 00:a0:cc:da:da:da. The physical media selection is on autoselection mode (media: Ethernet autoselect (100baseTX <full-duplex>)).
If the output shows something like:

```
dc0: flags=8843<BROADCAST,SIMPLEX,MULTICAST> mtu 1500
ether 00:a0:cc:da:da:da
```

it indicates the card has not been configured. In this case you should edit the file /etc/rc.conf (the main system configuration file) to add the following line:

```
ifconfig_dc0=''inet 192.168.1.3 netmask 255.255.255.0''
```

B.2.2 Starting Network Services

Many Internet services such as TELNET and FTP can be enabled by editing the file /etc/inetd.conf. By default the Internet services are disabled. For example, FTP service is disabled if the file inetd.conf contains the following line:

```
#ftp   stream   tcp   nowait   root   /usr/libexec/ftpd   ftpd   -l
```

To enable the FTP service, simply remove # at the beginning of the line and run the command #netstart as the superuser (root).

B.3 KERNEL MODIFICATION

FreeBSD kernel is the core of the FreeBSD operating system. It is responsible for memory management, security control, networking, storage management, and so on. To change the kernel's behavior to support the new functionalities, you need to modify the kernel configuration file, modify the kernel source file, compile a new kernel, install the new kernel, and then reboot your computer with the new kernel.

B.3.1 Modify Kernel Configuration Files

First you need to modify the kernel configuration files. The most important kernel configuration file is GENERIC, which is located in the directory /usr/src/sys/arch/conf (Arch represents either i386, alpha, or pc98). In the kernel configuration file GENERIC, each line contains a keyword and one argument; #(hash) is used for the comment. For example, some networking-related options are shown like:

```
options        INET        #InterNETworking
options        INET6       #IPv6 communications protocols
```

The above two options enable the machine to support the internetworking of both IPv4 and IPv6. You can disable the services by adding # at the beginning of the line.

To enable the new functionality, copy GENERIC to the name you want to give your kernel (such as MYKERNEL) and add the new options in your kernel configuration file. In the following example, we use NEW_FUNCTION as the options argument to support a new kernel function.

```
#cd /usr/src/sys/i386/conf
#cp GENERIC MYKERNEL
```

Add the following line in file MYKERNEL:

```
options    NEW_FUNCTION
```

Again, this new kernel function can be disabled by commenting it out.

Another configuration file that must be modified is the file options located at the directory /usr/src/sys/conf. This file presents the mapping between the options in the configuration file and the options definition in the kernel source file. For the above example, the following line should be added in file options:

```
NEW_FUNCTION    opt_newfunction.h
```

If option NEW_FUNCTION is enabled in the kernel configuration file, it will be defined in file opt_newfunction.h:

```
#define    NEW_FUNCTION    1
```

The file opt_newfunction.h is automatically created when the kernel source is generated by command #config, and it is included by the kernel source files, which are modified to support the new kernel functionality.

B.3.2 Modify Kernel Source Files

The kernel source code is located at /usr/src/sys (or /sys). If you cannot access this directory, it means kernel source has not been installed in your computer. You can install the kernel source by simply running the command #/stand/sysinstall as root, choosing Configure, then Distributions, then Src, then Sys.

Now you can modify the kernel files (*.h or *.c files). The network-related files are located in the directory /usr/src/sys/netinet (for IPv4) and /usr/src/sys/netinet6 (for IPv6). You can simply add some new files or modify the existing files to represent your new kernel functionality. In Figure B.1, code 2 represents the original code in the kernel source file and the other code is the newly added code to support the new kernel functionality.

If NEW_FUNCTION is defined in opt_newfunction.h, which means option NEW_FUNCTION is enabled in the kernel configuration file, code 1, which supports the new functionality, will be executed; otherwise, the original kernel code 2 will be executed. In this way, you can simply switch on and off the options in the kernel configuration file to change the functionality of the kernel.

```
#include opt_newfunction.h

#ifdef NEW_FUNCTION
code 1 (code to support new kernel functionality)
#else
code 2 (original code)
#endif
```

FIGURE B.1: Kernel source modification.

B.3.3   Build and Install the New Kernel

Now, you are ready to compile and install your new kernel. Follow the following steps:

1. Generate the kernel source code.

   ```
   #/usr/sbin/config MYKERNEL
   ```

2. Change into the kernel source code directory.

   ```
   #cd ../../compile/MYKERNEL
   ```

   Make sure the file where the new kernel options is defined (for example, file opt_newfunction.h) is created in this directory.

3. Compile the kernel.

   ```
   #make depend
   #make
   ```

   "Make depend" takes about 5 minute and "make command" takes about 10 minutes to generate the new kernel binary file.

4. Install the new kernel.

   ```
   #make install
   ```

   The new kernel is copied to the root directory as /kernel and the old kernel is moved to /kernel.old. Now you can reboot the system to use your new kernel. Usually, the kernel reboot takes about 5 minutes.

B.3.4   Kernel Error Recovery Technique

There are four kinds of kernel error that can occur when building a new kernel.

1. **Config Fails.** Config command usually fails because of a simple error in your kernel configuration file such as misspelling of a keyword or argument. Config command prints the line number where the error happens, so you can quickly skip to it to find the error. The easiest way to correct the error is to compare your new kernel configuration file to the kernel file GENERIC.

2. **Make Fails.** Failure of "make command" may signal an error in your kernel description, but it may not be severe enough for config command to catch it. Again, check your new configuration file. "Make command" also fails due to some compile and link errors of the kernel source files. "Make command" prints the line number where the error happens. You should look over the modified and newly added kernel source code to find and correct the errors.

3. **Installing the New Kernel Fails.** If the kernel fails to install, you should check the system secure level of your computer using command #init. The kernel installation needs to be performed at secure level 0 or lower.

4. **The Kernel Fails to Work Properly.** If your new kernel fails to boot, you have to boot your machine using another kernel that works properly. When the system counts down from 10 in the booting process, hit any key except the Enter key, type *unload*, and then type *boot proper_kernel_file_name* (e.g., kernel.old). If your new kernel is not able to perform as you expected, you may need to debug the binary kernel file using your favorite debug tools such as gdb or DDD. You can also check the file /var/log/messages to find all the kernel log messages.

B.3.5   Kernel Modification Example

In this example, we increase the maximum TCP retransmission times from the default value of 12 to 17, so that the TCP connection reset duration is increased from 511 seconds to 831 seconds. Large TCP connection reset time prevents TCP resets during temporary blackouts in mobile networking (see the case study at the end of Chapter 7). FreeBSD 4.7 is used in this example. There are seven steps:

Step 1: Modify Kernel Configuration File

```
# cd /usr/src/sys/i386/conf
# cp GENERIC MYKERNEL
```

In file MYKERNEL, add the following line:

```
options    TCP_INCREASETIMER        #increase the TCP connection
reset timer from 511 seconds to 831 seconds.
```

It enables the new kernel functionality to increase TCP connection reset timer duration from 511 seconds to 831 seconds.

Step 2: Modify Kernel Configuration File options

```
#cd /usr/src/conf
```

In file options, add the following line:

```
TCP_INCREASETIMER      opt_tcpincreasetimer.h
```

It maps the configuration options TCP_INCREASETIMER to the kernel source file opt_tcpincreasetimer.h. In this case, the definition of

TCP_INCREASETIMER is enabled in the file opt_tcpincreasetimer.h. This definition is used in kernel source file tcp_timer.h and tcp_timer.c.

Step 3: Modify Kernel Source .h File

```
#cd /usr/src/sys/netinet
#ee tcp_timer.h
```

Figures B.2 and B.3 represent the original and modified code of tcp_timer.h respectively. According to the modified tcp_timer.h, if TCP_INCREASE TIMER is defined in the file opt_tcpincreasetimer.h, which means the option TCP_INCREASETIMER is enabled in file MYKERNEL, the maximum TCP retransmission times is 17 instead of 12.

Step 4: Modify Kernel Source .c File

```
#ee tcp_timer.c
```

Figures B.4 and Figure B.5 represent the original and modified code of tcp_timer.c, respectively. According to the modified tcp_timer.c, if TCP_INCREASETIMER is defined in the file opt_tcpincreasetimer.h, which means the option TCP_INCREASETIMER is enabled in file MYKER-NEL, the TCP backoff time will be increased to 831 seconds because of five additional 64-seconds backoffs.

Step 5: Generate Kernel Source Code

```
#cd /usr/src/sys/i368/conf
#/usr/sbin/config MYKERNEL
```

```
#define TCP_MAXRXTSHIFT 12
```

FIGURE B.2: Original code of tcp_timer.h.

```
#include <sys/compile/MYKERNEL/opt_tcpincreasetimer.h>

#ifdef TCP_INCREASTIMER
#define TCP_MAXRXTSHIFT 17
#else
#define TCP_MAXRXTSHIFT 12
#endif
```

FIGURE B.3: Modified code of tcp_timer.h.

```
int tcp_backoff[TCP_MAXRXSHIFT + 1] =
{1, 2, 4, 8, 16, 32, 64, 64, 64, 64, 64, 64, 64};
static int tcp_totbackoff = 511;
```

FIGURE B.4: Original code of tcp_timer.c.

```
#include <sys/compile/MYKERNEL/opt_tcpincreasetimer.h>

#ifdef TCP_INCREASETTIMER
int tcp_backoff[TCP_MAXRXSHIFT + 1] =
  {1, 2, 4, 8, 16, 32, 64, 64, 64, 64, 64, 64, 64, 64, 64, 64, 64, 64};
static int tcp_totbackoff = 831;
#else
int tcp_backoff[TCP_MAXRXSHIFT + 1] =
  {1, 2, 4, 8, 16, 32, 64, 64, 64, 64, 64, 64, 64};
static int tcp_totbackoff = 511
#endif
```

FIGURE B.5: Modified code of tcp_timer.c.

All the .h files declared in file `/usr/src/sys/conf/options` will be automatically generated. Check the file `opt_tcpincreasetimer.h` and make sure it includes the following line:

```
#define   TCP_INCREASETIMER      1
```

Step 6: Compile the New Kernel

```
# cd ../../compile/MYKERNEL
# make depend
# make
```

Step 7: Install the New Kernel

```
# make install
```

Now reboot your computer. You will be able to enjoy the new kernel with increased TCP reset time running on your machine!

APPENDIX C

TCP Auto-Tuning

In previous chapters, we have discussed advanced TCP modifications needed to optimize performance in different networking environments. In some cases, however, advanced modifications to TCP algorithms and semantics are not necessary to improve performance; rather simple tuning of key parameters can eliminate performance bottleneck. One such tuning often used is the setting of an appropriate TCP buffer (or window) size so that the full bandwidth of the underlying channel can be utilized without being bottlenecked by window flow control. Automatically tuning the buffer size is referred to as *TCP auto-tuning*. This appendix presents the motivation for TCP auto-tuning, followed by a brief introduction to available auto-tuning techniques and products.

C.1 MOTIVATION FOR TCP AUTO-TUNING

In today's computing and communication infrastructure, most TCP/IP implementations set a 64 KB buffer size. Although this default setting works well in some cases, it fails to achieve optimal performance in others. For example, users working from home with a 56 Kbps modem connection to their office have a bandwidth-delay product on the order of 56 Kbps × 5 ms = 36 B. In this case, 99% of memory allocated is wasted. In contrast, a long-distance, 622 Mbps ATM link with 100 ms RTT needs a buffer size of 7.8 MB to fill the pipe. In this case, a default 64 KB buffer setting would waste 99% network bandwidth. It is, therefore, necessary to tune the buffer size to optimize performance without wasting memory or network resources[1].

Manual tuning requires kernel configurations that cannot be accomplished by end applications. System administrators have to do such configurations at both ends of a TCP connection (a tedious and time-consuming process). Furthermore, manual tuning only works for the pair of TCP hosts for which buffers have been configured. To avoid such manual tuning, techniques are needed to automatically and transparently tune TCP buffers without any human intervention. In the following section, we discuss the available techniques and products for TCP auto-tuning.

C.2 TCP AUTO-TUNING TECHNIQUES AND PRODUCTS

There are six known auto-tuning techniques and products [318]:

1. PSC tuning [288]. Pittsburgh Supercomputing Center (PSC) developed a TCP auto-tuning technique that allows a sender to estimate bandwidth-delay product of a connection using TCP header information and the timestamp option.

---

[1]Tuning helps improve TCP performance for large data transfers. For short transactions, where propagation delay plays a major role, buffer tuning is irrelevant.

2. Dynamic Right Sizing (DRS) [318]. Similar to PSC's technique, except here the receiver estimates the delay bandwidth product and advertises a large enough window to sender.

3. Linux 2.4 auto-tuning [309]. This is basically a memory management technique in the kernel of Linux 2.4. Buffer size is reduced (some memory is freed) if most of it remains unused, and it is increased (more memory is allocated) if it becomes full. As a side effect of this memory management, TCP enjoys auto-tuning of its buffers.

4. Enable tuning [306]. It runs a daemon to gather data on the pair of hosts between which auto-tuning is required and saves information regarding bandwidth-delay products in a database. Hosts then look up this database before opening a connection and set the buffer size accordingly.

5. Auto-tuned ncFTP [252]. It estimates bandwidth-delay product using the control connection before starting the data connection.

6. DRS FTP [151]. This technique is similar to auto-tuned ncFTP. The difference is that it continues to adjust the buffer during the lifetime of the data connection.

C.3   SELECTING AUTO-TUNED TCP

For a given communication task at hand, one auto-tuning technique may be more suitable than the others. In their recent article, Weigle and Feng [318] compared six tuning techniques based on the following four criteria (see Table C.1 for a summary of this comparison):

User-level versus kernel-level refers to whether the tuning can be accomplished at the user level or kernel configuration is required.

Static versus dynamic refers to whether the buffer size is adjusted once at the start of a connection or it is dynamically adjusted throughout the lifetime of a connection.

In-band versus out-band refers to whether bandwidth-delay product information of the connection is estimated directly from the connection or obtained through separate process.

Transparent versus visible refers to how intrusive the technique is. For completely transparent solutions, users do not notice that they are using an auto-tuned TCP.

TABLE C.1: A comparison of TCP auto-tuning techniques.

Tuning	*Level*	*Setting*	*Band*	*Visibility*
PSC	Kernel	Dynamic	In	Transparent
Linux 2.4	Kernel	Dynamic	In	Transparent
DRS	Kernel	Dynamic	In	Transparent
Enable	User	Static	Out	Visible
ncFTP	User	Static	Out	Opaque
DRS FTP	User	Dynamic	Both	Opaque

C.4 FURTHER READING

The Web100 [23] and Net100 [10] projects aim to develop software and tools for end hosts to automatically achieve high data rates over the high-performance research networks. The data intensive distributed computing research (DIDC) group at the Lawrence Berkeley National Laboratory (LBNL) maintains a TCP tuning guide [16], which, among other things, includes a summary of how to manually set the buffer size in popular operating systems, including Linux, Solaris, IRIX, and FreeBSD. If there are multiple TCP connections in a host trying to set large buffers, there may be a memory depletion problem. If memory is not available, a TCP connection will not be able to set the desired buffer size. In such cases, a fair-share algorithm helps allocating memory resources fairly among competing TCP connections. Semke [287] describes the implementation issues of auto-tuning fair-share algorithms.

Bibliography

1. *Analyzer homepage.* http://analyzer.polito.it.

2. *CAIDA homepage.* http://www.caida.org/tools/.

3. *CISCO Systems home page.* http://www.cisco.com.

4. *FreeBSD handbook.* http://www.freebsd.org/doc/en_US.ISO8859-1/books/handbook/index.html.

5. FreeBSD website. http://www.freebsd.org.

6. *Internet2 Land Speed Record.* http://www.internet2.edu/lsr.

7. *Juniper Networks home page.* http://www.juniper.net.

8. *Los Alamos National Laboratory.* URL:http://public.lanl.gov/radiant/research/measurement/traces.html.

9. *The National Laboratory for Applied Network Research (NLANR).* URL:http://pma.nlanr.net/Traces/.

10. *Net100 home page.* http://www.net100.org.

11. *Netspec homepage.* http://www.ittc.ku.edu/netspec.

12. *Nettest homepage.* http://www-itg.lbl.gov/nettest.

13. *Pathrate homepage.* http://www.pathrate.org.

14. *SkyX GatewayTechnology, White Paper.*

15. *Surveyor homepage.* http://www.advanced.org/surveyor/.

16. Tcp tuning guide. http://www-didc.lbl.gov/TCP-tuning/.

17. *TCP Westwood home page.* http://www.cs.ucla.edu/NRL/hpi/tcpw/index.html.

18. *Tcpillust homepage.* http://www.csl.sony.co.jp/person/nishida/tcpillust.html.

19. *Tcptrace homepage.* http://www.cs.ohiou.edu/software/tcptrace/tcptrace.html.

20. *Telecommunication Networks Group (TKN), Technical University of Berlin.* URL:http://www-tkn.ee.tu-berlin.de/research/trace/trace.html.

21. *Traceroute homepage.* http://www.traceroute.org.

22. *Ttcp homepage.* ftp://ftp.arl.mil/pub/ttcp.

23. *Web100 home page.* http://www.web100.org.

24. *The WIDE Project in Japan.* URL:http://mawi.wide.ad.jp/mawi/.

25. *Proceedings of the IEEE, Special Issue on Satellite Communications*, November 1984.

26. *Proceedings of the IEEE, Special Issue on Satellite Communications*, July 1990.

27. A possible method to enhance TCP/IP performance on satellite links. document 4b/61, ITU, September 2001.

28. Ian Akyildiz, Giacome Morabito, and Sergio palazzo. Research issues for transport protocols in satellite IP networks. *IEEE Personal Communications*, pages 44–48, June 2001.

29. Ian F. Akyildiz, Giacomo Morabito, and Sergio Palazzo. TCP-Peach: a new congestion control scheme for satellite ip networks. *IEEE Transaction on Networking*, 9(3):307–321, June 2001.

30. Ian F. Akyildiz, Xin Zhang, and Jian Fang. TCP-Peach: Enhancement of TCP-Peach for satellite IP networks. *IEEE Communications Letters*, 6(7):303–305, July 2002.

31. T. Alanko, M. Kojo, H. Laamanen, M. Liljeberg, M. Moilanen, and K. Raatikainen. Measured performance of data transmission over cellular telephone networks. *Computer Communications Review*, 24(5):24–44, October 1994.

32. M. Allman. TCP congestion control with Appropriate Byte Counting ABC. RFC 3465, IETF, February 2003.

33. M. Allman et al. Ongoing TCP research related to satellites. RFC 2760, IETF, February 2000.

34. M. Allman, S. Floyd, and C. Partridge. Increasing TCP's initial window. RFC 3390, IETF, October 2002.

35. M. Allman, D. Glover, and L. Sanchez. Enhancing TCP over satellite channels using standard mechanisms. RFC 2488, IETF, January 1999.

36. M. Allman, V. Paxon, and W. Stevens. TCP congestion control. RFC 2581, IETF, April 1999.

37. Mark Allman. Improving TCP performance over satellite channels. Master's thesis, Ohio University, June 1997.

38. Mark Allman. On the generation and use of TCP acknowledgements. *ACM Computer Communication Review*, 28(5): 4–21, October 1998.

39. Mark Allman. TCP byte counting refinements. *ACM Computer Communication Review*, 29(3): 14–22, July 1999.

40. Mark Allman, Jim Griner, and Alan Richard. TCP behavior in networks with dynamic propagation delay. In *Proceedings of IEEE Globecom 2000*, pages 1103–1108, November 2000.

41. Mark Allman, Chris Hayes, Hans Kruse, and Shawn Osterman. TCP performance over satellite links. In *Proceedings of 5th International Conference on Telecommunication Systems*, 1997, pp. 456–469.

42. Mark Allman, Hans Kruse, and Shawn Ostermann. Data transfer efficiently over satellite circuits using a multi-socket extension to the file transfer protocol FTP. In *Proceedings of ACTS Results Conference*, September 1995.

43. Mark Allman, Hans Kruse, and Shawn Ostermann. An application level solution to TCPs satellite inefficiencies. In *Proceedings of the First International Workshop on Satellite-based Information Services*, Nov 1996.

44. Mark Allman, Vern Paxson, and W. Stevens. TCP congestion control. RFC2581, IETF, April 1999.

45. G. Almes, S. Kalidindi, and M. Zekauskas. *A One-way Delay Metric for IPPM*. RFC2679, IETF, September 1999.

46. G. Almes, S. Kalidindi, and M. Zekauskas. *A One-way Packet Loss Metric for IPPM*. RFC2680, IETF, September 1999.

47. G. Almes, S. Kalidindi, and M. Zekauskas. *RFC2681: A Round-trip Delay Metric for IPPM*, September 1999.

48. E. Altman, K. Avrachenkov, and C. Barakat. A stochastic model of TCP/IP with stationary random losses. *Proceedings of ACM SIGCOMM*, August 2000.

49. Farooq M. Anjum and Leandros Tassiulas. Balanced RED: An algorithm to achieve fairness in the Internet. Technical Report TR99-17, 1999, Department of Electrical Engineering and Institute for Systems Research, University of Maryland at College Park.

50. Vivek Arara, Narin Suphasindhu, and Douglas Dillon. Asymmetric Internet access over satellite-terrestrial networks. In *Proceedings of AIAA: 16th International Communications Satellite Systems and Exhibits, Part 1*, pages 476–482, February 1996.

51. Sanjeewa Athuralyia, Steven H. Low, Victor H. Li, and Qinghe Yin. REM:active queue management. *IEEE Network Magazine*, pages 48–53, May/June 2001.

52. D. O. Awduche, Y. Rekhter, J. Drake, and R. Coltun. *Multi-Protocol Lambda Switching: Combining MPLS Traffic Engineering Control With Optical Crossconnects*. IETF Draft draft-awduche-mpls-te-optical-03.txt, 2001.

53. Editor B. Carpenter, ed. Architectural principles of the internet. RFC 1958, IETF, June 1996.

54. A. Bakre and B. R. Badrinath. I-TCP: Indirect TCP for mobile hosts. In *Proceedings of the 15th International COnference on Distributed COmputing Systems*, May 1995, pp. 136–143.

55. A. Bakre and B. R. Badrinath. Implementation and performance evaluation of Indirect-TCP. *IEEE Transactions on Computers*, 46(3):260–278, March 1997.

56. H. Balakrishnan. *Challenges to Reliable Data Transport over Heterogeneous Wireless Networks*. PhD thesis, University of California at Berkeley, August 1998.

57. H. Balakrishnan and R. Katz. Explicit loss notification and wireless web performance. In *IEEE Globecom* Internet Mini Conference, November 1998.

58. H. Balakrishnan, V. N. Padmanabhan, S. Seshan, and R. H. Katz. A comparison of mechanisms for improving TCP performance over wireless links. *IEEE/ACM Transactions on Networking*, 5(6):756–769, December 1997.

59. H. Balakrishnan, S. Seshan, E. Amir, and R. Katz. Improving TCP/IP performance over wireless networks. In *Proceedings of ACM Conference on Mobile Computing and Networking*, November 1995, pp. 2–11.

60. H. Balakrishnan, S. Seshan, and R. H. Katz. Improving reliable transport and handoff performance in cellular wireless networks. *Wireless Networks*, 1(4):469–481, 1995.

61. Hari Balakrishnan, Randy Katz, and Venkata N. Padmanabhan. The effects of asymmetry on TCP performance. *Mobile Networks and Applications*, 4(3):219–241, 1999.

62. Gaurav Banga and Jeffrey C. Mogul. Scalable kernel performance for Internet servers under realistic loads. In *Proceedings of the USENIX Annual Technical Conference*, pages 1–12, June 1998.

63. J. Banks and J. S. Carson. *Discrete-Event System Simulation*. Upper Saddle River, NJ: Prentice Hall, 1984.

64. Robert Bauer. New opportunities with the advanced communications technology satellite (acts), satellite networks: Architectures, applications, and technologie. In *Workshop NASA/CP-1998-208524, Cleveland, Ohio*, June 1998.

65. D. Bertsekas and R. Gallager. *Data Networks*. Upper Saddle River, NJ: Prentice Hall, 1987.

66. V. Bharghavan, A. Demers, S. Shenker, and L. Zhang. MACAW: A Medium Access Protocol for Wireless LANs. In *Proceedings of ACM SIGCOMM*, 24(4):212–225, August 1994.

67. David A. Borman. Implementing TCP/IP on a Cray computer. *ACM SIGCOMM, Computer Communication Review*, 19(2):11–15, April 1989.

68. C. Bormann. The Multi-Class Extension to Multi-Link PPP. RFC 2686, IETF, September 1999.

69. B. Braden, D. Clark, J. Crowcroft, B. Davie, S. Deering, D. Estrin, S. Floyd, V. Jacobson, G. Minshall C. Partridge, L. Peterson, K. Ramakrishnan, S. Shenker, J Wroclawski, and L. Zhang. Recommendations on queue management and congestion avoidance in the Internet. RFC 2309, IETF, April, 1998.

70. R. Braden. Requirements for internet hosts—communication layers. RFC 1123, IETF, October 1989.

71. R. Braden. T/TCP-TCP extensions for transactions, functional specifications. RFC 1644, IETF, July 1994.

72. L. Brakmo, S. O'Malley, and L. Peterson. TCP vegas: New techniques for congestion detection and avoidance. In *Proceedings of the ACM SIGCOMM*, pages 24–35, August 1994.

73. J. Broch, D. B. Johnson, and D. A. Maltz. The Dynamic Source Routing Protocol for Mobile Ad Hoc Networks. *Internet Draft draft-ietf-manet-dsr-03.txt*, October 1999.

74. J. Broch, D. A. Maltz, D. B. Johnson, Y.-C. Hu, and J. Jetcheva. A Performance Comparison of Multi-Hop Wireless Ad Hoc Network Routing Protocols. In *Proceedings ACM MOBICOM*, October 1998, pp. 85–97.

75. K. Brown and S. Singh. M-TCP: TCP for mobile cellular networks. *Computer Communications Review*, 27(5):19–43, October 1997.

76. Jose Brustoloni and Peter Steenkiste. The effects of buffering semantics on I/O performance. In *Proceedings of the Second USENIX Symposium on Operating System Design and Implementation (OSDI)*, pages 277–291. USENIX Association, October 1996.

77. Greg Buzzard, David Jacobson, Milon Mackey, Scott Marovich, and John Wilkes. An implementation of the Hamlyn sender-managed interface architecture. ACM SIGOPS Operating Systems Review, 30(51): pp. 245–259.

78. C. Perkins. IP Mobility Support. *RFC 2002*, IETF, October 1996.

79. CACI Products Company, La Jolla, CA, USA. *COMNET III User's Manual*. URL:http://www.caciasl.com/.

80. CACI Products Company, La Jolla, CA, USA. *GPSS/H User's Manual*. URL:http://www.caciasl.com/.

81. CACI Products Company, La Jolla, CA, USA. *Network II.5 User's Manual*. URL:http://www.caciasl.com/.

82. CACI Products Company, La Jolla, California, USA. *SIMSCRIPT II.5 Reference Handbook*. URL:http://www.caciasl.com/.

83. F. Callegati. Optical buffers for variable length packets. *IEEE Communications Letters*, 4(9):292–294, 2000.

84. F. Callegati, H. C. Cankaya, Y. Xiong, and M. Vandenhoute. Design issues for optical ip routers. *IEEE Communication Magazine*, 37(12):124–128, 1999.

85. F. Callegati, M. Casoni, G. Corazza, C. Raffaelli, D. Chiaroni, F. Masetti, and M. Sotom. Architecture and performance of a broadcast and select photonic switch. *Optical Fiber Technology*, 4:266–284, 1998.

86. F. Callegati and W. Cerroni. Wavelength selection algorithms in optical buffers. In *IEEE International Conference on Communications*. June 2001, Vol. 2, pp. 499–503.

87. F. Callegati and C. Raffaelli. End-to-end delay evaluation for an optical transparent packet network. *Photonic Network Communications* 1(2):147–160, 1999.

88. C. Casetti, M. Gerla, S. Mascolo, M. Y. Sanadidi, and R. Wang. TCP westwood: Bandwidth estimation for enhanced transport over wireless links. Wireless Networks, 8(5):467–479, 2002.

89. G. Yang, R. Wang., M. Y. Sanadidi and, M. Gerla. Performance of TCPW BR in next generation wireless and satellite networks. UCCLA CSD Technical report no. 020025, 2002, Los Angeles, CA90095, USA.

89a. V. Cerf. *TCP Version 2 Specification*, USC/Information Sciences Institute, IEN-5, March 1977.

90. V. Cerf. *TCP Specification 3*, IEN21, IETF, January 1978.

91. V. Cerf, Y. Dalal, and C. Sunshine. *Specification of Internet Transmission Control Program*, RFC 675, IETF, December 1974.

92. V. Cerf and R. Kahn. A protocol for packet network interconnection. *IEEE Transactions on Communications*, volume COM22, May 1974.

93. A. Chandra, V. Gummalla, and J. O. Limb. Wireless medium access control protocols. *IEEE Communications Surveys and Tutorials*, 3(2), 2000.

94. Abhishek Chandra and David Mosberger. Scalability of Linux event-dispatch mechanisms. In *Proceedings of the USENIX Annual Technical Conference*, pages 231–244, June 2001.

95. K. Chandran, S. Raghunathan, S. Venkatesan, and R. Prakash. A Feedback Based Scheme for Improving TCP Performance in Ad-hoc Wireless Networks. *IEEE Personal Communications*, 8(1):34–39, Feb. 2001.

96. Wu Chang Feng and Wu chi Feng. The impact of active queue management on multimedia congestion control. In *IEEE IC3N98*, Louisiana, Oct, 1998, pp. 214–218.

97. Wu Chang Feng, Dilip D Kandlur, and Debanjan Saha. Adaptive packet marking for maintaining end to end throughput in a differentiated service Internet. *IEEE/ACM Transactions on Networking*, 7(5):685–697, Oct, 1999.

98. Wu Chang Feng, Dilip D Kandlur, Debanjan Saha, and G Kang. Self-configuring RED gateway. In *IEEE INFOCOM99*, pages 1320–1328, New York, March, 1999.

99. Wu Chang Feng, Dilip D. Kandlur, Debanjan Saha, and Kang G. Shin. BLUE: A new class of active queue management algorithm. Technical Report CSETR-387-99, University of Michigan, April, 1999.

100. Wu Chang Feng, Dilip D. Kandlur, Debanjan Saha, and Kang G. Shin. Stochastic fair blue: A queue management algorithm for enforcing fairness. In *IEEE INFOCOM2001*, Anchorage, Alaska, USA, April 22–26, 2001, Vol. 3, pp. 1520–1529.

101. C. P. Charalambos, G. Y. Lazarou, V. S. Frost, J. Evans, and R. Jonkman. Experimental and simulation performance results of tcp/ip over high-speed atm over acts. In *IEEE International Conference on Communication (ICC)*, volume 1, pages 72–78, 1998.

102. Jeffrey S. Chase, Andrew J. Gallatin, and Kenneth G. Yocum. End system optimizations for high-speed TCP. *IEEE Communications, Special Issue on High-Speed TCP*, 39(4):68–74, April 2001.

103. B. Chatschik. An overview of the Bluetooth wireless technology. *IEEE Communications Magazine*, 39(12):86–94, December 2001.

104. Girish Chiruvolu and Saravut Charcranoon. An efficient edge-based congestion management for a differentiated services domain. In *IEEE IC3N2000*, pages 75–80, Las Vegas, Nevada, USA, Oct 16–18, 2000.

105. Prakash Chitre. Satellite communications and interoperability, satellite networks: Architectures, applications, and technologies. In *Workshop NASA/CP-1998-208524, Cleveland, Ohio*, pages 3–9, June. 1998.

106. Mikkel Christiansen, Kevin Jeffay, David Ott, and F. Donelson Smith. Tuning RED for web traffic. In *Proceedings of ACM SIGCOMM2000*, Stockholm, Sweden, August, 2000, Vol. 30, No. 4, pp. 139–150.

107. K. Claffy, G. Miller, and K. Thompson. The nature of the beast: recent traffic measurements from an internet backbone. In *http://www.caida.org/Papers/Inet98/index.html*, July 1998.

108. David D. Clark, Van Jacobson, John Romkey, and Howard Salwen. An analysis of TCP processing overhead. *IEEE Communications Magazine*, 27(6):23–29, June 1989.

109. David D. Clark and David L. Tennenhouse. Architectural considerations for a new generation of protocols. In *SIGCOMM Symposium on Communications Architectures and Protocols*, pages 200–208. ACM, September 1990.

110. R. Cohen and Y. Hamo. Balanced packet discard for improving tcp performance in atm networks. In *Infocom*. IEEE, 2000, Vol. 3, pp. 1556–1565.

111. Comdisco Systems, Inc. (acquired by Cadence), Foster City, CA, USA. *BONeS DESIGNER User's Guide*. URL:http://www.cadence.com.

112. D. Comer and D. Stevens. *Internetworking with TCP/IP Vol. II: ANSI C Version: Design, Implementation and Internals*. Upper Saddle River, NJ: Prentice Hall, 1991.

113. D. E. Comer. *Internetworking with TCP/IP Vol 1: Principles, Protocols, and Architecture*, 2nd edition. Upper Saddle River, NJ: Prentice Hall, 1991.

114. C. Qiao. Labeled optical burst switching for ip over dwdm integration. *IEEE Communications Magazine*, 38(9):104–114, 2000.

115. B. P. Crow, I. Widjaja, J. Geun Kim, and P. T. Sakai. IEEE 802.11 wireless local area networks. *IEEE Communications Magazine*, 35(9):116–126, September 1997.

116. Ole-Johan Dahl and Kristen Nygaard. *The Simula Programming Language*. Norwegian Computing Center (NCC), Oslo, Norway. URL:http://www.idiom.com/free-compilers/TOOL/Simula-1.html.

117. E. Dahlman, B. Gudmundson, M. Nilsson, and A. Sköld. UMTS/IMT-2000 based on wideband CDMA. *IEEE Communications Magazine*, 36(9):70–80, September 1998.

118. B. Davie, P. Doolan, and Y. Rekhter. *Switching in IP Networks*. Morgan Kaufmann, San Francisco, 1998.

119. M. Degermark, Mathias Engan, Bjorn Nordgren, and Stephen Pink. Low-loss TCP/IP header compression for wireless networks. *Wireless Networks*, 3(5):375–387, 1997.

120. M. Degermark, B. Nordgren, and S. Pink. IP header compression. RFC 2507, IETF, February 1999.

121. IEEE Standards Department. Wireless LAN medium access control (MAC) and physical layer (PHY) specifications. 18 Nov 1997, pp. 1–445, IEEE Std 802.11—1997.

122. A. DeSimone, M. C. Chuah, and O. C. Yue. Throughput performance of transport-layer protocols over wireless LANs. In *Proceedings of the IEEE GLOBECOM '93*, pages 542–549, December 1993.

123. Peter Druschel, Larry L. Peterson, and Bruce S. Davie. Experience with a high-speed network adaptor: A software perspective. In *Proceedings of the SIGCOMM Symposium on Communications Architectures and Protocols*. ACM, August 1994, Vol. 24, No. 4, pp. 2–13.

124. D. Duchamp and N. F. Reynolds. Measured performance of a wireless LAN. In *Proceedings of the 17th IEEE Conference on Local Computer Networks*, pages 494–499, September 1992.

125. Robert C. Durst, Gregory J. Miller, and Eric J. Travis. TCP extension for space communications. In *Proceedings of Mobicom '96*, pages 15–26, 1996.

126. D. Eckhardt and P. Steenkiste. Measurement and analysis of the error characteristics of an in-building wireless network. In *Proceedings of the ACM SIGCOMM '96*, pages 243–254, August 1996.

127. D. Eckhardt and P. Steenkiste. Improving wireless LAN performance via adaptive local error control. In *Proceedings of the ICNP'98*, 1998, pp. 370–378.

128. C. Bormann Editor. Robust header compression ROHC. RFC 3095, IETF, July 2001.

129. G. Pelletier Editor. Robust header compression ROHO, TCP/IP profile ROHC-TCP. INTERNET-DRAFT draft-ietf-rohc-tcp-03.txt, work in progress, IETF, November 2002.

130. Bruce R. Elbert. *Introduction to satellite communication*. Boston: Artech House, 1999.

131. Bruce R. Elbert. *Ground Segment and Earth Station Handbook*. Boston: Artech-House, 2001.

132. C. Guillemot, et al. Transparent optical packet switching: the European acts keops project approach. *IEEE Journal on Lightwave Technology*, 16(12):2117–2134, 1998.

133. D. K. Hunter, et al. Waspnet: A wavelength switched packet network. *IEEE Communication Magazine*, 37(3):120–129, 1999.

134. L. Chlamtac, et al. Cord: contention resolution by delay lines. *IEEE Journal on Selected Areas in Communications*, 14(5):1014–1029, 1996.

135. P. Gambini, et al. Transparent optical packet switching: network architecture and demonstrators in the KEOPS project. *IEEE Journal on Selected Areas in Communications*, 16(7):1245–1259, 1998.

136. J. Border, et al. Performance enhancing proxies intended to mitigate link-related degradations. RFC 3135, IETF, June 2001.

137. B. G. Evans, editor. *Satellite Communication Systems*, Third Edition. London: IEE, 1999.

138. J. V. Evans. The US proposed new multimedia communications satellite systems. In *Proceedings of 2000 IEEE Aerospace Conference, Big Sky, Montana*, March 2000, Vol. 1, pp. 229–240.

139. K. Fall and S. Floyd. Simulation-based comparisons of Tahoe, Reno, and SACK TCP. *ACM Computer Communication Review*, 26(3):5–21, July 1996.

140. Wenjia Fang and Larry Peterson. TCP mechanisms for diff-serv architecture. Technical Report TR-605-99, Computer Science Department, Princeton University, Princeton, NJ, September 1999.

141. R. Fielding et al. Hypertext transfer protocol—HTTP/1.1. RFC 2068, IETF, January 1997.

142. Victor Firoiu and Marty Borden. A study of active queue management for congestion control. In *IEEE INFOCOM2000*, Tel-Aviv, Israel, March 26–30, 2000, Vol. 3, pp. 1435–1444.

143. S. Floyd. TCP and explicit congestion notification. *ACM Computer Communication Review*, 24(5):10–23, October 1994.

144. S. Floyd, M. Handley, J. Padhye, and J. Widmer. Equation-based congestion control for unicast applications. *Proceedings of ACM SIGCOMM*, August 2000.

145. S. Floyd and T. Henderson. The NewReno modification to TCP's fast recovery algorithm. RFC 2582, April 1999.

146. S. Floyd and V. Jacobson. Random early detection gateways for congestion avoidance. *IEEE/ACM Transactions on Networking*, 1(4):397–413, August 1993.

147. Sally Floyd. Highspeed TCP for large congestion windows. Internet draft draft-floyd-tcp-highspeed-01.txt, IETF, August 2002.

148. Sally Floyd and Kevin Fall. Promoting the use of end-to-end congestion control in the internet. *IEEE/ACM Transaction on Networking*, August 1999, Vol. 7, Issue 4, pp. 458–472.

149. B. A. Forouzan. *TCP/IP Protocol Suite*. New York: McGraw Hill, 2000.

150. A. Furuskär, S. Mazur, F. Müller, and H. Olofsson. EDGE: Enhanced data rates for GSM and TDMA/136 evolution. *IEEE Personal Communications*, 6(3):56–66, June 1999.

151. M. K. Gardner, W-C. Feng, and M. Fisk. Dynamic right-sizing in ftp (drsftp): Enhancing grid performance in user-space. In *IEEE International Symposium on High Performance Distributed Computing*, pages 42–49, 2002.

152. Nasir Ghani and Sudhir Dixit. TCP/IP enhancements for satellite networks. *IEEE Communications Magazine*, 37(7):64–72, July 1999.

153. Daniel R. Glover and Hans Kruse. TCP performance in a geostationary satellite environment. In *Annual Review of Communications 1998, International Engineering Consortium*, April 1998.

154. T. Goff, J. Moronski, and D. S. Phatak. Freeze-TCP: A True End-to-End TCP Enhancement Mechanism for Mobile Environments. In *IEEE INFOCOM*, pages 1537–1545, 2000.

155. Yurong H. and Victor O. K. Li. Satellite-based internet: A tutorial. *IEEE Communications Magazine*, 39(3):154–162, March 2001.

156. Z. J. Haas and M. R. Pearlman. The Zone Routing Protocol (ZRP) for Ad Hoc Networks. *Internet Draft draft-zone-routing-protocol-01.txt*, August 1998.

157. Go Hasegawa, Takahiro Matsuo, Masayuki Murata, and Hideo Miyahara. Comparisons of packet scheduling algorithms for fair service among connections on the Internet. In *IEEE INFOCOM2000*, pages 1253–1262, Tel-Aviv, Israel, March 26–30, 2000.

158. M. Hassan and M. Atiquzzaman. *Performance of TCP/IP over ATM Networks.* Artech House, Boston 2000.

159. M. Hassan and H. Sirisena. Optimal Control of Queues in Computer Networks. In *IEEE International Conference on Communications (ICC)*, Helsinki, Finland, June 2001.

160. J. Heinanen, F. Baker, W. Weiss, and J Wroclawski. Assured forwarding PHB. RFC 2597, IETF, June, 1999.

161. T. Henderson. Design principles and performance analysis of SSCOP: a new atm adaptation layer protocol. In *ACM SIGCOMM Computer Communications Review*, 25(2):47–59, April 1995.

162. Thomas Henderson and Randy Katz. Transport protocols for internet-compatible satellite networks. *IEEE Journal on Selected Areas of Communications*, February 1999, Vol. 17, Issue 2, 326–344.

163. Thomas R. Henderson. *Networking over next-generation satellite systems.* PhD thesis, University of California at Berkeley, 1999.

164. Thomas R. Henderson and Randy H. Katz. TCP performance over satellite channels. UCB Computer Science Technical Report 99-1083, UCB, December 1999.

165. Urs Hengartner, Jurg Bolliger, and Thomas Gross. TCP vegas revisited. In *INFOCOM (3)*, pages 1546–1555, 2000.

166. Paul Herman. *tcpstat*, 2000. Manual Page. http://frenchfries.net/paul/tcpstat.

167. J. Hoe. Improving the start-up behavior of a congestion control scheme for TCP. In *Proceedings of the ACM SIGCOMM*, pages 270–280, August 1996.

168. Christopher F. Hoeber. 2000: The year of the network access satellite. In *51st International Astronautical Congress, Rio de Janeiro, Brazil*, IAF-00.M.1.0.3, October 2000.

169. Hsiao-Keng and Jerry Chu. Zero-copy TCP in Solaris. In *Proceedings of the USENIX Annual Technical Conference*, January 1996.

170. Tino Hutschenreuther and Alexander Schill. Content based discarding in IP router. In *IEEE IC3N2000*, pages 122–126, Las Vegas, Nevada, USA, Oct. 16–18, 2000.

171. ITU-T Recommendation I.380. *Internet Protocol (IP) Data Communication Service—IP Packet Transfer and Availability Performance Parameters*, February 1999.

172. J. Mitola III and G.Q. Maguire Jr. Cognitive radio: making software radios more personal. *IEEE Personal Communications*, 6(4):13–18, August 1999.

173. Loral CyberStar Inc. *TCP/IP Performance over Satellite Links—Summary Report.* http://www.adec.edu/nsf/tcpip-performance.pdf.

174. Intelsat. Impacts of FSS performance objectives and delay on the transmission of TCP/IP over satellites. Contribution ITU-R 4B/38-E, ITU, April 2001.

175. IP Performance Metrics (ippm) Working Group. *Internet Engineering Task Force (IETF).* http://www.ietf.org/html.charters/ippm-charter.html.

176. Joseph Ishac and Mark Allman. On the performance of TCP spoofing in satellite networks. In *Proceedings of IEEE Milcom*, IAF-00.M.1.0.2, October 2001, Vol. 1, pp. 700–704.

177. ITU-T. *G.872—Architecture for Optical Transport Networks.* ITU, 1999.

178. Irwin Mark Jacobs, Richard Binder, and Estil V. Hoversten. General purpose packet satellite networks. In *Proceedings of IEEE*, vol.66, no.11, November 1978, pp. 1448–1467.

179. V. Jacobson. Congestion avoidance and control. In *Proceedings of the ACM SIG-COMM*, 314–329, August 1988.

180. V. Jacobson. Compressing TCP/IP Headers for Low-Speed Serial Links. RFC 1144, February 1990.

181. V. Jacobson, R. Braden, and D. Borman. TCP extensions for high performance. RFC 1323, IETF, May 1992.

182. Van Jacobson. 4BSD header prediction. *ACM Computer Communication Review*, 20(2):13–15, April 1990.

183. Van Jacobson, Robert Braden, and David Borman. Internet Engineering Task Force, RFC 1323: *TCP Extensions for High Performance*, May 1992.

184. Van Jacobson, Craig Leres, and Steven McCanne. *tcpdump*, 1997. Manual Page. http://www.tcpdump.org.

185. Amit K. Jain and Sally Floyd. Quick-start for TCP and IP. Internet draft draft-amit-quick-start-01.txt, IETF, August 2002.

186. R. Jain. *The Art of Computer Systems Performance Analysis*. John Wiley and Sons, New York 1991.

187. S. Jha and M. Hassan. *Engineering Internet QoS*. Artech House, Boston 2002.

188. Rick Jones, Karen Choy, and Dave Shield. *Netperf*, 1996. Manual Page. http://www.netperf.org.

189. L. Kalampoukas, A. Varma, and K. K. Ramakrishnan. Improving TCP Throughput over Two-Way Asymmetric Links: Analysis and Solutions. In *Proc. ACM SIGMETRICS*, June 1998, pp. 78–89.

190. R. Kalden, I. Meirick, and M. Meyer. Wireless Internet access based on GPRS. *IEEE Personal Communications*, 7(2):8–18, April 2000.

191. P. Karn. MACA—A New Channel Access Method for Packet Radio. In *ARRL/CRRL Amateur Radio Computer Networking Conference*, September 1990, pp. 134–140.

192. P. Karn. The Qualcomm CDMA digital cellular system. In *Proceedings of the USENIX Mobile and Location-Independent Computing Symposium*, pages 35–39, August 1993.

193. Dina Katabi, Mark Handley, and Charlie Rohrs. Congestion control for high bandwidth-delay product networks. In *Proceeding of ACM SIGCOMM 2002*, August 2002, pp. 89–102.

194. R. H. Katz, S. Seshan, and H. Balakrishnan. Handoffs in Cellular Wireless Networks: The Daedalus Implementation and Experience. *Kluwer International Journal on Wireless Personal Communications*, March 1997, 4(2):141–162.

195. R. H. Katz and E. A. Brewer. The case for wireless overlay networks. *Proceedings of the SPIE*, 2667:77–88, 1996.

196. I. Katzela. *Modeling and Simulating Communications Networks: A Hands-on Approach Using OPNET*. Upper Saddle River, NJ: Prentice Hall, 1998.

197. Jonathan Kay and Joseph Pasquale. The importance of non-data touching processing overheads in TCP/IP. In *Proceedings of the SIGCOMM Symposium on Communications Architectures and Protocols*, pages 259–268. ACM, September 1993.

198. F. P. Kelly, A. K. Maulloo, and D. K. H. Tan. Rate control for communication networks: Shadow prices, proportional fairness and stability. *Journal of the Operational Research Society*, 49(3):237–252, March 1998.

199. S. Kent and R. Atkinson. Security architecture for the Internet protocol. RFC 2401, IETF, November 1998.

200. J. H. Kim, J. M. DeFilipps, N. P. Impert, C. F. Derheim, M. Y. Thompson, and S. Ray. ATM network–based integrated battlespace simulation with multiple uav-awacs-fighter platforms. In *IEEE Military Communication Conference (MILCOM)*, volume 1, pages 101–107. 1998.

201. Woo-June Kim and Byeong Gi Lee. The FB-RED algorithm for TCP over ATM. In *IEEE GLOBECOM98*, pages 551–555, Sydney, Australia, Nov 8–12, 1998.

202. L. Kleinrock. *Queueing Systems, Vol. 1*. John Wiley and Sons, New York, 1975.

203. L. Kleinrock and M. Gerla. On the measured performance of packet satellite access schemes. In *Proceedings of IEEE NTC*, pages 535–542, December 1977.

204. S. Knowles. IESG advice from experience with Path MTU Discovery. RFC 1435, IETF, March 1993.

205. C. E. Koksal, H. Kassab, and H. Balakrishnan. An analysis of short-term fairness in wireless media access protocols. In *Proceedings of ACM SIGMETRICS*, June 2000.

206. Sastri Kota. Demand assignment multiple access (DAMA) techniques for satellite communications. In *Proceedings of IEEE NTC*, pages c8.5.1–c.8.5.7, December 1981.

207. Sastri Kota. Multimedia satellite networks: Issues and challenges. In *Proceedings of SPIE International Symposium on Voice and Data Communications*, November 1998, pp. 600–618.

208. R. Krishnan, M. Allman, C. Partridge, J. Ster-benz, and W. Ivancic. Explicit transport error notification (ETEN) for error-prone wireless and satellite networks. In *Earth Science Technology Conference, California*, July 2002.

209. H. Kruse, M. Allman, and J. Griner and D. Tran. HTTP page transfer rates over geo-stationary satellite links. In *Proceedings of the sixth International Conference on telecommunication Systems*, March 1998.

210. H. Kruse, M. Allman, J. Griner, and D. Tran. Experimentation and modeling of HTTP over satellite channels. *International Journal of Satellite Communications*, 19(1), January 2001, pp. 51–68.

211. T. V. Lakshman, U. Madhow, and B. Suter. Window-based Error Recovery and Flow Control with a Slow Acknowledgement Channel: A Study of TCP/IP Performance. In *Proc. IEEE Infocom*, Kobe, Japan, April 1997, Vol. 3, pp. 1199–1209.

212. T. V. Lakshman, Arnold Neidhardt, and Teunis J. Ott. The drop from front strategy in TCP and in TCP over ATM. In *IEEE INFOCOM96*, pages 1242–1250, San Francisco, CA, March 26–28, 1996.

213. T. V. Lakshman and U. Madhow. The performance of tcp/ip for networks with high bandwidth-delay products and random loss. *IEEE/ACM Transactions on Networking*, June 1997, Vol. 5, Issue 3, pp. 336–350.

214. J-P. Laude. *DWDM Fundamentals, Components and Applications*. Artech House, Boston 2002.

215. A. M. Law and W. D. Kelton. *Simulation Modeling and Analysis* 3rd ed. New York: McGraw-Hill, third edition, 1991.

216. W. E. Leland and D. V. Wilson. High time-resolution measurement and analysis of LAN traffic: Implications for LAN interconnection. In *IEEE MILCOM*, volume 3, pages 101–107, 1991.

217. Will E. Leland, Murad S. Taqqu, Walter Willinger, and Daniel V. Wilson. On the self-similar nature of ethernet traffic (extended version). *IEEE/ACM Transactions on Networking (TON)*, 2(1):1–15, 1994.

218. Dong Lin and Robert Morris. Dynamics of random early detection. In *Proceedings of ACM SIGCOMM97*, pages 127–137, Cannes, France, Sept. 14–18, 1997.

219. Y-B. Lin and I. Chlamtac. *Wireless and Mobile Network Architectures*. John Wiley and Sons, New York, 2000.

220. S. Low and D. Lapsley. Optimization flow control I: Basic algorithm and convergence. *IEEE/ACM Transactions on Networking*, 7(6):861–874, December 1999.

221. S. Low, L. Peterson, and L. Wang. Understanding Vegas: A duality model. *Journal of ACM*, 49(2):207–235, March 2002.

222. S. H. Low, F. Paganini, J. Wang, S. Adlakha, and J. C. Doyle. Dynamics of TCP/AQM and a scalable control. In *Proceeding of IEEE INFOCOM 2002*, June 2002, Vol. 1, pp. 239–248.

223. R. Ludwig and R. H. Katz. The Eifel algorithm: making TCP robust against spurious retransmissions. *Computer Communications Review*, 30(1):30–36, January 2000.

224. R. Ludwig, A. Konrad, and A. D. Joseph. Optimizing the end-to-end performance of reliable flows over wireless links. In *Proceedings of the ACM/IEEE MOBICOM '99*, pages 113–119, August 1999.

225. R. Ludwig and B. Rathonyi. Link layer enhancements for TCP/IP over GSM. In *Proceedings of the IEEE INFOCOM '99*, pages 415–422, March 1999.

226. R. Ludwig, B. Rathonyi, A. Konrad, K. Oden, and A. D. Joseph. Multilayer tracing of TCP over a reliable wireless link. In *Proceedings of the ACM SIGMETRICS '99*, pages 144–154, June 1999.

227. E. Lutz, M. Werner, and A. Jahn. *Satellite Systems for Personal and Broadband Communications*. Berlin, Springer, 2000.

228. B. Mah. An empirical model of HTTP network traffic. In *Proceedings of IEEE Infocom '97*, 1997, Vol. 2, pp. 592–600.

229. J. Mahdavi and V. Paxson. *IPPM Metrics for Measuring Connectivity*, RFC 2678, IETF, September 1999.

230. P. Mähönen, T. Saarinen, Z. Shelby, and L. Muñoz. Wireless Internet over LMDS: Architecture and experimental implementation. *IEEE Communications Magazine*, 39(5):126–132, May 2001.

231. D. Maltz and P. Bhagwat. MSOCKS: An architecture for transport layer mobility. In *Proceedings of the IEEE INFOCOM '98*, pages 1037–1045, March 1998.

232. G. Maral and M. Bousquet. *Satellite Communications Systems*. New York: John Wiley and Sons Inc., 1993.

233. M. Marchese. Study and performance evaluation of TCP modifications and tuning over satellite links. *Computer Communications*, 24(9):877–888, May 2001.

234. M. Mathis and M. Allman. *Framework for Defining Empirical Bulk Transfer Capacity Metrics*, RFC 3148, IETF, July 2001.

235. M. Mathis and J. Mahdavi. Forward acknowledgment: Refining TCP congestion control. In *Proceedings of the ACM SIGCOMM*, August 1996, Vol. 2, No. 4, pp. 281–292.

236. M. Mathis, J. Mahdavi, S. Floyd, and A. Romanow. TCP selective acknowledgement options. RFC 2018, October 1996.

237. M. Mathis, J. Semke, and J. Mahdavi. The macroscopic behavior of the TCP congestion avoidance algorithm. *ACM Computer Communications Review*, 27(3), July 1997, pp. 67–82.

238. Martin May, Jean-Chrysostome Bolot, Alain Jean-Marie, and Christophe Diot. Simple performance models of differentiated services schemes for the internet. In *IEEE INFOCOM99*, New York, March, 1999, Vol. 3, pp. 1385–1394.

239. Martin May, Thomas Bonald, and Jean-Chrysostome Bolot. Analytic evaluation of RED performance. In *IEEE INFOCOM2000*, Tel-Aviv, Israel, March 26–30 2000, Vol. 3, pp. 1415–1424.

240. Martin May, Christophe Diot, Bryan Lyles, and Jean Bolot. Influence of active queue management parameters on aggregate traffic performance. Research Report, Institut National de Recherche en Informatique et en Automatique, April, 2000.

241. Paul E. McKenney and Ken F. Dove. Efficient demultiplexing of incoming TCP packets. In *SIGCOMM Symposium on Communications Architectures and Protocols*, pages 269–279. ACM, August 1992.

242. MIL 3 Inc., Washington DC, USA. *OPNET Modeling Manual*. URL:http://www.mil3.com.

243. V. Misra, W. Gong, and D. Towsley. Fluid-based analysis of a network of AQM routers supporting TCP flows with an application to RED. *Proceedings of ACM SIGCOMM*, August 2000.

244. J. Mo and J. Walrand. Fair end-to-end window-based congestion control. *IEEE/ACM Transactions on Networking*, 8(5):556–567, October 2000.

245. Jeffrey C. Mogul. Network locality at the scale of processes. *ACM Transactions on Computer Systems (TOCS)*, 10(2):81–109, May 1992.

246. Jeffrey C. Mogul and Steve E. Deering. Internet Engineering Task Force, *Path MTU Discovery*, RFC 1191, IETF, November 1990.

247. D. Mosberger, L. Peterson, P. Bridges, and S. O'Malley. *Analysis of Techniques to Improve Protocol Processing Latency*. Technical Report TR96-03, Department of Computer Science, The University of Arizona, Tucson, AZ 85721, 1996.

248. David Mosberger, Larry L. Peterson, Patrick G. Bridges, and Sean O'Malley. Analysis of techniques to improve protocol processing latency. In *Proceedings of the SIGCOMM Symposium on Applications, Technologies, Architectures and Protocols for Computer Communication*. ACM, August 1996, Vol. 21, No. 4, pp. 73–84.

249. Yukio Murayama. *DBS User's Manual Ver. 1.1*, 1998. Manual Page. http://www.ai3.net/products/dbs.

250. Yukio Murayama and Suguru Yamaguchi. Dbs: A powerful tool for tcp performance evaluations. In *Proceedings of SPIE Performance and Control of Network Systems*, volume 3231, pages 570–581, 1997.

251. S. Nanda, R. Ejzak, and B. T. Doshi. A retransmission scheme for circuit-mode data on wireless links. *IEEE Journal on Selected Areas in Communications*, 12(8):1338–1352, October 1994.

252. G. Navlakha and J. Ferguson. *Automatic TCP Window Tuning and Applications*, April 2001. http://dast.nlanr.net/Projects/Autobuf/autotcp.html.

253. G. T. Nguyen, R. H. Katz, B. Noble, and M. Satyanarayanan. A trace-based approach for modeling wireless channel behavior. In *Proceedings of the Winter Simulation Conference*, pages 597–604, December 1996.

254. K. Nicols, S. Blake, F. Baker, and D. Black. Definition of the differentiated services field (ds field) in the ipv4 and ipv6 headers. RFC2474, IETF, December 1998.

255. Teunis J. Ott, T. V. Lakshman, and Larry Wong. SRED: Stabilized RED. In *IEEE INFOCOM99*, pages 1346–1355, New York, March, 1999.

256. J. Padhye, V. Firoiu, D. Towsley, and J. Kurose. Modeling TCP throughput: A simple model and its empirical validation. *IEEE/ACM Transactions on Networking*, 8(2):133–145, April 2000.

257. V. N. Padmanabhan. *Addressing the Challenges of Web Data Transport*. PhD thesis, University of California at Berkeley, September 1998.

258. Vivek S. Pai, Peter Druschel, and Willy Zwaenepoel. IO-Lite: A unified I/O buffering and caching system. *ACM Transactions on Computer Systems (TOCS)*, 18(1):37–66, February 2000.

259. S.-Y. Park, J. Lee, and S. Hariri. Performance evaluation of ATM and gigabit networks. In *IEEE Information Technology Conference (ITC)*, pages 145–148, 1998.

260. Mark Parris, Kevin Jeffay, and F. Donelson Smith. Lightweight active router queue management for multimedia networking. In *Proceedings of SPIE*, pages 162–174, San Jose, CA, USA, Jan 25–27, 1999.

261. C. Partridge and T. J. Shepard. TCP/IP performance over satellite links. *IEEE Network Magazine*, pages 44–49, September/October 1997.

262. Craig Partridge and Timothy J. Shepard. TCP/IP performance over satellite links. In *IEEE Network*, September/October 1997, Vol. 11, Issue 5, pp. 44–49.

263. K. Pawlikowski. Steady-State Simulation of Queueing Processes: A Survey of Problems and Solutions. *ACM Computing Surveys*, 22(2):123–170, June 1990.

264. K. Pawlikowski, H.-D. J. Jeong, and J.-S. R. Lee. On Credibility of Simulation Studies of Telecommunication Networks. *IEEE Communications Magazine*, 40(1):132–139, January 2002.

265. Vern Paxson and Mark Allman. Internet Engineering Task Force, RFC 2988: *Computing TCP's Retransmission Timer*, November 2000.

266. Vern Paxson, Mark Allman, Scott Dawson, William Fenner, Jim Griner, Ian Heavens, Kevin Lahey, Jeff Semke, and Bernie Volz. Internet Engineering Task Force, RFC 2525: *Known TCP implementation problems*, RFC 2525, IETF, March 1999.

267. Vern Paxson and Sally Floyd. Wide area traffic: the failure of Poisson modeling. *IEEE/ACM Transactions on Networking*, 3(3):226–244, 1995.

268. Joseph N. Pelton. Satellite communications 2010. In *IEEE Military Communications*, pages 670–675, October 28–31 2001.

269. C. E. Perkins, E. M. Royer, and Samir Das. Ad Hoc On Demand Distance Vector (AODV) Routing. *Internet Draft draft-ietf-manet-aodv-04.txt*, October 1999.

270. Spiros Philopoulos and Ken Ferens. Proxy-based connection-split architecture for improving tcp performance over satellite channels. In *Proceedings of the 2002 IEEE Canadian Conference on Electrical and Computer Engineering*, 2002, pp. 1430–1435.

271. J. Postel. *Comments on Internet Protocols and TCP*, IEN 2, IETF, August 1977.

271a. J. Postel. DOD Standard Transmission Control Protocol. USC/Information Sciences Institute, IEN-129, RFC 761, NTIS ADA082609, January 1980.

272. J. Postel. Transmission control protocol. RFC 793, IETF, September 1981.

273. Jon Postel. Internet Engineering Task Force, RFC 793: Transmission Control Protocol, September 1981.

274. C. Qiao and M. Yoo. Optical burst switching—a new paradigm for an optical internet. *Journal of High Speed Networks*, 8(1):69–84, 1999.

275. R. Braden. Requirements for Internet Hosts—Communication Layers. *RFC 1122*, IETF, October 1989.

276. S. Ramanathan and R. Cohen. TCP for High Performance in Hybrid Fiber Coaxial Broad-Band Access Networks. *IEEE/ACM Transactions on Networking*, February 1998, Vol. 6, Issue 1, pp. 15–29.

277. K. Ramakrishnan and S. Floyd. A proposal to add explicit congestion notification (ECN) to IP. RFC 2481, IETF, January 1999.

278. K. Ramakrishnan, S. Floyd, and D. Black. The addition of explicit congestion notification (ECN) to IP. RFC 3168, IETF, September 2001.

279. B. Davie and Y. Rekhter. *MPLS: Technology and Applications*. San Francisco; Morgan Kaufmann, 2000.

280. M. Richharia. *Satellite Communications Systems*, Second Edition. London: Macmillan Press; 1999.

281. Dennis Roddy. *Satellite Communications*. Boston: McGraw-Hill, 2001.

282. E. Rosen, A. Viswanathan, and R. Callon. *Multiprotocol Label Switching Architecture*. RFC 3031, IETF, 2001.

283. S. M. Ross. *Introduction to Probability and Statistics for Engineers and Scientists*. New York: John Wiley & Sons, 1987.

284. N. K. G. Samaraweera. Return Link Optimization for Internet Service Provision Using DVB-S Networks. *ACM SIGCOMM CCR*, July 1999, 29(3):4–13.

285. J. Schiller. *Mobile Communications*. Reading, MA: Addison-Wesley, 2000.

286. N. Seddigh, B. Nandy, P. Pieda, J. Hadi Salim, and A. Chapman. Experimental study of assured services in a diffserv IP QoS network. In *Proceedings of SPIE*, pages 217–230, 1998.

287. J. Semke. Implementation issues of the autotuning fair share algorithm. Technical Report CMU-PSC-TR-2000-0002, Carnegie Mellon University, May 2000.

288. J. Semke, J. Mahdavi, and M. Mathis. Automatic tcp buffer tuning. In *ACM SIGCOMM*, October 1998, Vol. 28, No. 4, pp. 311–323.

289. S. Floyd. RED: Discussions of setting parameters. http://www.aciri.org/floyd/REDparameters.txt, November, 1997.

290. S. Sharma and Y. Viniotis. Convergence of a dynamic policy for buffer management in shared buffer ATM switches. *Performance Evaluation*, 36–37:249–266, August, 1999.

291. S. Shi, G. Parulkar, and R. Gopalakrishnan. *TCP/IP Implementation with Endsystem QoS*. Technical Report WUCS98-03, Department of Computer Science, Washington University, St. Louis, MO, 1998.

292. W. Simpson. *PPP over SONET/SDH*. RFC 1619, IETF, May 1994.

293. P. Sinha, J. Monks, and V. Bharghavan. Limitations of TCP-ELFN for Ad hoc Networks. In *Proceedings of IEEE International Workshop on Mobile Multimedia Communications*, October 2000.

294. P. Sinha, N. Venkitaraman, R. Sivakumar, and V. Bharghavan. WTCP: A Reliable Transport Protocol for Wireless Wide-Area Networks. In *Proceedings of ACM MOBICOM*, August 1999, pp. 231–241.

295. H. Sirisena and M. Hassan. Generalised minimum variance control of queues in packet switching networks. *Communications in Information and Systems*, 2(4):419–432, 2002.

296. H. Sirisena, M. Hassan, and A. Haider. Optimal TCP Congestion Control. In *IEEE International Conference on Telecommunications*, pages 732–736, Beijing, China, June 2002.

297. K. Sklower, B. Lloyd, G. McGregor, D. Carr, and T. Coradetti. The PPP Multilink Protocol (MP). RFC 1990, IETF, August 1996.

298. Quinn Snell and Guy Helmer. *NetPIPE*, 1998. Manual Page. http://www.scl.ameslab.gov/netpipe.

299. A. Snoeren and H. Balakrishnan. An End-to-End Approach to Internet Host Mobility. In *Proceedings of ACM MOBICOM*, August 2000.

300. Dr. J. Scott Stadler and Jay Gelman. Performance enhancement for TCP/IP on a satellite channel. In *Proceedings of IEEE MILCOM*, pages 270–276, 1998.

301. W. Stallings. *High-Speed Networks TCP/IP and ATM Design Principles*. Upper Saddle River, NJ: Prentice Hall, 1998.

302. Richard W. Stevens. *TCP/IP Illustrated*, volume 1. Reading, MA: Addison-Wesley, 1994.

303. Bernhard Suter, T. V. Lakshman, Dimitrios Stiliadis, and Abhijit K. Choudhury. Buffer management schemes for supporting TCP in gigabit routers with per-flow queuing. *IEEE Journal on Selected Areas in Communications*, 17(6):1159–1169, June, 1999.

304. Systems Modeling Corporation (acquired by Rockwell Automation), Sewicky, PA, USA. *SIMAN V Reference Guide*. URL:http://www.rockwell.com/.

305. L. Tancevski, S. Yegnanarayanan, G. Castanon, L. Tamil, F. Masetti, and T. McDermott. Optical routing of asynchronous, variable length packets. *IEEE Journal on Selected Areas in Communications*, 18(10):2084–2093, 2000.

306. B. L. Tierney, D. Gunter, J. Lee, and M. Stoufer. Enabling network-aware applications. In *IEEE International Symposium on High Performance Distributed Computing*, August 2001, pp. 281–288.

307. Fouada A. Tobagi. Multiaccess protocols in packet communication systems. *IEEE Transactions on Communications*, 28(4): 468–488, April 1980.

308. C. K. Toh. *Ad-hoc Mobile Wireless Networks: Protocols and Systems*. Upper Saddle River, NJ: Prentice Hall, 2001.

309. L. Torvalds and The Free Software Company. *The Linux Kernel*. http://www.kernel.org.

310. UCB/LBNL/VINT groups. UCB/LBNL/VINT Network Simulator. http://www.isi.edu/nsnam/ns/, May 2001.

311. V. Visweswaraiah and J. Heidemann. Improving restart of idle TCP connections. Technical report 97-661, Los Angeles: University of Southern California, 1997.

312. Thomas M. Wallett, Vijaya K. Konangi, and Kul B. Bhasin. Simulation of a NASA LEO satellite hybrid network, satellite networks: Architectures, applications, and technologies. In *Workshop NASA/CP-1998-208524, Cleveland, Ohio*, June 1998.

313. J. Walrand. *An Introduction to Queueing Networks*. Upper Saddle River, NJ: Prentice Hall, 1988.

314. Ren Wang, Massimo Valla, M. Y. Sanadidi, and Mario Gerla. Using adaptive bandwidth estimation to provide enhanced and robust transport over heterogeneous networksTCP westwood: Bandwidth estimation for enhanced transport over wireless links. In *Proceedings of 10th IEEE International Conference on Network Protocols, Paris, France*, 2002, pp. 206–215.

315. DirecPC Webpage. http://www.direcpc.com.

316. Ricochet Networks Webpage. http://www.ricochet.com.

317. E. Weigle and Wu Chun Feng. A comparison of tcp automatic tuning techniques for distributed computing. In *IEEE International Symposium on High Performance Distributed Computing (HPDC)*, pages 1–8, March 26–28, 2002.

318. E. Weigle and W. Feng. Dynamic right sizing: A simulation study. In *IEEE International Conference on Computer Communications and Networks*, pages 152–158, 2001.

319. Arun Welch. *Improving TCP/IP performance over satellites—Gateway and Proxy testing*, May 1999. Available at http://www.internet-2.org.il/satellite-testing.html.

320. W. Willinger, M. S. Taqqu, R. Sherman, and D. V. Wilson. Self-Similarity Through High-Variability: Statistical Analysis of Ethernet LAN Traffic at the Source Level. *IEEE/ACM Transactions on Networking*, 5(1):71–86, 1997.

321. G. Xylomenos and G. C. Polyzos. TCP and UDP performance over a wireless LAN. In *Proceedings of the IEEE INFOCOM '99*, pages 439–446, March 1999.

322. G. Xylomenos and G. C. Polyzos. Link layer support for Quality of Service on wireless Internet links. *IEEE Personal Communications*, 6(5):52–60, October 1999.

323. Guang Yang, Ren Wang, Fei Wang, M. Y. Sanadidi, and Mario Gerla. Performance of tcpw br in next generation wireless and satellite networks. Technical report no. 020025, UCLA, 2002.

324. Guang Yang, Ren Wang, Fei Wang, M. Y. Sanadidi, and Mario Gerla. TCP westwood with bulk for heavy loss environments. Technical report no. 020023, UCLA, 2002.

325. Y. R. Yang, M. S. Kim, and S. S. Lam. Transient Behaviors of TCP-Friendly Congestion Control Protocols. In *Proceedings of the IEEE INFOCOM*, April 2001.

326. R. Yavatkar and N. Bhagawat. Improving end-to-end performance of TCP over mobile internetworks. In *Proceedings of the IEEE Workshop on Mobile Computing Systems and Applications*, pages 146–152, December 1994.

327. I. Yeom and A. Reddy. Modeling TCP behavior in a differentiated-services network. *IEEE/ACM Transactions on Networking*, 9(1):31–46, February 2001.

328. Bing Zheng and Mohammed Atiquzzaman. DSRED:An active queue management scheme for next generation networks. In *IEEE LCN2000*, pages 242–251, Tampa, Florida, Nov. 8–10, 2000.

329. Bing Zheng and Mohammed Atiquzzaman. A framework to determine the optimal weight parameter of RED in next generation Internet routers. Technical Report, The University of Dayton, Department of Electrical and Computer Engineering, July, 2000.

330. Bing Zheng and Mohammed Atiquzzaman. DSRED: improving performance of active queue management over heterogeneous networks. In *IEEE ICC2001*, Helsinki, Finland, June 11–15, 2001, Vol. 8, pp. 2375–2379.

331. Bing Zheng and Mohammed Atiquzzaman. Low Pass Filter/Over Drop Avoidance(LPF/ODA): An algorithm to improve the response time of RED gateways. *Intl. J. of Communication Systems*, Vol. 15, No. 10, 2002, pp. 899–906.

332. Thomas Ziegler, serge Fdida, Christof Brandauer, and Bernhard Hechenleitner. Stability of RED with two way TCP traffic. In *IEEE IC3N2000*, pages 214–219, Las Vegas, Nevada, USA, Oct 16–18, 2000.

333. Mary Jo Zukoski and Rafols Ramirez. A transport protocol for space communications. *Network and Communications: The Edge Newsletter*, November, 1998.

334. G. Holland and N. Vaidya. Analysis of TCP Performance over Mobile Ad-Hoc Networks. In ACM MOBICOM, August, 1999.

335. C. Casetti and M. Meo. A New Approach to Model the Stationary Behavior of TCP Connections. In IEEE INFOCOM. 26–30 March, 2000. Volume 1, pp: 367–375.

336. C. Casetti and M. Meo. An Analytical Framework for the Performance Evaluation of TCP Reno Connections. Computer Networks, 2001, Vol. 37, pp. 669–682.

337. A. Kumar. Comparative performance analysis of versions of TCP in a local network with a lossy link. IEEE/ACM Transactions on Networking. Aug 1998. Vol. 6, No. 4, pp. 485–498.

338. A. Wierman, T. Osogami and J. Olsén. A Unified Framework for modeling TCP-Vegas, TCP-SACK, and TCP-Reno. Technical Report CMU-CS-03-133. Carnegie Mellon University, Pittsburgh, PA15213.

Index